Jeroen van de Weijer (Ed.)
Representing Phonological Detail
Part II: Syllable, Stress, and Sign

Phonology and Phonetics

Edited by
Aditi Lahiri

Volume 33

Representing Phonological Detail

Part II: Syllable, Stress, and Sign

Edited by
Jeroen van de Weijer

DE GRUYTER
MOUTON

ISBN 978-3-11-162037-4
e-ISBN (PDF) 978-3-11-073008-1
e-ISBN (EPUB) 978-3-11-073014-2
ISSN 1861-4191

Library of Congress Control Number: 2022943754

Bibliographic information published by the Deutsche Nationalbibliothek
The Deutsche Nationalbibliothek lists this publication in the Deutsche Nationalbibliografie;
detailed bibliographic data are available on the internet at http://dnb.dnb.de.

© 2024 Walter de Gruyter GmbH, Berlin/Boston
This volume is text- and page-identical with the hardback published in 2023.
Typesetting: Integra Software Services Pvt. Ltd.

www.degruyter.com

Dedicated with fondness to Harry van der Hulst by
his teacher, colleagues, students and friends

'Whiting' (2018) by Helga Humbert

Preface

A few years ago a colleague was visiting Shanghai to give a number of talks. He also visited Shanghai International Studies University and gave a presentation on a sign language topic. At that time, it struck me that we both had been PhD students supervised by Harry van der Hulst at Leiden University, and how similarly we had both been affected by Harry's training and philosophy in life and in linguistics. All of his students have been struck by, and I think are now passing on to their own students, a sense of critical wonder about language, a penchant for "logical thinking". It was then that the idea for a celebratory volume was born. We were fortunate to contact a large number of colleagues, including Harry's own teacher in linguistics, who readily promised (and some time later delivered) their articles around the broad theme of "representing phonological detail", also touching upon the interfaces with phonetics, morphology and semantics, i.e. reflecting the broad range of Harry's linguistic interests. We thank all of them here, also as reviewers and critical readers of other articles. A number of external reviewers also kindly contributed their comments. Special thanks to Helga Humbert, who contributed two pieces of artwork, reproduced in the preceding pages.

Part I of this collection deals with segments and representation in general, in phonology and morphology. There is ample attention for vowels, and especially for vowel harmony-related processes. The other chapters touch on consonant representation, first language acquisition, recursion, the phonology–syntax interface and morphological representation. Part II revolves around the themes of syllable structure, stress and sign language. We hope that, together, the two volumes give a good idea of current research strands in phonology and directly related fields, and that they form a fitting tribute to Harry van der Hulst, who has touched so many with his brilliance, expertise and friendship.

Jeroen van de Weijer
Shenzhen, May 2022

Contents

Preface —— IX

Marika Butskhrikidze
The Status of /m/ in #/m/C Sequences in Georgian —— 1

Andrea Calabrese
Gemination in Middle Indic —— 19

John Harris
A Fake Diphthong in English —— 55

Ksenia Bogomolets
Deconstructing Secondary Stress —— 69

Irene Vogel
Is There Foot Structure in Isolating Languages? —— 99

Bing Li
Word Stress Placement in Wakhi —— 115

Rob Goedemans and Jelena Prokic
Mining Metrical Data —— 133

Ana Lívia Agostinho and Larry M. Hyman
Interpreting Non-Canonical Word Prosody in Afro-European Contact —— 151

Matthew Gordon
The Phonetic Basis for Tone-Stress Interactions:
A Cross-Linguistic Study —— 171

B. Elan Dresher and Aditi Lahiri
Some Applications of the Primary Accent First Parameter —— 191

Anthi Revithiadou
Accent as Autosegment: A Unified Account of Lexical Accent and Lexical Stress Systems —— 209

Vincent J. van Heuven
Stress Deaf and Color Blind: Native Language Background and Perceptual Categories —— 233

Alexandre Vaxman
The Representation and Computation of Weight in Hybrid Accent Systems: The Case of Standard Eastern Mari —— 253

Wendy Sandler
From Latent to Blatant: Unmasking Phonological Iconicity in Sign Language Theatre —— 271

Rachel Channon
A New Feature Type: Functional Features in Sign Languages —— 291

Onno Crasborn and Els van der Kooij
The Emergence of the Second Hand in Sign Language Phonology: From Underlying to Surface Representations —— 319

Shengyun Gu
Phonological Processes in Shanghai Sign Language: Contexts, Constraints, and Structure —— 345

Language Index —— 363

Subject Index —— 367

Contents of Part I —— 369

Marika Butskhrikidze
The Status of /m/ in #/m/C Sequences in Georgian

Abstract: Consonant co-occurrence in Georgian largely complies to phonological principles such as the SSP and the OCP. However, these principles are violated in #/m/C sequences, because the sonorant *m* can precede any consonant, without any restriction. This raises questions concerning the status of /m/: are these #/m/C sequences true clusters or are they secondary, for instance, the result of morphological derivation or analogy? We consider various types of evidence: 1) synchronic constraints on consonant co-occurrence; 2) comparative and dialectal data; 3) diachronic studies involving /m/C sequences; and 4) reduplication data. Based on the findings the paper argues that the /m/ in #/m/C sequences should be analysed as a prefix. Henceforth, /m/ and C in #/m/C sequences belong to different morphemes and do not form true clusters.

Keywords: true clusters, consonant co-occurrence, phonological principles, morphological derivation, Georgian

The paper addresses various ways of analysing surface consonant sequences. In particular, it focuses on the case when an apparent consonant sequence does not form a true cluster, but a secondary/fake one. This occurs when constituents of the cluster belong to different morphemes. The data is drawn from the Georgian language.

There are four possible ways of analysis, to my mind, to consider when two consonants appear together. First, those two consonants could constitute a true cluster (obeying phonological principles, e.g. the SSP and the OCP). Secondly, the two consonants could constitute a complex segment (usually demonstrated by syllabification, peculiar behavior in phonological processes, the existence of minimal pairs, phonetic experiments, etc.). Thirdly, the first consonant could be syllabic (usually demonstrated by phonetic factors and participation in stress assignment). Finally, the two consonants might seem monomorphemic, but in actual

---

Note: I am indebted to Jeroen van de Weijer for his careful reading of the paper and many useful suggestions. I am very grateful to an anonymous reviewer for his helpful comments. The usual disclaimers apply.

Marika Butskhrikidze, AAB College

https://doi.org/10.1515/9783110730081-001

fact are not. In this case, the sequences could be referred to as "secondary"[1] or "fake" clusters (see also on the notion of "bogus" clusters in van der Hulst (1984). Interestingly, to establish the status of consonant sequences, the kind of evidence used is unique for each. To illustrate the distinct nature of the fourth type, one needs to consider a wide range of linguistic evidence, both in terms of time and space: historical and dialectal/comparative data can be used to check the status of certain constructions, and what are the core and peripheral syllabic structures within the language system. All four kinds of clusters can be demonstrated based on Georgian data, but the focus of the present paper is on the last one.

The sonorant *m* is the only consonant that can precede any consonant in Georgian (see examples in (1) below). To restate this observation, there are no co-occurrence restrictions on the sequence #/m/C. While it is very odd not to have co-occurrence restrictions on clusters belonging to one morpheme, such freedom of co-occurrence might be less surprising if the consonants belong to different morphemes. Besides, #/m/C sequences violate phonological principles such as the Sonority Sequencing Principle (SSP) and the Obligatory Contour Principle (OCP). The domain of these principles is the stem/root (Butskhrikidze 2002; see also Clements (1990) and Selkirk (1984), who suggest that the syllable is the relevant domain). Consider the following examples:

(1) Word-initial consonant clusters
    a. CC   **mp**arveli   'patron'
    b. CCC   **mk'**lavi   'arm'
                  mtvare   'moon'
    c. CCCC   **msx**vili   'thick'
    d. CCCCC   **msxv**reva   'breaking'

The consonant sequence *mp* in *mparveli* violates the OCP as both, *m* and *p*, are bilabial consonants, while all the above-listed sequences violate the SSP as in all examples, the more sonorous consonant *m* precedes less sonorous ones, such as *p*, *k'*, *t* and *s*.

This paper argues that the /m/ in #/m/C sequences should be analysed as a prefix. Thus, *m* and C belong to different morphemes. Consequently #/m/C sequences do not form true clusters. To substantiate this claim, the Georgian phonological inventory, and the synchronic patterns of consonant clustering in general and specifically those of /m/C type will be considered in Section 1. Some

---

[1] In line with this suggestion is also the claim made by van der Hulst and Ritter (1999: 16): "... clusters that are grammatical at the left edge of words are not necessarily true onsets".

typological observations and morpho-phonological patterns of Georgian are discussed in Section 2. Comparative data on dialectal forms of Georgian and another Kartvelian language, Megrelian, are considered in Section 3. Historical studies on #mC sequences are considered in Section 4. Reduplication data and aspects of child language development are considered as relevant pieces of evidence concerning this issue in Section 5. Finally, some tentative conclusions are drawn.

1 The Phonemic Inventory and the Synchronic Patterns of Consonant Clustering

Georgian belongs to the Kartvelian (South Caucasian) language family. The name of the language group is related to the ethnonym *kartveli* 'Georgian'. Georgian is the official state language of Georgia, with more than four million speakers. Outside Georgia, there are Georgian-speaking populations in Azerbaijan (Saingilo),[2] Turkey (Shavsheti, Imerkhevi), Iran (Fereidan) and the North Caucasus (Sochi, Kizlar-Mozdok, Orjonikidze). Besides Georgian, the Kartvelian language family comprises three other languages, Megrelian (Mingrelian), Laz (Chan) and Svan. According to Shanidze's (1973) classification, which is mainly based on geographical factors, there are six groups of Georgian dialects: 1. Pkhouri (Khevsuruli, Mokheuri, Tushuri); 2. Mtiulur-Pshauri (Mtiulur-Gudamakruli, Pshauri); 3. Kartlur-Kakhuri (Kartluri, Kakhuri, Javakhuri, Meskhuri, Kizikuri); 4. Dasavluri (Imeruli, Guruli, Rachuli, Lechkhumuri); 5. Samkhret-Dasavluri (Acharuli, Imerkheuli); and 6. Ingilouri.

Georgian has 28 consonants in its phonemic inventory. To account for the syntagmatic patterns of consonant combinations, it is convenient to classify them according to place and manner of articulation, as in (2):

(2) Consonants grouped according to the place of articulation and manner.

Manner Place	Stop			Nasal	Fricative/affricate					Liquid	
Bilabial/labio-dental	b	p	p'	m	v						
Alveolar	d	t	t'	n	dz	dʒ	ts'	z	s	l	r
Palato-alveolar					ts	tʃ	tʃ'	ʒ	ʃ		
Velar	g	k	k'					ɣ	x		
Uvular									χ'		

---

2 Names of the geographical areas are given in brackets.

There are many co-occurrence restrictions of the OCP type in Georgian, referring primarily to the place of articulation.

Geminates are disallowed in monomorphemic contexts.[3] The classification discussed below is based on Uturgaidze (1976), which accounts for most of the Georgian data.

The first restriction concerns the labial sounds (including the labio-dental /v/). This class is denoted as C1 and contains the sounds /b p p' m v/.

It is not permissible to have two adjacent labial consonants in a monomorphemic environment. Any combination between the members of this class is disallowed. Thus, *mb-, *mp-, *mp'-, *mv-, *bm-, *bp-, *bp'-, *bv-, *pm-, *pb-, *pv-, *vm-, etc. are not found. Combinations of rounded vowels, as well as rounded vowels and the labio-dental /v/, are also disallowed (Butskhrikidze 2002).

The second class, C2, contains the coronals, /d t t' ʣ ts ts' z s ʤ tʃ tʃ' ʒ ʃ/, in which three places of articulation are distinguished:

(3) Dentals: /d t t'/
     Alveolars: /ʣ ts ts' z s/
     Palato-alveolars: /ʤ tʃ tʃ' ʒ ʃ/

Two restrictions that pertain to C2 consonants:
a) Combinations of homorganic phonemes are not accepted (i.e. the same restriction as for labials);
b) A posterior coronal may precede an anterior coronal, but never follow it. Thus, the combinations ʃt, ʤd, tsd are attested (for instance in words like ʃtantkva 'absorption', ʤdoma 'to sit', tsda 'attempt'), while *tʃ *dʤ, *dts never occur.

The third class, C3, contains the sonorants, /r l n/, which are subject to the restriction that the members of this class never combine within the same morpheme (i.e. the same restriction as for the first and the second classes).

The velar and uvular consonants are grouped, including a glottal voiceless fricative /h/. This class is referred to as C4 and contains /g k k' ɣ x χ' h/. The members of this class also never co-occur.

To conclude, the generalisation is as follows:

---

[3] There are no geminates in Georgian. However, identical consonants do occur across morpheme boundaries, e.g. /xaz-ze/ 'on the line', /v-varʤiʃob/ 'I am training', /mat-tan/ 'with them'. In order to avoid gemination, one of the consonants undergoes deletion, e.g. /t'ani-samosi/ /*t'anis-samosi/ 'cloth', etc. Foreign words with geminates (whether orthographic or phonetic) always enter the Georgian lexicon with only one consonant, e.g. /alegoria/ 'allegory', /k'lasi/ 'class', etc.

(4) Obstruents with the identical place of articulation never combine.[4]

Two additional factors are of importance when consonant sequences are discussed, viz. the places of articulation of the members of the consonant sequence (i.e. directionality involved) and their laryngeal specifications. Regarding the first factor, regressive and non-regressive consonant sequences can be distinguished. 'Regressive' refers to anterior + posterior consonant sequences (i.e. labial-coronal, coronal-dorsal, labial-dorsal). 'Non-regressive' refers to posterior + anterior consonant sequences (i.e. dorsal-coronal, coronal-labial, dorsal-labial). Concerning the second factor, clusters are defined as 'homogeneous' or 'heterogeneous'. In 'homogeneous' clusters, members share the laryngeal feature. Thus, they are voiced, voiceless, or glottalized. Regressivity and homogeneity are the preferred patterns for Georgian consonant sequences (see Akhvlediani 1949; Vogt 1961; Melikishvili 1997).

Regressivity and homogeneity are observed in long consonant sequences as suggested by Gvinadze (1970) in the following generalisation:

(5) I   /b p p' m/
    II /r/
    III /d t t' dz ts ts' dʒ tʃ tʃ' z s ʒ ʃ/
    IV /g k k' ɣ x χ'/
    V   /v/
    VI /r l m n/

One consonant from each set can combine in the strict order given and form maximally a six-member cluster, e.g. /brdɣvna/ 'to fight', /prtskvna/ 'to peel'. Any set can be skipped, but the order between the sets should be respected. Consonants in the sequence must have the same laryngeal specification and must be regressive. For instance, permissible five-member sequences are *bdɣvr-*, *p'rtʃχ'v-*, etc. Non-permissible would be e.g. **pdɣvr-/* p'dɣvr-* (violating homogeneity), or **dbɣvr-/ *bɣdvr-* (violation regressivity).

As shown in (5), the sonorant /m/ is included in the first set suggesting that word-initial /m/C combinations were considered as true clusters by Gvinadze (1970). The double occurrence of /r/, in both the second and sixth sets, is explainable by the optionality of the first /r/ in long consonant sequences.

---

[4] In other words, sequences of homorganic consonants are disallowed in Georgian. This claim does not apply to the class of sonorants since combinations of e.g. coronal obstruents and coronal sonorants are well-formed. For instance, sequences such as dn, dr, t'l, etc. are attested. These obstruent-sonorant clusters are "true clusters" in the sense above.

It can also be seen from (5) that the first set consists of bilabial stops. The appearance of bilabials in the initial position of long consonant sequences can be related to the phonotactic restrictions that hold in general for the bilabials (including rounded vowels) in Georgian phonotactics. This generalisation is in accordance with the cross-linguistic observation that bilabials commonly appear as the first member of long consonant sequences, e.g. in Polish (see Cyran and Gussmann 1999: 235). Cross-linguistically, as Zubkova (1990) and Chrétien (1965) report, there is a tendency for bilabials to occur word-initially. The asymmetric distributional characteristics of the nasals /m/ and /n/ could be attributed to this generalisation. The nasal /m/ is commonly found in the word-initial position, while the nasal /n/ commonly occurs in the word-final position (Zubkova 1990; van der Torre 2003). The asymmetry is confirmed by the neutralisation of the opposition /m/ vs. /n/ in word-final position in a number of languages, where only the nasal /n/ is attested, e.g. in Old Greek, Italian, Finnish, Avar, Lak and Japanese (Zubkova 1990: 108).[5] Thus, the initial position in the sequence is taken by bilabials because they have less combinatory power than other segments, such as coronals. The behaviour of the Georgian bilabials shows their marked character and reflects the cross-linguistic observation that bilabials are marked obstruents (Melikishvili 1976).[6]

Based on the above-mentioned restrictions on consonant clustering, we can conclude that there are certain principles governing consonant co-occurrence in Georgian. However, this does not apply to /m/C sequences, because the sonorant *m* can precede any consonant, without any restriction. The question that thus arises is whether these #/m/C sequences are true clusters (just like other clusters, i.e. sequences of consonants within a morpheme) or whether they are secondary, for instance, the result of morphological derivation or analogy. One could also consider the possibility of analysing them as complex segments or explore whether *m* is syllabic in these contexts: these are all possible options.

The proposal that we would like to make is that #/m/C sequences are the result of morphological derivation and analogy. Thus, they are secondary, and should not be treated as true clusters in Georgian. There are parallels within Georgian morpho-phonology. In monomorphemic words, /v/ can never be the first member of a cluster (the only exceptions to this are two words: *vrtseli* 'vast' and *vseba* 'filling'). Apart from these, there are no /v/C clusters in Georgian. /v/ does occur in word-

---

[5] Jeroen van de Weijer points out to me that this generalization holds also in some varieties of Chinese (personal communication). An anonymous reviewer suggested the following generalization: "... in many dialects of Chinese, /n/ may occur in the onset and the coda positions of a syllable, while /m/ occurs in the onset position only".

[6] Markedness is determined by the structure of phonemic inventory, frequency of occurrence, combinatoric power, etc.

initial position in clusters, but always as a prefix. Illustrative examples are given in (6):

(6) a. *v-rtʃeb-i*　　　　b. *v-muʃa-ob*
　　　1SG-stay-1SBJ PRS　　1SG-work-THEM SUFF
　　　'I am staying'　　　 'I am working'

Two the most prominent cases when the grammatical function of /m/ is obvious are when /m/ is a prefix, a nominalizer, or a part of a confix (or circumfix). This is the reason why constructions like 7(a) and 7(b) are tolerated, which otherwise would violate two phonotactic constraints of Georgian: 1. Geminates are disallowed in monomorphemic contexts, and 2. It is not permissible to have two adjacent labial consonants in a monomorphemic context. Illustrative examples are given in (7).

(7) a. **m-martv-el-i**　　　　　　**m-mal-av-i**
　　　NMLZ-rule-THEM SUFF-NOM　　NMLZ-hide-THEM SUFF-NOM
　　　'ruler'　　　　　　　　　　　'hider'

　　b. **m-brdʒaneb-el-i**　　　　　**m-brts'χ'in-av-i**
　　　NMLZ-order-THEM SUFF-NOM　　NMLZ-shine-THEM SUFF-NOM
　　　'sovereign'　　　　　　　　　 'shining'

Nobody disputes that *m* in these forms is a grammatical morpheme. The morphological origin of /m-/ is also obvious in forms such as: /m-ts'eral-i/ 'writer', /m-k'vlel-i/ 'killer' and /m-ts'vrtnel-i/ 'trainer'. Nevertheless, there are some words such as: /mze/ 'sun', /mgel-i/ 'wolf', /mta/ 'mountain', /msxal-i/ 'pear' and /mt'red-i/ 'pigeon' in which it is difficult to trace the morphological origin of /m-/. These are words that are often cited when illustrating the complexity of consonant clustering in Georgian (Nepveu 1994; Bush 1997). In the rest of the paper, we will try to demonstrate that the initial /m/ in these words is secondary, has a morphological origin, and thus that #mC does not constitute a true cluster. Next, we consider morphological and morpho-phonological characteristics of Georgian.

2 Some Typological Observations and Morpho-phonological Patterns in Georgian

Georgian has a rich morphology, with very productive inflectional and derivational systems. Morpheme combinations can be both agglutinative and inflectional. Grammatical affixes attach before or after a root and may sometimes even violate the integrity of the root if metathesis takes place. Both the noun and the verb are characterized by prefixing and suffixing morphology, but verbal morphology is much more complex. Consider the morphologically complex nominal (8a) and verbal (8b) forms:

(8) a. *kud-ian-eb-is-tvis*
hat-POSS-PL-GEN-PURP
'for people wearing hats'

b. *ga-u-k'et-eb-in-eb-i-a*
PREV-OBJ VER-do-THEM SUFF-CAUS-THEM SUFF-PRF-3SBJ
'somebody made somebody else do something'

When affixes attach to a root, several phonological processes can take place, e.g. vowel deletion, metathesis and epenthesis (see Butskhrikidze and van de Weijer (2003) for an analysis of metathesis in Georgian). The deletion of the root vowel is the most widespread process in both nominal and verbal morphology. As a result of vowel deletion, consonant sequences emerge, as illustrated in (9).

(9) a. NOM   GEN
xmal-i   xml-is   'sword'
tsxvar-i tsxvr-is 'sheep'

b. *da-tʃ'er-i*   *da-tʃ'r-a*
PREV- cut-2IMP   PREV - cut -3PST
'cut IMP'   'he cut'

Surface consonant sequences also emerge because of simply adding consonantal prefixes or suffixes to a root, e.g.:

(10) a. *gv-ts'er*
2OBJ- write
'you write us'

b. *gv-xat'-av*
2OBJ- draw-THEM SUFF
'you draw us'

c. *m-ts'er-al-i*
NMLZ-write- PTCP-NOM
'writer'

Thus, one of the ways to account for the surface consonant sequences of Georgian is to study the morphological structure of such words. Sequences may be the result either of the deletion of a root vowel, which generally happens when a vowel-initial affix is added to a root, as illustrated in (9), or of the addition of a consonantal affix to a root, as illustrated in (10).

Cross-linguistically, lexical and grammatical morphemes differ in their use of the phonological inventory. A common discrepancy between the two is that grammatical morphemes use a subset of the phonological inventory of a language, whereas the full set is employed for lexical morphemes, and this is also attested in Georgian. Of the total of 28 consonants of Georgian, only 13 can occur in both lexical and grammatical (derivational and inflectional) morphemes, while the other 15 occur exclusively in lexical morphemes.

(11) a. Consonants appearing only in lexical morphemes:
/p p' t' k tʃ dz ts' tʃ' dʒ z ʃ ʒ χ' x h/

b. Consonants appearing in lexical and grammatical morphemes:
/b t d g k' ts s χ' v m l r n/

It is interesting to note that the set in (11a) includes almost all affricates (i.e. consonants with a complex stop + fricative constituency), e.g. /tʃ ts' tʃ' dz dʒ/, and other marked consonants, e.g. /h/ and /ʒ/, the distribution of which is quite restricted, e.g. /h/ occurs only in word-initial position, while the fricative /ʒ/ occurs only in a few words of Georgian origin.

Consonants in grammatical affixes given in the set in (11b) have different distribution patterns depending on their position in a derived word.

(12) a) Word-initial consonants: /v m n s[7] d g/
     b) Word-medial consonants: /v m l r n t d g b k' dʒ/
     c) Word-final consonants: /v m n s t d t b[8] ts/

It is interesting to observe that the velars /k'/ and /ɣ/ appear only in word-medial position, and that the affricate /ts/, which is the only affricate consonant that appears in grammatical morphemes, occurs only in word-final position and that

---

[7] It should be noted that depending on the root-initial sound, the person marker /s-/ has several allomorphs, for instance, /h-/ and /ʃ-/. In Old Georgian, the morpheme also had an allomorph /x-/.

[8] Word-final /d/ and /b/ devoice and are pronounced as [t] and [p], respectively, e.g. /k'arg-ad/ 'well' is pronounced as [k'argat] and /v-a-k'eteb/ 'I do' is pronounced as [vak'etep].

the liquids /r/ and /l/ occur only in word-medial position. Coronals, nasals and the sonorant /v/ appear to be quite free in their distribution. All of this has direct consequences for the surface complexity of consonant sequences in Georgian, and I return to this issue later. One more thing to notice is that of the 11 consonants given in (12b), only eight, /v m n s t d g b/, occur in inflectional affixes, e.g. the following:

(13) /v-/ 1st SUBJECT MARKER
/m-/ 1st OBJECT MARKER
/s-/ 3rd OBJECT MARKER
/-t/ PL MARKER
/-d-/ POSS MARKER
/g-/ 2nd OBJECT MARKER
/-b/ is attested in the thematic suffix /-eb/

The constituency of the set is reminiscent of 'primary' consonants (the distinction between 'primary' and 'secondary' sounds was first proposed by Jakobson (1941) and later extended by Milewski (1967, 1969) and Skalička (1970)), which appear to be the most unmarked consonants not only in Georgian, but also cross-linguistically (see also an interesting study on "basic" set of consonants by Lindblom and Maddieson 1988).

The rest of this section will focus on different prefixes and confixes in which the sonorant /m/ is manifested. There are many such grammatical morphemes and in most cases they are polysemous. Consider some illustrative examples:

/m/ as the first-person object marker appears in verb forms, e.g. *m-mal-av-s* 'somebody hides me', *m-xat'-av* 'you paint me'. The same marker expresses the first-person subject in *verba sentiendi*, e.g. in forms such as *m-sur-s* 'I want', *m-tsˈχ'uria* 'I am thirsty', *m-tsiv-a* 'I feel cold', *m-ʃi-a* 'I am hungry'.

/m/ is also manifested in prefixes like /mi-/ and /mo-/ denoting direction. They attach to the verbal root, e.g. *mi-di-s* 'somebody goes there' and *mo-dis* 'somebody comes here'; *mi-akv-s* 'somebody is taking something away' and *mo-akv-s* 'somebody is bringing something'.

There are many other cases of the occurrence of the sonorant /m/ as a prefix in nominal forms:

/m/ is attested as a part of the confix *m-e* in adjectival forms like: *m-laʃ-e* 'salty', *m-tsˈutx-e* 'salty', *m-tsˈar-e* 'hot', *m-tsˈvav-e* 'acute', *m-tʃˈl-e* 'lean', *m-k'vax-e* 'unripe', *m-tsˈip-e* 'ripe', *m-dzim-e* 'heavy', *m-tsir-e* 'small, little', *m-tʃat'-e* 'light', *m-dzay-e* 'rancid', *m-rud-e* 'curved', *m-tsˈk'lart'-e* 'astringent', *m-t'k'its-e* 'solid'. In some cases, the adjectival forms are more complex having an -ar-/-al- infix, e.g. in forms such as *m-tʃ'munv-ar-e* 'mournful', *m-tʃ'ux-ar-e* 'sad', *m-tsxunv-ar-e* 'hot', *m-xurv-al-e* 'hot', *m-tsˈχ'urv-al-e*/*m-tsˈχ'urv-al-i* 'thirsty', etc.

/m/ is also attested as a part of the confix *m-e* where this confix denotes an agent: *m-x'ep-ar-e* 'barking', *m-ʃob-i-ar-e* 'woman in childbirth', *m-tsin-ar-e/m-tsin-ar-i* 'a laughing person', *m-glovi-ar-e* 'a mourning person', *m-tsodn-e* 'expert'. The same meaning is expressed by the *m-al/ar*, *m-el*, *m-ul/ur*, *m-av* confixes:

(14) | *m-al/ar* | *m-el* | *m-ul/ur* | *m-av* |
|---|---|---|---|
| m-ts'er-al-i | m-tsv-el-i | m-sax-ur-i | m-t'virt-av-i |
| m-xatv-ar-i | m-k'vl-el-i | m-sadʒ-ul-i | m-k'er-av-i |
| m-t'arv-al-i | m-ts'vrtn-el-i | | m-retsx-av-i |

The prefix /m/, denoting meaning of an agent, is attested in words like *m-saxiob-i* 'artist, actor', *m-sadʒ-i* 'referee', *m-ts'x'ems-i* 'shepherd', *m-gzavr-i* 'passenger'.

/m/ is attested as a part of the confix *m-al/ar* in participial forms like *m-ʃr-al-I* 'dry', *m-t'k'n-ar-i* 'sweet, about water', *m-tsdar-i* 'false', *m-x'r-al-i* 'stinking', etc.

We will not discuss other participial forms such as the *ma-el*, *me-al*, *me-e*, *mo-e* confixes (Shanidze 1973).

Thus far we have illustrated that this sort of derivation is very productive (including loanwords) in Georgian. Besides, these examples illustrate that prefixes are more phonologically independent than suffixes. Such a discrepancy between prefixes and suffixes is cross-linguistically well attested (Greenberg 1966; Plank 1998). Stems in Georgian can end either in a vowel or in a consonant, while underived words can only end in a vowel.[9] Nominal word formation is stem-dependent; more specifically, the affixes attached to the stem alternate depending on whether the stem ends in a vowel or in a consonant. For example, the ergative case has the allomorphs /-m/ and /-ma/, respectively:

(15) a. *Vowel-final stems*

NOM	ERG	
xe	xe-m	'tree'
sok'o	sok'o-m	'mushroom'
deda	deda-m	'mother'

b. *Consonant-final stems*

NOM	ERG	
k'ac-i	k'ac-ma	'man'
saxl-i	saxl-ma	'house'
ts'ign-i	ts'ign-ma	'book'

---

9 Note that there are a number of adverbs ending in a consonant, e.g. *utseb* 'suddenly', *k'idev* 'again', *guʃin* 'yesterday', *k'argad* 'well', etc.

As shown in the examples in (15), the allomorph /-m/ is chosen when the stem ends in a vowel (see (15a)), while the allomorph /-ma/ is chosen when the stem ends in a consonant.

A similar asymmetric pattern at the prefix-stem and stem-suffix boundaries is also attested in resolving vowel hiatus in Georgian. Hiatus is tolerated at the prefix-stem boundary, while at the stem-suffix boundary it is not. The most common way of resolving hiatus across the stem-suffix boundary is epenthesis (Akhvlediani 1949). For the prefix /m/ this means that it can freely precede any stem-initial consonant, resulting in the types of unusual sequences of consonants presented above.

3 Comparative Data

Comparative data could shed some light on the constituency of the forms with #/m/C sequences. Consider, for example, the following correspondences between the forms of Modern Georgian and Megrelian, another Kartvelian language.

(16) *Modern Georgian*   *Megrelian*
      mxari   xuʤi   'shoulder'
      msxali   sxuli   'pear'
      mxali   xuli   'name of a meal'
      mtʃʼadi   tʃʼkʼidi 'maize-bread'

The Megrelian forms lack the word-initial /m-/ (see the Megrelian cognates in (16)). The absence of /m/ before consonants in word-initial position in Megrelian was first noticed by Gudava (1979: 82–84). This shows that either /m/ developed later in Georgian or that it was lost in Megrelian. In any case, language change must have been involved here and shows that, crucially, the first consonant of the word is a prefix and not a part of the stem.

In addition, there are correspondences between Literary Georgian and other Georgian dialects (e.g. the West Georgian dialects of Acharuli, Guruli and Imeruli) involving parallel forms with and without word-initial /m-/. Consider the correspondences in (14). The data come from Gudava (1979).

(17) a. *Literary Georgian*   *Acharuli*
           mze   ze   'sun'
           mtsʼare   tsʼre   'hot, bitter'
           mkʼlavi   kʼlavi   'arm'
           mtsʼχʼemsi   tsʼχʼesi 'shepherd'

b. *Literary Georgian*   *Imeruli*
    mta   ta   'mountain'
    mgeli[10]   geli   'wolf'
    mdidari[11]   didari 'rich'
    mʃobeli[12]   ʃobeli 'parent'

The dialectal forms systematically lack /m-/. These correspondences once again substantiate the claim that /m-/ should be analyzed as a prefixal morpheme rather than a part of the lexical morpheme in Literary Georgian.

4 Historical Studies on #*m*C Sequences

Melikishvili (1997) argues that all Proto-Kartvelian (PK) *mC(C)(V)* roots given in different etymological dictionaries should be reconstructed without *m*. The author considers 19 roots with root-initial /m/ and argues that in all of them /m/ is secondary: it is either a prefixal morpheme or the result of analogy. We consider only three roots to illustrate the arguments advanced by Melikishvili (1997).

The PK root **mze* has correspondences in Georgian such as *mze* 'sun', in Megrelian as *mʒa/bʒa*, and in Svan as *miʒ*. Melikishvili compares Georgian *mze* with the root *zu-* attested in the Georgian form *m-zu-ar-e* 'sunny place' (in this form only *-zu-* is the root, the rest are grammatical morphemes: *m-e is* a circumfix, while *-ar-* is a participial suffix). Melikishvili (1997) suggests that *mze* could be a participial form, derived by the circumfix *m-ar-em-z-e* (see also Klimov 1964). She notes that the Georgian *zu-* root has parallels with Proto-Indo-European (PIE) **sāu-*, with the same meaning. We would like to suggest a parallel with the semantically related Georgian form *mtvare* 'moon', and suggest that this form is also derived with the *m-ar-e* circumfix, i.e. *m-tv/(u)-ar-e*. Thus, these semantically related forms are derived participial forms and *m* in both forms is secondary. Compare these forms with *m-din-ar-e*, which has two meanings, 'river' and 'something that is flowing'. This is a participial form that most likely later acquired the meaning 'river'. The same process can be anticipated for *mze* and *mtvare*.

The PK root **mk'rd-* corresponds to Georgian *mk'erd-i* 'chest', and Megrelian *k'irid*. This form is also related to the PIE root **kerd-* 'heart'. Melikishvili (1997) suggests that this root should also be reconstructed without /m/. We would like to suggest there are

---

10 Compare Armenian gail 'wolf'.
11 The word seems to be semantically related to didi 'big'.
12 This word is derived from the verb ʃoba 'to give birth'.

parallel derivations for other body parts in Georgian like *mxari* (compare the verbal form *mo-xar-a* 'twisted') 'shoulder', *mk'lavi* 'arm'. 'Chest', 'arm' and 'shoulder' are semantically related body parts and the derivations of the Georgian forms *m-k'erd-i*, *m-k'lav-i* and *m-xar-i* could be the result of similar analogy, respectively.

The PK root **msxal-* corresponds to Georgian *msxal-* (in Old Georgian *sxal-* is attested), and Megrelian *sxul-*, Laz *mtsxul-* and Svan *itsx-*. Melikishvili (1997) suggests reconstructing this root as **sxal-*. We suggest that this root could be related to the verbal root *sx* attested in the forms *mo-sx-m-a, da-sx-m-a* 'bearing fruits', and *m-sxmoiar-e* 'fruit-bearing tree'. Thus, the word-initial *m* is secondary. The ending *l-i/al-i* in *msxali* could be the result of analogy. Consider other forms denoting fruits in Georgian, e.g. *vaʃli* 'apple', *ts'abli* 'chestnut', *txili* 'nuts', *k'ak'ali* 'walnut', *maχ'vali* 'blackberry', *martsvali* 'grain, seed'.

Thus, Old Georgian and comparative data (the Megrelian and Svan forms) suggest that the word-initial *m* preceding consonants is secondary, in the sense that it has (or had) a grammatical function. It is not part of the stem/root and, as Melikishvili also suggests, /m/ should not be reconstructed as a part of the Proto-Kartvelian consonant-initial roots.

5 Evidence from Reduplication and Child Language Acquisition

One interesting aspect of reduplication is that it is sometimes iconic in nature, or alternatively, as characterized by "self-evident symbolism" (Sapir 1921: 79). According to Jakobson (1949), reduplication is an iconic relation between the linear order of morphemes and the meaning which the word denotes (e.g. plurality, iteration, continuance, an increase in size, repetition or duration).[13] This peculiar type of form-meaning mapping in reduplication requires a specific phonotactic organization of the reduplicated form. Iconicity yields predictability, which is manifested in transparent phonological structure. Transparency is related to the notion of simplicity, which is a characteristic feature of unmarked structures in a language.

Reduplication is a type of affixation process which takes into account the phonology of the base (the reduplicant). A cross-linguistic study of reduplication has shown that reduplicants are less marked in particular ways than the remain-

---

[13] Note that not all types of reduplication are strictly iconic, e.g. in Leti reduplication is used to change a lexical category, e.g. *luli* 'taboo' and *lululi* 'taboo (adj)' (van der Hulst and Klamer 1996: 115).

der of the outputs of a language. In Optimality Theory, for instance, this is captured by the 'emergence of the unmarked' ranking (McCarthy and Prince 1994, 1995; Carlson 1997, among others). Since reduplication generally yields a less marked subset of what a language may allow in the way of prosodic and featural structures, reduplicative patterns of Georgian are discussed to substantiate the proposal that /m/ in #mC sequences is secondary.

There are numerous compounds in Georgian that are formed by reduplication. Reduplication occurs in verbal forms, e.g. to mark continuative aspect or intensity and in nominal forms, e.g. to form the collective plural. Reduplication is widely used in onomatopoeia, too. The reduplicant commonly attaches to a base as a suffix. Total reduplication, which involves the copying of a complete base, is quite common, but partial reduplication is also found. Both obey the general co-occurrence restrictions of the language.

If /m/C are true, genuine clusters in Georgian, then we would expect stems/roots with *mc* to reduplicate just like other consonant clusters in Georgian. Consider e.g. the reduplication forms in (18) and (19) (The glosses were omitted in purpose as all the examples in (18) and (19) are imitative (onomatopoetic) words denoting some movements and sounds emitted with various degrees of pitch or loudness):

(18) *The reduplication of stem-initial harmonic clusters*
  tkar-tkar-i
  tkon-tkor-i   sk'up'-sk'up'-i
  txap'-txap'-i   dgan-dgar-i

(19) *The reduplication of C + /v/ combinations*
  k'vink'vil-i   gvangval-i
  xvarxvar-i   xvanxval-i
  tʃvartʃval-i kvankval-i

The only attested cases of reduplicated forms with /m/C are **mta-mta, mtel-mteli**, and **mza-mzareuli**, all of them expressing some sort of intensity. Since there are many other words with /m/C sequences in Georgian, these three reduplicated forms present exceptions rather than the norm (more on reduplication in Georgian see Butskhrikidze 2002).

Evidence from child language acquisition could also shed some light on the treatment of /m/C sequences in Georgian. We do not have sufficient data to make any conclusive proposals at this point, but based on our personal experience, we can suggest that there is a delay in the acquisition of /m/C sequences compared to clusters that do obey the SSP and the OCP. What is more interesting is that kids (until around the age of two) often pronounce /m/C sequences without /m/, e.g. instead of *mgeli* 'wolf', we find *geli*, instead of *mtvare* 'moon', we find *tvare*, etc. Other consonant clusters that are well-formed onsets are pronounced without any problem, e.g. *k'ravi* 'lamb' or *byavili* 'mooing'. More research is needed to see what the regularities are, and how and when kids start mastering the actual literary forms such as *mgeli* and *mtvare*.

6 Conclusions

It has been demonstrated that there are phonological principles governing consonant co-occurrence in Georgian. However, these principles, at first sight, do not apply to #/m/C sequences, because the sonorant *m* can precede any consonant, without any restriction. The questions concerning the status of /m/ are the following: are these #/m/C sequences true clusters (just like other clusters complying with phonological principles such as the OCP, SSP, etc.) or are they secondary, for instance, the result of morphological derivation or analogy? We have considered various types of evidence: 1) synchronic patterns of consonant co-occurrence; 2) comparative data and diachronic patterns involving /m/C sequences, and 3) reduplication data. We have noted that a study on child language acquisition could also shed some light on this issue. The material discussed here suggests that the word-initial *m* preceding consonants has a grammatical function and is thus secondary. Hence, /m/ in #/m/C sequences belong to different morphemes and initial /m/C sequences are not true clusters.[14]

References

Akhvlediani, Giorgi. 1949. *Zogadi ponet'ik'is sapudzvlebi*. [Foundations of general phonetics]. Tbilisi: Tbilisis Sakhelmc'ipo Universit'et'is Gamomcemloba.
Bush, Ryan. 1997. *Georgian syllable structure*. Santa Cruz, CA: University of California Santa Cruz MA thesis.
Butskhrikidze, Marika. 2002. *The consonant phonotactics of Georgian*. Leiden: Leiden University Doctoral Dissertation. LOT: Utrecht. LOT 63.
Butskhrikidze, Marika & Jeroen M. van de Weijer. 2003. On the formal representation of metathesis in phonological theory: *v*-metathesis in Modern Georgian. *Lingua* 113. 765–778.

---

[14] Concerning syllabification, I think, /m/ should be analysed as extrasyllabic in #/m/C sequences.

Carlson, Katy. 1997. Reduplication and sonority in Nakanai and Nuxalk. In John Austin & Aaron Lawson (eds.), *Proceedings of the Fourteenth Eastern Student Conference on Linguistics '97*, 23–33. Ithaca: CLC Publications.
Chrétien, Douglas C. 1965. The statistical structure of the Proto-Austronesian morph. *Lingua* 14. 243–270.
Clements, George. 1990. The role of sonority cycle in core syllabification. In John Kingston & Mary Beckman (eds.), *Papers in Laboratory Phonology.* Vol. 1: *Between the Grammar and Physics of Speech*, 283–333. Cambridge: Cambridge University Press.
Cyran, Eugeniusz & Edmund Gussmann. 1999. Consonant clusters and governing relations: Polish initial consonant sequences. In Harry van der Hulst & Nancy Ritter (eds.), *The Syllable: Views and Facts*, 219–248. Berlin/Boston: De Gruyter.
Greenberg, Joseph H. 1966. Some universals of grammar with particular reference to the order of meaningful elements. In Joseph H. Greenberg (ed.), *Universals of Language*, 73–113. Cambridge, MA: MIT Press.
Gudava, Togo. 1979. Bagismieri tankhmovnebi chkamierta c'in Megrulshi. [Bilabial consonants in front of obstruents in Megrelian]. *Saenatmecniero K'rebuli.* Tbilisi.
Gvinadze, Tsira. 1970. Tavk'idura tankhmovantk'omp'leksebi kartulshi. [Word-initial consonant sequences in Georgian]. *Student'ta Samecniero K'onperencia* 32, 21–24. Mokhsenebat-atezisebi. Tbilisi: Tbilisis Sakhelmc'ipo Universit'et'is Gamomcemloba.
Hulst, Harry G. van der. 1984. *Syllable Structure and Stress in Dutch.* Dordrecht: Foris
Hulst, Harry G. van der & Marian Klamer. 1996. Reduplication in Leti. In Crit Cremers & Marcel den Dikken (eds.). *Linguistics in the Netherlands*, vol. 13, 109–120. Amsterdam: John Benjamins.
Hulst, Harry G. van der & Nancy Ritter. 1999. Theories of the syllable. In Harry G. van der Hulst & Nancy Ritter (eds.), *The Syllable: Views and Facts*, 13–52. Berlin: Mouton de Gruyter.
Jakobson, Roman. 1941. *Kindersprache, Aphasie und allgemeine Lautgesetze.* Uppsala: Uppsala Universitets Arsskrift.
Jakobson, Roman. 1949. The phonetic and grammatical aspects of language and their interrelation. *Proceedings of the Sixth International Congress of Linguistics*, 103–114. Paris: Klincksiek.
Klimov, Giorgi. 1964. *Etymological Dictionary of Kartvelian Languages* (in Russian). Moscow: Nauka.
Lindblom, Björn & Ian Maddieson. 1988. Phonetic universals in consonant systems. In Charles Li & Larry M. Hyman (eds.), *Language, Speech and Mind*, 62–78. London: Routledge.
McCarthy, John & Alan Prince. 1994. The emergence of the unmarked: Optimality in prosodic morphology. In Merce Gonzalez (ed.), *Proceedings of the North East Linguistic Society* 24. Graduate Linguistic Student Association, University of Massachusetts, Amherst.
McCarthy, John & Alan Prince. 1995. Faithfulness and reduplicative identity. *University of Massachusetts Occasional Papers in Linguistics* 18. 249–384.
Melikishvili, Irine. 1976. *Mark'irebis mimarteba ponologiashi.* [Markedness relations in phonology]. Tbilisi: Mecniereba.
Melikishvili, Irine. 1997. *Saerto-kartveluri dziri st'rukt'uruli da t'ip'ologiuri tvalsazrisit.* [The Proto-Kartvelian root in structural and typological aspects]. Tiblisi: Tbilisi State University Doctoral dissertation.
Milewski, Tadeusz Z. 1967. *Językoznawstwo.* [Linguistics]. Warsaw: Państwowe Wydawnictwo Naukowe.

Milewski, Tadeusz Z. 1969. *Z zagadnień językoznawstwa ogólnego i historycznego* [General and historical linguistics]. Warsaw: Państwowe Wydawnictwo Naukowe.

Nepveu, Denis. 1994. Georgian and Bella Coola: Headless Syllables and Syllabic Obstruents. Santa Cruz: University of California Santa Cruz MA thesis.

Plank, Frans. 1998. The co-variation of phonology with morphology and syntax: A hopeful history. *Linguistic Typology* 2. 195–230.

Sapir, Edward. 1921. *Language: Introduction to the Study of Speech*. New York: Harcourt, Brace & World.

Selkirk, Elisabeth O. 1984. On the major class features and syllable theory. In Mark Aronoff & Richard T. Oerhle (eds.), *Language Sound Structure*, 107–136. Cambridge, MA: MIT Press.

Shanidze, Akaki. 1973. *Kartuli gramat'ik'i s sapudzvlebi* [Foundations of Georgian grammar]. Tbilisi: Tbilisis Sakhelmc'ipo Universit'et'is Gamomcemloba.

Skalička, Vladimir. 1970. Die Typologie der Lautsysteme. *Proceedings of the International Congress of Phonetic Sciences* 6. Prague.

Torre, Erik Jan van der. 2003. Dutch sonorants: The role of place of articulation in phonotactics. Leiden: University of Leiden Doctoral dissertation. LOT: Utrecht. LOT 81.

Uturgaidze, Tedo. 1976. *Kartuli enis ponemat'uri st'rukt'ura.* [The phonemic structure of the Georgian language]. Tbilisi: Mecniereba.

Vogt, Hans. 1961. *Kartuli enis ponemat'uri st'rukt'ura.* [The phonematic structure of the Georgian Language]. Tbilisi: Tbilisis Sakhelmc'ipo Universit'et'is Gamomcemloba.

Zubkova, Ludmila G. 1990. *Fonologičeskaija typologija slova.* [The phonological typology of the word]. Moscow: Izdatel'stvo Universiteta Druzhby Narodov.

Andrea Calabrese
Gemination in Middle Indic

Abstract: Since Saussure (1889), we know that stops in clusters stop+sonorant/ sonorant+stop were geminated in Sanskrit, although this gemination may not be represented orthographically in this language. The same gemination is observed in the outcomes of these clusters in Middle Indic languages. Gemination in these languages will be the focus of this paper, e.g. Pāli: *arabh + ya-→arabbha-*Passive of *arabh* 'begin', *kar + tum-→kattuṃ* Inf. of. *kar* 'make'.

Gemination, however, was not the only process removing these consonantal cluster in Middle Indic. As shown in Pischel (1981), there are dialects in which epenthesis is used instead of gemination (plus single consonant deletion): Apabhraṁśa *garāsa* 'swallowing' < Sanskrit *grāsa;* Ardha-Magadhi *usiṇa* 'hot, warm' < Sanskrit *usna*. Evidence for a dialectal distinction in Middle Indic is also provided by the Aśoka inscriptions: As observed by Cardona (2003), there is epenthesis, instead of gemination (+single consonant deletion) in these cluster in the Jaugada dialect of these inscriptions. I will propose that an adequate analysis of these processes is most adequately accounted for by assuming the X-skeletal model of syllable structure (Levin 1985, van der Hulst and Ritter 1999).

Keywords: Gemination, skeletal positions, syllable structure, phonological rules, constraints & repairs, complex onsets, codas, consonantal cluster removal

1 Introduction

Since Saussure (1889), we know that stops in clusters stop+sonorant/sonorant+ stop were geminated (e.g., VprV→VpprV, VrpV→VrppV) in Sanskrit, at least in a late stage of this language. The same gemination is observed in the outcomes of these clusters in Middle Indic languages that developed from Sanskrit. Gemination in Sanskrit and in these languages will be the focus of this paper.

I will propose that this gemination results from a process removing complex onsets and codas. This analysis assumes the following: i) the X-skeletal model of

---

Note: I offer this article to Harry van der Hulst in great appreciation of the theoretical contributions of a scholar of outstanding ability. The article develops, clarifies and refines some of the analyses of the same phenomena proposed in Calabrese (2009b).

Andrea Calabrese, University of Connecticut

https://doi.org/10.1515/9783110730081-002

syllable structure (Levin 1985; van der Hulst and Ritter 1999). ii) The phonological model developed in Calabrese (2005, 2009a, 2019). This model includes both negative constraints and rules, which are considered different types of phonological instructions (see the quoted works for detailed discussion). Establishing the nature of the operations triggered by these instructions is thus of crucial importance, and emphasis is given to what happens when phonological changes are implemented; in fact, these implementations are not hidden in GEN as in OT (Prince and Smolensky 2002 [1993]). So, this paper will look at what happens when configurations in violation of constraint against complex onsets and codas are repaired by the realignment of melodic roots and skeletal positions in the onset (root spreading). As will be seen, this is the repair that leads to gemination in Sanskrit and Middle Indic.

2 Theoretical Preliminaries

2.1 The X-Skeletal Model of Syllable Structure

I will propose that an adequate analysis of Sanskrit and Middle Indic requires assuming the X-skeletal model of syllable structure against the currently popular moraic model of syllable structure. In the X-skeletal model of syllable structure, skeletal positions must be considered as the interface level between the melodic component and syllable structure. A skeletal position represents the syllabic segment, the structural unit that is relevant for syllable structure. A skeletal position is to be distinguished from the melodic root whose function is to represent the temporal overlap or simultaneity among the features it dominates. A root represents the melodic segment, a bundle of simultaneously articulated features.

Such a distinction between syllabic segments and melodic segments is, for example, needed to describe sounds such as the labio-coronal /ps/ of Margi (Ladefoged 1968), the velarized coronal affricate /tx/ of Xũ (Snyman 1970) or the double fricatives [fs, ff, βʃ] of SePedi (Ladefoged and Maddieson 1996). The languages where these sounds are found have simple CV syllables and therefore do not allow consonantal clusters. Hence, these sounds must involve a single syllabic unit but two melodic elements. For example, in the case of SePedi (Northern Soto), a language with CV syllables, the following spectrograms of the double fricatives in words such as βofsa 'youth', and leʃʃera 'coward' demonstrate that these are phonetic sequences. One articulation follows the other, so that for example SePedi fs is not very different from the fs in an English word as *offset* (Lagefoged and Maddieson 1996: 330–331). This dissociation between melodic structure and syllabic behavior is most adequately represented as in (2):

(1)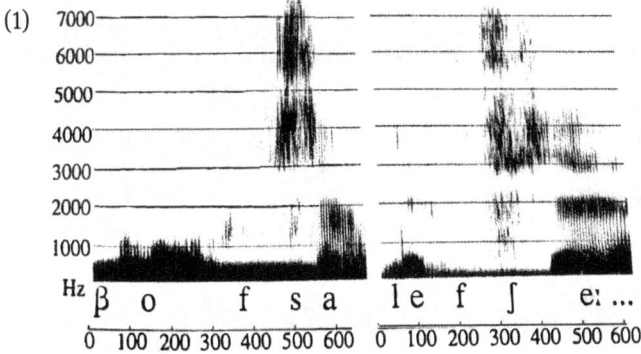

(2) SePedi /fs/ (see Clements 1992)

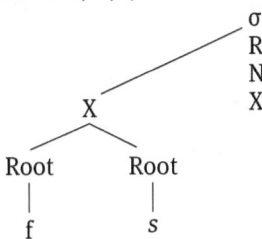

Further evidence in support of structures in which a single skeletal slot dominates more melodic segments also comes from Kinyarwanda, an eastern Bantu language spoken in Rwanda. Sagey (1986) shows that like many Bantu languages, Kinyarwanda has only open syllables. However, she points out that a first look at a typical word in Kinyarwanda seems to suggest quite complex onset consonant clusters.

(3) u.mu.ga.bo   'man'
    i.mɲee.ru .mɲe   'male dig'
    u.bgaa.nŋwa   'beard'
    kwaa.ka   'to ask'

(4) a. tkwaa.ŋga   'we hate'
        mɲaa.nho.re.ye   'you (pl.) worked for me'
        nda.me.sa   'wash'
    b. ka.rii .ndgwi   'seven'

At the same time, the syllabification in Kinyarwanda of loan words with consonant clusters shows a pattern in which almost no clusters are allowed. This contrasts with the complex clusters seen above. Thus, the *rg* and the *st* in *Burgermeister* are split by epenthesis, yielding [*burugumesitiri*]. Similarly, the *ks* in *Alexander* is split, yielding [*aregisaanderi*]. Other sample German loan-word clusters split by epenthesis are given in (5)

(5) Republik   repuburika
    Präsident perezida
    Patrizia   paatirisiya
    Petroleum peeterorii
    Präfekt   perefe

Relying on the preceding arguments, Sagey (1986) proposes that the maximal syllable in Kinyarwanda is CV(V). Therefore, the words in (3) and (4) cannot be analyzed as containing consonant clusters: a syllable such as *tkwaa* does not conform to the requirement for a maximum onset of one, consonant if [*tkw*] is analyzed as a consonant cluster. Rather, the evidence from syllabification in Kinyarwanda suggests that the onsets must involve single segments from the syllabic point of view.

Ladefoged and Maddieson (1996), however, show that while the labial-velar stop is characterized by the simultaneous use of the dorsal and labial articulators, the same cannot be said of Kinyarwanda tk^w. In this case we are dealing with a sequence of melodic segments. They, in fact, show that sequences such as *tk*, *dg* are quite unambiguously phonetic sequences of two stops, as also shown by Jouannet (1983). They use data from the Zezuru dialect of Shona (Maddieson 1990), similar to Kinyarwanda from this point of view. So, for example, the audio waveforms of the phrase *tkwana tkwangu* 'my little child' in two male speakers ((6)) indicates that the release of *t* clearly precedes *k*. The alveolar and velar closures do not overlap at all (Ladefoged and Maddieson 1996: 346).

(6)
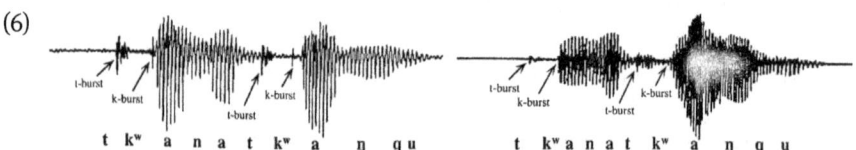

The sequence tk^w involving a single syllabic position and a multiple melodic constituency is most adequately represented as in (7) (using the feature model of Halle, Vaux, and Wolfe 2000):

(7)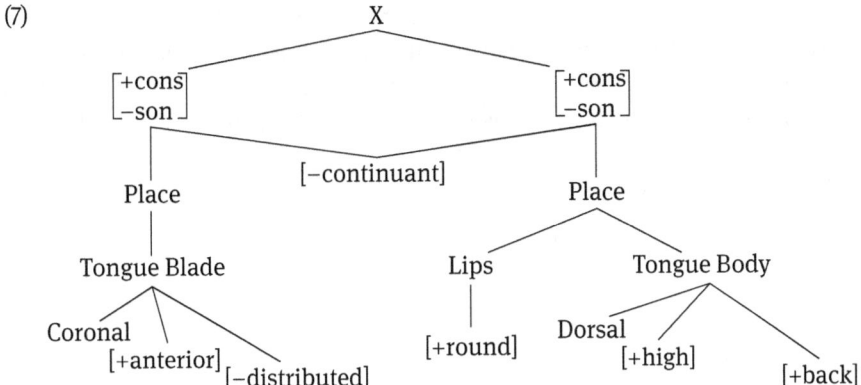

2.2 Root Spreading

Assuming phonological representations as those argued above, consider the structures in (8). To have an onset cluster, one needs two or more skeletal positions, each exhaustively associated with a melodic segment. A given melodic segment is assigned a given syllabic status through its association with a skeletal position. By changing its association relations to the skeletal positions, we can change its syllabic status.

(8) a. a simple onset. b. a complex onset.

 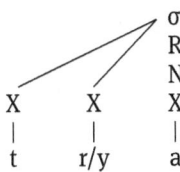

It follows that syllable structure configurations are governed by constraints targeting the relations between classes of melodic segments and syllabic positions such as the one in (9) in the case of complex onsets of rising sonority.

(9) No Complex onsets:

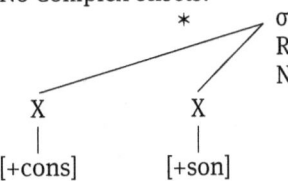

In Calabrese (2005) I therefore argued that a possible way of repairing violation of the constraint in (9) involves a realignment of the relation between melodic roots and syllabic segments as in (10), what I called root spreading. This operation must be recognized as an alternative repair strategy to epenthesis and deletion:

(10) Root spreading:

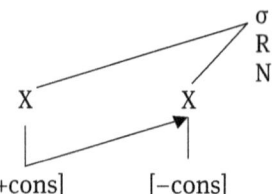

Consider the structure in (10). When the root node of the first onset consonant is expanded onto the skeletal position dominating the glide, we are no longer dealing with an onset cluster. As mentioned above, to have an onset cluster one needs two or more skeletal positions, each exhaustively associated with a melodic segment. Thus, by the change in (10), the onset cluster is removed from the syllabic interface, and can no longer be targeted by the constraint in (5). Observe that the root that spreads is the one of the least sonorous segments, the one that forms the best onset – and the best syllable margin – according to Clements' (1990) Sonority Dispersion principle.

The application of root spreading creates an onset geminate, which is disallowed by the constraint in (11). This onset geminate is then repaired by delinking its first member from the onset position as in (12):

(11) *

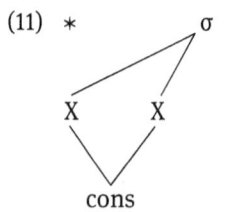

(12) a.

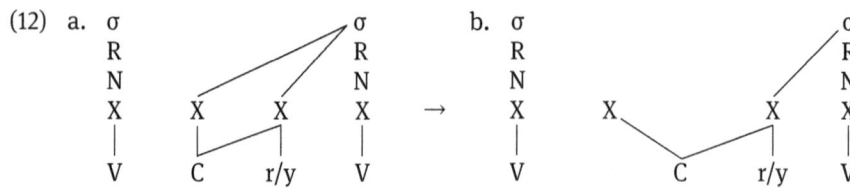

The unsyllabified consonant that results is incorporated into the preceding syllable thus generating a legitimate geminate.

(13)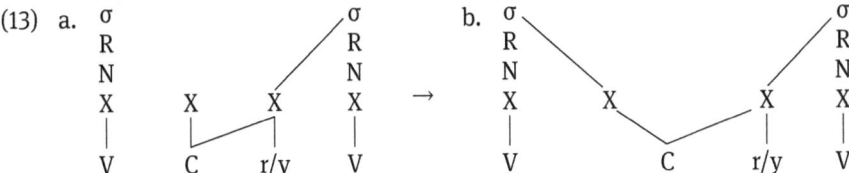

If there no no preceding open syllable, one can assume that the first skeletal position of the onset geminate is deleted as in (14):

(14)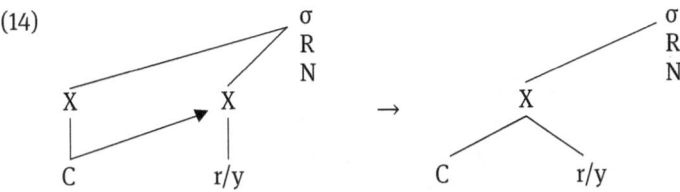

As discussed in Calabrese (2005), the first palatalization of Romance provides an example of root spreading. This historical process deals with the treatment of pre-glide consonants. In this context, consonants were geminated and if the glide was palatal, nonlabial consonants were also palatalized (the process of palatalization will not be discussed here (see Calabrese 2005; Petrosino and Calabrese 2021) (see (17) for the change *sepia→seppya* 'cuttlefish'):

	Proto-Romance	Italian
(15)	*sepya*	*seppya* 'cuttlefish'
	simya	*ʃimmya* 'monkey'
	manwa	*mannwa* ((\[w\] was subsequently lost) → *manna*) 'bundle'
	futwo	*fottwo* (→ It. *fotto*) 'I fuck'

	Proto-Romance	Italian	
(16)	*pretyu*	*prettso*	'price'
	putyu	*pottso*	'well'
	brakyu	*brattʃo*	'arm'
	[e]rikyu	*rittʃo*	'hedgehog'

(17) a.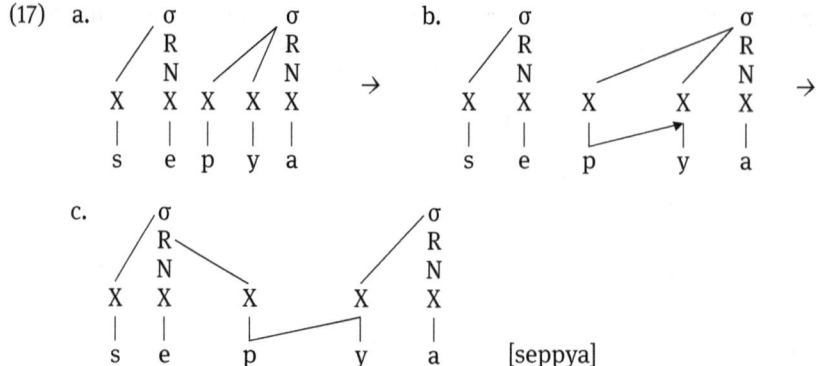

c.

Other examples of this type of gemination are listed below:

(18) Ancient Greek Gemination:
kēruk-y-ō →	kērussō, Attic kēruttō	'herald'
tarakʰ-y-ō →	tarassō, Attic tarattō	'disturb'
eret-y-ō →	eressō, Attic erettō	'row'
koruth-y-ō →	korussō, Attic koruttō	'equip'
tetwar →	tesseres, tettares	
ekwos →	ippos	

(19) West Germanic gemination (GO=Gothic, OS=Old Saxon, OE=Old English):
sat.jan GO	settian OS	settan OE	'to set'
kun.jis GO	kunnies OS	cynnes OE	'race' (gen.)
hal.ja GO	hellia OS	helle OE	'hell'
bid.jan GO	biddian OS	biddan OE	'to ask for'

In this article, I would like to propose that gemination in Sankrit and Middle Indic was due to a root spreading process that eliminated complex onsets in these languages. As will be discussed in more detail later, a similar process eliminated codas by spreading the root associated with onset--the best syllable margin – onto the coda position:

3 Facts

3.1 Sanskrit

According to Wackernagel (1896: 278), Kurylowicz (1948: 199), ancient Sanskrit grammarians prescribe the following rules of syllabification for their own language:

(20) a. A single consonant is the onset of the following syllable:
      ta . pas-
   b. In the same way the last consonant of a bisegmental cluster, but crucially not the first.
      tap . ta-, put . ra-, vid . ya-
   c. The last two consonants of a cluster of 3 members are syllabified as part of the onset of the following syllable when the last consonant is a sibilant (ś, ṣ, s), or a sonorant (r, l, n):
      astam.psit,   *can.drá*

Rule (20)b) explicitly states that bisegmental clusters, and in particular also clusters of rising sonority such as *-tr-, -dy-*, are hetero-syllabic. Observe, however, that according to (20)c), in the case of clusters such as *mps, ndr* the last two segments are considered as part of the complex onset of the following syllable. From this, it should follow that complex onsets are actually possible, despite what seems to be implied by the statement in (20) b). We can account for all of these cases if we assume that the first member of intervocalic bisegmental clusters makes position, i.e., make the preceding syllable heavy. I assume that this is the issue the grammarians try to address with the statements in (20). This is what we can expect if the first consonant in these clusters is geminated.

Evidence for this hypothesis is provided by Saussure (1889), who observed that there was a lack of contrast between the Sanskrit forms in (21)a) as discussed in the passage in (21)b):

(21) a. *śara-trayam*   (trois flèches)   *śarattrayam (< śarad-trayam)* (trois automnes),
   b. Saussure (1889: 426–427):
      "Devant liquide, nasale ou semi-consonne, le catégories de la consonne double et de la consonne simple sont absolument confondues en sanskrit. Etant donnés les composés *śara-trayam* (trois flèches) et *śarad-trayam* (trois automnes), nous croyons devoir en Europe observer la différence

étymologique dans l'orthographe, écrire l'un *śaratrayam* et le second *śarattrayam*. Si nous consultons la tradition indigène, nous apprenons qu'il faut écrire:
a. D'après nombre de manuscripts dans les deux cas *śaratrayam*. Aucune occlusive n'est marquée double devant [r, w].
b. D'après certains Prātiśākhyas: dans les deux cas *śarattrayam*. Aucune occlusive n'est marquée simple devant [r, w].
c. D'après Pāṇini (8, 4, 47); cf. avec critique 48 et 50–52): dans les deux cas *śaratrayam* ou dans le deux cas *śarattrayam*. Emploi à volonté de la lettre double ou simple devant [r, w].

Cette dernière doctrine, pour etre fidèlement rapportée, doit plutot se formuler comme suit: toute occlusive est supposée simple devant [r, w], mais on peut toujours la redouble."

According to Saussure, the reason for the lack of contrast in the Sanskrit forms in (21)a is that the stop in clusters stop+ sonorant was geminated.

In fact, in many Sanskrit manuscripts, the first consonant of clusters of rising sonority is written as double as shown in (22) (Whitney 1868; Wackernagel 1896: 112) and especially Varma (1929: chapters 2 and 5), for a detailed discussion of the facts. See also Suzuki (2015).

(22) *dádhyátra*   →   *daddhyatra*   'sour milk + here'
      mádhvátra   →   *máddhvátra*   'delicious + here'
      agní   →   *aggní*   'fire'
      putráḥ   →   *puttráḥ*   'son, child'
      satyáḥ   →   *sattyáḥ*   'true'

Detailed accounts of the conditions under which graphic doubling occurs in Sanskrit: Panini 8.4.46–52, Whitney (1868: 284–313),

(23) Panini 8.4.46–52:
The first consonant of a cluster is doubled, but when the first member of the cluster belongs to the set {r l v h}, it is the second member which is doubled.

Note that Panini observes that gemination is found also in clusters such as that in (24)a where we have a simple coda containing a liquid followed by a simple onset. It is the simple onset that is geminated in this case (Pischel 1981: 233; Masica 1991: 176). Gemination of a consonant is also found when followed by a consonant of the same sonority as in (24)b)(see below for more sample cases):

(24) *artha* [*arttha*] 'purpose' *sapta* [*saptta*] 'seven'

Let us focus on onset clusters and first consider clusters of a labiovelar high vocoid before a palatal glide, as in the forms in (25):[1]

(25) *gávya-*   'relating to cows'   (< gau + ya-)
      návya-   'praise-Gerundive'   (< nau + ya-)
      plaːvya-   'float-Gerundive'   (< plau + ya-)
      bhavya-   'be-Gerundive'   (< bhau + ya-)
      divyá-   'heavenly'   (< diu + ya-)

By rule, a postvocalic high vocoid before a non-syllabic segment merges with the preceding vowel into a diphthong, which is later monophthongized when the vowel is short, as shown in (26):

(26) *góbhiḥ*   'cow-Instr. Pl.'   (< gau + bhis)
      ánuːnot   'praise-Aorist'   (< a + nu + nau + t)
      ploṣyáti   'float-Future'   (< plau + sya + ti)
      bodhí   'be-Aor. Imperative'   (< bhau + dhi)
      juhóti   'pour a libation-PR'   (ju + (g)hau + ti)

The process of merging we see in the forms in (26) can be accounted for by assuming that the high vocoid in these forms is in coda position and that there is a process of coda incorporation that incorporates the coda high vocoid into the preceding nucleus, as shown in (27):

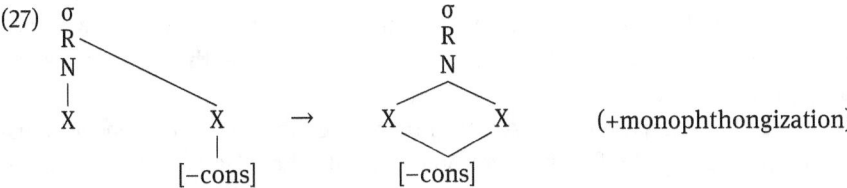

Now, if the labiovelar high vocoids occurring before the palatal glide in (25) were actually in coda position we should expect them to merge with the preceding

---

1 All the forms in (23) often have a trisyllabic scansion in the Rigveda (e.g., *gavi(y)a*, *bhavi(y)a*). Crucially disyllabic scansions such as those mentioned in (23) are also found (cf. Seebold 1972). My analysis is based on these disyllabic scansions. See Calabrese (2019: IV.3.4–5) for discussion of the variations in the syllabic scansion of high vocoids in the Rigveda.

vowel as in (28)a. This is not what actually happens. We can hence conclude that the labiovelar glide in (25) cannot be in coda position, but must be in the same onset as the following glide as in (28)b. Complex onsets with a glide as a last member must therefore be possible.

(28) a. * *gáu . ya-* [*góya-*]   'relating to cows'   (< gau + ya)
       * *náu . ya-* [*nóya-*]   'praise-Gerundive'   (< nau + ya-)
       * *plau . ya-* [*ploya-*] 'float-Gerundive'   (< plau + ya-)
       * *bháu . ya-* [*bhóya-*] 'be-Gerundive'   (< bhau + ya-)

   b. *gá. vya-*   'relating to cows'   (< gau + ya-)
      ná. vya-   'praise-Gerundive'   (< nau + ya-)
      pla:. vya- 'float-Gerundive'   (< plau + ya-)
      bhá. vya- 'be -Gerundive'   (< bhau + ya-)

The syllabification we have in (28)b is accounted for by assuming a syllabification rule incorporating a preceding sonorant as an onset of a syllable beginning with the glide [y] stated in (29):

(29)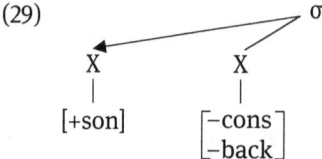

Observe that there is no evidence for the syllabification in (28)a in the historical development of Sanskrit, and we can exclude that it ever appeared. Still, as mentioned above, the fact is that clusters of rising sonority, such VwyV, always make the preceding syllable heavy (cf. Varma 1929: 77). Therefore, the [w] must also be syllabified as a coda.

There is an apparent contradiction then. The labio-velar high vocoid must be in the onset of the following syllable since it otherwise would be monophthongized with the preceding vowel. This is in fact what happens to high vocoids in coda position, as shown in (26). However, the labiovelar high vocoids in (25) also makes the preceding vowel heavy. Therefore, it must also be in the coda of that syllable.

How can this contradiction be solved? The solution is simple. Let us assume that (29) applies before (27) bleeding its application. After application of (29) and the subsequent root spreading, a word like *gavya* is then syllabified as in (30).

(30)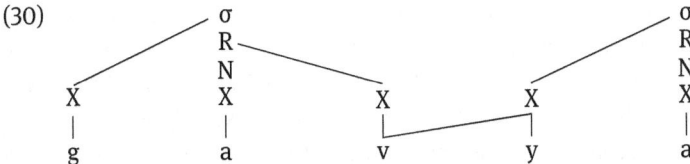

It follows that the first consonant of intervocalic clusters of rising sonority has a double identity: it is the coda of the preceding syllable, thus making it heavy, but at the same time, it is in the onset of the following syllable. I assume that this is due to root spreading as a repair of an active constraint against complex onsets.

Other evidence pointing to the syllabification of intervocalic onset clusters is provided by the reduplicated aorist (Jamison 1983; Vaux 1992). This verbal form is characterized by the fixed prosodic template in (31) with the reduplicated prefix heavy and the root syllable light. If the prefixal syllable is not heavy by position, the template is satisfied by lengthening its vowel as shown in (32). A consonantal cluster blocks this lengthening, as shown in (33):

(31) [σ_{Prefix} - σ_{Root}]
         H   L

(32) á-niːnaś-am   (naś 'be lost')   á-jiːjan-am   (jan 'beget')
     á-buːbhuv-aḥ   (bhuː 'be')   á-ciːkr̥ṣ-am   (karṣ 'plough')

(33) á-cukrudh-at   (kraudh 'be angry')   á-titras-an   (tras 'be terrified')
     á-śuśruv-at   (śrau 'hear')   á-dudruv-at   (drau 'run')
     á-didyut-at   (dyaut 'shine')   siṣvap-aḥ   (svap 'sleep')

The short vowel in the reduplicated syllable in the forms in (33) shows that clusters of rising sonority make the preceding syllable heavy. This fact hints at a syllabification of clusters of rising sonority in which the first member is a coda of the preceding syllable, thus making it heavy. One can assume that it is geminated as argued above.[2]

---

[2] Further possible evidence for this syllabification in Sanskrit is provided the metrical behavior of consonantal clusters. In fact, the Vedic meter appears to consider all intervocalic consonantal clusters as hetero-syllabic regardless of the relative sonority of their constituents. Thus, in the Vedic metric system, all obstruent + sonorant clusters make position, i.e., is metrically heavy. We can see this in the hendecasyllable in (i) (, = caesura, | =cadence, L = Light syllable, H = Heavy syllable). The cluster /tr/ in (i) makes the preceding syllable heavy. This suggests the syllabification in (ii)b, and not that in (iii)c:

The best way to account for the Sanskrit facts is that the situation we observe is due to a change in syllabification patterns. In an early stage of the language complex onsets and codas were allowed. In a later stage they became disallowed. This led to root spreading and gemination as argued above. Note, however, that the synchronic evidence seems to indicate that this diachronic change still has an effect on the synchronic syllabification insofar as the simplest analysis of the facts leads to the postulation of two passes of syllabification. In an initial pass complex onsets and simple and complex codas are allowed.[3] In a subsequent pass, in contrast, both complex onsets and simple and complex codas are disallowed. This is due to the fact that constraints against these configurations are actively implemented. Configurations violating these constraints are repaired by root spreading. According to Varma (1929), graphic doubling in the manuscripts represents actual gemination: wherever a consonant is graphically double in the Sanskrit manuscripts, later stages of Sanskrit, and in particular Middle Indic, display an actual geminate in its place (see also Jacobi 1881: 609). Thus, we can assume that in the case of the words in (22) and (24) we have the structure in (34)a) and b), respectively:

(34) a. Sanskrit *putra*: b. Sanskrit: *art^{h}a*

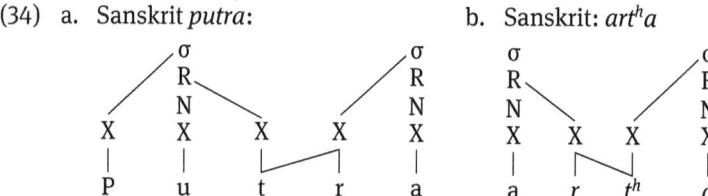

It is important to notice that gemination was not the only strategy used to repair consonantal clusters in Middle Indic. As shown in Pischel (1981), there are dialects in which epenthesis is used instead of gemination (plus deletion):

(i) L H   L H ,   L L L | H L   H H
     amī́   t[u]vā jahati putra   devā́ḥ   (RV 4.18.11b)
     'these gods are abandoning you, son'

(ii) a. putráḥ 'son'   b. put.ráh   not   c. pu.tráḥ

These facts could be interpreted as pointing to a syllabification where the first member of a cluster of rising sonority is geminated.

Unfortunately, the metrical behavior of clusters is often not a reliable source of information on syllable structure as pointed out by Steriade (1982) insofar as it is often influenced by traditional conventions established by poets and grammarians.

3 For the sake of brevity, I will ignore the important issue of whether the two passes correspond to different morphological stages of the derivation; something that is really not relevant for the analysis developed here (see Calabrese 2019 for discussion).

(35) Apabhraṁśa　　　　　　　　　　Sanskrit
　　　garāsa　　'swallowing'　　　　　grāsa
　　　tarāsai　　'be terrifiedP3s'　　　trasyati
　　　paramāna　'measure, scale'　　　pramāna
　　　parasanna　'clear, right'　　　　prasanna

(36) Ardha-Magadhi　　　　　　　　　Sanskrit
　　　rayana　　'gift'　　　　　　　　ratna
　　　usiṇa　　　'hot, warm'　　　　　usna
　　　sināi　　　'bathe3Pr.'　　　　　snāti
　　　kiriya　　 'the sign Aries'　　　kriya
　　　śiloka　　 'sound, noise'　　　　śloka
　　　suviṇa　　'sleep'　　　　　　　 svapna

In Ardha-Magadhi, clusters with a glide are repaired by assigning nuclear status to the glide – This treatment is common after long vowels and word-initial position (cf. Sievers' Law).

(37) Ardha-Magadhi　　　　　　　　　Sanskrit
　　　ciyatta　　'left, abandoned'　　tyakta
　　　baliya　　 'boyhood'　　　　　　bālya
　　　āriya　　　'respectable man'　　ārya
　　　tuvarai　　'hasten-Pr3sg.'　　　tvarate
　　　suvo　　　'dog'　　　　　　　　śvah

Evidence for a dialectal distinction in Middle Indic is also provided by the Aśoka inscriptions: As observed by Cardona (2003), there is epenthesis, instead of assimilation (gemination+single consonat deletion in my terms), in cluster in the Jaugada dialect of these inscriptions.

The dialectal variation we observe in Middle Indic points to a situation where consonantal clusters were avoided and eliminated by different strategies. Gemination appears to be one of these strategies, and it can be naturally accounted for if one assumes root spreading.

The dialectal variation also allows us to reconstruct a stage of Indic where clusters were allowed and there was no gemination. Pre-Classical Sanskrit may be close to this stage, an exception must be made for clusters with glides, which according to Calabrese (2019) were already excluded in Vedic Sanskrit. Given Panini's statement in (23), one must assume that the Sanskrit language of his time was already changing its syllabification patterns. This is assumed here, although, further philological research on this point is obviously required.

3.2 Gemination in Middle Indic Languages

As mentioned above, gemination in consonantal clusters characterizes the Middle Indic languages that developed from Sanskrit (cf. Geiger 2013 [1916]. Sample cases of the development of Sanskrit clusters of rising sonority are given below (where the Sanskrit surface syllabifications as expected from the discussion in the preceding section is given in column b.)[4,5,6]

---

[4] Synchronic alternations in Pāli, one of these middle Indic languages, are given below (Aissen and Hankamer 1979):

(i) arabh + ya-   →   arabbha-   pass. arabh 'to begin'
     pac + ya-   →   pacca-   pass. pac 'to cook'
     kas + ya-   →   kassa-   pass. kas 'to farm'
     lag + na-   →   lagga-   pp. lag 'to attach'
     kar + tum-   →   kattuṃ   inf. kar 'to make'

[5] Two rules of palatalization are needed to account for the clusters such as those in (i–ii). They cannot be discussed here.

(i) Skt. Input   Middle Indic
     satya   'truth'   sacca
     madhya.   'middle'   majjha

(ii) Skt.   Middle Indic
     matsara   'exhilarating' macchara
     apsaras   'nymph'   acchara

[6] Note that gemination is not controlled by prosodic structure. Gemination can occur anywhere in the word and is independent of the position of accent. It depends only of the segmental composition of the string, its syllable structure as proposed in the next section.

(i) Sanskrit input   Sanskrit surface   Middle Indic
     catvā́ras   'four'   cattvā́ras   cattaro
     supyáte   'sleeps'   suppyate   suppati
     víklava   'alarmed'   vikklava   vikkava-
     prajválati 'ignites'   prajjválati   pajjalati
     sahásra   'thousand'   sahássra   sahassa
     adhyātmám   'concerning self'   addhyāttmám   ajjhappa
     dā́kṣiṇā́tya 'southern, from the south' dā́kkṣiṇā́ttya   dakkhiṇattā
     dā́kṣinya   'skill'   dā́kkṣinnya   dakkhiṇṇa

Suzuki (2015) also observes that graphic gemination in Sanskrit manuscripts is independent from stress placement.

(38) a. Skt. Input   b. Skt. Surface   c. Middle Indic
    aśakya   'impossible'   aśakkya   asakka
    supyatē 'sleeps'   suppyatē   suppati
    ramya   'enoyable'   rammya   ramma
    catvaras 'four'   cattvaras   cattaro
    pakva   'cooked, ripe'   pakkva   pakka
    aśva   'horse'   aśsva   assa
    viklava 'alarmed'   vikklava   vikkava
    cakra   'wheel'   cakkra   cakka
    vajra   'thunderbolt'   vajjra   vajja
    aśru   'tear'   aśśru   assu
    agnih   'fire'   aggnih   aggi

Observe, though, that there is no gemination in this type of clusters after long vowels:

(39) *Pāṇini* 8.4.52: [There is no doubling] after long vowels, according to all teachers
    mātra- → *māttra- 'measure'

(40) Sanskrit   Middle Indic
    āsya   āsa
    ātman   āda
    saumya   soma
    mātrā   māyā
    dīrgha   dīha
    pārsva   pāsa

Furthermore, there is no gemination in clusters of rising sonority in word-initial position neither in Sanskrit (41) – as hinted by the absence of graphic doubling especially post-pausally,[7] nor in any of the Middle Indic developments. In this latter case, the clusters are simplified by eliminating the most sonorous one.

---

[7] Instances of graphic doubling in word-initial clusters may be found in Sanskrit manuscripts (Suzuki 2015: 4):

(i) a. manasā d^hyāyati > manasādd^{h}yāyati 'considers with the mind'
    b. uru prat^{h}asva > urupprat^{h}assva 'spread wide'
    c. mad^{h}u atra > madd^{h}vatra 'there is honey here'

(41) Skt. Input
    śruta 'heard'
    dhvani 'sound'
    grāma 'village'
    śyāma 'dark'

(42) Sanskrit   Middle Indic
    kvathati → *kaḍhai* 'boils'
    dvija → *dia* 'sister-in-law'
    trasati → *tasati* 'tremble'
    grāma → *gāma* 'village'

As mentioned above, gemination is found also in clusters of falling sonority where we have a simple coda containing a liquid followed by simple onset. It is the simple onset that is geminated in this case (Pischel 1981: 233; Masica 1991: 176).[8]

(43) a. Skt. Input   b. Middle Indic
    ardha 'half'   *addha*
    mārga 'road'   *magga*
    arpita 'entrusted'   *appita*
    artha 'purpose'   *attha*
    phalgu 'spring season'   *phaggu*
    alpa 'small'   *appa*

However, there is no gemination in homorganic clusters nasal + stop (see Masica 1991: 178; Pischel 1981: 222). This is consistent with the Grammarians'

I assume that here one is dealing with across-word re-syllabification (see the example in (ic) in particular where [u] undergoes glide formation insofar it is followed by the vowel [a].

8 Clusters of both rising and falling sonority containing a coronal fricative display aspiration in Middle Indic (Varma 1929: 75; Pischel 1981: 238, 258; Masica 1991: 177):

(i) a. Skt. Input   b. Skt. Surface   c. Middle Indic
    kṣata 'wounded'   *kṣata*   *khata*
    akṣi 'eye'   *akkṣi*   *akkhi* (also *acchi*)
    śikṣita 'learned'   *śikkṣita*   *sikkhida*

(ii) a. Skt. Input   b. Skt. Surface   c. Middle Indic
    hasta 'the hand'   *hastta*   *hattha*
    puṣṭa 'well-fed'   *puṣṭṭa*   *puṭṭha*
    puṣkara 'blue lotus'   *puṣkkara*   *pŏkkhara*
    aṣṭā 'eight'   *aṣṭṭā*   *attha*

statement: TP 14.23: *Consonants followed by a homogeneous or identical consonants are not doubled* (Whitney 1868: 308).

(44) a. Skt. Input   b. Middle Indic
    antara 'interior'   antara
    andha   'blind'   andha
    aŋkuśa 'elephant'   aNkusa
    kaṇṭha 'throat'   kaṇṭha
    lamba   'pendent'   lamba

There is always gemination in clusters of equal sonority (Masica 1991: 174; Pischel 1981: 221).

(45) a. Skt. Input   b. Skt. Surface   c. Middle Indic
    bhakta 'meal, food'   bhaktta   bhatta
    dugdha 'milk'   dugddha   duddha
    ṣaṭka   'set of six'   ṣaṭkka   chakka
    mudga   'mung bean'   mudgga   mugga
    utpāta 'sudden portent' utppāta   uppāta
    śadba   'sound'   śadbba   sabba
    sapta   'seven'   saptta   satta
    labdha 'taken'   labddha   laddha

Note that in clusters of rising sonority where a coronal fricative is followed by a nasal, given the pattern observed above, one should expect the fricative to be geminated. There are a few sample cases of this type ((46)). However, it is usually the nasal that is doubled in the manuscripts in this case (cf. *brahmma, raśmmiṣu* (Varma 1929: 123) and in Middle Indic, these clusters developed into a geminated aspirated nasal (see footnote 3 about the digraph *nh*).[9]

---

[9] The digraph nasal+h represents an aspirated nasal (Masica 1991: 178). Its geminate status is shown by the fact that it triggers shortening of the preceding vowel as all other geminates (Masica 1991: 183):

(i) Skt. *grīsma* 'summer heat'   MI *gimha*
    Skt. *śleṣman* 'mucus, phlegm' MI *silemha/silimha*

This shortening is due to Geiger's Law according to which syllable rimes in MI cannot exceed two moras.

(46) a. Skt. Input | | b. Skt. Surface | c. Middle Indic
raśmi 'rope' | rassmi | rassi
etasmin 'this-Lsg.' | etassmin | edassim

(47) -sn- clusters
a. Skt. Input | | b. Skt. Surface | c. Middle Indic
praśna 'question' | praśnna | paṇha
prasnava 'flow' | prasnnava | paṇhava
Kṛṣṇa 'dark blue' | Kṛṣnna | Kaṇha
grīṣma 'summer heat' | grīṣmma | gimha
aśman 'stone' | aśmman | amha
vismaya 'wonder' | vismmaya | vimhaya

Analysis

4.1 Gemination in Middle Indic Bisegmental Clusters

As already proposed, the main purpose of the root spreading is the elimination of complex onsets and codas.

Let us consider Sanskrit again. I proposed that in an initial syllabification pass, complex onsets and codas are allowed. However, these complex onsets and codas are eliminated in a second pass of syllabification through the operation of root spreading (Pischel 1981: 225, 233; Masica 1991: 174–175):

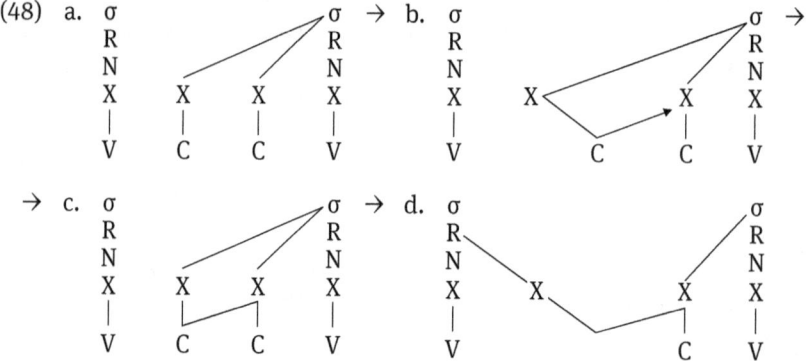

The Middle Indic outcomes can be accounted for by assuming a process delinking branching roots in (49). The Uniformity Applicability Condition (UAC) in (55) allows the application of (49) only to singly-linked branching roots.

(49)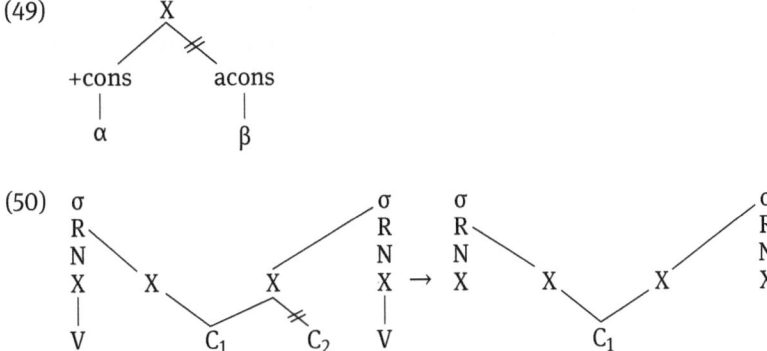

(50)

I assume that root spreading also applied to complex onsets in word-initial position. No gemination in Sanskrit or in Middle Indic is observed here (e.g. *śruta* 'heard' *suta*, *grāma* 'village' *gāma*). This can be accounted for by assuming that the onset geminate resulting from the application of root spreading as in (51)b) is eliminated by skeletal deletion:

(51) a. 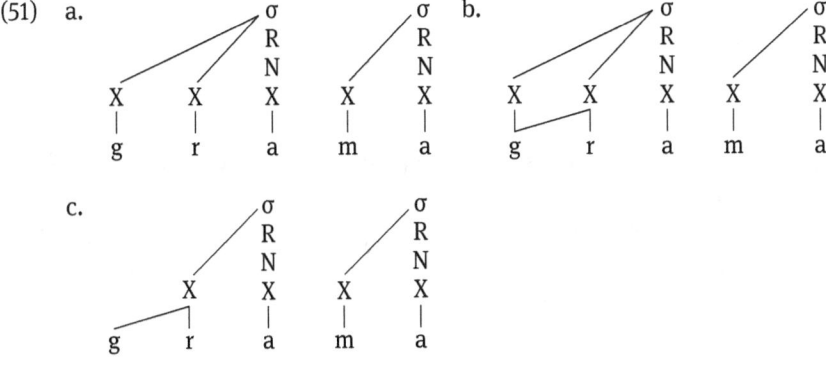 b.

c.

The same analysis could be assumed for clusters of rising sonority after a long vowel (or a heavy syllable). We saw that in this case there is no gemination in Sanskrit and Middle Indic (cf. (39)-(40)). One can propose that root spreading applies also in this case. The geminate created by this process is eliminated by skeletal deletion as in word initial position because of the constraint in (52).

(52) NoGeminateAfterHeavyσ:

$\quad$ *[X X X]$_{\text{Rhime}}$ X

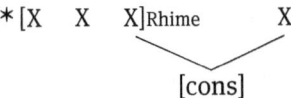

$\qquad$ [cons]

Let us consider clusters with a sonorant followed by an obstruent. Observe that a true coda involves a violation of the constraint in (53), where we have a root node exhaustively linked to the coda X.

(53) NOCODA:

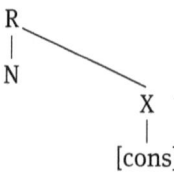

Now, the only codas that are allowed after the application of root spreading are the first member of a geminate as shown in (54), which are licit due to the Uniformity Applicability Condition (Schein and Steriade (1986)) insofar as the coda constraint in (53) does not exhaustively applies to them.[10]

(54)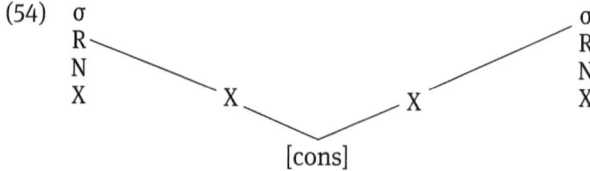

(55) The Uniformity Applicability Condition (Schein and Steriade 1986) (as reformulated in Calabrese (1999)):

Given a node n and a set S consisting of all nodes linked to n, and given a rule or a constraint T, if T refers to n and any member of S, it must refer to all members of S to be active.

The constraint in (53) does not hold for (54) since the root in (54) is also part of the onset. Therefore, the coda in (54) does not violate (53) and is not a true coda. Therefore, the root spreading process eliminates true codas.[11]

One can then assume that Sanskrit was characterized by the constraint disallowing codas in (53) and that applications of Root spreading were used to repair a violation of this constraint:

---

[10] Codas in Middle Indic can also contain nasals homorganic with the following onset. They behave like geminates, as discussed later.

[11] Observe that the final /m̩/ of *kattum̩* inf. *kar* 'make' is an *anusvara* which according to Calabrese (2019) is part of the syllabic Nucleus and therefore is not a true coda.

(56) a. NoCoda: 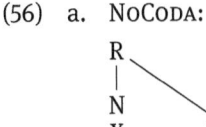   b. Repair of NoCoda by Root Spreading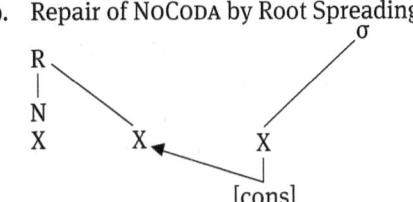

This is shown in the case of Sanskrit *artha* 'purpose' Middle Indic *attha*. The coda consonant in (57)a violates (53). Root spreading repairs this violation as in (57)b. In fact, according to the UAC, the coda skeletal position is not affected by the constraint in (56) because it dominates a root that is also dominated by the onset of the following syllable.

(57) a. Sanskrit: b. Middle Indic:

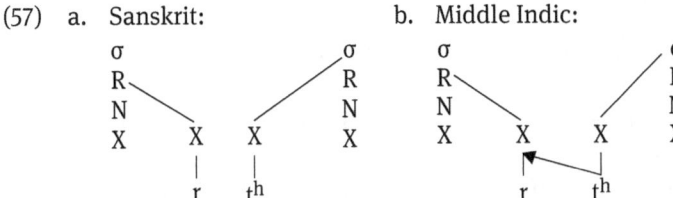

The Middle Indic outcomes are accounted by application of (49) as shown below:[12]

(58)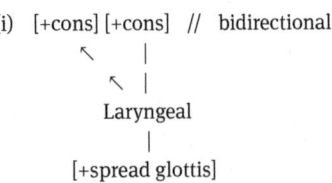

---

[12] A rule of aspiration is required to account for the evolution of other consonantal clusters from Sanskrit to Middle Indic (cf. footnote 7 (e.g. *kṣata* 'wounded' *khata*, *akṣi* 'eye' *akkhi*, *hasta* 'the hand' *hattha*, *puṣkara* 'blue lotus' *pŏkkhara*). First, it must be assumed that coronal fricatives are characterized by the feature [+spread glottis] (Vaux's Law (Vaux 1998)). Then, the rule in (i) can be assumed. This rule is bidirectional, affecting the non-fricative member of the cluster. After it has applied, the geminate that is the outcome of the simplification of the cluster in Middle Indic is aspirated.

(i) [+cons] [+cons] // bidirectional
          ↖ |
            ↖ |
          Laryngeal
             |
       [+spread glottis]

Root spreading immediately explains the gemination we find in clusters of equal sonority in (45) (e.g., *bhakta* 'meal, food' *bhatta*, *dugdha* 'milk' *duddha*, *sapta* 'seven' *sutta*.) The input configuration for these clusters is shown in (59)a. The stop in coda position is disallowed by (56). Root spreading applies to repair this configuration and geminates the second stops as in (59). This is the Sanskrit situation. The Middle Indic outcomes are derived by applying (49), as in (59)b.

(59) a. Sanskrit: b. Middle Indic:

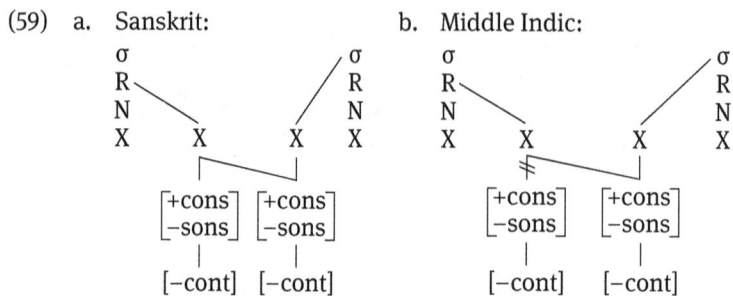

In (44) we saw that there is no gemination in Middle Indic in the case of homorganic nasal stop clusters (e.g. *antara* 'interior' *antara*, *lamba* 'pendent' *lamba*). Nasals followed by a homorganic stop have the structure in (60). This structure is produced by a previous application of a process of nasal place assimilation given in (60)b.

(60) a. b.

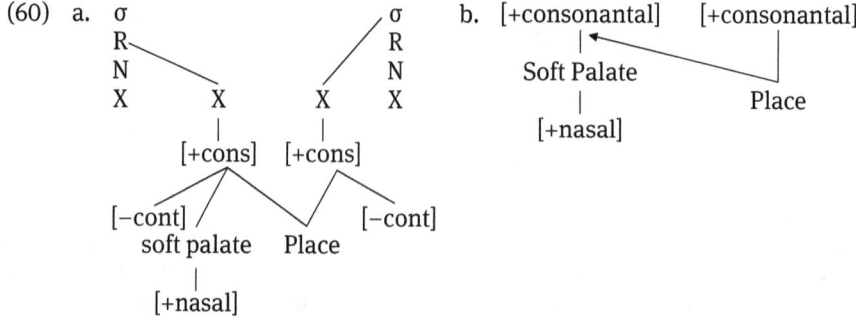

I propose that the structure in (60)a is automatically changed into (61) In other words, a homorganic nasal+ sequence is automatically changed into a prenasalized geminate stop:[13]

---

[13] I therefore predict that there should not be phonetic contrast between a homorganic nasal+ stop sequence and a homorganic nasal + geminate stop sequence. As far as I know this predic-

(61)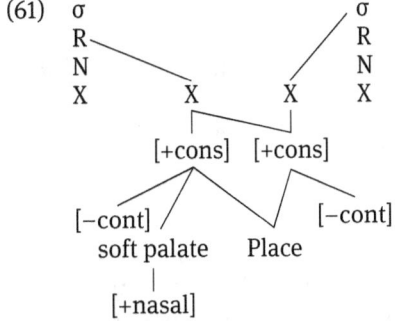

The coda skeletal position is therefore licensed by the onset root according to the UAC. No root spreading is therefore needed in this case. Therefore, there is no gemination in Sanskrit and subsequently these structures are preserved as such in Middle Indic.

Finally, we can now consider the sequence of a fricative plus a nasal. Here application of root spreading as a repair of a complex onset should give us gemination of /s/ (see (62)) and (63) for the Middle Indic outcome with loss of the nasal due to (49).

(62) Sanskrit gemination

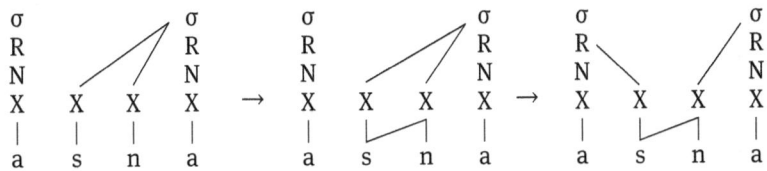

tion is correct. Ladefoged and Maddieson (1996) discuss two languages with a contrast between a single and a geminate prenasalized stop: Sinhala and Fula. In both languages it is the nasal component that is longer in the geminate stop. In the representation proposed here the single prenasalized stop is represented as in (61) and the geminate one as in (i) by reverting the line between the nasal root and the X-skeletal positions (representation simplified):

(i)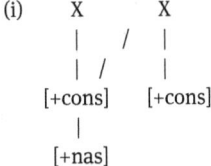

(63) Middle Indic outcome

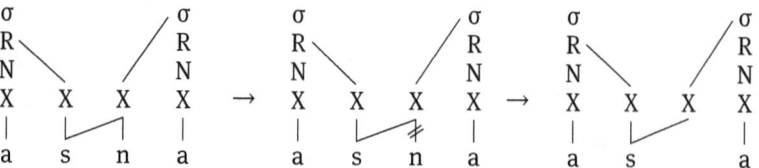

As already discussed, there are a few of such outcomes (see (46)), but this is not the most common development. The most common development is that in (47) (e.g. *praśna* 'question' *paṇha*) (Remember that the digraph [nh] represents a geminated aspirated nasal. See footnote 8).

Observe that although onset clusters fricative + nasal need to be reconstructed for common Indo-European, they were eliminated in Indo-European languages such as Greek and Latin. They can be considered quite instable and marked onset clusters. We should expect a tendency to eliminate them before other clusters. To account for the Middle Indic development leading to geminated aspirated nasals from clusters of a fricative+nasal, one can then propose that at a later stage of Sanskrit, there was a change in what was allowed in initial syllabification. In particular, onset clusters of a fricative followed by a nasal became disallowed.

(64)

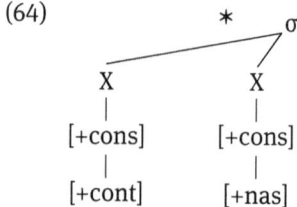

Therefore, sequences of this type were syllabified as in (65)a) in initial syllabification. In the second pass of syllabification these configurations were removed by root spreading as in (65)b):

(65) a.   b.

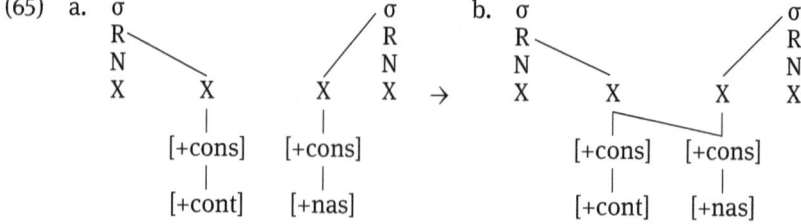

The Middle Indic outcomes are accounted for by applying the rule of aspiration in Footnote 11 as shown in (66)a. (49) applies as in (66)b and (66)c is generated.

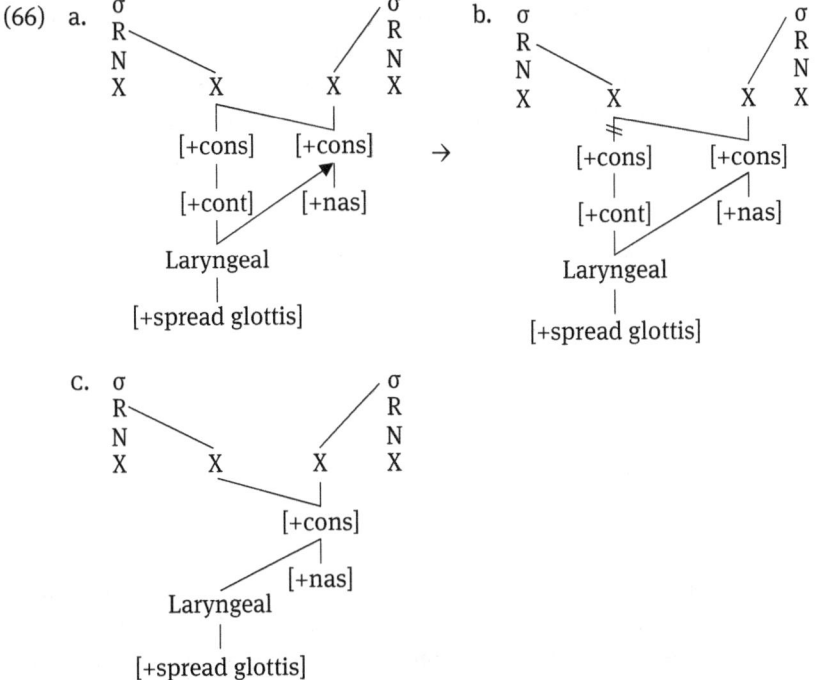

The treatment of these clusters demonstrates that it is syllable structure and not sonority that accounts for gemination.[14,15]

---

14 Root spreading followed by skeletal deletion applies when these clusters occur in word-initial position:

(i) snāti 'bathes' nhāi
snāru 'sinew' nhāru
snūsā 'son's wife' nhusā

In the case of these cluster also epenthesis can be observed:

(ii) snigdha 'sticky' siniddha / saniddha

There are also cases with deaspiration:

(iii) snigdha ṇiddha

15 Varma (1929: 123) accounts for the special treatment of /sn/ clusters in the forms in (1) in the same Modern Indic languages by assuming a stage with an intrusive stop as in (ii). Root spreading, aspiration and delinking proposed here would then generate the final outcomes:

4.2 Gemination in Multi-segmental Clusters

In the preceding sections I restricted my attention to bisegmental clusters. Sanskrit also has clusters containing more than two consonants. They developed in Middle Indic in the same way as bisegmental clusters, and became geminates. I consider what happens in clusters of rising sonority containing three or more consonants. Sample cases from Sanskrit and their outcomes in Middle Indic are given in (67) (Remember that the sequence *nh* represents a geminated aspirated nasal):

(67) a. *kṛtasapatnya*   *kayàsāvatta* AMg
       sāmagryaka   *sāmaggaa*
       akṣni   *akkhihi*
       tikṣna   *tinha/ tikkha* (Pischel, p. 254)
       lakṣmi   *lacchi*

   b. *pakṣmala*   *pamhala*
      jyotsna   *jŏnha*
      ślokṣṇa   *saṇha*
      parislakṣṇa *parisaṇha*

The difference between the sets of cases in (67)a and the set in (67)b will be discussed below. The first generalization that can be drawn from these examples is that in all of them a cluster of onset consonants, regardless of their size, develops into a single geminate consonant in Middle Indic. Therefore, any string of skeletal positions in an input syllabification in Sanskrit survives simply as two skeletal positions in Middle Indic.

Consider a trisegmental cluster such as [tny] first. The initial Sanskrit syllabification for the word *patnya* is given in (68)a, and the eventual outcome of this word in Middle Indic is in (68)b.

(68) a. Input syllabification in Sanskrit   b. Eventual outcome in Middle Indic:

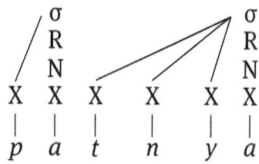   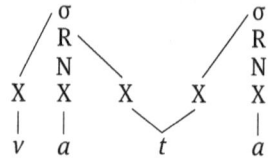

(i) *Viṣnu* → Marathi, Canarese: *Viṭṭhu*
     Kṛṣṇa → Marathi, Canarese: *Kiṭṭa*
(ii) *Viṣnu* → *Viṣṭnu*
     Kṛṣṇa → *Kṛṣṭna*

Let us derive this form in Sanskrit from the Input syllabification in (68)a). I propose that the complex onset is eliminated by root spreading starting from the most internal string, as shown in (69)a). Root spreading applies to clusters from inside out. The onset geminated thus created is fixed up by skeletal deletion as shown in (69)b). Now root spreading takes care of the remaining complex onset and generates (69)c). We again have an onset geminate that must be fixed up. It can be fixed up by delinking as shown in (69)d). The delinked consonant can now be incorporated into the coda of the preceding syllable thus producing the surface form in (69)e).

(69) a. Input syllabification in Sanskrit   b.

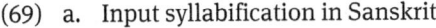
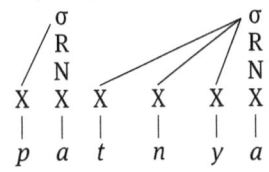
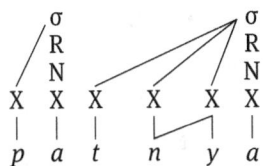

c.   d.

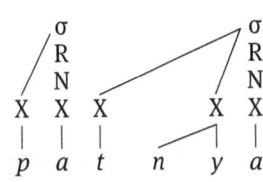
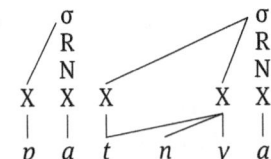

e.

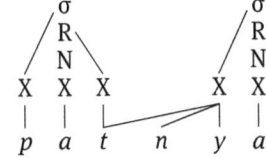

The Middle Indic outcome can be accounted for as proposed earlier by delinking all the roots that are singly linked by rule in (49).

(69) f.

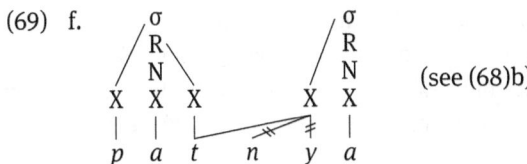

(see (68)b)

However, when the cluster contains a fricative and a nasal, there are two different outcomes. In one case it is the expected consonant that survives, the doubly linked stop in (67)a), in the other it is the nasal that survives ((67)b)). These two outcomes are shown again in (70). In both cases, the surviving consonant is aspirated. This aspiration is due to the process in (i), Footnote 11, which spreads the feature [+spread glottis] from a fricative to the other members of the same cluster.

(70) Sanskrit   Middle Indic
      tikṣna   a)   tikkha   (Pischel; 254)
                b)   tinha   (Pischel; 254)

The two outcomes can be accounted in the following way. I begin with the development in (71)a). Consider the input in (71)a). If we apply the derivation in (69), we obtain (71)b):

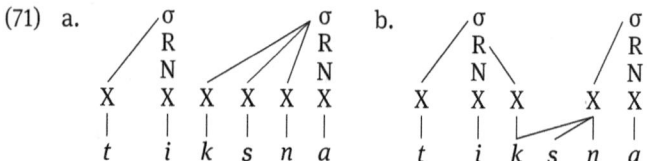

This is the Sanskrit situation. The Middle Indic outcome is derived as follows. Aspiration will apply and produce (72)a). Now application of (49) generates (72)b)

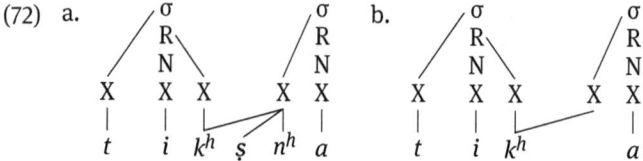

Let us turn to (71)b. In the input in (71), the cluster was syllabified as a complex onset. Now remember that in some varieties of Sanskrit the onset cluster fricative + nasal was not allowed. It follows that also the onset cluster stop + fricative+nasal was not allowed. As proposed earlier in these varieties the fricative was resyllabified into a coda position. Hence, also the preceding stop is forced to be in coda position as in (73)a). The complex coda cluster in this form is repaired by root spreading as in (71)b). The coda geminate is eliminated by skeletal deletion as in (71)c):

(73) a.

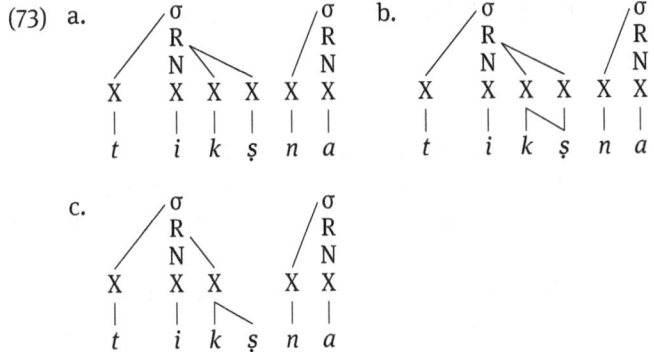

Root spreading triggered by the constraint against codas generates (74):

(74)

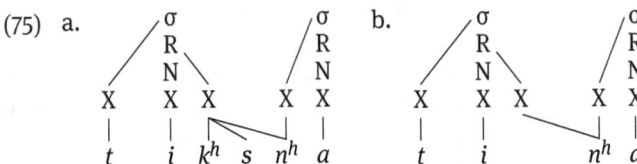

This is the situation in some variety of Sanskrit. The alternant Middle Indic outcome follows from the application of aspiration, which produces (75)a) and the subsequent application of (49), which produces (75)b):

(75) a.

5 Previous Accounts of Middle Indic Gemination

I will end with a brief discussion of the previous accounts of Middle Indic gemination.

The traditional account of gemination in the middle Indic languages (cf. Geiger 1916; Hankamer and Aissen 1974) and the essentially similar stricture-based account of Suzuki (2002, 2015), assumes that it is directly driven by the sonority hierarchy, so that in any given cluster the more sonorous will assimilate to the less sonorous.

(76) 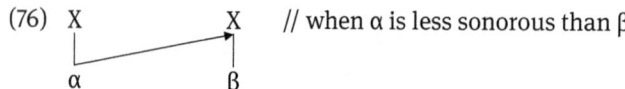 // when α is less sonorous than β

This account faces various problems. First of all, it fails to address the crucial role that syllable structure plays in the gemination process, and to provide an account for the development of multi-segmental clusters. Secondly, it fails to account for the fact that there is gemination in clusters of equal sonority (45) (e.g., *bhakta* 'meal, food' *bhatta*, *dugdha* 'milk' *duddha*, *sapta* 'seven' *sutta*. Thirdly, it fails to account for why there is no gemination in homorganic clusters nasal + stop (44) (e.g. *antara* 'interior *antara*, *aṅkuśa* 'elephant' *aṅkusa*, *lamba* 'pendent'*amba*). Furthermore, note that the sonority-based account predicts the gemination of the less sonorous coronal fricative in clusters where this consonant is followed by a nasal. However, as shown before (cf. (47)) it is the nasal that is doubled in the manuscripts in this case (cf. *brahmma*, *raśmmiṣu* and geminated as an aspirated nasal in Middle Indic (e.g. *praśna* 'question' *paṇha*, *griṣma* 'summer heat'*gimha*).

A different account of Middle Indic gemination was proposed by Vaux (1992). He assumes that this process is due to resyllabification which however preserves the weight of a syllable in a sequence as shown below:

(77)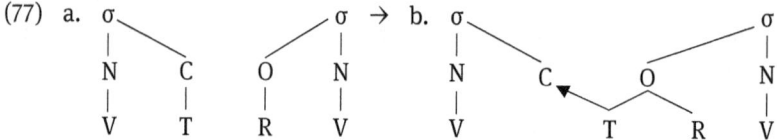

Problems for Vaux's account are the same as those of the sonority-based accounts. On the one hand, (77) fails to account for what happens in clusters where a coronal fricative is followed by a nasal. In fact, given (78), one expects gemination of the fricative instead of the gemination of the nasal

(78)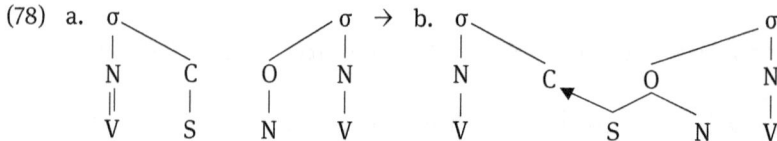

(77) also fails to account for gemination of stops after stops in (45) and for why no gemination is found in homorganic nasal + stop clusters. Furthermore, (77) fails to account for gemination of obstruents after sonorants that is instead accounted for by the sonority-based account. On the other hand, this account also fails to deal with the development of multi-segmental clusters. In addition, the change in

syllabification in (77) is incompatible with the fact that the initial syllable parsing for Sanskrit require complex onsets as discussed earlier. It is plausible to assume that this initial syllabification represents the syllabification characteristic of an older stage of the language. Then, the evidence is for an older stage of Sanskrit with complex onsets that were later eliminated, that is, for a sequence of events that is the opposite from the one assumed in Vaux's account.

Another possible way to account for Middle Indic gemination is to assume that Root spreading is the repair of a bad syllable contact (cf. Vennemann 1988; Murray 1982):

(79) a.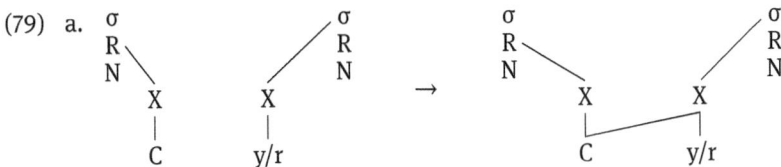

This hypothesis would simply account for what happens in intervocalic position (after short vowel (see below). However, if root spreading is a repair triggered only by a bad syllable contact, there is no account for gemination in cluster of falling sonority that are perfectly fine according to this law.

(80)

Furthermore, the process in (79) could not account for what happens in onset clusters in word-initial position since they are apparently preserved in this position in Sanskrit and then simplified by deleting the sonorant in Middle Indic. An operation like root spreading (followed by application of (14), readily accounts for this but not in this account. The same holds for the fact that there is no gemination in clusters after long vowels which can be readily accounted for as proposed earlier by using root spreading followed by simplification but not in this account. Given (79) it is also unclear how to deal with the development of multi-segmental clusters. It follows that for all these cases, independent processes and principles must be postulated with the consequence that a unitary account for gemination is not proposed

The account proposed in the preceding sections appears to be the most adequate and simpler.

6 Conclusion

In this paper, I have shown that if we assume that an operation like root spreading can repair disallowed syllabic configurations, we can readily account for the gemination processes we find in Sanskrit and Middle Indic. Root spreading must be recognized as another possible source for gemination, in addition to processes such as assimilation, lengthening under stress, reanalysis (see Blevins 2005)

Root spreading can provide an alternative account for the gemination processes, similar to those found in Sanskrit, although restricted to clusters containing consonants followed by glides, which are found in other Indo-European languages such as Italian, Ancient Greek and West Germanic. My hypothesis is that in these cases, root spreading is also operating as a repair of the constraint in (9).

References

Blevins, Juliette J. 2005. The typology of geminate inventories: Historical explanations for recurrent sound patterns. *Seoul Linguistics Forum* 2005, 121–137. Seoul: Language Education Institute, Seoul National University.

Calabrese, Andrea. 1999. Sievers' law in Vedic. In H. van der Hulst and N. A. Ritter (eds.), *The Syllable: View and Facts*. 673–751. Berlin: Mouton de Gruyter.

Calabrese, Andrea. 2005. *Markedness and Economy in a Derivational Model of Phonology*. Berlin: Mouton De Gruyter.

Calabrese, Andrea. 2009a. Markedness theory vs. phonological idiosyncracies in a realistic model of language. In C. Cairns & E. Raimy (eds.), *Contemporary Views on Architecture and Representations in Phonological Theory*, 261–304. Cambridge, MA: MIT Press.

Calabrese, Andrea. 2009b. Cluster syllabification, gemination and syllabic repairs in Sanskrit. In Rajat Mohanty & Mythili Menon (eds.), *Universals and Variation*, 205–225. Hyderabad: EFL University Press.

Calabrese, Andrea. 2019. Morphophonological investigations: A theory of PF. From syntax to phonology in Sanskrit and Italian verb system. Ms., University of Connecticut. [/https://andrea-calabrese.uconn.edu/publications]

Cardona, George. 2003. Sanskrit. In George Cardona & Dhanesh Jain (eds.), *The Indo-Aryan Languages*, 104–160. London: Routledge.

Clements, George N. 1990. The role of the sonority cycle in core syllabification. In J. Kingston & M. Beckmann (eds.), *Papers in Laboratory Phonology 1*, 283–333. Cambridge: Academic Press.

Clements, Nick G. 1992. Place of articulation in consonants and vowels: A unified theory. In B. Laks & A. Rialland (eds.), *L'architecture et la géometrie des représentations phonologiques*, 101–147. Paris: CNRS Editions. (Also appeared in *Working Papers of the Cornell Phonetics Lab* 5 (1991)).

Geiger, Wilhelm. 2013 [1916]. *A Pāli Grammar*. Translated by Batakrishna Ghosh; revised and edited by K. R. Norman. Bristol: The Pali Text Society. (Original German work published

1916; English translation first published 1943; revised English translation first published 1994.)
Halle, Morris, Bert Vaux & Andrew Wolfe. 2000. On feature spreading and the representation of place of articulation. *Linguistic Inquiry* 31. 387–444.
Hankamer, Jorge & Judith Aissen. 1974. The sonority hierarchy. In A. Bruck, R. Fox & M. La Galy (eds.), *Papers from the Parasession on Natural Phonology*, 131–144. Chicago: Chicago Linguistic Society.
Hulst, Harry van der & Nancy Ritter. 1999. Head-driven phonology. In H. van der Hulst & N. Ritter (eds.), *The Syllable: Views and Facts*, 113–168. Berlin: Mouton de Gruyter.
Jacobi, H. 1881. Zur Genesis der Präkritsprachen. *Zeitschrift fur Vergleighende Sprachforschung* 25. 603–609.
Jamison, Stephanie. 1983. *Function and Form in the -áya-Formations of the Rig Veda and the Atharva Veda*. Göttingen: Vandenhoeck & Ruprecht.
Jouannet, François. 1983. Phonetique et phonologie. Lesysteme consonantique du Kinyarwanda. In F. Jouannet (ed.), *Etudes linguistiques*, 55–74. Paris: SELAF.
Kurylowicz, Jerzy. 1948. Contribution à la théorie de la syllabe. *Bulletin de la Societe Polonaise de Linguistique* 8. 80–114.
Ladefoged, Peter. 1968. *A Phonetic Study of West African Languages*. Cambridge: Cambridge University Press.
Ladefoged, Peter & Ian Maddieson. 1996. *The Sounds of the World Languages*. Cambridge, MA: Blackwell.
Levin, Juliette. 1985. *A metrical theory of syllabicity*. Cambridge, MA: MIT Ph.D. dissertation.
Maddieson, Ian. 1990. Shona velarization: Complex consonants or complex onsets. *UCLA Working Papers in Phonetics* 74. 16–34.
Masica, Colin P. 1991. *The Indo-Aryan Languages*. Cambridge: Cambridge University Press.
Murray, Robert W. 1982. Consonant cluster developments in Pāli. *Folia Linguistica Historica* 3. 163–184.
Petrosino, Roberto & Andrea Calabrese. 2021. Palatalization in romance. In Christoph Gabriel, Randall Gess & Trudel Meisenburg (eds.), *Manual of Romance Phonetics and Phonology*, 173–214. Berlin: De Gruyter.
Pischel, R. 1981. *A Grammar of the Prākrit Languages*. Translated by Subhadra Jha. Dehli: Motilal Barnasidass.
Prince, Alan & Paul Smolensky. 2002/2004 [1993]. *Optimality Theory: Constraint Interaction in Generative Grammar*. Blackwell Publishers. Originally distributed as Technical Report #2, Rutgers University Center for Cognitive Science and Computer Science Department, University of Colorado at Boulder (1993).
Sagey, E. C. 1986. *The representation of features and relations in non-linear phonology*. Cambridge, MA: MIT Doctoral dissertation.
Saussure, Ferdinand de. 1922 [1889]. Sur un point de la phonétique des consonnes en indo-européen. In *Recueil de publications scientifique*, 420–432. Geneva: Sonor.
Schein, Barry & Donca Steriade. 1986. On geminates. *Linguistic Inquiry* 17. 691–744.
Seebold, Elmar. 1972. *Das system der Indogermanischen Halbvokale*. Heidelberg: Winter.
Snyman, Jan. 1970. *An Introduction to the !Xū Languages*. Cape Town: Balkema.
Steriade, Donca. 1982. *Greek prosodies and the nature of syllabification*. Cambridge, MA: MIT Doctoral dissertation.
Suzuki, Yasuko. 2002. Consonant cluster changes in Pali: Toward restricting the phonological patterns. *Journal of Inquiry and Research* 75. 97–125.

Suzuki, Yasuko. 2015. On characterizing Sanskrit gemination. *Journal of Inquiry and Research* 102. 1–18.

Varma, Siddheshwar. 1929. *Critical Study in the Phonetic Observations of the Indian Grammarians.* London: Royal Asiatic Society.

Vaux, Bert. 1992. Gemination and syllabic integrity in Sanskrit. *The Journal of Indo-European Studies* 20. 3–4.

Vaux, Bert. 1998. The laryngeal specifications of fricatives. *Linguistic Inquiry* 29(3). 497–511.

Vennemann, Theo. 1988. *Preference Laws for Syllable Structure and the Explanation of Sound Change.* Berlin: Mouton.

Wackernagel, Jacob. 1896. *Altindische Grammatik*, 3 vols. Göttingen: Vandenhoek und Ruprecht; vol. 1: *Lautlehre*, repr. with a new introduction by Louis Renou and addenda by Albert Debrunner, 1957.

Whitney, William D. 1868. *The Taittirīya Pratiśākhya and Tribhāṣyatna.* New Haven, CT: Yale University Press; reprinted Delhi: Motilaal Barnasidass.

John Harris
A Fake Diphthong in English

Abstract: English is generally agreed to have true diphthongs: vowel-glide sequences contained within the same syllable nucleus. There is evidence that it also has at least one fake diphthong, in which the glide falls outside the nucleus: the /ow/ that occurs post-tonically in words such as *yellow, tomorrow, potato*.

At stake here is the wider question of whether we can maintain the otherwise robust generalisation that stress in English is quantity-sensitive, one symptom of which is that diphthongs render a syllable heavy and thus attract stress. Post-tonic /ow/ appears to breach this pattern. If it were a heavy diphthong, quantity-sensitivity would require it to bear subsidiary stress (e.g. *yéllòw). However, evidence to be reviewed here clearly points to /ow/ being unstressed in this position.

The apparent contradiction is resolved if we treat unstressed /ow/ as a fake diphthong, consisting of a short nucleus followed by a non-nuclear position (i.e. VC). Metrically, this makes *yellow* just like *rabbit*: in both cases, the final consonant is extra-metrical, meaning that the preceding syllable is light and unstressed, in accord with quantity-sensitivity.

Keywords: English phonology, true vs fake diphthongs, quantity-sensitive stress, extrametricality

1 Introduction

English is generally agreed to have true diphthongs, i.e. vowel-glide sequences contained within the same syllable nucleus. There is evidence that it also has at least one fake diphthong, in which the glide falls outside the nucleus: the /ow/ that occurs post-tonically at the end of words such as *yellow, tomorrow, potato*.[1]

At stake here is the wider question of whether we can maintain the otherwise robust generalisation that stress in English is quantity-sensitive. One symptom of quantity-sensitivity is that diphthongs render a syllable heavy and thus attract stress. Post-tonic /ow/ appears to breach this pattern. If it were a heavy diph-

---

[1] There may be one or two other fake diphthongs in English. Another prime suspect is post-tonic final /uw/, e.g. in *value, curlew, curfew*. (On the reasons for describing this vowel as an upgliding diphthong rather than a long monophthong /u:/, see Lindsey (2012).)

John Harris, University College London

thong, quantity-sensitivity would require it to bear subsidiary stress (e.g. *yéllòw). However, phonological evidence to be reviewed here clearly points to /ow/ being unstressed in this position.

The apparent contradiction is resolved if we treat unstressed /ow/ as a fake diphthong, consisting of a short nucleus followed by a non-nuclear position (i.e. VC). Metrically, this makes *yellow* just like *rabbit*: in both cases, the final consonant is extrametrical, meaning that the preceding syllable is light and unstressed, in accord with quantity-sensitivity.

§2 reviews the difference between true and fake diphthongs. §3 considers what the stress status of final post-tonic /ow/ means for quantity-sensitivity in English. §4 presents several pieces of evidence confirming that post-tonic /ow/ is unstressed. §5 shows how post-tonic /ow/ started life as a fake diphthong. §6 explains how a VC analysis of the diphthong saves the generalisation that stress in English is quantity-sensitive. §7 cautions against treating all diphthongs in English as fake.

2 Diphthongs: How to Spot a Fake

The term DIPHTHONG was originally used to describe a sequence of two vowel letters in alphabetic writing. Since the term came to be applied to the description of vowel sounds, it has often been used to refer to any sequence of vocalic segments written as two phoneme characters. From a phonological viewpoint, this usage is at best vague and at worst downright misleading. It can obscure the different ways in which vocalic sequences are syllabified in different languages. For this reason, it is useful to draw a distinction between what can be called true and fake diphthongs.

IPA-style phonetic transcriptions are of little help in establishing the syllabification of vocalic sequences. First, being fundamentally alphabetic, they typically do not represent syllable structure. Second, conventions vary with respect to whether vocalic sequences should be transcribed with vowel or glide characters, e.g. [au] versus [aw]. As shown in (1a), a true diphthong can be defined as a vocalic sequence (ωω) that is contained within the same syllable nucleus (N). A fake diphthong can take one of two forms. One, shown in (1b), is where the two vocalic units belong to separate nuclei and thus to separate syllables. The other, shown in (1c), is where one unit belongs to a nucleus and the other to a neighbouring non-nuclear position; whether the latter is a coda (Co) or an onset (O) is not immediately relevant here.

(1) (a) True   (b) Fake I   (c) Fake II

```
     σ           σ   σ         σ           σ   σ
     |           |   |         | \         |   |
     N           N   N         N   Co      N   O
     |\          |   |         |    \      |   |
     ω ω         ω   ω         ω     ω     ω   ω
```

There are various ways of telling when we are dealing with a true diphthong. For one thing, it exhibits prosodic integrity: it counts as a single landing site for stress or tone, and in languages with quantity-sensitive stress it defines a single domain of weight. For another, since a true diphthong forms a single nucleus, its phonological distribution parallels that of monophthongs. For example, if a language allows word-final consonants, they can be preceded by any vowel, be it a monophthong or a diphthong. Both of these criteria are met by up-gliding diphthongs in English, including the /ow/ of the GOAT lexical set, the vowel we are interested in here. /ow/ belongs to a single syllable unit for the location of stress and the calculation of weight. It can also appear before a word final consonant (e.g. *rope, loaf, loan*), just like monophthongs can (e.g. *step, deaf, ten*).

Compare this behaviour with that of fake diphthongs. A vocalic hiatus split over two syllables, as shown in (1b), presents two separate landing sites for stress or tone. For example, in Saramaccan each vowel in a vocalic sequence potentially bears its own tone, giving rise to contrasts such as /léi/ 'learn' versus /seí/ 'ant type', /pái/ 'father-in-law' versus /paí/ 'give birth' (McWhorter and Good 2012). A vocalic sequence split between a nucleus and, say, a coda (as in (1c)) is subject to the same phonotactic restrictions as hold of VC sequences. For example, in French, fake diphthongs such as /aj, ɛj, uj/ (e.g. in *paille* 'straw', *veille* 'eve', *grenouille* 'frog') cannot be followed by a word-final consonant because of general restrictions on final consonant clusters (Dell 1995).

As I'll try to show here, there is good evidence that post-tonic /ow/ in English is a fake diphthong of the type shown in (1c), where the two vocalic units are split between a nuclear and a non-nuclear position, i.e. VC. Towards the end of the paper, I will argue that /ow/ only has this structure when it is post-tonic. There is no reason to suspect that it is anything other than a true diphthong when tonic. As depicted by the contrast between *below* and *bellow* in (2), this means that syllabically there are actually two /ow/ vowels in English.

(2) (a) Tonic /ow/: *belów*   (b) Post-tonic /ow/: *béllow*

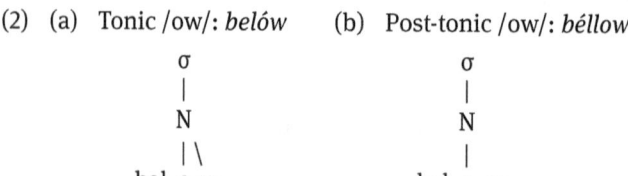

The precise syllabic status of the upglide is left undetermined in (2b), in acknowledgement of a diversity of opinion among phonologists about whether word-final C is syllabified as a coda or not (see Harris and Gussmann (1998) and van der Hulst and Ritter (1999) for discussion of the different views). For the purposes of the analysis to be defended here, all that matters is that the glide in post-tonic /ow/ falls outside the nucleus.

It might seem odd to suggest that a language can accommodate both true and fake diphthongs. However, there are good precedents, perhaps the best studied of which are to be found in Frisian and Dutch (Booij 1989, 1999). There are clear parallels here with consonant clusters. Consonants forming a genuine cluster can be defined as syllabically adjacent, one symptom of which is that they are subject to systematic phonotactic restrictions (such as a steeply rising sonority slope within complex onsets, e.g. [pl, tr, kw]). Consonants forming a fake cluster show no such restrictions, an indication that they are not syllabically adjacent, which can be captured by assuming they are separated by a silent nucleus. As with diphthongs, we can find true and fake consonant clusters within the same language, as Harry van der Hulst (1984) has shown for Dutch.

3 Post-tonic /ow/: Stressed or Not?

For various reasons, I will follow the tradition of symbolising diphthongs in English as vowel plus glide rather than the vowel-plus-vowel notation that is usual in British dictionaries. For the GOAT lexical set, this means /ow/ in preference to something like /əʊ/. (The decision to use [o] to represent the quality of the first element of the diphthong is largely a matter of accent choice: besides being characteristic of General American, it happens to be a broadly accurate reflection of Harry van der Hulst's pronunciation (not to mention my own).) A more important criterion lies behind the choice of the off-glide notation. The historical pedigree of this format runs from Thomas Gataker (1646), through Henry Sweet (1877) and the American Structuralists (Trager and Bloch 1941), up to the present day in the form of the

Current British English online dictionary (CuBE).[2] The off-glide design embodies a more insightful analysis of the English vowel system than the vowel-vowel design of /əʊ/. For detailed arguments in favour of this analysis, see Lindsey (2012) and Szigetvári (2016). Harry van der Hulst (1984) offers similar arguments for a parallel analysis of diphthongs in Dutch. Moreover, vowel-plus-glide more readily accommodates the specific phonological analysis of /ow/ that I will try to defend below.

Like all long monophthongs and diphthongs in English, /ow/ can appear in syllables bearing a main stress, e.g. *go, road, token, below*. It can also appear after a main stress in words such as *yellow, tomorrow, potato, photo, bellow*. Does this post-tonic /ow/ bear a subsidiary stress, or is it unstressed? Stress in English is generally agreed to be quantity-sensitive, one implication of which is that heavy syllables must bear some degree of stress. Since a diphthong in English makes a syllable heavy, this would lead us to expect that post-tonic /ow/ in words such as *yellow* and *photo* should bear a subsidiary stress. However, there is plenty of evidence, to be reviewed below, which indicates that it is unstressed. On the face of it, this undermines the claim that stress in English is quantity-sensitive: at least some heavy syllables can apparently be unstressed in English.

Describing post-tonic /ow/ as unstressed accords with transcriptions found in most current dictionaries of English. Not that this is much of an endorsement: post-tonically, dictionaries tend to be quite inconsistent in marking a distinction between unstressed and subsidiary-stressed syllables. This is in spite of good evidence that the distinction is perceptually real (Mattys 2000) and can be phonologically and lexically sensitive, not just in English (Pater 2000) but also – as Harry van der Hulst's work amply demonstrates – in other languages as well (1996, 2012; see also Bogomolets, this volume). In what follows, we can take the *Cambridge Dictionary* as representative of this inconsistency.

Two-word compounds provide us with a useful check on the inconsistency, since the routine pattern in English is for the first word to bear main stress and the second to bear subsidiary stress, as in *seagull, towpath, pinecone*. That is, in compounds we have a reference point against which to judge whether a post-tonic syllable bears subsidiary stress or not. The *Cambridge Dictionary* lists both *yellow* and *hedgerow*, for example, without a stress on the final syllable. Since *hedgerow* is a compound, we know that its second syllable in fact bears a subsidiary stress: *hédgeròw*. The problem is that, since the dictionary ignores the subsidiary stress in *hedgerow*, we could be left wondering whether it has also ignored a subsidiary stress in *yellow*.

Not marking a distinction between post-tonic unstressed and subsidiary-stressed syllables has its roots in the British phonetic tradition of classifying English vowels

---

[2] http://cube.elte.hu.

into a 'full' set (the maximal inventory of contrasts) and a 'reduced' set (Jones 1950). Reduced vowels only occur in unstressed syllables, while full vowels occur in syllables that may or may not be marked for stress. The unrecorded distinction between subsidiary stress and lack of stress can be partially reconstructed by drawing on this classification: if a vowel unmarked for stress belongs to the full set, there is a good chance it actually bears a subsidiary stress. This certainly works for compounds. For example, we know that the full vowel in the second element of *greenhouse* bears a subsidiary stress, even though *Cambridge* does not mark it. This contrasts with the second syllable of *Venus*, where the schwa quality of the reduced vowel confirms it as unstressed. Rhythmically, there is a very clear difference between the two words: *gréenhòuse* with two stresses (and thus two feet) versus *Vénus* with one stress (and thus one foot).

Does the full-vs-reduced classification help determine whether the vowel at the end of *yellow* bears a subsidiary stress or not? Since /ow/ belongs to the set of full vowels, this suggests it bears a subsidiary stress in *yellow*. However, we will now examine several pieces of evidence that clearly point to it being unstressed.

4 Final Post-tonic /ow/ Is Unstressed

4.1 Foot Binarity

The first piece of evidence has to do with the requirement that feet in English are minimally binary. If a post-tonic syllable containing /ow/ bears subsidiary stress, it and the preceding tonic syllable must belong to separate feet (represented here in parentheses), e.g. *(phó)(tò), (wín)(dòw)*. The problem here is that, in many of the relevant words, the tonic is light, i.e. monomoraic: it contains a short vowel in an open syllable, e.g. *yellow, marrow, pillow, minnow, widow*. Being monomoraic, the tonic is thus too small to form an independent foot, since feet in English are minimally bimoraic (Hayes 1995). To satisfy foot binarity, the /ow/ needs to be co-footed with the tonic syllable, i.e. as the weak syllable of a bisyllabic trochee: *(yéllow), (márrow)*. This forces the conclusion that post-tonic /ow/ in these words is unstressed.

4.2 /ow/ and Schwa

The next piece of evidence points to a close affinity between post-tonic /ow/ and word-final schwa in English.

In many varieties, post tonic /ow/ reduces to a weak vowel – a vowel independently known to be unstressed. Most often this is schwa, reflected in folk spellings such as *fella* and *yella* for *fellow* and *yellow*. Weak outcomes of reduction that are regionally more restricted include rhotic schwa (e.g. *feller* for *fellow*, *yeller* for *yellow*) and /-i/ (e.g. *swally* for *swallow*) (Wright 1898–1905). One interpretation of this effect is that the post-tonic syllable is changed from having subsidiary stress to having no stress, which in turn triggers vowel reduction. Another is that reduction is evidence that the post-tonic syllable is already unstressed, which then encourages a more typically weak vowel to emerge in its place. For reasons that will emerge below, the second of these explanations is much more plausible than the first.

If vowel reduction suggests schwa makes a good match for post-tonic /ow/, history tells us that the relationship also works in the other direction. Word-final schwa has had something of a chequered history in English. Once firmly ensconced in Old English, by mediaeval times it had been ejected from the system by apocope, e.g. /biːtə/ > /biːt/ (later > /bajt/) *bite* (Jespersen 1909; Lass 1992). It has since re-infiltrated the system by various routes. One has been via borrowings of words, especially proper names, spelt with final -*a*, e.g. *idea, Belinda, Shakira*. Another is via the loss of final /r/ in non-rhotic accents. At the time when final schwas were being apocopated, all of English was rhotic, and the /r/ in final-/ər/ words like *better, letter, latter* shielded the schwa from deletion. Later loss of /r/ then triggered a new influx of final-schwa words in non-rhotic accents. A historical connection with /r/ has been retained in those non-rhotic accents that allow it to re-emerge before a vowel in a cross-word linking /r/ environment; hence r-less *tear down* versus r-ful *tea/r/ up*. The extension of linking /r/ to novel final-*a* words produces non-etymological 'intrusive' /r/, e.g. *Pizza/r/ Express*.

What has all this to do with post-tonic /ow/? Well, the initial stages of final schwa's re-entry into English were far from straightforward. The earlier apocope of schwa meant there was no indigenous vowel to adapt the incoming words to. One alternative that was taken up was to use final /ər/ as a stand-in. This has produced intrusive pronunciations such as *idea*/r/, where the /r/ appears as [ɚ] in some regional rhotic accents and as linking /r/ in non-rhotic accents. But an alternative substitute was also made use of: /ow/. Now obsolescent, this pronunciation is attested in some earlier vernacular varieties of the southern United States. It shows up as dialect spellings such as *hammo (hammer)* and *Saro (Sarah)* in folksongs, a well-known repository of archaic accent features.[3] Since final schwa is unstressed, this adaptation suggests that final post-tonic /ow/ is itself also unstressed.

---

[3] Listen for example to Huddie 'Lead Belly' Ledbetter's version of *Take this Hammo* or Hedy West's version of *Pretty Saro*.

4.3 Suffixing -o

The inventory of segments appearing in English word-level suffixes is quite limited, e.g. *-(e)s, -(e)d, -er, -est, -y, -ly, -ness, -ish*. With few exceptions, consonants are coronal, and vowels are drawn from a reduced set that, depending on the accent, includes some selection from /i, ɪ, ɨ, ə, ɚ/. Note that all of these vowels are unstressed. Some of these suffixes attach to monosyllabic stems created by truncative morphology, such as /-i/ in *Jenny, Andy, Marty*.

The fact that these suffix vowels are unstressed is significant when we consider that there is a full vowel that can also appear as a word-level suffix in English: /ow/. It attaches to stems that are already monosyllabic (see (3a)) or become so via truncation (see (3b)). It is a favoured suffix in truncative morphology when the written form of the stem contains *-o* (see (3c)).

(3) (a) Deano, Ringo, Jacko, wino, weirdo, whacko, cheapo, pinko, sicko, kiddo, doggo, fatso
    (b) Robbo, Tommo, journo, muso, ammo, combo, aggro, defo
    (c) condo, limo, promo, hippo, rhino, psycho, porno, paedo

In its suffixing behaviour, /ow/ patterns with weak unstressed vowels, indicating that it too is unstressed in this position

4.4 *t*-lenition

Lenition of /t/ in English is sensitive to stress, so it provides a good test for whether post-tonic /ow/ is stressed or not. Leaving aside certain segmental details, we can summarise the lenition environments as follows (see Harris (1994) for a summary of the large literature on this topic). In tapping (or flapping) accents, postvocalic /t/ lenites to [ɾ] (a) before an unstressed vowel within the same word (e.g. in *better, city, Rita*) or (b) word-finally before any vowel regardless of stress (e.g. in *gét a, gèt ón*). In glottalling accents, postvocalic /t/ lenites to [ʔ] (a) before an unstressed vowel within the same word (e.g. in *better, city, Rita*) or (b) word-finally (e.g. in *get*). Word-internally, both tapping and glottalling are blocked before a vowel with any level of stress, whether this be main (e.g. *retáin, curtáil, betíde*) or subsidiary (e.g. *détàil, prótèin, quárantìne*).

What of post-tonic /ow/? Tapping and glottalling occur here too, e.g. in *pota̱to, toma̱to, photo*. The evidence from /t/-lenition is thus pretty clear: post-tonic /ow/ is unstressed.

5 Post-tonic /ow/: A Short History

It's worth looking at the history of post-tonic /ow/ in more detail, because it not only sheds light on the stress status of the vowel but also flags it up as a potentially fake diphthong.

The commonest spellings of post-tonic /ow/ are *-ow* and *-o*. Let us first examine the *-ow* words, all of which are inherited from Germanic:

(4) (a) -llow   bellow, billow, callow, fallow, fellow, follow, gallows, hallow, hollow, mallow, mellow, pillow, sallow, shallow, swallow, tallow, wallow, willow, yellow
    (b) -rrow   arrow, barrow, borrow, burrow, farrow, furrow, harrow, marrow, morrow, narrow, sorrow, sparrow, tomorrow, yarrow
    (c) -nnow   minnow, winnow
    (d) -dow   meadow, shadow, widow
    (e) window, elbow

Of the various generalisations that can be extracted from the 40 words in (4), two will turn out to have a particular bearing on our analysis of /ow/. First, all but two of these words contain a light tonic syllable (see (4a–d)). As noted above, this means they form disyllabic trochees, with /ow/ occupying the weak syllable of the foot. (The two exceptions – *window* and *elbow* in (4e), with a heavy tonic syllable – were originally compounds.) Second, in the 38 words with a light tonic, the consonants preceding /ow/ are all coronals, and most often these are liquids – see (4a) and (4b).

In all the Germanic words with post-tonic /ow/, the vowel derives historically from a sequence of a short vowel followed by a separate glide (see Jespersen (1909), on which the historical aspect of the following account is based). The glide has two main historical sources: a glide that was already present in continental Germanic, or an original dorsal fricative or lenis stop that was subsequently weakened. The short vowel is historically epenthetic, inserted between the glide and a preceding heterorganic consonant. In Old English, the vowel alternates with zero depending on the morphological paradigm it finds itself in. This can be seen in the examples in (5), which includes assorted inflected forms to illustrate the alternation.[4]

---

4 Examples from Bosworth Toller's Anglo-Saxon Dictionary online (https://bosworthtoller.com).

(5)		OE ROOT	OE INFLECTED FORMS
	shadow	sceadw-	sceadwe, sceaduwe
	widow	widw-	widewe, weoduwe, widwe
	winnow	windw-	windwian
	yellow	geolw-	geolwe, gealewe
	narrow	nearw-	nearwe

The glide in the examples in (5) originates in continental Germanic. The epenthetic effect is also seen in words that originally contained a dorsal fricative or lenis stop, which later underwent spirantisation and/or vocalisation:

(6) lg > ləg > ləɣ > ləw   follow, gallows, swallow
     rg > rəg > rəɣ > rəw   borrow, morrow, sorrow
     rx > rəɣ > rəw   furrow, farrow

The original sequence of liquid plus heterorganic consonant is still observable in cognate forms in English's West Germanic sisters, cf. German *folgen* 'follow', *Morgen* 'morrow', *Furche* 'furrow'. Some varieties of Dutch provide us with a present-day analogue of the vowel-epenthesis effect that was once active in Old English, cf. *vilg* /vɪl(ə)x/ 'willow', *merg* /mer(ə)x/ 'marrow' (Ewen and van der Hulst 2001: 190–193; Warner et al. 2001).

Armed with these historical facts, we are now in a position to explain the two generalisations we extracted from the *-ow* examples in (4a–d). Both have to do with the fact that the consonants preceding what is now /ow/ were originally codas, e.g. OE *fol.gian* 'follow', *bor.gian* 'borrow'. First, the consonants are sonorants because these made good codas in Old English. Second, the vowel of the tonic syllable is short because the codas conditioned closed-syllable shortness.

To summarise: present-day post-tonic /ow/ derives historically from a sequence of an epenthetic vowel plus an independent glide. There are two lessons to be drawn from this. First, the vowel was born as a fake diphthong, i.e. a vowel nucleus followed by an extra-nuclear glide. Second, we can be confident that it emerged in an unstressed position, since epenthetic vowels are always unstressed in Germanic (and other languages).

What of words in which post-tonic /ow/ is written as -o? These greatly outnumber -ow spellings – roughly 13 to one, according to CuBE. As far as I can tell, all are relatively recent borrowings. 20 of the most frequent are listed in (7).

(7) video, photo, radio, info, cargo, solo, studio, zero, volcano, euro, retro, hero, patio, polo, bingo, portfolio, maestro, casino, piano, auto

The simplest assumption, in line with research on loanword phonology, is that these borrowed words were assimilated into English by adapting them to an existing syllabic pattern, namely with an unstressed fake diphthong. In support of this, we observe that reduction of post-tonic /ow/ to schwa affects high-frequency *-o* loans e.g. (*potato̦, tomato̦*) just as it does inherited-Germanic *-ow* words (e.g. *fellow, yellow*).

Note that, in some of the examples in (7), /ow/ is separated from the tonic by an unstressed syllable, e.g. *video, radio, studio*. Under an analysis where feet in English are maximally binary, this means the syllable housing /ow/ is unfooted: *(vide)o, (radi)o, (studi)o*. Since unfooted syllables are by definition unstressed, this further confirms the unstressed status of post-tonic /ow/.

Analysing present-day post-tonic /ow/ as unstressed VC remains true to the vowel's historical origins. While this is not in and of itself proof that the synchronic analysis is correct, there is no reason to suppose that post-tonic /ow/ has subsequently been spontaneously restructured so as to acquire subsidiary stress or achieve true dipththonghood. The present-day facts reviewed in §4 above speak against that. Post-tonic /ow/ is still fake after all these years.

6 Maintaining Quantity-Sensitivity

Having established that post-tonic /ow/ is unstressed, we return to the issue of quantity-sensitivity. If the vowel were a true diphthong, it would render its syllable heavy. The existence of unstressed heavy syllables would subvert the otherwise robust generalisation that stress in English is sensitive to syllable weight.[5]

However, establishing that post-tonic /ow/ is a fake diphthong means that the quantity-sensitivity of English stress remains intact. The vowel does not constitute a heavy nucleus but is rather a light nucleus followed by a separate non-nuclear position, i.e. VC. Word-final consonants in English are extrametrical, in that they do not contribute to the weight of a preceding syllable (Hayes 1982). If the preceding syllable is thereby light, it does not attract stress; hence the penultimate stress in C-final words such as those in (8a) (extrametrical consonants marked by <>).

(8) (a) rápi<d>, cábi<n>, métho<d>
    (b) píllo<w>, yéllo<w>, tomórro<w>

---

[5] The British tradition of English phonetics is only accidentally right in not marking a stress on post-tonic /ow/, since it also doesn't mark post-tonic subsidiary stress. To be fair, this tradition has rarely troubled itself with the question of whether English stress is quantity-sensitive or not.

Since the /w/ of final post-tonic /ow/ is C, it too is extrametrical, just like any other final consonant. The nuclear portion of the sequence (V) is light, with the result that stress defaults to the penult in words such as those in (8b).

7 Not All Diphthongs Are Fake in English

Having established that post-tonic /ow/ is VC, we might be tempted to extend the analysis to all instances of /ow/, including in stressed position in words such as *road, go, blow, token*. Stretching this point even further, we might go on to propose that all diphthongs in English are VC (and maybe in other languages for that matter), as for example Szigetvári (2016) has proposed. Let me outline just one of several reasons that this would risk throwing the baby out with the bathwater.

The advantage of the VC analysis of unstressed /ow/ lies in prosodically decoupling the glide from the preceding nucleus. This is exactly the result we want for post-tonic position: it ensures the glide is extrametrical, thereby leaving the preceding syllable light and therefore not stress-attracting. However, consider the consequences of extending the VC analysis to diphthongs in stressed position. In particular, consider the consequences for consonant phonotactics in the most relevant environment: post-vocalic position. Here clusters of two consonants are subject to quite strict sonority and place constraints. Very broadly speaking, there is a clear preference for a falling sonority slope across syllable boundaries (e.g. *after, winter, filter*) or at the end of a word (e.g. *graft, stint, guilt*).

Generalising a VC analysis to stressed diphthongs suddenly increases the length of the consonant clusters involved in these patterns by one. One effect of this is to create internal complex codas where none are otherwise attested, e.g. internal VCC.CV in *shoulder, council, oyster*, or word-final VCCC# in *bold, bounce, moist*. Moreover, under this analysis, it's a surprise that the initial glide consonant is largely insulated from the tight phonotactic restrictions that hold over the following two consonants. Under a traditional analysis, this falls out from the fact that the glide and the following consonants are in different syllabic constituents. There are probably ways of reconfiguring syllable theory so as to enable a generalised VC analysis of diphthongs to accommodate the phonotactics of three-consonant clusters. But at the very least this will inevitably make the theory more complex than anything required by a true-diphthong analysis.

8 Conclusion

There are actually two /ow/ vowels in modern English. One occurs in stressed syllables, e.g. *goat, hope, go, own, token*. This is a true diphthong: the two vocalic units of which it is composed are contained within the same syllable nucleus. The other occurs in post-tonic unstressed syllables, e.g. *yellow, borrow, photo, potato*. This one is a fake diphthong: the off-glide lies outside the nucleus housing the first unit. Recognising this difference allows us to maintain the generalisation that English stress is robustly quantity sensitive.

If there's a lesson to be drawn from this episode, one that goes beyond English, it is this: when confronted with alleged diphthongs, beware of fakes.

References

Booij, Geert. 1989. On the representation of diphthongs in Frisian. *Journal of Linguistics* 25. 319–332.
Booij, Geert. 1999. *The Phonology of Dutch*. Oxford: Oxford University Press.
Dell, François. 1995. Consonant clusters and phonological syllables in French. *Lingua* 95. 5–26.
Ewen, Colin J. & Harry van der Hulst. 2001. *The Phonological Structure of Words*. Cambridge: Cambridge University Press.
Gataker, Thomas. 1646. *De diphthongis, sive bivocalibus*. London: Clifton.
Harris, John. 1994. *English Sound Structure*. Oxford: Blackwell.
Harris, John & Edmund Gussmann. 1998. Final codas: Why the West was wrong. In Eugeniusz Cyran (ed.), *Structure and Interpretation: Studies in Phonology*, 139–162. Lublin: Folium.
Hayes, Bruce. 1982. Extrametricality and English stress. *Linguistic Inquiry* 13. 227–276.
Hayes, Bruce. 1995. *Metrical Stress Theory*. Chicago: University of Chicago Press.
Hulst, Harry van der. 1984. *Syllable Structure and Stress in Dutch*. Dordrecht: Foris.
Hulst, Harry van der. 1996. Separating primary accent and secondary accent. In Rob Goedemans, Harry van der Hulst & Ellis Visch (eds.), *Stress Patterns of the World*, Part I, 1–26. (HIL Publications 2). The Hague: Holland Academic Graphics.
Hulst, Harry van der. 2012. Deconstructing stress. *Lingua* 122. 1494–1521.
Hulst, Harry van der & Nancy A. Ritter. 1999. Theories of the syllable. In Harry van der Hulst & Nancy A. Ritter (eds.), The Syllable: Views and Facts, 13–52. Berlin: Mouton de Gruyter.
Jespersen, Otto. 1909. A Modern English Grammar on Historical Principles, Part 1: Sounds and Spellings. London: Allen & Unwin.
Jones, Daniel. 1950. *The Phoneme: Its Nature and Use*. Cambridge: Heffer.
Lass, Roger. 1992. Phonology and morphology. In Norman Blake (ed.), *The Cambridge History of the English Language*, Vol. 2: *1066–1476*, 23–155. Cambridge: Cambridge University Press.
Lindsey, Geoff. 2012. The British English vowel system. https://www.englishspeechservices.com/blog/british-vowels/.
Mattys, Sven L. 2000. The perception of primary and secondary stress in English. *Perception & Psychophysics* 62. 253–265.

McWhorter, John H. & Jeff Good. 2012. *A Grammar of Saramaccan Creole*. Berlin: de Gruyter Mouton.
Pater, Joe. 2000. Non-uniformity in English secondary stress: The role of ranked and lexically specific constraints. *Phonology* 17. 237–274.
Sweet, Henry. 1877. *A Handbook of Phonetics*. Oxford: Clarendon Press.
Szigetvári, Péter. 2016. No diphthong, no problem. In Jolanta Szpyra-Kozłowska & Eugeniusz Cyran (eds.), *Phonology, Its Faces and Interfaces*, 123–141. Frankfurt am Main: Peter Lang.
Trager, George L. & Bernard Bloch. 1941. The syllabic phonemes of English. *Language* 17. 223–246.
Warner, Natasha, Allard Jongman, Ann Cutler & Doris Mücke. 2001. The phonological status of Dutch epenthetic schwa. *Phonology* 18. 387–420
Wright, Joseph. 1898–1905. *The English Dialect Dictionary*. 6 vols. Oxford: Henry Frowde.

Ksenia Bogomolets
Deconstructing Secondary Stress

Abstract: Inspired by the Accent-First Theory (van der Hulst 1996, 2009, 2010, 2012), this chapter proposes a novel view on the organization of word-level prosody. I argue that the word-level prosodic system is not *bipartite*: primary accent vs. rhythm, but *tripartite*: primary accent vs. secondary accent vs. rhythm. Secondary accent is defined as abstract marking for inherent prominence phonetically realized as non-primary stress. Rhythm is defined as automatic alternation of strong and weak syllables. I show that secondary accent and rhythm regularly exhibit non-trivial discrepancies in their phonological behavior and propose that these discrepancies stem from two different sets of parameters governing the two properties.

Keywords: Secondary accent, secondary stress, rhythm, prosody, accent, stress, prosodic typology

1 Introduction

Traditionally, in the study of word-level prominence, a broad distinction is made between primary stress/accent and non-primary stress (or rhythm).[1] In this paper, I propose that the notion of *rhythm* and the notion of *secondary accent* ought to be treated separately. It will be shown that a large number of genetically unrelated languages provide evidence for treating *rhythm* and *secondary accent* as distinct prosodic phenomena. I will show that the notion of *rhythm* as commonly used in the prosodic literature, in fact, is used to analyze two different prosodic properties which regularly exhibit non-trivial discrepancies in their phonologi-

---

[1] I adopt the view of *accent* and *stress* proposed in van der Hulst (1996, 2012, 2014a, 2014b and other works). In this view, the term *accent* is used to mean an abstract property of a unit, a mark which does not provide any information about the phonetic cues, while *stress* (or 'stress-accent') is used to mean the phonetic manifestation of accent (see also Hyman 2006, 2009 for a discussion of the two terms). *Accent* is thus viewed as *underlying stress*.

Note: I would like to thank Jeroen van de Weijer and Marc van Oostendorp for helpful suggestions. I am also grateful to an anonymous reviewer for their comments and questions. Many thanks go to Harry van der Hulst, Jonathan Bobaljik, and Matthew Gordon for comments on earlier versions of this paper.

Ksenia Bogomolets, University of Auckland

https://doi.org/10.1515/9783110730081-004

cal and morpho-phonological behavior. The theory proposed here explains these discrepancies and predicts that they would occur regularly, which accords with the empirical facts.

I propose to reserve the term *rhythm* for secondary prominence which is (i) automatic, (ii) iterative, and (iii) is governed by a specific set of parameters discussed below (6). *Secondary accent*, on the other hand, by the definition proposed in this paper (4), is not dependent on iterative application of the rhythmic pattern, and as such, its assignment is governed by other, non-rhythmic, parameters (4). It will be evident that secondary accent assignment in fact parallels primary accent assignment, and I will argue that this parallelism is not accidental but is due to the identical set of parameters governing the two.

1.1 Separation of Primary Stress and Rhythm

The key proposal of this paper is based on the formal theory of word accent/stress that separates the representation of primary accent and the representation of rhythmically strong syllables (also known as rhythmic beats), detailed in van der Hulst (1996, 1997 2009, 2010, 2012). Primary accent in the Separation Theory is calculated first and independently of the rhythmic structure, while rhythm is assigned at a later derivational stage and may have some reference to the already assigned accent. The Separation Theory is in opposition to the assumptions of standard Metrical Phonology (Liberman and Prince 1977; Hayes 1995; Halle and Vergnaud 1987; Idsardi 1992), which treats primary stress and rhythm as derived by a single computation whereby primary stress is 'promoted' from one of the rhythmic beats. Below, I mostly focus on summarizing the motivations for separating primary stress and rhythm leaving aside the issue of the ordering in assignment of accent and rhythm.

Van der Hulst (1996, 2009, 2010, 2012) draws evidence for separating accent and rhythm from systems in which different algorithms govern their assignment. Firstly, as shown in Goedemans and van der Hulst (2013) on the basis of StressTyp (Goedemans and van der Hulst 2009), it is not unusual for primary stress and rhythm to be assigned from the opposite edges of a word. These so-called *polar rhythm* systems (van der Hulst 1984)[2] crucially require contrasting settings of the relevant parameters for the assignment of stress and rhythm (see also Moskal 2012). Secondly, stress and rhythm may differ in the setting of the Extrametrical-

---

[2] These systems are sometimes referred to as *dual rhythm systems* (Gordon 2002), or *bidirectional rhythm systems* (Kager 2005).

ity parameters. Thus, Goedemans and van der Hulst (2013) mention languages like Khalkha Mongolian, Munsee, and Unami where primary stress assignment is sensitive to right-edge extrametricality while rhythm is not. Thirdly, Goedemans and van der Hulst (2013) show that primary stress and rhythm may differ in the settings of parameters dealing with foot structure: weight-sensitivity, headedness, boundedness, and foot size – binary or ternary (see also McGarrity 2003 for a thorough study of asymmetries in primary stress and rhythm).

Additionally, primary stress and rhythm often display properties suggesting that they are assigned at different stages of prosodic derivation. While it is typical for primary stress to exhibit lexical exceptions and/or sensitivity to morphological classes of words, as well as to morphological structure and stratal differences, such sensitivities are typically not involved in the calculation of rhythm. Rhythm is typically fully automatic, 'post-lexical', and implementational.[3]

Importantly, the Separation Theory thus argues that primary stress is non-metrical, rejecting the major postulates of the Metrical Theory. I adopt the main idea of the Separation Theory, namely that primary accent and rhythm are assigned by different prosodic modules. However, I argue that this separation is not sufficient. Specifically, I propose that the word-level prominence system is not bipartite: primary accent vs. secondary accent, but tripartite: primary accent vs. secondary accent vs. rhythm. I propose that rhythm is post-cyclic and automatic while secondary accent assignment occurs in parallel to primary accent assignment and thus can potentially interact with segmental phonology, morphological structure, and lexical information. Although this approach at first glance may seem less parsimonious, it will be shown that (i) it is in fact formally more economical as it reduces the number of parameters required to account for accentual and rhythmic patterns, and (ii) it provides a better empirical coverage for the prosodic systems with complex interactions between primary and non-primary prominence.

1.2 Parametric Approach to Accent and Rhythm

Within the Separation Theory, van der Hulst (1996, 2012, 2014a, 2014b) proposes to account for the variety of accent behaviors on one hand, and for the variety of rhythmic patterns on the other hand with a set of Accent parameters and a set of Rhythm parameters. Let us review these two sets.

---

[3] Goedemans and van der Hulst (2013) note, however, that 'apparent counterexamples' exist, including languages in which secondary prominence needs to be specified as unpredictable – a note crucial for the theory of separation of secondary stress and rhythm proposed in this paper; see Section 2.3 in this chapter for details on phonologically unpredictable secondary prominence.

Firstly, the source of accent in languages is parametrically determined, and a distinction is made between languages where accent is sensitive to phonological properties of words or syllables and lexical accent languages. Van der Hulst does not provide a formalism to capture this parametric choice, but for the purposes of the current discussion, let us formalize it as in (1) below:

(1) LEXICAL ACCENT (Y/N)

Secondly, the mechanism of accent assignment is governed by the Domain parameters and the Accent Placement parameters within the designated domain:

(2) Accent parameters

Accent Domain	(BOUNDED) (R/L)
	(SATELLITE) (R/L)
Accent Placement	WEIGHT-TO-ACCENT (Y/N)
	(SELECT) (R/L)
	(DEFAULT) (R/L)

The parameters in (2) can be briefly defined as follows. The first parameter – BOUNDED (R/L) – determines whether stress is assigned within a bounded domain at one of the domain edges, Right or Left. If a language assigns stress in a bounded domain, a primary stress has to surface within the first or the last two or three syllables of the domain (as opposed to being assigned anywhere within a word). The parentheses indicate that this parameter can be active or inactive. In case the BOUNDED parameter is inactive, the domain of accent assignment is equivalent to the word, producing an unbounded accent system. In case this parameter is active, it determines the edge of the word which coincides with the accent domain. The second domain parameter – SATELLITE (R/L), if active, produces a trisyllabic domain and determines whether an extra syllable is adjoined to the right or to the left of a disyllabic accent domain in a bounded accent system. The notion of *satellite* in van der Hulst (2012) captures the notion of Extrametricality in the Metrical Theory, which involves an extension of the accentual domain at the word periphery (such a satellite is called *external*), but it also includes a possible extension of the accent domain with an internal syllable. Unlike an extrametrical syllable, a satellite can be accented either regularly or in a limited set of language-specific circumstances (see van der Hulst 2012: 1502–1504 for some examples). Consider, for instance, a schematic representation of the accentual domain in a language where an accent must be assigned within a bounded trisyllabic domain at the right edge of the word in (3). The representation in (3) below groups the three syllables at the right edge of a word into a constituent where the binary stress domain is within the parentheses and the binary stress domain with the adjunct of an external satellite is in curly brackets; the square bracket represents the word boundary:

(3) Trisyllabic accent domain oriented to the right edge of the word
    BOUNDED(R)   SATELLITE(R)
    ... σ {(σ σ)+ σ}]

The Accent Placement parameters govern the particulars of accent assignment. WEIGHT-TO-ACCENT parameter determines the source of accent: if this parameter receives a positive setting, accent placement in the language is weight-sensitive. SELECT (R/L) and DEFAULT (R/L) deal with a competition of more than one accent (SELECT), and with absence of accent (DEFAULT), assigning accent to the leftmost or the rightmost accentable unit in a domain. Bogomolets (2020: 190–218) argued for adding two additional parameters to the list of accent parameters in (2), based on the parametric view of Culminativity and Obligatoriness of accent (Hyman 2006, 2009): thus, CULMINATIVITY (Y/N) and OBLIGATORINESS (Y/N) determine whether words with multiple stresses or no stresses are allowed (see examples in §2–3 and discussion in §4). Different combinations of the settings of the parameters in (1)–(2) create the typological diversity found in primary accent systems. I propose that the same set of parameters is responsible for the diversity of secondary accent systems presented in the following section. More specifically, I propose that the algorithm of primary accent assignment and the algorithm of secondary accent assignment are formally identical, and this is due to them being governed by the same set of parameters. *Secondary accent* is defined as (4) with the full list of accent parameters in (4a):

(4) Secondary accent
    Abstract marking for inherent prominence phonetically realized as secondary stress and governed by the set of parameters in (4a).
    a. Accent parameters

Accent Domain	(BOUNDED) (R/L)
	(SATELLITE) (R/L)
Accent Placement	WEIGHT-TO-ACCENT (Y/N)
	(SELECT) (R/L)
	(DEFAULT) (R/L)
	CULMINATIVITY (Y/N)
	OBLIGATORINESS (Y/N)

In the Separation Theory (van der Hulst 1996, 2009, 2010, 2012), a different set of parameters has been proposed to account for the rhythmic patterns since, crucially for the Separation Theory, accent and rhythm are treated as two different kinds of prosodic phenomena. The following parameters governing rhythm have been proposed in van der Hulst's work:

(5) Rhythm parameters (van der Hulst 2014b)
   POLAR BEAT (Y/N)
   RHYTHM (POLAR/ECHO)
   WEIGHT (Y/N)
   LAPSE (Y/N)
   NONFINALITY (Y/N)

The list of parameters in (5) includes the POLAR BEAT parameter which, if active, assigns a secondary prominence (a 'beat') at the edge of the word opposite to the primary accent. However, note that a remark is made in van der Hulst (2014b) that this 'edge prominence' is independent of rhythm. Languages which exhibit this pattern are discussed in detail in §2.1 of this paper. The RHYTHM parameter governs the directionality of rhythm propagation: the 'echo' rhythm is assigned to alternating syllables from primary stress, while the 'polar' rhythm in the terms proposed in van der Hulst (2014b), is assigned to alternating syllables from the 'polar beat'. The WEIGHT parameter determines whether rhythm is weight-sensitive. The LAPSE parameter determines whether rhythm is binary or ternary, and the NONFINALITY parameter decides whether the final syllable is provided with a rhythmic beat or not. Although adopting the main ideas of this approach to rhythm, I will propose that rhythmic patterns cross-linguistically can in fact be accounted for with a subset of the parameters in (5). I define *rhythm* as (6) with the updated list of rhythmic parameters in (6a).

(6) Rhythm
   Automatic iterative alternation of strong and weak syllables within a word, governed by the set of parameters in (6a).
   a. Rhythm parameters
      RHYTHM (POLAR/ECHO)
      LAPSE (Y/N)
      NONFINALITY (Y/N)

I will thus argue that not only do *rhythm* and *primary* accent require separate algorithms in their assignment (as is argued in the Separation Theory), but that *secondary* accent and rhythm require separate algorithms in their assignment as well. Crucially, it will be shown that secondary accent assignment does not require any parameters that are not already required for primary accent assignment, while the rhythm patterns can be accounted for with just three parameters in (6a).

1.3 Outline of the Paper

The remainder of this paper is organized as follows. Section **2** presents a typology of secondary accent systems. In Section **3**, I show that some languages present evidence for all three prosodic properties, and all the logical combinations of rhythm and secondary accent are attested. Importantly, rhythm and secondary accent in languages which have both exhibit discrepancies, which are unaccounted for if both rhythm and secondary accent are assigned by a single algorithm. Finally, conclusions and a brief discussion of the implications of the proposed theory are provided in Section **4**.

2 Secondary Accent Typology

In this section, I present empirical evidence for and the theoretical implementation of further deconstruction of the notion of word-level prominence. The empirical evidence for the proposed theory centers around two general observations. Firstly, secondary accent assignment parallels the assignment mechanisms common in primary accent assignment and does not parallel the mechanisms common in the assignment of rhythm. Secondly, some languages present evidence for all three prosodic properties.

I begin with evidence for the first point: secondary accent behaves as *accent* proper and is assigned cross-linguistically in the same way as primary accent. The following three strategies of primary accent assignment are common across languages (see Bogomolets and van der Hulst (forthcoming) for an overview). Firstly, primary accent can be *fixed*, i.e. primary accent always falls on the same syllable. The most common patterns cross-linguistically involve fixed primary stress on one of two edge-most syllables at either of the word edges. Examples of such systems are multiple and include, for instance, such languages as Amur Nivkh (initial, Mattissen 2003, forthcoming), Dakota (peninitial, Shaw 1985), Apurinã (penultimate, Facundes 2000), Trumai (final, Guirardello 1999). In §2.1, I propose that in parallel to *fixed* primary accent, *fixed* secondary accent is regularly found cross-linguistically. Secondly, primary accent assignment may depend on the sensitivity to phonological prominence of some syllables in a wordform. Such prominence most often is conditioned by phonological weight distinctions. Vast descriptive and theoretical literature is available on the role of syllable weight in primary accent assignment; however, the role of syllable weight in secondary accent assignment has received far less attention and has been a subject of controversy even for the best-studied systems like English (see for example Pater 2000 and references therein). In §2.2, I review evidence for the weight sensitivity in secondary accent assignment. Finally, I will consider accent conditioned by underlying phonologically unpredictable prominence of some syllables, i.e. *lexical* accent. Contrary to the predictions of some theories of accent (e.g. de Lacy 2019), and to descriptive claims (e.g. Goedemans and van der Hulst 2014), I will argue that secondary accent, in parallel to primary accent, can in fact be *lexical*. I provide examples of lexical secondary accent in §2.3.

2.1 Fixed Secondary Accent

The first type of secondary accent is predictably located in a fixed position within a word. *Fixed* secondary accent, in parallel to *fixed* primary accent, may be located at the edge of a domain (e.g. at one of the edges of a morphological word or another morphological domain). These patterns can be accounted for by the active status of the BOUNDED (L/R) parameter for secondary accent assignment and the negative setting of the WEIGHT-TO-ACCENT parameter. An active status of the SATELLITE (L/R) parameter produces a trisyllabic bounded domain for secondary accent assignment, while its inactive status produces a disyllabic domain. The appropriate setting of the DEFAULT (L/R) parameter determines the accent placement within the bounded edge-oriented domain. Finally, fixed accent is normally culminative and obligatory, which is expressed through the positive settings of the CULMINATIVITY and OBLIGATORINESS parameters:

(7) Parameters governing fixed accent placement

Accent Domain	BOUNDED (L/R)
	(SATELLITE) (L/R)
Accent Placement	WEIGHT-TO-ACCENT (N)
	DEFAULT (L/R)
	CULMINATIVITY (Y)
	OBLIGATORINESS (Y)

Below I provide examples of three systems with fixed secondary accent: Passamaquoddy (Eastern Algonquian; initial secondary accent), Border Lakes Ojibwe

(Central Algonquian; final secondary accent), and Tahltan (Athabaskan; penultimate secondary accent). Let us first consider the general pattern observed in Passamaquoddy, where primary accent falls on the penultimate syllable, and secondary accent falls on the initial syllable:

(8) a. ˌle.ˈwes.to b. ˌwi.ke.ˈwes.to c. ˌseh.ta.ye.ˈwes.to
    l-ewesto   wik-ewesto   sehtay-ewesto
    thus-speak   like-speak   backwards-speak
    'He speaks.'   'He likes to talk.' 'He speaks while walking backwards.'
                                        (adapted from Hagstrom 1995: ex. 5)[4]

Examples in (8) show the regular assignment of *fixed* primary accent and *fixed* secondary accent in Passamaquoddy. An identical pattern has been reported in van der Hulst (2012) for Maithili, Biangai, and South Conchucos Quechua. The following parameter settings account for the placement of fixed primary accent (9a) and fixed secondary accent (9b) in Passamaquoddy:

(9) Passamaquoddy accent placement parameters
   a. Primary accent parameters

Accent Domain	BOUNDED (R)
	(SATELLITE)
Accent Placement	DEFAULT (L)
	CULMINATIVITY (Y)
	OBLIGATORINESS (Y)

   b. Secondary accent parameters

Accent Domain	BOUNDED (L)
	(SATELLITE)
Accent Placement	DEFAULT (L)
	CULMINATIVITY (Y)
	OBLIGATORINESS (Y)

The result of the settings of the accent parameters in (9) is schematically illustrated in (10):

---

[4] Note that in addition to *fixed* secondary accent and primary accent, Passamaquoddy also has rhythm. I do not mark rhythm in these examples for clarity of exposition, but see §3.1 below where this pattern is discussed.

(10) Passamaquoddy accent placement
    a. Primary accent   b. Secondary accent

         x   DEFAULT (L)   x   DEFAULT (L)
         ...σ σ (σ σ)]   BOUNDED (R)   [(σ σ) σ σ...   BOUNDED (L)

As evident from the settings of the BOUNDED (L/R) parameter in (9) and from the implementation in (10), Passamaquoddy shows a common type of *fixed* secondary accent which has previously been termed *polar* (van der Hulst 2014b).⁵ The *polar accent* term refers to its characteristic positioning at the edge opposite to the edge of the word where the primary accent is found in the language. This is, however, not the only possible pattern of fixed secondary accent placement.

Fixed *non-polar* secondary accent is found in several dialects of another Algonquian language, Ojibwe. Both, accounts of the so-called syncopating dialects of Odawa and Eastern Ojibwe (Hayes 1995: 216–218; Kaye 1973; Newell 2008; Piggott 1980, 1983) and the so-called non-syncopating dialects, for example, Border Lakes Ojibwe (Swierzbin 2003) describe a stress pattern where, in addition to primary stress, at least in some parts of the lexicon, secondary stress is obligatory on the last syllable of the word. This obligatory word-final secondary prominence is most accurately analyzed as *fixed* secondary accent. Consider data from Border Lakes Ojibwe where one of the regular stress patterns is the following: primary accent assignment is sensitive to syllable weight and is assigned to the rightmost non-final heavy syllable in a word, and secondary accent is required on the final syllable of a word (Swierzbin 2003).⁶ Thus, in the examples in (11), the initial syllable receives primary stress because it is the only, and thus the rightmost, heavy (CVV) while secondary stress falls on the final syllable:

(11) a. ˈaːndʒɪgoˌzɪ   'S/he is moving to a new place.'
      b. ˈʃaːboniˌgʌn   'needle'   (Swierzbin 2003: 357)

In the examples in (11), primary stress is word-initial while secondary stress is word-final, which creates a seemingly 'polar' pattern (minimally different from the Passamaquoddy pattern (10)). However, primary stress can be located at the

---

5 Van der Hulst (2012) provides multiple examples of such systems.
6 As reported in detail in Swierzbin (2003), this is not the only stress pattern observed in the language as stress assignment appears to also be sensitive to lexical marking of some suffixes as well as to word-internal prosodic domains. I refer the reader to Swierzbin (2003) for a detailed description and a possible analysis.

same edge as the word-final secondary stress, since primary stress is not *fixed* in the language, but is assigned to the rightmost heavy syllable in a word. Thus, consider the example in (12), where weight-sensitive primary stress and word-final secondary stress are located at the same edge of the word:

(12) aːnd͡ʒɪˈnaːgo‚zɪ 'S/he looks different.'[7] (Swierzbin 2003: 358)

Thus, while primary accent in the language is unbounded and weight-sensitive, secondary accent is fixed and weight-insensitive. This pattern is accounted for by the following parameter settings:

(13) Border Lakes Ojibwe accent placement parameters
 a. Primary accent parameters

Accent Domain	(BOUNDED)
	(SATELLITE)
Accent Placement	WEIGHT-TO-ACCENT (Y)
	SELECT (R)
	CULMINATIVITY (Y)
	OBLIGATORINESS (Y)

 b. Secondary accent parameters

Accent Domain	BOUNDED (R)
	(SATELLITE)
Accent Placement	WEIGHT-TO-ACCENT (N)
	DEFAULT (R)
	CULMINATIVITY (Y)
	OBLIGATORINESS (Y)

The SATELLITE parameter is not active in Ojibwe, and by (13b), a secondary accent in Ojibwe is assigned within a disyllabic domain at the right edge of a word. Within that disyllabic domain, accent is assigned to the rightmost syllable, which results in a fixed final secondary accent in the language. Consider the schematic representation of these patterns in (14); in (14a), the bold-facing represents heavy syllables:

---

[7] This form in the source also includes a rhythmic beat on the initial syllable, omitted here for clarity of exposition.

(14) Border Lakes Ojibwe accent placement
  a. Primary accent
     x   SELECT (R)
     x x   WEIGHT-TO-ACCENT (Y)
     [σ σ σ σ σ σ]
  b. Secondary accent
                              x   DEFAULT (R)
     ...σ σ (σ σ)] BOUNDED (R)[8]

Additional evidence for the claim that *fixed* secondary accent is not required to only occur at the edge of the word opposite to the primary stress (as previously proposed for the notion of *polar accent*) can be found. We also find *fixed* secondary accent in languages which do not associate primary accent with a particular distance from the word edges. Consider, for instance, the pattern found in the Athabaskan language Tahltan. In the majority of cases, primary accent in this language is assigned to the initial syllable of the root, but a secondary accent is required in the prefixal domain. Secondary accent is penultimate in the prefixal domain, but is also obligatory even if the root is only prefixed with a single monosyllabic prefix, in which case a clash between the primary and the secondary accent occurs (Bob and Alderete 2005). The clashing secondary and primary stress pattern is exemplified in (15a–c), and the secondary stress assigned to the penultimate syllable in the prefixal domain is exemplified in (15d–f); the root morpheme in all examples is bold-faced:

(15) Tahltan primary and secondary stress
  a. ˌme-ˈlaʔ   'his/her hand'
  b. ˌkaː-ˈtsʼet   'I scratched it out.'
  c. ˌʔes-ˈθone   'my star'
  d. ˌmeʔe-ˈkʼahe   'his/her fat'
  e. ʔuˌdeθiː-ˈdlet 'We (dual) melted it.'
  f. ʔeˌdʒi-da-ˈdaɬ 'S/he is going hunting.'   (Bob and Alderete 2005: 374)

---

[8] I thank an anonymous reviewer who has brought to my attention that an even "cleaner" example of both fixed primary and fixed secondary accent aligned to the same edge can be found in Plains Cree. In this Central Algonquian language, primary stress in the default case falls on the antepenultimate syllable, and secondary stress is assigned to the final syllable (as reported in Wolfart 1996). In addition to the fixed right-edge-aligned primary and secondary stress, Plains Cree also has a fully automatic rhythmic pattern propagating from the primary stress leftward. See § 3.1.1 for a discussion of systems which have all three phenomena – primary stress, secondary stress, and rhythm.

In (15), the root receives primary stress while the prefixal domain receives secondary stress. Both primary accent and, crucially, secondary accent in Tahltan can be analyzed as *fixed* within the relevant domains – the root domain in the case of the primary accent, and the prefixal domain in the case of secondary accent.

A number of typologically and theoretically important generalizations have been made in this section. Firstly, primary and secondary accent can be governed by conflicting settings of the same accent parameters. Secondly, this section has presented a number of accent systems where non-primary prominence is most accurately analyzed as *fixed secondary accent*. Finally, in contrast to the previously held assumption that *fixed* secondary accent can only ever be present in the form of the *polar accent*, I have demonstrated that the position of fixed secondary accent in a language can be calculated without a reference to the position of primary accent, which results in non-polar patterns. I therefore propose to treat *polar accent* as just one kind of *fixed* secondary accent.

2.2 Weight-Sensitive Secondary Stress

The second type of secondary accent, which also finds a parallel in primary accent assignment, is *weight-sensitive* secondary accent. Let us consider some examples.

The Australian language Waalubal has been reported to have a fixed primary accent and a weight-sensitive secondary accent (Crowley 1978; Hammond 1986). Primary accent is invariably assigned to the initial syllable in Waalubal, while secondary accent is assigned to all heavy syllables. Syllables with branching nuclei are treated as heavy by the accent assigning algorithm while all other syllable structures are treated as light; consider the data in (16) below:

(16) a. ˈbandaŋ 'other'
 b. ˈŋaˌmaːlu 'tree goanna.ERG'
 c. ˈwurguˌluːm 'magpie'
 d. ˈbaɲɖaniˌbeː 'only covered' (Hagberg 2006: 108)

What we observe in Waalubal, thus, is an asymmetry between the primary accent and the secondary accent, where only the latter is weight-sensitive. This crucially results in a clearly non-rhythmic secondary prominence pattern: for instance, in (16b) the two accents create a clash, and in (16d) we observe a lapse. The Waalubal accent patterns are formally accounted for with the parameter settings in (17):

(17) Waalubal accent placement parameters
    a. Primary accent parameters.

Accent Domain	BOUNDED (L)
	(SATELLITE)
Accent Placement	WEIGHT-TO-ACCENT (N)
	DEFAULT (L)
	CULMINATIVITY (Y)
	OBLIGATORINESS (Y)

    b. Secondary accent parameters

Accent Domain	(BOUNDED)
	(SATELLITE)
Accent Placement	WEIGHT-TO-ACCENT (Y)
	CULMINATIVITY (N)
	OBLIGATORINESS (N)

Consider the schematic representation of (17) in (18) below; the bold-facing in (18b) represents heavy syllables:

(18) Waalubal accent placement
    a. Primary accent   b. Secondary accent
        x   DEFAULT (L)   x   x WEIGHT-TO-ACCENT (Y)
      [(σ σ) σ σ... BOUNDED (L)   [σ **σ** σ σ σ **σ**]

While Waalubal and a number of other languages show an asymmetrical pattern where only secondary accent is weight-sensitive, other languages have been shown to have both primary and secondary accent assignment conditioned by syllable weight.[9] One such pattern is found in the East Mongolian languages Khalkha and Buriat: primary stress falls on the last syllable if it is the only heavy in the word, otherwise on the rightmost nonfinal heavy, otherwise on the initial syllable. Secondary stress falls on all heavy syllables, including the final syllable (Walker 1995). Syllables with branching nuclei are heavy for the purposes of both primary and secondary stress assignment; syllables with non-branching nuclei including closed syllables are treated as light. Consider the examples from Buriat in (19):

---

9 McGarrity (2003: 16) lists the following languages showing the same asymmetry as Waalubal: Finnish, Koya, Cahuilla, Apalai, Cambodian, Cayapa, Estonian, Irish Gaelic, Gidabal, Tubatulabal, Western Shoshoni, Margany/Gunya, Alabama, Veps, Votic.

(19) a. ˈboːˌsoː b. ˌxyːxenˈgeːˌreː c. ˌbuːzaˌnuːˈdiːje
'bet, wager' 'by one's own girl' 'steamed dumplings.ACC'
(Walker 1995: 88)

As can be observed in (19), secondary accents in Buriat are assigned to all heavy syllables. Interestingly, clashes between primary accent and secondary accent are allowed, and secondary accent assignment does not obey the same constraints as primary accent in this language, which is evident from the fact that final primary accent is dispreferred while secondary accent can fall on the final syllable (I refer the reader to Walker 1995, 1997 for a detailed analysis of these patterns within the OT framework).

2.3 Phonologically Unpredictable Secondary Stress

Finally, the third type of secondary accent, in parallel with primary accent, is phonologically unpredictable, or *lexical*. In this section, I adopt a broad definition of *lexical accent* as accent whose position cannot be predicted form phonological properties of the word (e.g. closeness to word edges or number of syllables) or of the syllables (i.e. syllable weight) and thus has to be underlyingly marked in the lexicon (for a general discussion of lexical accent see van der Hulst 1999, 2010; for competing analyses of lexical accent systems see Alderete 1999, 2001; Bogomolets 2020; Revithiadou 1999). The source of accent in languages which exhibit this pattern is thus specified as in (20):

(20) LEXICAL ACCENT (Y)

Nez Perce (Crook 1999), a Sahaptian language, shows a (cyclic) lexical secondary accent pattern. In Nez Perce, multiple morphemes in a morphologically complex word can be underlyingly marked for accent. In such cases, one of the underlying accents receives primary stress (see Bogomolets 2020: 113–133 for a detailed analysis). It is shown in Crook (1999: 383–387) that the remaining underlying accents, however, do not get deleted, but receive secondary stress. Consider the following form of the verb ˈ*weeyik* 'to cross'. In (21), the underlyingly accented root is combined with an underlyingly accented prefix ˈ*nees-* marking a plural object, and an underlyingly accented directional suffix -ˈ*uu*. The first line in the example presents the surface form, and the second line presents the underlying form:

(21) hi-ˌnes-ˌweyiˈk-uu-se
hii-ˈnees-ˈweeyik-ˈuu-see
3-PL.OBJ-cross-toward-INC
'He is crossing toward them.' (adapted from Crook 1999: 480)[10]

In (21), we observe that the root, one of the prefixes, and the suffix realize their underlying accents as stress. The primary stress is on the suffix, and the root and the prefix carry phonologically unpredictable, i.e. *lexical* (*cyclic*) secondary stress.

Phonologically unpredictable secondary accent of similar nature is also attested in the Austronesian language Chamorro. In morphologically simple words in Chamorro, primary accent is obligatorily assigned in the trisyllabic window at the right edge of a word, and penultimate syllable is the default position. In morphologically complex words, primary accent is assigned cyclically: primary accent is assigned to an underlyingly accented affix in the outermost derivational layer (Chung 1983). Accents assigned at all cycles are retained as secondary.[11]

Fijian is an example of non-cyclic lexical secondary accent, which is evident in loanword phonology. Fijian stress has received much attention in the formal literature (see, for example, Hayes 1995: 142; Kenstowicz 2007) with most of the data coming from a series of papers by Schütz (1978, 1983, 1999). Primary stress in the language is weight-sensitive in the bounded disyllabic domain at the right

---

10 In Nez Perce, in addition to lexical secondary stress, there is also regular rhythm. In these examples, I omit the marking of rhythm for clarity of exposition. Refer to Crook (1999: 352–382) for a detailed description and a possible analysis.

11 Secondary stress resulting from the retained accents of simpler morphological forms in Nez Perce and Chamorro are in some way reminiscent of the well-known examples of phonologically unpredictable secondary accent in English, which has received a considerable amount of attention in the formal literature (Chomsky and Halle 1968; Halle and Kenstowicz 1991; Pater 2000). The classic example of such stress is in words like ˌconˌdenˈsation where the secondary stress on the second syllable conflicts with the tendency for a syllable immediately preceding the syllable with primary stress to be stressless and reduced. This phonologically unexpected secondary stress is usually assumed to be retained from the morphologically simpler form, i.e. to be *cyclic* – *con*ˈ*dense*. However, Halle and Kenstowicz (1991: 460) showed that English has a parallel secondary stress pattern where secondary accent has to be lexically specified and not result from primary stress at the earlier cycle in words like ˌchimˌpanˈzee, ˌinˌcarˈnation, ˌosˌtenˈtation. Based on these examples, Halle and Kenstowicz (1991) proposed to treat all *condensation*-type words as having a lexically conditioned weight-to-stress rule. In the terms adopted here, all phonologically unpredictable accent is *lexical*, thus secondary accent in forms like ˌconˌdenˈsation would be treated as cyclic lexical accent (see Pater 2000 and references therein for various analyses of this pattern).

edge of the word where it is assigned to the final syllable if it is heavy (CVV) and otherwise to the penultimate syllable. The secondary accent pattern relevant for the current discussion is found in loanwords from English (refer to Kenstowicz 2007 for a detailed analysis within the OT framework). Fijian is an open syllable language, which results in pervasive vowel epenthesis to repair consonant clusters found in the source forms. It is particularly interesting that Fijian preserves the main stress of the English source as secondary stress, consider examples in (22) below from Kenstowicz (2007: 319):

(22) Lexical secondary accent in Fijian

	English	Fijian
a.	ˈcolony	ˌkoːˈloni
b.	ˈcabin	ˌkeːˈbini
c.	ˈestimate	ˌesitiˈmeti
d.	ˈtelegraph	ˌtalekaˈravu
e.	ˈtelevision	ˌteleviˈsoni

Note that primary stress in all the forms in (22) is predictable from the general primary accent assignment pattern. Secondary stress in loanwords must, however, be underlyingly marked. Thus, as with the accent systems exemplified in the previous sections, primary and secondary accent assignment in languages with phonologically unpredictable secondary accent may be governed by conflicting settings of the relevant parameters.

2.4 Summary

In this section, I presented a typology of secondary accent systems. On one hand, we find that secondary accent and primary accent within a single language are often governed by conflicting parameter settings – an observation which was first made in van der Hulst's work and which influenced the creation of the Separation Theory. On the other hand, we find striking parallels between primary accent assignment and secondary accent assignment in that they are overall governed by the same set of parameters, resulting in the same overall types of primary and secondary accent (i.e. fixed accent, weight-sensitive accent, and phonologically unpredictable accent). This is not expected to occur under the predictions of the Separation Theory.

3 Combination of Secondary Accent and Rhythm

The model of word-level prominence proposed in this paper predicts that some languages should distinguish between all three of the proposed types of prominence: primary accent, secondary accent, and rhythm. Notably, this prediction is unique to the theory of prominence proposed here: neither the Separation Theory, nor the standard Metrical Theory distinguish between more than two levels of word-level prominence. In this section, I show that this prediction is borne out: some languages present independent evidence for each prosodic property. Thus, we find languages with only primary accent and rhythm, languages with primary accent and secondary accent but no rhythm, and languages with primary accent, secondary accent, and rhythm.

In the previous section, I argued that secondary accent patterns in all cases can be accounted for with the set of parameters which accounts for primary accent placement cross-linguistically, i.e. only the parameters, which have been independently shown to play a role in primary accent assignment, are needed to account for secondary accent patterns. In this section, I review the parameters proposed for rhythm in van der Hulst (2012, 2014b) and I argue that a smaller set of parameters than previously proposed is sufficient to account for rhythm. Recall that the following parameters governing rhythm were proposed in van der Hulst (2014b):

(23) Rhythm parameters in van der Hulst (2014b)
    a. POLAR BEAT (Y/N)
    b. RHYTHM (POLAR/ECHO)
    c. WEIGHT (Y/N)
    d. LAPSE (Y/N)
    e. NONFINALITY (Y/N)

Notably, parameters (a) and (c) in (23) determine the assignment of prominence which does not create a rhythmic pattern. Under the account proposed for secondary accent in this paper, the 'polar beat' is analyzed as a type of fixed secondary accent. The role of syllable weight in non-primary prominence in the current approach is also restricted to accent proper. Specifically, I argued that weight-sensitivity is a property of accent stemming from the WEIGHT-TO-ACCENT parameter. I thus propose that only three out of five parameters in (23) are needed to account for rhythm (24):[12]

---

[12] It is possible that one more parameter might be relevant for rhythm assignment – DIRECTION (of propagation) with possible settings being 'leftward' or 'rightward'. Positing this parameter

(24) Rhythm parameters: revised
   a. RHYTHM (POLAR/ECHO)
   b. LAPSE (Y/N)
   c. NONFINALITY (Y/N)

By (24), three properties are definitional of a rhythm system: a specified anchor (primary or secondary accent), the size of a rhythmic unit – binary or ternary, and whether the final syllable in a domain is visible to the rhythm-assigning mechanism. The remaining part of this section presents evidence for the sufficiency of the parameters in (24) and for separating rhythm from secondary accent.

3.1 Languages with Secondary Accent and Rhythm

Let us first consider languages which show evidence for all three prosodic properties. Crucially, it will be shown that in all cases, parameters governing the assignment of secondary accent versus rhythm are different, which is predicted to be the case under the theory proposed in this paper, but is unaccounted for otherwise. Below, I review examples of languages where secondary accent must be assigned independently of rhythm in systems with a fixed secondary accent (§3.1.1) and in systems with phonologically unpredictable secondary accent (§3.1.2).[13]

---

would be warranted if rhythm systems may differ in the direction of rhythmic alternation, regardless of the rhythm anchor. Thus, if indeed such parametric variation exists, we should find 'echo' systems differing solely in the direction of rhythmic beats assignment. Consider (i) vs. (ii) below; the syllable carrying primary accent is represented with a bold-faced capital sigma, syllables in rhythmically strong positions are underlined:
   (i) Binary 'Echo' rhythm L-R
       σ σ σ σ Σ σ $\underline{σ}$ σ $\underline{σ}$ σ
   (ii) Binary 'Echo' rhythm R-L
       $\underline{σ}$ σ $\underline{σ}$ σ Σ σ σ σ σ σ

I am not aware of such pairs of languages, and it is possible that rhythmification is always automatic and exhaustive, in which case specifying the anchor (i.e. primary accent or secondary accent) is sufficient.

[13] Languages with weight-sensitive secondary accent and an independent regular rhythmic pattern are attested as well, but are not discussed here for the reasons of space. One such example comes from the Muskogean language Chickasaw, where primary accent is weight-sensitive and is assigned to the rightmost heavy syllable within the word, secondary accent is weight-sensitive and is assigned to all heavy syllables, and a regular iambic rhythm is assigned left-to-right (Munro and Ulrich 1984; Munro and Willmond 1994; Gordon 2004).

3.1.1 Fixed Secondary Accent and Rhythm

Let us consider first languages which in the previous section have been shown to have a *fixed* secondary accent. Recall from §2.1, in Passamaquoddy, fixed primary accent is assigned on the penultimate syllable, and fixed secondary accent falls on the initial syllable, a pattern accounted for by the parameter settings in (9). In addition, a regular rhythm falls on alternate syllables from the primary accent right-to-left (*echo* rhythm in the terminology of van der Hulst 2012, 2014b). Consider the forms in (25); both rhythm and secondary accent are marked in the examples with the IPA diacritic <ˌ>, but rhythmically prominent syllables are additionally underlined for clarity of exposition:

(25) a. ˌteh.ˌsah.kwa.ˌpa.sol.ˈti.ne
'Let's walk around on top.'

b. ˌwi.ˌcoh.ke.ˈke.mo
'He helps out.'

c. ˌwi.coh.ˌke.ta.ˈha.mal
'He thinks of helping the other.' (LeSourd 1988: 140–143)

Note in (25), the mechanism of secondary accent assignment and that of rhythm assignment may result in a clash (25a). The following parametric settings derive the rhythmic pattern observed in Passamaquoddy:

(26) Passamaquoddy rhythm parameters
RHYTHM (ECHO)
LAPSE (N)
NONFINALITY (N)

The settings of the rhythm parameters in (26) and the accent parameters in (9) capture the account proposed in this paper for secondary accent as separate from rhythm in application to the prosodic system of Passamaquoddy.

Given the rhythm parameters in (24) and the independent status of secondary accent, we expect that we should find languages with the reverse-Passamaquoddy pattern, i.e. a pattern where rhythm would be anchored to the fixed secondary accent position (and not primary accent) and would thus result in a lapse at the primary accent edge of the word (if clashes with primary accent are disallowed) or in a clash with the primary accent (if clashes with primary accent are allowed). This is indeed what we find. The former pattern is found, for instance, in Piro

(Arawakan; Matteson 1965), while the latter pattern is found in South Conchucos Quechua (Quechuan; Hintz 2006).

In South Conchucos, primary accent is assigned to the initial syllable, and a secondary fixed accent is assigned to the penultimate syllable. An alternating rhythm is anchored to the penultimate syllable accent. Consider examples in (27):

(27) a. ˈʃu.maq 'pretty'
 b. ˈi.ma.ˌku.na 'things'
 c. ˈtʃu.pan.ˌki.man.ˌła.chi̥ 'you would likely have just gotten drunk'
 d. ˈtu.ʃu.ku.ˌna.qḁ 'dancers'
 e. ˈwa.ˌraː.ka.ˌmun.qa.ˌna.tʃi̥ 'hopefully it will appear at dawn'

The South Conchucos data exhibit two interesting properties. Firstly, the system allows for clashes of rhythm with the primary accent (27c–d). Secondly, a variation has been reported between the discourse realization of stress and the realization of stress in elicited data (Hintz 2006). In elicited forms, the stress on the penultimate syllable is judged by speakers as the primary stress, whereas in discourse data the stress on the initial syllable is primary and the stress on the penultimate syllable is secondary. Data illustrating stress in South Conchucos Quechua in (27) thus reflects the discourse pronunciation. Notably, no such variation is possible between the primary stress (on either initial or penultimate syllable) and any of the rhythmic beats between the initial and the penultimate syllable, supporting the claim made in this paper, namely that primary accent and secondary accent are prosodic properties of the same type while rhythm is a prosodic property of a formally different nature.[14]

3.1.2 Lexical Secondary Accent and Rhythm

Evidence for the separate systems of secondary accent and rhythm can also be found in languages where secondary accent is phonologically unpredictable,

---

[14] Goedemans and van der Hulst (2013) also note that fixed secondary accent (of the 'polar beat' type) can get reanalyzed as primary accent diachronically, for example, leading a system with penultimate accent to become a system with initial accent or vice versa. They list as examples of such possible historical reanalysis the aboriginal languages of Australia (see Goedemans 2010) and the Slavic languages (with penultimate accent in Polish and initial accent in Czech; see Dogil 1999). Perhaps, another example can be added to this list, namely the change from penultimate accent reconstructed for Proto-Algonquian (Goddard 2016) to second-syllable accent in Blackfoot (Plains Algonquian; Van Der Mark 2003; Weber 2016). Importantly for the proposal put forward in this paper, such reanalysis seems more plausible if it involves a 'swap' between two instances of *accent* rather than between a *rhythmic* beat and a primary accent.

i.e. *lexical*. Rhythm in these languages, however, just as in languages like Passamaquoddy, Piro or South Conchucos is fully predictable, regular, and automatic. The case in point here comes from Chamorro. Recall from §2.3, all lexical accents in morphologically complex words with multiple underlying accents are retained as stresses in Chamorro: one of them is realized as primary stress, and all the others are realized as secondary stresses. Secondary stress in Chamorro results from phonologically unpredictable cyclic lexical accents. However, in addition, Chamorro also has a regular rhythm assigned to alternating syllables right-to-left from the primary stress. In contrast to the secondary accent assignment, morphological complexity is not a pre-requisite for rhythm to occur (28a–b), although it may also appear in morphologically complex forms (28c–d) and (28e–f). Consider examples in (28) below; rhythmically prominent syllables are underlined:

(28) a. ˌat.may.ˈgo.su
'vegetable'

b. ˌki.ma.ˈson
'to burn'

c. ba.ˈpot
ship
'ship'

d. ˌba.pot.-ˈni.ha
ship-3PL
'their ship'

e. ka.ˈdu.ku
crazy
'crazy'

f. ˌman.-ka.ˈdu.ku
PL-crazy
'crazy (pl.)' (adapted from Chung 1983: 43)

In (28a–b), primary stress is assigned to the penultimate syllable, and a rhythmic beat is predictably found on the initial syllable. In (28c), primary stress is assigned to the final syllable of the simplex form. In (28d), when the root is suffixed with the 3Pl possessive agreement marker, primary stress predictably falls on the penultimate syllable of the newly formed word. Note that in this case, the primary stress of the 'ship' form (28c) is not preserved as a secondary stress due to Chamorro not allowing for a syllable preceding a syllable with primary stress to bear stress (the so-called *Destressing Rule*, Chung 1983: 42). However, we observe that a rhythmic beat surfaces in (28d) on the initial syllable. The same is observed in (28e–f). The rhythmic pattern in Chamorro can be accounted for with the following settings of the rhythm parameters:[15]

---

[15] I should note that no examples are available in the sources where both secondary accent and rhythm would be observable in the same form. However, it is possible for both to be

(29) Chamorro rhythm parameters
 RHYTHM (ECHO)
 LAPSE (N)
 NONFINALITY (N)

Secondary accent and rhythm in Chamorro not only are assigned by different parameters (secondary accent being phonologically unpredictable and rhythm being fully automatic), their interaction with morpho-phonology differs. This is to be expected under the theory proposed here since rhythm is post-cyclic while secondary accent assignment occurs in parallel to primary accent assignment and thus can potentially interact with segmental phonology and with lexical information. The difference in morpho-phonological interactions between rhythm and secondary accent in Chamorro is evident in the processes of Umlaut and Gemination (Chung 1983; Kaplan 2008). Both only are triggered by secondary accent and cannot be triggered by rhythm, firstly supporting the idea that secondary accent and rhythm are different properties; secondly, supporting the idea that secondary accent is *accent*, i.e. is a property of the same class as primary accent, which in this language also triggers umlaut and gemination.

3.2 Languages with Secondary Accent and No Rhythm

In the previous section, I demonstrated that some languages present evidence for having both secondary accent and a rhythmic structure. In this section, I turn to languages which have secondary accent, but lack rhythm. One such example comes from an Austronesian language Sibutu Sama (Elenbaas and Kager 1999; Gordon 2002). This language has a fixed primary accent on the penultimate syllable and a fixed secondary accent on the initial syllable.[16] Consider examples in (30) below, note that clashes between primary and secondary stresses are disallowed in Sibutu Sama, thus only penultimate primary stress surfaces in (30a):

(30) a. bisˈsala   'talk'
     b. ˌbissaˈlahan   'persuading'
     c. ˌbissalaˈhanna   'he is persuading'
     d. ˌbissalahanˈkami 'we are persuading'   (Gordon 2002: 505)

---

present within one word if the word is long enough and is morphologically complex (Sandra Chung, p.c.).
16 Kager (1997) provides a discussion and an analysis of prefixed words in the language, which do not necessarily exhibit the same stress pattern.

Sibutu Sama thus presents a clear example of a language where primary stress assignment and secondary stress assignment are governed by different settings of the same accent parameters (to produce the penultimate and the initial fixed stress respectively). Crucially, there is no evidence of rhythm, as is clear from lapses in (30c–d) above.

Weight-sensitive secondary accent but no evidence of a regular rhythmic alternation is found in Waalubal (Pama-Nyungan; Hagberg 2006: 108) and in Khalka and Buriat (East Mongolian; Walker 1995) discussed in §2.2.

3.3 Languages with Rhythm and No Secondary Accent

Finally, let us briefly consider examples of languages with a clear rhythmic structure, but no secondary accent. Languages which have rhythm but no secondary accent have in fact been the center of attention for most of metrical stress typology (see, for instance, Hayes 1995; Goedemans and van der Hulst 2013; Gordon, forthcoming; Rice 2010), and for that reason I only provide one illustrative example here.

Apurinã (Arawak; Facundes 2000) has a fixed primary accent and a regular binary rhythm echoing the primary accent. In Apurinã, primary stress is fixed on the penultimate syllable, and rhythm is assigned to alternating syllables right-to-left from the penult; consider examples in (31):

(31) a. ta.ˈka   'to put/plant'
     b. nɨ.ˈta.ka   'I put/plant.'
     c. ˌnɨ.ta.ˈka.rɨ   'I put/planted it.'
     d. nɨ.ˌta.ka.ˈrɨ.ko   'I will put/plant it.'
     e. ˌnɨ.ta.ˌka.pe.ˈrɨ.ko 'I will have put/planted it.'
     f. nɨ.ˌta.ka.ˌpe.ka.ˈrɨ.ko 'I will put/plant it.'   (Facundes 2000: 103)

The Apurinã prominence patterns are straightforwardly accounted for with the following parameter settings:

(32) Apurinã accent parameters

Accent Domain	Bounded (R)
	(Satellite)
Accent Placement	Default (L)
	Culminativity (Y)
	Obligatoriness (Y)

(33) Apurinã rhythm parameters
RHYTHM (ECHO)
LAPSE (N)
NONFINALITY (N)

Importantly for the discussion in this paper, languages like Apurinã show no evidence of secondary accent in addition to primary stress (which is *fixed* in the language) and rhythm (which is regularly echoing the primary stress).

4 Discussion

In this paper, building on the insights of the Separation Theory (van der Hulst 1996, 2009, 2010, 2012, 2014a, 2014b), I have argued that not only do rhythm and *primary accent* require separate algorithms in their assignment, but that *secondary accent* and rhythm require separate algorithms in their assignment as well. I have presented empirical data in favor of treating primary accent and secondary accent as prosodic phenomena of the same type. Specifically, I have argued that primary and secondary accent are formally united by virtue of being dependent on the same set of parameters. Rhythm, on the other hand, is treated as a formally different prosodic property.

Since the approach put forward in this paper formally unites primary accent and secondary accent as belonging to the same type of word-level prominence, while rhythm is regarded as belonging to a different type, some of the issues which were unresolved in the Separation Theory of van der Hulst receive an explanation. For instance, it is unexplained in the Separation Theory why some properties may be shared between primary accent and secondary prominence since the two types of prominence are regarded as unrelated phenomena. Under the account proposed here, it is predicted that primary accent would be sharing some properties with secondary accent. Thus, for instance, cases mentioned in Goedemans and van der Hulst (2014) like English swapping of primary and secondary stresses in *àbsolùte/ àbsolútely* is problematic for the Separation Theory, but not for the theory proposed here (recall also similar examples from South Conchucos discussed in §3.1.1 and examples of similar diachronic patterns from footnote 17).

Relatedly, in van der Hulst (2009, 2012, 2014a, 2014b), it is argued that the 'irregularity' observed in prosody cross-linguistically is to be attributed to the accentual module which belongs to the 'lexical phonology'. Van der Hulst also proposed that the rhythmic module is 'post-grammatical', fully regular, and automatic. I propose that both primary and secondary accent are assigned at a point of the prosodic derivation when morpho-lexical and morpho-phonological material is accessible. This is generally assumed to be true of primary accent assignment in order to ensure that primary accent can be (i) sensitive to segmental phonology, (ii) sensitive to morpho-lexical information, and (iii) can drive phonological (segmental) processes. I have proposed that secondary accent, being formally *accent*, is assigned in parallel to primary accent. This predicts that secondary accent might exhibit morpho-lexical and morpho-phonological interactions comparable to primary accent because it is assigned in the same way as primary accent. Rhythm, on the other hand, following the Separation Theory, is fully automatic and is assigned at a later point in the prosodic derivation when it cannot drive segmental processes and is insensitive to morpho-lexical information. As shown in this paper, this prediction is borne out. The Chamorro case discussed in §3.1.2 can be taken as an illustration.

As has been shown throughout this paper, primary and secondary accent systems cross-linguistically vary within the limits defined by the set of accent parameters (4). It has also been observed above that some of the parameters active for the primary accent assignment might not be active for the secondary accent assignment. This is most easily observed in the CULMINATIVITY and OBLIGATORINESS parameters. In evaluating this issue, it is useful to address the functional role of stress and the place of CULMINATIVITY and OBLIGATORINESS in performing that role. The "prototypical" one-per-domain stress is traditionally seen as assisting in demarcation of the relevant domain. Demarcation as the main function of stress can be considered responsible for the near-universal status of culminativity and obligatoriness of primary stress. Importantly, however, in primary stress assignment, the demarcative function of stress can compete with the demand that primary stress be assigned to prominent syllables. Such prominence can result from syllable weight, sonority considerations, or underlying (*lexical*) marking for accent. Thus, for instance, in a weight-sensitive primary accent system, in a word with multiple heavy syllables, the demarcative function of stress ensured by the positive settings of the CULMINATIVITY and OBLIGATORINESS parameters, demands that only one of the heavy syllables receive primary stress. The demand that inherently prominent syllables must be realized with stress is thus subordinate to the requirements of CULMINATIVITY and OBLIGATORINESS.[17] The demarcating function of secondary stress, however, appears to be 'losing' to the demand of associating a prominent syllable with stress at least in some cases. For example, this is the case in languages with weight-sensitive secondary accent discussed

---

[17] This can be straightforwardly expressed with a ranking of groups of constraints in Optimality Theory models, see McGarrity (2003).

above – Waalubal and the East Mongolian languages, where SELECT crucially does not apply resulting in multiple secondary stresses within a word if multiple heavy syllables are present. The subordinate status of the demarcative function of secondary stress in such systems is also supported by the inactive status of DEFAULT: indeed, if no heavy syllables are present within a word, secondary stress simply does not get assigned – a pattern virtually unattested in primary accent systems. However, we do find languages where secondary accent is culminative and obligatory within some domain. This, for instance, was shown to be the case in Tahltan (cf. §2.1) where a single obligatory secondary stress is assigned in the relevant domain. The conclusion that can be drawn then is that CULMINATIVITY and OBLIGATORINESS are (nearly) universally active in primary accent assignment, while they can be inactive for secondary accent assignment purposes.[18] Crucially, the proposal put forward in this paper predicts that we should not find any systems where secondary accent assignment would require any additional parameters (i.e. parameters which are not already required for primary accent assignment cross-linguistically), and this prediction is borne out

References

Alderete, John. 1999. *Morphologically-governed accent in optimality theory*. Amherst, MA: University of Massachusetts, Amherst Doctoral dissertation.
Alderete, John. 2001. Root-controlled accent in Cupeño. *Natural Language & Linguistic Theory* 19(3). 455–502.
Bob, Tanya & John Alderete. 2005. A corpus-based approach to Tahltan stress. In Sharon Hargus & Keren Rice (eds.), *Athabaskan Prosody*, 369–391. Amsterdam: John Benjamins.
Bogomolets, Ksenia. 2020. *Lexical accent in languages with complex morphology*. Mansfield, CT: University of Connecticut Doctoral dissertation.
Bogomolets, Ksenia & Harry van der Hulst. Forthcoming. Word prominence and polysynthetic languages. In Ksenia Bogomolets & Harry van der Hulst (eds.), *Word Prominence in Languages with Complex Morphologies*. Oxford: Oxford University Press.

---

[18] An anonymous reviewer has pointed out another potential gap between the attested combinatorial possibilities for primary and secondary accent parameters – namely, there appears to be an asymmetry in the availability of the positive setting of the SATELLITE parameter. Indeed, although typologically rare, a primary accent bounded within a trisyllabic domain at either edge of a word is attested. Trisyllabic stress windows for secondary accent appear to be virtually non-existent (see, however, Karvonen (2005) for a possible case of antepenultimate secondary accent in Finnish). The question of whether such gaps are accidental or meaningful is left for future research (but refer to McGarrity 2003 for a relevant account of asymmetries between primary and secondary accent).

Chomsky, Noam & Morris Halle. 1968. *The Sound Pattern of English*. New York: Harper and Row.
Chung, Sandra. 1983. Transderivational relationships in Chamorro phonology. *Language* 59(1). 35–66.
Crook, Harold David. 1999. *The phonology and morphology of Nez Perce stress*. Los Angeles: University of California, Los Angeles Doctoral dissertation.
Crowley, Terry. 1978. *The Middle Clarence Dialects of Bandjalang*. Canberra: Australian Institute of Aboriginal Studies.
Dogil, Grzegorz. 1999. West Slavic. In Harry van der Hulst (ed.), *Word Prosodic Systems in the Languages of Europe*, 814–839. Berlin/New York: Mouton de Gruyter.
Elenbaas, Nine & René Kager. 1999. Ternary rhythm and the lapse constraint. *Phonology* 16(3). 273–329.
Facundes, Sidney da Silva. 2000. *The language of the Apurina people of Brazil (Maipure/Arawak)* Buffalo: State University of New York at Buffalo Doctoral dissertation.
Goddard, Ives. 2016. Arapaho historical morphology. *Anthropological Linguistics* 57(4). 345–411.
Goedemans, Rob. 2010. An overview of word stress in Australian Aboriginal languages. In Harry van der Hulst, Rob Goedemans & Ellen van Zanten (eds.), *A Survey of Word Accentual Patterns in the Languages of the World*, 55–85. Berlin/New York: Mouton de Gruyter.
Goedemans, Rob & Harry van der Hulst. 2009. StressTyp: A database for word accentual patterns in the world's languages. In Martin Everaert, Simon Musgrave & Alexis Dimitriadis (eds.), *The Use of Databases in Cross-Linguistics Research*, 235–282. New York/Berlin: Mouton de Gruyter.
Goedemans, Rob & Harry van der Hulst. 2013. Rhythm types. *The World Atlas of Language Structures Online*.
Goedemans, Rob & Harry van der Hulst. 2014. The separation of accent and rhythm: Evidence from StressTyp. In Harry van der Hulst (ed.), *Word Stress: Theoretical and Typological Issues*, 119–145. Cambridge: Cambridge University Press.
Gordon, Matthew. 2002. A factorial typology of quantity insensitive stress. *Natural Language & Linguistic Theory* 20(3). 491–552.
Gordon, Matthew. 2004. A phonological and phonetic study of word-level stress in Chickasaw. *International Journal of American Linguistics* 70(1). 1–32.
Gordon, Matthew. Forthcoming. Word stress and intonational prominence in highly synthetic languages. In Ksenia Bogomolets and Harry van der Hulst (eds.), *Word Prominence in Languages with Complex Morphology*. Oxford: Oxford University Press.
Guirardello, Raquel. 1999. *A reference grammar of Trumai*. Houston, TX: Rice University Doctoral dissertation.
Hagberg, Lawrence Raymond. 2006. *An Autosegmental Theory of Stress*. [Dallas]: SIL International.
Hagstrom, Paul. 1995. When a Passamaquoddy unstressable schwa, that's a mora. Ms. Massachusetts Institute of Technology.
Halle, Morris & Michael Kenstowicz. 1991. The free element condition and cyclic versus noncyclic stress. *Linguistic Inquiry* 22(3). 457–501.
Halle, Morris & Jean-Roger Vergnaud. 1987. *An Essay on Stress*. Cambridge, MA: MIT Press.
Hammond, Michael. 1986. The obligatory-branching parameter in metrical theory. *Natural Language & Linguistic Theory* 4. 185–228.

Hayes, Bruce. 1995. *Metrical Stress Theory: Principles and Case Studies*. Chicago: University of Chicago Press.
Hintz, Diane M. 2006. Stress in South Conchucos Quechua: A phonetic and phonological study. *International Journal of American Linguistics* 72(4). 477–521.
Hulst, Harry van der. 1984. *Syllable Structure and Stress in Dutch*. Dordrecht: Foris.
Hulst, Harry van der. 1996. Separating primary accent and secondary accent. In Rob Goedemans, Harry van der Hulst & Ellis Visch (eds.), *Stress Patterns of the World. Part I*, 1–26. (HIL Publications 2). The Hague: Holland Academic Graphics.
Hulst, Harry van der. 1997. Primary accent is non-metrical. *Rivista di linguistica* 9(1). 99–127.
Hulst, Harry van der. 1999. Word accent. In Harry van der Hulst (ed.), *Word Prosodic Systems in the Languages of Europe*, 3–116. Berlin/New York: Mouton de Gruyter.
Hulst, Harry van der. 2009. Brackets and grid marks or theories of primary accent and rhythm. In Eric Raimy & Charles E. Cairns (eds.), *Contemporary Views on Architecture and Representations in Phonological Theory*, 225–245. Cambridge, MA: MIT Press.
Hulst, Harry van der. 2010. Representing accent. *Phonological Studies* 13. 117–128.
Hulst, Harry van der. 2012. Deconstructing stress. *Lingua* 122. 1494–1521.
Hulst, Harry van der. 2014a. The study of word accent and stress: Past, present, and future. In Harry van der Hulst (ed.), *Word Stress: Theoretical and Typological Issues*, 3–55. Cambridge: Cambridge University Press.
Hulst, Harry van der. 2014b. Representing rhythm. In Harry van der Hulst (ed.), *Word Stress: Theoretical and Typological Issues*, 325–365. Cambridge: Cambridge University Press.
Hyman, Larry M. 2006. Word-prosodic typology. *Phonology* 23(2). 225–257.
Hyman, Larry M. 2009. How (not) to do phonological typology: The case of pitch-accent. *Language Sciences* 31(2–3). 213–238.
Idsardi, William James. 1992. *The computation of prosody*. Cambridge, MA: Massachusetts Institute of Technology Doctoral dissertation.
Kager, René. 1997. Generalized alignment and morphological parsing. *Rivista di linguistica* 9. 245–282.
Kager, René. 2005. Rhythmic licensing theory: An extended typology. In *Proceedings of the Third International Conference on Phonology*, 5–31. Seoul National University.
Kaplan, Aaron. 2008. Stress is the trigger of Chamorro umlaut. In Emily Tummons & Stephanie Lux (eds.), *Proceedings of the 2007 Mid-America Linguistics Conference*, 135–149. Kansas Working Papers in Linguistics.
Karvonen, Daniel H. 2005. *Word prosody in Finnish*. Santa Cruz: University of California, Santa Cruz Doctoral dissertation.
Kaye, Jonathan. 1973. Odawa stress and related phenomena. *Odawa Language Project: Second Report*, Centre for Linguistic Studies, University of Toronto, 42–50.
Kenstowicz, Michael. 2007. Salience and similarity in loanword adaptation: A case study from Fijian. *Language Sciences* 29(2–3). 316–340.
Lacy, Paul de. 2019. The feature [stress]. In Harrison Adeniyi, Olyesye Adesola, Francis Egbokhare & Eno-Abasi Urua (eds.), *Festschrift for Akinbiyi Akinlabi*, 86–101. Nigeria: Zenith BookHouse.
LeSourd, Philip S. 1988. *Accent and syllable structure in Passamaquoddy*. Cambridge, MA: Massachusetts Institute of Technology Doctoral dissertation.
Liberman, Mark & Alan Prince. 1977. On stress and linguistic rhythm. *Linguistic Inquiry* 8(2). 249–336.
Matteson, Esther. 1965. *The Piro (Arawakau) Language*. Berkeley: University of California Press.

Mattissen, Johanna. 2003. *Dependent-Head Synthesis in Nivkh: A Contribution to a Typology of Polysynthesis*. (Typological Studies in Language 57). Amsterdam/Philadelphia: John Benjamins.

Mattissen, Johanna. Forthcoming. Phonological and morphological wordhood in Nivkh. In Ksenia Bogomolets & Harry van der Hulst (eds.), *Word Prominence in Languages with Complex Morphology*. Oxford: Oxford University Press.

McGarrity, Laura W. 2003. *Constraints on patterns of primary and secondary stress*. Bloomington: Indiana University Doctoral dissertation.

Moskal, Beata. A. 2012. Clashes and lapses: Responses to edge prominence. Paper presented at CUNY Conference on the Phonology of Endangered Languages, CUNY, USA.

Munro, Pamela & Charles Ulrich. 1984. Structure-preservation and Western Muskogean rhythmic lengthening. In *West Coast Conference on Formal Linguistics*, 3, 191–202.

Munro, Pamela & Catherine Willmond. 1994. *Chickasaw: An Analytical Dictionary*. Norman: University of Oklahoma Press.

Newell, Heather. 2008. *Aspects of the morphology and phonology of phases*. Montreal: McGill University Doctoral dissertation.

Pater, Joe. 2000. Non-uniformity in English secondary stress: The role of ranked and lexically specific constraints. *Phonology* 17(2). 237–274.

Piggott, Glyne L. 1980. *Aspects of Odawa Morphophonemics*. New York: Garland.

Piggott, Glyne L. 1983. Extrametricality and Ojibwa stress. *McGill Working Papers in Linguistics* 1. 80–117.

Revithiadou, Anthi. 1999. *Headmost accent wins: Head dominance and ideal prosodic form in lexical accent systems*. The Hague: Holland Academic Graphics Doctoral dissertation.

Rice, Keren. 2010. Accent in the native languages of North America. In Harry van der Hulst, Rob Goedemans & Ellen van Zanten (eds.), *A Survey of Word Accentual Patterns in the Languages of the World*, 155–248. Berlin/New York: Mouton de Gruyter.

Schütz, Albert J. 1978. English loanwords in Fijian. In Albert J. Schütz (ed.), *Fijian Language Studies: Borrowing and Pidginization*, 1–50. (Bulletin of the Fiji Museum 4). Suva: Fiji Museum.

Schütz, Albert J. 1983. The accenting of English loanwords in Fijian. In Frederick B. Agard, Gerald Kelley, Adam Makkai & Valerie Becker Makkai (eds.), *Essays in Honor of Charles F. Hockett*, 565–572. Leiden: E. J. Brill.

Schütz, Albert J. 1999. Fijian accent. *Oceanic Linguistics* 38(1). 139–151.

Shaw, Patricia A. 1985. Coexistent and competing stress rules in Stoney (Dakota). *International Journal of American Linguistics* 51(1). 1–18.

Swierzbin, Bonnie. 2003. Stress in Border Lakes Ojibwe. In H. C. Wolfart (ed.), *Papers of 34th Algonquian Conference*, 341–369. Winnipeg: University of Manitoba.

Van Der Mark, Sheena Chantal. 2004. *The phonetics of Blackfoot pitch accent*. Calgary: University of Calgary Master's thesis.

Walker, Rachel. 1995. Mongolian stress: Typological implications for nonfinality in unbounded systems. *Phonology at Santa Cruz* 4. 85–102.

Walker, Rachel. 1997. Mongolian stress, licensing, and factorial typology. Rutgers Optimality Archive; ROA-171-0197.

Weber, Natalie. 2016. Initial extrametricality and cyclicity in Blackfoot accent. *UBC Working Papers in Linguistics* 44. 1–16.

Wolfart, Hans Christoph. 1996. Sketch of Cree, an Algonquian language. *Handbook of North American Indians* 17. 390–439.

Irene Vogel
Is There Foot Structure in Isolating Languages?

Abstract: This chapter addresses a fundamental issue that arises in relation to the prosodic hierarchy: whether the constituents proposed in a model such as that of Nespor & Vogel (1986/2007) are universal, both with regard to their presence in all languages and their definition across languages. The constituent considered here is the Foot, which is particularly controversial in isolating languages, two of which are examined here, Mandarin Chinese and Vietnamese. Although these languages have much in common prosodically, recent research has treated them quite differently with regard to their Foot structure. While Mandarin is generally argued to include a Foot constituent, Vietnamese is argued to dispense with it. I consider several types of evidence and propose not only a similar type of analysis for both languages, but also how the Foot may be defined in these languages in conformity with generally recognized notions of the Foot in other types of languages.

Keywords: Foot, Isolating languages, Mandarin Chinese, Prosody, Prosodic structure, Vietnamese

1 Introduction

A question that arises in relation to the prosodic hierarchy is whether the constituents proposed in a model such as that of Nespor and Vogel (1986/2007) are universal. In considering this question we may ask not only whether all of the constituents are present in all languages, but also whether they are defined in the same way across languages. Over the years, various constituents have been argued to be present or absent in specific languages and / or universally, and when present, they have been defined in different ways in some cases. The constituent considered here is the Foot, which - if present in the prosodic hierarchy - is the largest of the strictly phonological constituents (i.e., those that are not defined in relation to morpho-syntactic structures like the larger, interface constituents).

Isolating languages such as Mandarin Chinese (henceforth Mandarin) and Vietnamese pose a challenge for the universality of the Foot in two fundamental respects. First, the canonical, binary, Foot typically contains two syllables, but in

---

Irene Vogel, University of Delaware

https://doi.org/10.1515/9783110730081-005

isolating languages, most words are monosyllabic. While it might be possible in such cases that the Foot binarity requirement is met at the moraic level (i.e., two moras instead of two syllables), it is not the case that all words in Mandarin and Vietnamese have two moras, nor is there evidence that the languages are quantity-sensitive at all (i.e., mora counting). Second, Feet are usually invoked in lexical stress assignment, but isolating languages are generally not stress languages, since many (or most) of their words do not contain multiple syllables that are in relative prominence relations to each other. It may be observed that isolating languages frequently make use of compounding to create words longer than one syllable; however, if a crucial aspect of the universality of prosodic constituents is the uniformity of their definition across languages, defining Feet as components of a Phonological Word in some cases and as consisting of multiple Phonological Words in others, fails to satisfy that requirement.

This paper examines the role and representation of the Foot in the two isolating languages, Vietnamese and Mandarin, which have been treated in recent investigations quite differently with respect to the Foot and its potential as a universal prosodic constituent. In the former, it has been argued that the Foot is absent, and thus not a universal constituent, while in the latter, is has been argued to be present, and thus a universal constituent, but its definition is somewhat different from that found in other, non-isolating, languages. In Section 2, I briefly outline some general properties associated with Feet, as well as the recent, divergent approaches to Foot structure in Vietnamese and Mandarin. In Section 3, I introduce some additional observations regarding Vietnamese and Mandarin, and show how the Foot might be defined in conformity with universal notions of this constituent. Section 4 offers a general discussion of the role of the Foot in the prosodic hierarchy, and Section 5 concludes.

2 The Foot Constituent in General, and in Isolating Languages

2.1 The Foot Constituent

In prosodic hierarchies that include the Foot, it appears between the syllable and the Phonological (or Prosodic) Word (PW). It may also be referred to as the "metrical" or "stress" Foot, indicating its fundamental role in rhythmic patterns, typically involving alternations between stronger and weaker syllables. The strong syllable, or head of the Foot, is considered to be stressed, and if there are multiple

Feet in a PW, one stressed syllable will be more prominent than the other(s) - signaling the main or primary stress of the word. It has also been argued that the Foot, like other prosodic constituents, may serve as the domain for different types of phonological phenomena and phonotactic constraints (e.g., Nespor and Vogel 1986/2007).

It is widely, though not universally, assumed that Feet come in two types with regard to their composition: bounded, containing two syllables, and unbounded, containing any number of syllables (e.g., Hayes 1995). Bounded Feet are either iambic, exhibiting a weak-strong (W-S) prominence pattern, or trochaic, with a strong-weak (S-W) pattern. While iambic Feet tend to be quantity-sensitive, with the strong position being heavy, the corresponding requirement is not necessarily observed in trochaic Feet. In either case, words with multiple bounded Feet will present alternating rhythmic patterns. By contrast, the words in a language with unbounded Feet will not present such alternating patterns, but rather have a single prominent syllable, with the others all being weak, as in the case of Hungarian, which has primary stress on the first syllable of a word, followed by one or more unstressed syllables.[1]

The centrality of the bounded Foot type in phonological theory is reflected in the concept of the Minimal Foot, a binary branching Foot which typically contains two syllables (or in some cases, two moras). This Minimal, binary Foot, is in turn taken as the basis of the Minimal Word, which must consist of at least one Minimal Foot (e.g., McCarthy and Prince 1990). There are, nevertheless, numerous cases of words in different languages consisting of a single monomoraic syllable (e.g., Italian *re* [re] 'king', French *thé* [te] 'tea'). If a word must contain at least one Foot, however, these must be Feet, and indeed, are recognized as such, but they are referred to as "degenerate" Feet (e.g., Hayes 1995).

It must be noted that if the constituents of the prosodic hierarchy are all assumed to be universal, and this also entails that they are consistently and unambiguously defined across languages, degenerate Feet, although often accepted as a necessity, are potentially problematic since they do not meet the requirement of Foot (and consequently Word) minimality. Other proposed structures, such as ternary Feet, also introduce definitional challenges to the universality of the Foot constituent if only (binary) bounded and unbounded Feet are permitted. In a constraint-based phonological system, degenerate and ternary Feet need not

---

[1] It has been suggested that Hungarian may have alternating secondary stresses, accounted for by a unit referred to as the "cola" in Hammond (1987); however, in a systematic study of multisyllabic words which were controlled for the location of heavy syllables, Blaho and Szeredi (2011) found no evidence for word level secondary stress (cf. also Kálmán and Nádasdy 1994, cited in Blaho and Szeredi 2011).

be excluded, just considered less preferred than binary Feet. It must be borne in mind, however, that allowing such divergent configurations to count as Feet, even if they are dispreferred, weakens the original theory of Foot structure which defined only two types of Feet, binary bounded and unbounded, and is therefore not a decision that should be made lightly.

2.2 The Foot in Two Isolating Languages: Two Approaches

The most obvious question raised by isolating languages with regard to the Foot constituent is whether it is needed, given that words tend to be monosyllabic, whereas Feet are expected to be branching.[2] Moreover, if syllables correspond (and directly map) to PWs in isolating languages, an intervening level of representation would seem superfluous. These issues are illustrated in (1), with a sentence from Vietnamese, where σ, Σ and PW represent syllables, Feet and Phonological Words, respectively. The PWs would in turn be grouped into larger constituents, not shown here as they are not directly relevant to the discussion.

(1) Vietnamese isolating / monosyllabic sentence structure (Comrie 1981: 40)

PW	PW	PW	PW	PW	PW	PW	PW	PW	PW	PW	PW
|	|	|	|	|	|	|	|	|	|	|	|
Σ	Σ	Σ	Σ	Σ	Σ	Σ	Σ	Σ	Σ	Σ	Σ
|	|	|	|	|	|	|	|	|	|	|	|
Khi$_\sigma$	tôi$_\sigma$	đến$_\sigma$	nhà$_\sigma$	bạn$_\sigma$	tôi$_\sigma$	chúng$_\sigma$	tôi$_\sigma$	bắt$_\sigma$	dầu$_\sigma$	làm$_\sigma$	bài$_\sigma$
when	I	come	house	friend	I	pl	I	begin[3]		do	lesson

'When I came to my friend's house, we began to do lessons.'

As can be seen, the monosyllabic morphemes are all assigned to their own Feet, and the Feet to PWs, so we may ask whether all three levels of structure are needed. It must be noted, though, that strings of monosyllabic words can arise in other types of languages as well, and crucially in languages with stronger evidence for distinct syllable, Foot, and PW constituents, as illustrated in the English sentence in (2).

---

[2] Somewhat analogous questions may also be raised in relation to other languages, with different morphological structures. For example, as pointed out by a reviewer, the status of the syllable is often questioned in Japanese (e.g., Labrune 2012).
[3] Note that *bắt dầu* 'begin' is a compound, and thus shown as consisting of two (phonological) words, each consisting of a syllable.

(2) English monosyllabic sentence structure

PW	PW	PW	PW	PW	PW	PW	PW	PW	PW
|	|	|	|	|	|	|	|	|	|
Σ	Σ	Σ	Σ	Σ	Σ	Σ	Σ	Σ	Σ
|	|	|	|	|	|	|	|	|	|
While$_\sigma$	Sam$_\sigma$	ate$_\sigma$	fresh$_\sigma$	fruit$_\sigma$	Fran$_\sigma$	drank$_\sigma$	hot$_\sigma$	tea$_\sigma$	

Since such non-branching structures do exist cross-linguistically, and are simply considered in other languages to be a type of (degenerate) Foot, one could argue that there is no fundamental difference between the Vietnamese and English cases. Instead, it is only a matter of the degree of overlap: the overlap of syllable, Foot and Phonological Word is relatively uncommon in English, while it is quite typical in, and in fact characterizes, isolating languages such as Vietnamese (and Mandarin). As will be seen in the next sections, recent approaches to these structural considerations in Vietnamese and Mandarin have been divergent, despite the similarities in their morphological properties.

2.2.1 Vietnamese

Focusing on the frequent overlap between the syllable, Foot and PW, as illustrated in (1), Schiering, Bickel, Hildebrandt and others (e.g., Schiering, Bickel, and Hildebrandt 2010) have argued that there is no need for either the Foot or PW constituent in Vietnamese. That is, both the Foot and the PW are superfluous since there is no evidence for word level prosodic structure that is distinct from Phonological Phrase structure (2010: 673), and thus syllables are parsed directly into PPhs. They cite acoustic investigations by Nguyen and Ingram (e.g., Ingram and Nguyen 2006; Nguyen and Ingram 2007a) that show that pairs of compounds and matching phrases like *hoa hồng* 'rose' (compound) and *hoa hồng* 'pink flower' (phrase) are not acoustically distinct, and that listeners do not reliably perceive a difference between them.

It must be noted, however, that just because compounds and phrases sound the same, this does not necessarily mean that their prosodic structures are identical. For example, in Italian, both compounds and phrases have prominence on the rightmost element, so a compound *Croce Rossa* ('Red Cross' organization) sounds the same as the phrase *croce rossa* ('red-colored cross'). These items behave differently morphologically and syntactically, suggesting that they might correspond to distinct prosodic structures as well, despite their phonetic similarity.

It will be seen in Section 3 that there are more nuanced considerations to be made with regard to Vietnamese compounds and phrases, but the main point here is the nature of the argument advanced by Schiering, Bickel, and Hildebrandt, in particular the claim that a level in the prosodic hierarchy may be skipped if there is no evidence that it is distinct from some other constituent. Such an approach is fundamentally different from one that takes the constituents of the prosodic hierarchy, and grammar more generally, to be universal even if they are not overtly manifested or exhibit overlap with other constituents.

2.2.2 Mandarin

In contrast with Vietnamese, the approach to Mandarin has generally been to retain and motivate all of the prosodic constituents that have been proposed for other, non-isolating, languages, and in particular the Foot. In fact, contrary to the widely held view that Mandarin words characteristically consist of a single syllable, Duanmu (among others, 1999, 2000) argues that the language is undergoing a change in favor of longer words consisting of disyllabic Feet, which furthermore, exhibit a trochaic (strong-weak) prominence pattern. Thus, a single morpheme may acquire an additional element precisely for the purpose of making it disyllabic, and thus binary branching, without altering its meaning, as illustrated in (3); and the same process may apply multiple times, as illustrated in (4). (The diacritics (shown on "a") indicate the tones: ā = Tone 1 (high), á = Tone 2 (rising), ǎ = Tone 3 (dipping), à = Tone 4 (falling); a = Toneless syllable, sometimes referred to as Tone 5.)

(3) Formation of Disyllabic Foot (= PW) in Mandarin (Duanmu 1999)
    a. add morpheme with similar meaning
        zhòng 'plant' → [[[zhòng]$_\sigma$ [zhí]$_\sigma$]$_\Sigma$]$_{PW}$ 'to plant' (< plant+plant)

    b. add morpheme with (ignored) different meaning
        ěr 'ear' → [[[ěr]$_\sigma$ [duo]$_\sigma$]$_\Sigma$]$_{PW}$ 'ear' (< ear+petal)

(4) Formation of Multiple Disyllabic Feet (= PW) in Mandarin (Duanmu 1999)
    [[[zhòng]$_\sigma$ [zhí]$_\sigma$]$_\Sigma$ [[dà]$_\sigma$ [suàn]$_\sigma$]$_\Sigma$]$_{PW}$ 'garlic plant' (< plant + garlic, both lengthened words)

In fact, according to Duanmu, the role of the trochaic Foot in Mandarin is so important that a dummy weak syllable (0) may be inserted to ensure the desired Foot structure, as in (5).

(5) Formation of Multiple Disyllabic Feet with Dummy Syllable (= PW) in Mandarin (Duanmu 1999)
[[[zhòng]$_\sigma$ [zhí]$_\sigma$]$_\Sigma$ [[suàn]$_\sigma$ [∅]$_\sigma$]$_\Sigma$]$_{PW}$ 'garlic plant' (< plant + garlic, first lengthened word)

This approach to the prosodic structure of Mandarin does not raise the same challenge to the universality of the constituents of the prosodic hierarchy as was seen in the above analysis of Vietnamese. That is, it retains, and indeed, militates in favor of the Foot. It does, nevertheless, raise questions for the potential universality of the Foot with regard to its definition. If the Foot is the constituent in the prosodic hierarchy between the syllable and the PW, it should not dominate PWs. In the items in (3)–(5), the Foot is not shown as dominating PWs, but the structures in question contain pairs of (monosyllabic) words that would be considered compounds. Since the members of compounds are typically considered to constitute PWs, this would mean that the items with pairs of syllables labeled as Feet, actually contain one or more PWs (e.g., relevant labels underlined: [[[zhòng]$_\sigma$]$_\underline{PW}$ [[zhí]$_\sigma$]$_\underline{PW}$]$_\Sigma$ 'plant' (< plant+plant)). That is, the Foot effectively dominates constituents of a higher (PW) level. Moreover, if such Feet are then parsed into larger PWs before being parsed into the upper prosodic constituents (e.g., Phonological and Intonational Phrases), we would have a repetition of the PW constituent in two positions in the prosodic hierarchy: PW < Foot < PW (e.g., relevant labels underlined: [[[[zhòng]$_\sigma$]$_\underline{PW}$ [[zhí]$_\sigma$]$_\underline{PW}$]$_\Sigma$]$_\underline{PW}$ 'plant' (< plant+plant)). Additionally, the properties of the two PW constituents would be different. The lower PWs are monosyllabic, do not meet the minimal Foot requirement of binarity, and lack internal prominence relations. The upper Foot, by contrast, is binary branching and meets the minimality requirement with two syllables, even if one must be a dummy syllable as in (5), and it exhibits a trochaic prominence pattern. Thus, despite the apparent similarity of Mandarin prosodic structure to that of languages with more canonical Foot structures, we must question whether the type of analysis advanced by Duanmu and others is desirable. Although it supports a universal set of prosodic constituents including the Foot, it does so at the cost of invoking idiosyncratic definitions of the Foot and an atypical configuration of the prosodic hierarchy whereby the same constituent appears in two positions: the PW is below and above the Foot.

3 The Foot in Isolating Languages Revisited

On the one hand, the type of analysis advanced for Vietnamese argues that the Foot must be dispensed with. On the other, the type of analysis advanced for Mandarin argues that the Foot must be retained, but requires fundamental alterations in the nature of the Foot and aspects of the prosodic hierarchy. This section presents additional observations that indicate the need for groupings of the various phonological elements under consideration that motivate the Foot constituent in both Vietnamese and Mandarin, without fundamental alterations, thus supporting the Foot's status as a potentially universal constituent of the prosodic hierarchy.

3.1 The Foot as a Constituent in Vietnamese

While there may not be a significant acoustic or perceptual distinction between *hoa hồng* 'rose' (compound) and *hoa hồng* 'pink flower' (phrase), as noted above, further investigation of different types of reduplication and their relation to compounds and phrases has yielded more nuanced information regarding the prominence relations in Vietnamese. In full reduplication, a word is repeated in the same form, with the same tone (e.g., *sáng sáng* 'rather bright', tones: both rising), whereas in partial reduplication the reduplicated element exhibits a change in tone, a segment, or both (e.g., *sang sáng* 'rather bright', tones: level+rising). Acoustic and perceptual analysis of the different types of reduplication revealed that in full reduplications, the reduplicated (first) element was acoustically less prominent than the second one, although the two elements were perceived by listeners as prosodically similar. In partial reduplications, however, the reduplicated element was not only acoustically less prominent, it was perceived as less prominent than the base (second) element (Nguyễn and Ingram 2007a, 2007b, 2013). Additionally, a difference was observed between the relative prominence pattern of full reduplications and compounds (e.g., *sáng chói* 'dazzling', tones: both rising), the reduplicant being perceived as somewhat weaker than the first member of the compound (Nguyen and Ingram 2007b, 2013).

We thus have evidence of three prominence patterns, where the first element ranges from weakest to strongest in partial reduplications < full reduplications < compounds, in addition to the previously noted difference between compounds and phrases, yielding a total of four patterns. Taking prosodic structure to be the means by which prominence relations are encoded, the four levels of distinction make it clear that an analysis lacking the Foot (and PW), as proposed by Schiering, Bickel, and Hildebrandt (2010), is not adequate. Instead, if we include both of these constituents between the syllable and Phonological Phrase (PPh), we are able to distinguish four structures that correspond to the observed differences in prominence patterns, as shown in (6).

(6) Prominence Patterns and Prosodic Structure in Vietnamese
    a. Partial reduplication   [[sang$_\sigma$ sáng$_\sigma$]$_\Sigma$]$_{PW}$ 'rather bright'
    b. Full reduplication   [[sáng$_\sigma$]$_\Sigma$ [sáng$_\sigma$]$_\Sigma$]$_{PW}$ 'rather bright'
    c. Compound   [[sáng$_\sigma$]$_{\Sigma/PW}$ [chói$_\sigma$]$_{\Sigma/PW}$]$_{CompG}$ 'dazzling'
                          [[hoa$_\sigma$]$_{\Sigma/PW}$ [hồng$_\sigma$]$_{\Sigma/PW}$]$_{CompG}$ 'rose'
    d. Phrase   [[hoa$_\sigma$]$_{\Sigma/PW/CompG}$ [hồng$_\sigma$]$_{\Sigma/PW/CompG}$]$_{PPh}$ 'pink flower'

The Foot allows us to distinguish between partial and full reduplication by combining both elements into a single iambic Foot in the former (6a), while treating each as its own Foot and combining these Feet into the next constituent, the PW, in the latter (6b). Full reduplications and compounds have in common that their two elements are both Feet, but in the former they constitute a single PW (6b), while the latter they constitute two separate PWs (6c), which combine into the next larger constituent, shown as the CompG (Composite Group) (e.g., Vogel 2020). The same words in a phrase (6d) are not only PWs, but each one constitutes a CompG, and these combine to form a PPh.[4] Thus, while there is considerable overlap between syllables and other constituents in the structures in (6), a distinction is required between a binary branching Foot in (6a) and the non-branching Feet in the other structures. Moreover, while in many cases the PW is coextensive with a single Foot, this is crucially not the case in (6b). Nevertheless, it remains clear that most of the Feet appear to be "degenerate," consisting of a single syllable, a point we return to below.

3.2 The Foot as a Constituent in Mandarin

As noted above, the items previously identified as Feet in Mandarin fundamentally compromise the definition of the Foot by allowing it to dominate words (i.e., PWs), and in so doing, also potentially result in prosodic tree structures in which the Foot both dominates and is dominated by the PW constituent.[5] Moreover, if compounds are considered Feet, but similar strings of PWs may also constitute Phonological Phrases, we would expect a phonological distinction between the compound *niàn shū* 'study' and the phrase *niàn shū* 'read books'; however, native speakers of Mandarin report that they cannot, in fact, consistently distinguish between the two types of structures. This situation parallels the observations

---

[4] For additional motivation and discussion of the Composite Group as a necessary constituent of the prosodic hierarchy between the Phonological Word and the Phonological Phrase, see among others Vogel (2009, 2012, 2020).
[5] See also Zhang's (2014) discussion of problems with Foot structure in Mandarin.

about Vietnamese compounds and phrases. It thus further suggests the undesirability of the previous type of Foot analysis of compounds in Mandarin, and also that it might be possible to identify Foot structure in relation to additional types of constructions, along the lines of the Vietnamese analysis.

In reconsidering the need for a Foot in Vietnamese, it was seen that there are phonological phenomena that operate in different domains that could not be accounted for if all syllables were directly grouped into larger word or phrasal constituents. Although certain properties of Vietnamese and Mandarin are different (e.g., Vietnamese is iambic, Mandarin is trochaic), a similar strategy of identifying the prosodic patterns may be applied to Mandarin. While in Vietnamese all syllables appear to bear a tone, in Mandarin, several types of elements are identified as toneless, and thus prosodically weak or "unstressed" (e.g., Tiee 1979; Packard 2000), as illustrated in (7). These may be compared to tone-bearing affixes and bound roots, illustrated in (8). (The elements relevant for the comparison are underlined.)

(7) Mandarin toneless elements
 a. Affix: mǎi le 'bought' (< 'buy' + le = perfective)
 b. Bound Root: ěr duo 'ear' (< 'ear' + 'petal')

(8) Mandarin elements with tones
 a. Affix: pào shǒu 'cannoneer' (< pào 'cannon' + shǒu '-er')
 b. Bound Root: fēi jī 'airplane' (< 'fly' + 'machine')

The distinct prosodic patterns in (7) and (8) require distinct prosodic structures to account for them. Analogously to the Vietnamese forms in (6a), we may analyze the toneless, weaker, elements simply as syllables that combine with another syllable to form a Foot. In other cases, where the syllables bear tones, they are analyzed as Feet, like the Vietnamese items in (6b, c, d). The prosodic structures for the Mandarin items are shown in (9) and (10), where the full words are indicated as PWs in both cases.

(9) Prosodic Structure: Mandarin toneless elements
 a. Affix: [[mǎi$_\sigma$ le$_\sigma$]$_\Sigma$]$_{PW}$ 'bought'
 b. Bound Root: [[ěr$_\sigma$ duo$_\sigma$]$_\Sigma$]$_{PW}$ 'ear'

(10) Prosodic Structure: Mandarin elements with tones
 a. Affix: [[pào$_\sigma$]$_\Sigma$ [shǒu$_\sigma$]$_\Sigma$]$_{PW}$ 'cannoneer'
 b. Bound Root: [[fēi$_\sigma$]$_\Sigma$ [jī$_\sigma$]$_\Sigma$]$_{PW}$ 'airplane'

Again, as in the case of Vietnamese, these types of structures must remain distinct from more typical compounds consisting of two (or more) PWs, and the compounds must be distinguished from PPhs, at least for morpho-syntactic reasons, even if they are perceptually not consistently distinguished, as shown in (11). Longer compounds, such as those see in above in (4) and (5), are also accommodated by this approach, as in (12), where any number of PWs forming a compound are parsed in the Composite Group, and there is no need for dummy syllables as in (5).

(11) Prosodic Structure: Mandarin Compound and Phrase
    a. Compound: [[niàn$_\sigma$]$_{\Sigma/PW}$ [shū$_\sigma$]$_{\Sigma/PW}$]$_{CompG}$ 'study'
    b. Phrase: [[niàn$_\sigma$]$_{\Sigma/PW/CompG}$ [shū$_\sigma$]$_{\Sigma/PW/CompG}$]$_{PPh}$ 'read books'

(12) Prosodic Structure: Mandarin Longer Compounds
    a. Three Elements: [[zhòng$_\sigma$]$_{\Sigma/PW}$ [zhí$_\sigma$]$_{\Sigma/PW}$ [suàn$_\sigma$]$_{\Sigma/PW}$]$_{CompG}$ 'garlic plant'
    b. Four Elements   [[zhòng$_\sigma$]$_{\Sigma/PW}$ [zhí$_\sigma$]$_{\Sigma/PW}$ [dà$_\sigma$]$_{\Sigma/PW}$ 'garlic plant'
                       [suàn$_\sigma$]$_{\Sigma/PW}$]$_{CompG}$

Ultimately, all elements will be parsed within PPhs and any larger prosodic constituents in which they appear in a sentence.

4 Discussion: The Foot in the Prosodic Hierarchy

Although there may be considerable overlap between syllables and several larger phonological units in isolating languages, examination of somewhat more subtle distinctions than are typically considered shows that in both Vietnamese and Mandarin there are different relationships between the syllables in different types of structures. Taking prosodic constituent structure to be the means of representing these differences, it becomes clear that it is not possible to group the syllables into the same larger domain in all cases, as was proposed for Vietnamese (e.g., Schiering, Bickel, and Hildebrandt 2010). In particular, the Foot (as well as the PW) serves a crucial role in providing the appropriate domains for the prominence relations and other phonological patterns observed in different types of reduplications and compounds in Vietnamese, and in different types of affixed items and compounds in Mandarin.

We may also consider the nature of the Foot, not just its existence, in the languages in question. It was pointed out above that analyses such as those advanced for Mandarin by Duanmu (e.g., 1999, 2000) and others essentially involved redefining the Foot since it was taken as the domain for compounds, the members of which are typically considered PWs in other languages. As such, the Foot would not only dominate a larger (PW) constituent, but it would also presumably be parsed into another PW constituent before being included in higher constituents (e.g., PPh). Considering the individual members of some compounds to be Feet, without requiring that they also be PWs, however, permits the items in question to be consistent with Foot and PW structures as generally defined for the prosodic hierarchy.[6] Moreover, it allows the members of other types of compounds to consist of PWs, also as typically seen in other languages, where these are then combined into a Composite Group (e.g., Vogel 2020).

With regard to the nature of the Foot in the languages considered here, it must also be noted that the proposed analysis still results in substantial overlap of syllables and Feet, and to some extent also PWs, the original problem raised with regard to isolating languages. It was pointed out above, however, that similar types of Feet, that is, those consisting of a single syllable, are also found in many other (non-isolating) languages, and are recognized as a type of Foot, the so-called degenerate Foot. It is possible that languages simply differ with respect to their percentage of degenerate Feet, with isolating languages having more than other types of languages. We may also, however, consider another possibility. That is, the presence of tone may contribute additional weight to syllables that would otherwise appear to be degenerate, and thus make them appropriately heavy, and possibly binary branching (i.e., $[\sigma + T]_\Sigma$).[7] It is interesting to note in this regard that isolating languages frequently have tones, like Mandarin and Vietnamese, so considering the tones as contributing to the Foot structure would mean that we no longer need to view such languages as having a particularly high percentage of degenerate Feet. The same view of tones would also allow us to account for the difference in Mandarin between the toneless syllables, which are considered weak in terms of their relative prominence, exemplified above in (9), and the more typical syllables which bear one of the four contrastive tones, as seen in the other examples. Interestingly, Vietnamese does not seem to have

---

[6] Obviously, the dummy syllables proposed in items such as (5) would not form Feet, but rather would simply be absent in the reanalysis.

[7] It was noted in Nespor and Vogel (1989) that tonal properties may have an analogous effect to that of durational properties in certain languages. Specifically, it was suggested that Modern Greek, derived from the pitch accent system of Classical Greek, may compensate for clashes (two adjacent stressed syllables) by introducing a pitch change, serving to distance the stresses perceptually without adding duration (Beat Insertion), or reducing one stress (Beat Deletion). Thus, building on this observation, we may consider that the tones themselves provide the necessary content in isolating languages like Vietnamese and Mandarin, so that we effectively avoid sequences of degenerate Feet.

a similar presence of toneless syllables, which could be a difference between the languages; however, it must also be noted that tones are orthographically represented in Vietnamese, and it is possible that some elements do actually lose their tones, as in Mandarin, but this is not recognized due to orthographic practices. In fact, tonelessness may be what accounts for the perception of weakness noted above in relation to certain partial reduplications (e.g., 6a).[8]

5 Conclusions

The constituents of the prosodic hierarchy are widely, though not uncontroversially, viewed as universal, despite some differences in their definition. One of the constituents, the Foot, at first glance appears to be potentially expendable, in particular in isolating languages, where words typically consist of single morphemes, and these single morphemes typically consist of a single syllable. In this case, the question may be raised as to the relevance of the Foot, a constituent that most commonly groups together two (sometimes more) syllables. Two approaches to this challenge have been considered, one advanced for Vietnamese, where it was argued that the Foot was absent, and the other advanced for Mandarin, where it was argued that the Foot was binary branching, as in other types of languages, but where the branches were essentially equivalent to PWs in the other languages, or possibly even null.

Both of the previous approaches appear to be largely motivated by theoretical considerations, preferring either to present the case that prosodic constituents are not universal, or to present the case that they are, so that an isolating language like Mandarin is fundamentally the same prosodically as a language like English. In this paper, I have taken a more empirical approach, and shown that there is additional, more subtle, evidence that could be interpreted as supporting the need for prosodic constituents that group syllables in different ways within larger Foot and PW constituents. Acoustic analysis and perceptual data on Vietnamese, as well as other phonological phenomena, have revealed that there are, in fact, several distinct patterns of relative prominence and rule application that may only be accounted for if different structures are posited as their domains.

---

8 There do seem to be some reduced morphemes, including "clitics", but they are still written with tone specifications (Pham 2007). Further investigation is required, however, to determine the extent to which they actually bear tone, and consequently how they must be analyzed prosodically, especially since in some cases the elements lack a nucleus and thus would not even constitute full syllables on their own.

In Mandarin, a range of phonological behaviors of different types of syllables without and with tones was also seen to require different structures to provide the necessary variations in their domains of application. In both cases, by including the Foot as a prosodic constituent, it is possible to account for the observed distinctions among the domains of the phenomena under consideration, and also to retain essentially the same concept of Foot as is seen in other languages. The main potential difference is the relatively large role of so-called degenerate Feet in isolating languages like Vietnamese and Mandarin, compared to their role in other types of languages. It was suggested that it might be possible to interpret the presence of tone in many such syllables as the additional weight element required to make the Feet adequately heavy, and thus with this small modification, avoid considering them as atypical or degenerate. Further investigation of additional isolating languages as well as the relationship between syllable and Foot structure and tone is required in order to assess such possibilities.

References

Blaho, Sylvia and Dániel Szeredi. 2011. (The non-existence of) secondary stress in Hungarian. In Tibor Laczkó and Catherine. O. Ringen (eds.), *Approaches to Hungarian*, vol. 12: Papers from the 2009 Debrecen Conference, 39–62.
Comrie, Bernard. 1981. *Language Universals and Linguistic Typology*. Chicago: University of Chicago Press.
Duanmu, San. 1999. Stress and the development of disyllabic words in Chinese. *Diachronica* 16(1). 1–35.
Duanmu, San. 2000/2007. *The Phonology of Standard Chinese*. Oxford: Oxford University Press.
Hammond, Michael. 1987. Hungarian cola. *Phonology Yearbook* 4. 267–269.
Hayes, Bruce. 1995. *Metrical Stress Theory: Principles and Case Studies*. Chicago: University of Chicago Press.
Ingram, John and Thi Anh-Thư Nguyễn. 2006. Stress, tone and word prosody in Vietnamese compounds. In P. Warren and C. Watson (eds.), *Proceedings of the 11th Australian International Conference on Speech Science and Technology*. 193–198.
Kálmán, László and Ádám Nádasdy. 1994. [Cited in Blaho and Szeredi. 2011]. A hangsúly [Stress]. In F. Kiefer (ed.), *Strukturális magyar nyelvtan: fonológia [A structural grammar of Hungarian: phonology]*. 393–467. Budapest: Akadémiai Kiadó.
Labrune, Laurence. 2012. *The Phonology of Japanese*. (The Phonology of the World's Languages). Oxford: Oxford University Press.
McCarthy, John and Allen Prince. 1990. Foot and word in prosodic morphology: The Arabic broken plural. *Natural Language and Linguistic Theory* 8. 209–283.
Nespor, Marina and Irene Vogel. 1986/2007. *Prosodic Phonology*. Dordrecht: Foris.
Nespor, Marina and Irene Vogel. 1989. On clashes and lapses. *Phonology* 6. 69–116.

Nguyễn, Anh-Thư and John C. L. Ingram. 2006. Reduplication and word stress in Vietnamese. In P. Warren and C. Watson (eds.), *Proceedings of the 11th Australian International Conference on Speech Science and Technology*. 187–192.

Nguyễn, Anh-Thư and John C. L. Ingram. 2007a. Acoustic and perceptual cues for compound-phrasal contrasts in Vietnamese. *Journal of the Acoustical Society of America* 112(3). 1746–1757.

Nguyễn, Anh-Thư and John C. L. Ingram. 2007b. Word stress and compounding in Vietnamese. Ms. School of English, Media Studies, and Art History, University of Queensland, St. Lucia, Australia.

Nguyễn, Anh-Thư and John C. L. Ingram. 2013. Perception of prominence patterns in Vietnamese disyllabic words. *Mon-Khmer Studies* 42. 89–101.

Packard, Jerome. 2000. *The Morphology of Chinese: A Linguistic and Cognitive Approach*. Cambridge: Cambridge University Press.

Pham, Andrea Hoa. 2007. Cliticization in casual speech in Vietnamese. *Cahiers de linguistique - Asie orientale* 36(2). 219–244. DOI: 10.3406/clao.2007.1840.

Schiering, R., B. Bickel & K. Hildebrandt. 2010. The prosodic word is not universal, but emergent. *Journal of Linguistics* 46. 657–709. DOI: 10.1017/S0022226710000216.

Tiee, H. H.-Y. 1979. The productive affixes in Mandarin Chinese morphology. *Word* 30(3). 245–255. DOI: 10.1080/00437956.1979.11435670.

Vogel, Irene. 2009. The status of the clitic group. In Janet Grijzenhout and Barış Kabak (eds.), *Phonological Domains: Universals and Deviations*, 15–46. Berlin: Mouton de Gruyter.

Vogel, Irene. 2012. Recursion in phonology? In Bert Botma and Roland Noske (eds.), *Phonological Explorations: Empirical, Theoretical and Diachronic Issues*, 41–61. Berlin: De Gruyter.

Vogel, Irene. 2020. Life after the Strict Layer Hypothesis: Prosodic structure geometry. In Hongming Zhang and Youyong Qian (eds.), *Prosodic Studies: Challenges and Prospects*, 9–60. New York: Routledge.

Zhang, Hongming. 2014. Some issues on studies of prosodic phonology and Chinese prosody. *Contemporary Linguistics* 3. 303–327.

Bing Li
Word Stress Placement in Wakhi

Abstract: The description presented in the article shows that the domain of word stress placement is morphologically defined in Wakhi. The stress is located in the right-most edge of a lexical word. Where a derivative suffix is added to the stem, the stress shifts from the stem-final position to the right-most edge of the lexical word. Suffixes of non-finite verbs behave in a similar way as derivative suffixes do, causing the stress to shift to the right-most edge of the word. In contrast to derivative and non-finite verbal suffixes, inflectional suffixes do not trigger such a rightward shift. Based on these observations it is tentatively proposed that, functionally, word stress is morphological stress in Wakhi. The analysis given shows that surface regular and irregular locations of word stress are consequences derived by a set of ordered phonological rules, the operations of which are triggered by syllabification. The analysis also shows that word stress is assigned by the Word Stress Assignment (WSA) rule at an abstract level, and that the vowel, rather than the syllable, is the stress-bearing unit, for WSA applies prior to syllabification.

Keywords: morphological stress, stress placement, Wakhi

1 Introduction

This article presents a description of word stress placement in Wakhi, a Pamirian language belonging to the Eastern Iranian, the Indo-European family, spoken in the areas around the Wakhan Corridor shared by Afghanistan, Tajikistan, Pakistan and China (Shaw 1876; Morgenstierne 1938; Lorimer 1958; Bashir 2009; Li 2016).[1]

Wakhi is an SOV language and rich in inflectional morphology. Nominal inflection distinguishes numbers, persons and cases; adjectival inflection marks degrees; verbal inflection involves agreement in person/number, tense, voice, aspect, mood and finiteness. A grammatical category may be expressed either by external inflection (suffixation or clitics) or by internal inflection, or by both. Wakhi is a language with heavy suffixation and rich in prepositions and postpositions.

---

[1] The data presented here are based on fieldwork carried out in Tashkurgan, Xinjiang, China, since 2013.

Bing Li, Nankai University

https://doi.org/10.1515/9783110730081-006

In Wakhi, word stress would be regular in placement at the phonetic level if morphological factors and other phonological factors were excluded, based on the assumption that stress placement is rule-assigned (Chomsky and Halle 1968). Our analysis will show that word stress placement is morphologically sensitive, and that the regularity and irregularities in word stress placement at the phonetic level are the consequences of derivation based on a set of ordered phonological rules.

2 The Basics in Word Stress Placement

Wakhi is a stress language. Phonetically, stress is characterized by a number of acoustic properties: stressed syllables have a higher fundamental frequency (F_0), a lengthened duration, a greater amplitude and a well-formed formant structure of the vowel in the spectrum, relatively to unstressed and reduced syllables. Perceptually, stressed syllables sound louder than unstressed and reduced ones (Li, Hu, and Hou 2016).

2.1 Word Stress Placement in a Lexical Word

In Wakhi, word stress is fixed in location if the domain of stress placement is defined as a lexical word: it always falls on the ultimate syllable of a lexical word. There has been no evidence so far for assuming that syllable structure, syllable weight and grammatical category of the lexical word are factors relevant to the location of word stress. The location of the stress in lexical words is exemplified in (1).[2]

(1) **Nouns**   **Adjectives**
    aˈzo   'organ'   fəˈraχ   'wide'
    pɨˈzɨv   'heart'   dzaˈqlaj   'small; very young'
    ʂɨˈtɨr   'camel'   ʃiˈlaṭ   'warm'
    pərinˈda 'bird'   ʁəˈrung   'heavy'
    noʁərˈdum 'bear'   bɨroˈbar   'ordinary'

---

[2] Lexical exceptions are mostly loans, which may locate stress on the initial syllable of the stem, e.g., ˈχili 'very (good)' and ˈbazi 'some' from Persian; ˈχɨdi 'already' and ˈkɨli 'all', from Arabic.

Verbs		Adverbs	
ʒɨˈrəy-	'to be choked'	aˈwal	'firstly; at the beginning'
zɨˈgar-	'to stroll'	jinˈgum	'just'
zɨˈrənd-	'to scrape'	oˈzir	'now'
χɨˈroθ-	'to snore'	tʃuˈqum	'certainly'
nɨˈjup-	'to catch up'		

In native words, word stress does not distinguish lexical semantics. [aˈzo] ('organ') and [dzaˈqlaj] ('small; very young'), in each of which the ultimate syllable is stressed, are acceptable and grammatical, while the forms such as [ˈazo] and [ˈdzaqlaj] with a stressed initial syllable are believed to be unacceptable and ungrammatical.

Where a syllable-sized derivational suffix is added to the stem, that is, a new lexical word is formed by suffixation, word stress shifts from the stem-final syllable to the derivative suffix, as exemplified in (2).[3]

(2) a. nominal stem + diminutive suffix -ək

ˈwurk		wurˈk-ək	'sheep'
tʃinˈgol		tʃingoˈl-ək	'rake'
ʃirmaˈmad		ʃirmamaˈd-ək	'person's name'

b. adjective stem + nominalizer -iɣ

ˈbaf	'good'	baˈf-iɣ	'goodness'
jɨˈṣɨq	'unreasonable'	jɨṣɨˈq-iɣ	'unreasonableness'
ʁərdəmˈbits	'messy'	ʁərdəmbiˈts-iɣ	'messiness'

c. nominal stem + adjectivalizer -in

ˈwandʒ	'stomach'	wanˈdʒ-in	'having a big stomach'
qɨˈnat	'wing'	qɨnaˈt-in	'having wings'
ləˈwortʃ	'sand'	ləworˈtʃ-in	'there being a lot of sand'

d. nominal stem + suffix -ədʒ denoting 'one who lives in the place'

toʃqirˈʁan	Tashkurgan	toʃqirʁaˈn-ədʒ	'one who lives in Tashkurgan'
davˈdor	Dafdar	davdoˈr-ədʒ	'one who lives in Dafdar'
rəsˈkom	Reskam	rəskoˈm-ədʒ	'one who lives in Reskam'

e. ordinary numeral suffix -ing

ˈtruj	three	truˈj-ing	'the third'
tsɨˈbɨr	four	tsɨbɨˈr-ing	'the fourth'
ˈpandz	five	panˈdz-ing	'the fifth'

---

3 Disyllabic suffixes have not been found in Wakhi so far.

2.2 Word Stress Placement with Nominal and Adjectival Inflections

Different from derivational suffixes that cause word stress to shift from the stem-final syllable to the ultimate syllable of the newly created lexical word, nominal and adjectival inflectional suffixes do not cause such a shift, that is, where an inflectional suffix is added to a nominal or adjectival stem, the word stress remains where it was, as shown in (3).[4]

(3) a. 'za   'za-rə(k)   'child-DAT'
        'kənd   'kənd-əv-ən   'wife-PL-ABL'
        nɨ'pɨs   nɨ'pɨs-iʃt   'grandson-PL.NOM'
        dar'jo   dar'jo-rə   'river-DAT'
        noʁər'dum   noʁər'dum-əv-i   'bear-PL-ACC'

    b. 'sak   'sak-ər[4]   'PRON.1PL-DAT'
        'jət   'jət-əv-ən   'DEM2-PL-ABL'
        'pandz   'pandz-ər   'five-DAT'
        tsɨ'bɨr   tsɨ'bɨr-ən   'four-ABL'

    c. 'lup   'lup-tər   'big-COMP'
        dʑa'qlaj   dʑa'qlaj-tər   'small-COMP'
        'ʁaftʃ   'ʁaftʃ-tər   'much-COMP'
        'ʃak   'ʃak-tər   'bad-COMP'

So far, it seems to be the case that the stress location is determined simply by derivation, that is, derivational suffixes are stress-attractors and bearers, and that inflectional morphology does play a role in stress placement. However, as will be seen in the next section, it is actually more complicated: verbal inflection is interferential with stress placement in the language.

2.3 Word Stress Placement with Verbal Inflection

Since complexity in stress placement involves verbal inflectional morphology of the language, a few remarks about verbal inflection are necessary.

---

[4] The dative suffix has tree variants: -rək, -rə, and -ər. [k] in -rək may delete, and -rə occurs immediately after a vowel, while -ər, after a consonant.

In Wakhi, according to the forms, syntactic functions and the grammatical category of person/number, all the forms of a verb are classified into two general categories: finite forms and non-finite forms. The finite form functions as predicate in a sentence, always takes a marker indicating person/number and keeps an overt agreement with the exponence of the person/number that the subject of the sentence bears.

Non-finite verbs lack a marker of person/number and play various syntactic roles other than predicate. Based on syntactic functions and grammatical semantics, the non-finite forms of a verb are classified into infinitive, present participle and past participle; past participle is further divided into past participle I and past participle II.

Infinitive has six suffixes: -ak, -ɨk, -n, -g, -ng and -∅,[5] and the choice of any of them is determined by the verbal base. Functionally, the infinitive suffix is a nominalizer and therefore the infinitival phrase is a nominalized verb phrase, and able to take a case suffix and to play syntactic roles that a noun phrase does in the language.

Participles function basically as modifiers of nouns and verbs, and as subject complement, playing similar roles as an adjective phrase does syntactically. Present participles and past participles differ in temporal meaning; past participle I and Past participle II differ in aspectual meaning. The formations of the non-finite forms are given below.

Infinitive:	$[stem]_{BASE}$-ak (-ɨk, -n, -g, -ng, -∅)
Present Participle:	$[stem\text{-}ak\ (\text{-}ɨk, \text{-}n, \text{-}g)]_{BASE}$-kɨzg
Past Participle I:	$[stem]_{BASE}$-ətk
Past Participle II:	$[stem\text{-}ətk]_{BASE}$-ing

The form of the stem may vary, depending on the morphological category in which it is. For a more detailed description of Wakhi verbal inflectional morphology, see Hou (2020), Hou and Li (2020) and Li and Hou (2019). The reader may also refer to Lorimer (1958) and Bashir (2009) for some other dialects of the language. In addition to the external inflection that most verbs undergo, a small number of verbs undergo internal inflection. As observed, stress placement in verbs is involved mostly in external inflection, and therefore the internal inflections irrelevant to stress placement are ignored in the following description.

Stress placement in a verb is sensitive to the distinction between the finite and the non-finite. In a finite form, the inflectional suffix does not cause stress

---

[5] -∅ stands for a zero suffix.

to shift from the stem-final syllable to the ultimate syllable of the grammatical words. Even if a finite suffix is syllable-sized, it is not stressed, as exemplified in (4).

(4) Stress placement in finite inflected forms

Base	Finite forms	
ˈnəzd-	ˈnəzd-ən	'to sit-PRS.1PL'
ˈtʃuk-	ˈtʃuk-əm	'to smash-PRS.1SG'
zɨˈrənd-	zɨˈrəɣ-ni[6]	'to scrape-PST'[7]
niˈjup-	niˈjop-ti[8]	'to catch up-PST'
ˈnɨw-	ˈnɨw-ɨv-it	'to weep-CAUS-PRS.2PL'
ˈnow-	ˈnow-ov-d	'to weep-CAUS-PST'
ˈʃɨp-	ˈʃɨp-ɨv-ən	'to milk-CAUS-PRS.1PL'
ˈʃop-	ˈʃop-ov-d	'to milk-CAUS-PST'
ˈtʃɨlap-	ˈtʃɨlap-ov-d	'to spill-CAUS-PST'

---

6 The stem-final alternation of nd ~ ɣ can be ignored here.
7 In past tense, the person/number marker moves to the sentence-initial NP host, occurring there as a second position clitics, as illustrated below.

dzuɣ-iʃt=iv	tɨ	qir	rəɣ-di
yak-3PL.NOM=3PL	PREP	mountain	go-PST

'The yaks went onto the mountain.'

The clitics =iv is unstressed, as its suffix counterpart is in present tense.
Wakhi is a language that permits subject drop. Where the subject drops, the pronominal clitics appears in the position where the suffix of person/number is expected to occur. Compare the sentences below.

a. wuz=əm   gəfs-t
   I-NOM1SG =1SG   run-PST
   'I ran.'
b. gəfs-t=əm
   run-PST=1SG
   'I ran.'

In both a and b, the clitics =əm is unstressed. As we assumed, the clitics is added to the verbal stem in the lexicon, and its movement from its suffix site to the sentence-initial NP position takes place at the syntactic level. Therefore, whether the clitics receives word stress or not should be considered in terms of verbal inflection. For more details of Wakhi clitics, see Hu (2017) and Hu and Li (2017).
8 Stem-internally, there is [u] ~ [o] ablaut, where [u] occurs in the verb stem that takes a present tense suffix, while [o] occurs in past tense stems. Here the ablaut can be ignored. In addition, the past tense suffix has alternants -ti, -di, -ni, -t and -d, depending on the phonological and morphological context where the suffix occurs. The phonetic differences in these alternants can also be ignored here. For details see Hou (2020) and Li and Hou (2019).

Behaving differently from a finite suffix, a non-finite suffix causes stress to shift from the base-final syllable to the ultimate syllable of the grammatical word, i.e., suffixes of the non-finite category behave similarly as derivational suffixes do in that it attracts and bears word stress, as illustrated in (5).

(5) Stress placement in the non-finite forms
    a. Infinitive

Base	Suffixed forms	
x-	'x-ak	'to do'
'jit-	'jit-n	'to eat'
'rand-	rɨ'ðow-n	'to give'
'dʒoj-	dʒo'j-ɨk	'to read'
'gəfs-	gəf's-ɨk	'to run'
zɨ'gar	zɨga'r-ak	'to stroll'
dɨ'raw-	dɨra'w-ɨk	'to cut grass'

    b. Present Participle

Base	Suffixed forms	
'x-ak	x-a-'kɨzg	'to do'
'jit-n	jit-n-'kɨzg	'to eat'
rɨ'ðow-n	rɨðow-'kɨzg[9]	'to give'
gəf's-ɨk	gəfs-ɨ-'kɨzg[10]	'to run'
zɨga'r-ak	zɨgar-a-'kɨzg	'to stroll'
dɨra'w-ɨk	dɨraw-ɨ-'kɨzg	'to cut grass'

    c. Past Participles I

Base	Suffixed forms	
x-	'x-ətk	'to do'
'jit-	'ji-tk[11]	'to eat'
'ðə-	'ðə-tk[12]	'to give'
'tʃuk-	tʃu'k-ətk	'to smash'

---

9 We assume here that the underlying representation is rɨðow-n-kɨzg, and that /n/ deletes due to a phonotactic restriction on the word-internal consonant cluster -wnk-.
10 We assume here that the underlying representation is gəfs-ɨk-kɨzg and that /k/ in -ɨk deletes where a potential gemination /kk/ is created.
11 We may assume that the underlying representation is jit-ətk, but we do not have a ready answer to the question why the sequence /tət/ deletes and surfaces as [ji-tk].
12 It is reasonable to assume that the underlying representation is /ðə-ətk/ and the suffix-initial vowel /ə/ deletes, as the language has a strict restriction on vowel sequences. Phonemically, Wakhi does not have long vowels and diphthongs (Li 2016; Hou 2020).

zi'gar- ziga'r-ətk 'to stroll'
dɨ'raw- dɨra'w-ətk 'to cut grass'

d. Past Participles II
Base **Suffixed forms**
'x-ətk- x-ət'k-ɨng 'to do'
'ji-tk- ji-t'k-ɨng 'to eat'
'ðə-tk- ðə-t'k-ɨng 'to give'
tʃu'k-ətk- tʃuk-ət'k-ɨng 'to smash'
zɨga'r-ətk- zɨgar-ət'k-ɨng 'to stroll'
dɨra'w-ətk- dɨraw-ət'k-ɨng 'to cut grass'

To summarize so far, word stress is located on the ultimate syllable within the domain of a lexical word and a grammatical word defined as a non-finite verb, and the other inflectional suffixes (including nominal, adjectival and finite verbal inflectional suffixes) neither incur rightwards stress shift nor bear the word stress.

Based on the observations given so far, we tentatively propose that Wakhi word stress is the morphological stress in type, as opposed to the category of lexical stress that functions in distinguishing lexical semantics of words. In Wakhi, word stress does not distinguish lexical semantics, but functions as marker for indicating a morphological category, derivational or inflectional in general, and finite or non-finite in the verbal morphology in particular in the language.

3 Irregular Stress Location in Disyllabic Verbs

Irregularities in word stress location are found mostly in disyllabic verbs. Among the 310 known simplex verbs, there are 70 disyllabic, of which, 55 are found to have irregular stress location, that is, the stress is located on the first syllable of these disyllabic verbs. We will focus on these 55 verbs and explore the phonological factors that interfere with the word stress placement.

A close examination shows that these 55 verbs display two phonetic symptoms. Based on these symptoms, these verbs can be divided into two groups. In Group 1, verbs display an alternation [j] ~ [ɨ], palatal glide and hight front vowel, in the stem-final position. There are five verbs in all found so far that undergo the alternation. They are given in (6). For comparison, the infinitival forms of the verbs are also given.

(6) Base + PRS.3SG Base + PRS.1SG Base + INF
    'wəzi-t   'wəzj-əm   wə'zaj-n[13]   'to come'
    'məri-t   'mərj-əm   mi'raj-n   'do die'
    'təri-t   'tərj-əm   ti'n-ik   'to drive cattle'
    'wəṣi-t   'wəṣj-əm   wi'ṣ-ik   'to fear'
    'nəsi-t   'nəsj-əm   ni'si-n[14]   'to lie (in bed)'

As seen, in the finite form with the PRS.3SG suffix -t, the first syllable of the disyllabic base is unexpectedly stressed. [j] and [i] alternate, depending the suffix-initial segment: [j] occurs where it is immediately followed by a vowel, and [i] appears where it is immediately followed by a consonant. It is this [j]~[i] alternation that leads us to an assumption that these bases all have a stem that has one vowel in their lexical representation. Thus, each of the bases is assumed to be a string CəCj- in their lexical entry. Where a consonant suffix added to the base, a potential cluster of three consonants such as CjC is created.

Here, as assumed here, to syllabify the segments in the string, a vowel root (V_R) is inserted in the position between the two Cs and the consonantal root C dominating /j/ is replaced. (7) shows the process of insertion and replacement, using wəzi-t ('to come-PRS.3SG") as an example.

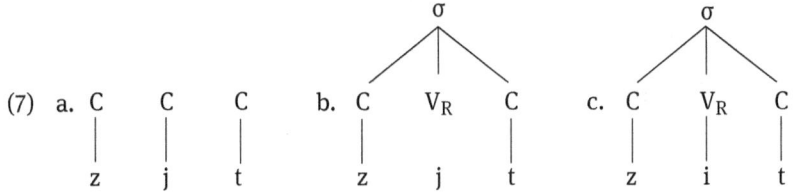

Vowel root insertion (VRI) in (7b) is incurred by syllabification. Once the V_R is inserted, syllable structure can be assigned as shown in (7c). As Lapointe and

---

13 In the base form of some verbs, but not all, there is a vowel /a/ that unexpectedly occurs in the stem-final syllable when the infinitival suffix -n is added. One of the unanimous reviewers suggests the possibility that the stressed vowel /a/ in the infinitival based wə'zaj-n ('to come-INF') be pre-specified. While we would not exclude this possibility, we prefer to treat the stressed /a/ as result from the rightwards stress shift incurred by adding the infinitival suffix -n. As will be seen, this treatment is consistent with the application of word stress assignment rule at the level of stem-formation, targeting the rightmost vowel in the domain. The idea behind this is that, where there are phonological and morphemic approaches are available for alternation with less evident motivations, the phonological approaches are preferred.

14 It is assumed here that ni'si-n ('to lie-INF') and 'nəsi-t ('to lie-PRS.3SG') differ in underlying base form.

Feinstein (1982) proposed, syllabification is part of phonological derivation. Here, this process is expressed in the form of VRI rule, as formulated in (8).

(8) VRI rule $\quad \emptyset \rightarrow V_R / \text{C\_\_C\#}$

The inserted V_R is an abstract segmental category defined as [−consonantal, +sonorant], which provides a structural basis on which segmental processes operate. For phonetic realization of such an abstract V_R, languages may mobilize various mechanisms. In Wakhi, where place features of /j/ delinked from its C root are mapped to the inserted V_R root node, and the segment is phonetically realized as [i], that is, literally, /j/ is vocalized to [i]. This glide vocalization (GV) rule is formulated as in (9).

(9) GV rule: $\quad$ /j/ $\rightarrow$ [i] / C__C\#

The vocalization of [j] to [i] is possible in that they are composed of the same segmental features [+high, −back] in a binary feature system (Chomsky and Halle 1968; Clements 1985; Anderson, Ewen, and Staun 1985), or the same element {I} in a unary feature system (van der Hulst and Smith 1985; Harris 1994). The only difference between [j] and [i] lies in the value of [±consonantal] that defines the root node of the segment, as shown in (10).

(10) a. C $\quad$ b. V
$\quad\quad\quad$ | $\quad\quad\quad$ |
$\quad\quad\quad$ j $\quad\quad\quad$ i

So far we have assumed three rules. Here we further assume that these rules apply in the order of (a) Word Stress Assignment rule (WSA rule), (b) VRI rule, and (c) GV rule.

Now we consider the disyllabic verbs in Group 2. As introduced, in Group 2, disyllabic stems have two identical vowels but the first syllable is stressed, as exemplified in (11).

(11) Base + PRS.3SG $\quad$ Base + PRS.1SG $\quad$ Base + INF
$\quad\quad$ ˈvaran-d $\quad\quad\quad\quad$ ˈvaran-əm $\quad\quad\quad$ vərənˈd-ak $\quad$ 'to scold'
$\quad\quad$ ˈniviʃ-t $\quad\quad\quad\quad\quad$ ˈniviʃ-əm $\quad\quad\quad\quad$ ˈniviʃ-n[15] $\quad\quad$ 'to write'
$\quad\quad$ ˈnəspər-d $\quad\quad\quad\quad$ ˈnəspər-əm $\quad\quad\quad$ nəspəˈr-ɨk $\quad\quad$ 'to tread'

---

15 The form niˈviʃ-n with regular stress is also found.

ˈvərəfs-t	ˈvərəfs-əm	vərəfˈs-ɨk	'to stop walking'
ˈðɨvɨj-d	ˈðɨvɨj-əm	ˈðɨvɨj-n	'to steal'
cf. ˈðovoj-d (past tense)			

Nevertheless, not all disyllabic stems with identical vowels are irregularly stressed in the language. A number of such disyllabic stems locate stress on the ultimate syllable of the base as predicted. Examples are given in (12).

(12)

	Base + PRS.3SG	Base + PRS.1SG	Base + INF	
	sɨˈtɨj-d	sɨˈtɨj-əm	sɨtɨˈj-ɨk	'to give (presents)'
	sɨˈðɨj-d	sɨˈðɨj-əm	sɨdɨˈj-ɨk	'to appear'
	zɨˈrɨj-d	zɨˈrɨj-əm	zɨˈrɨj-n	'to howl'
cf.	dɨˈraw-d	dɨˈraw-əm	dɨˈraw-n	'to cut grass'

For the difference between (11) and (12), we assume that each of the stem in (11) is a string of CVCC-, that is, the stem has one vowel in its lexical entry, while each of the stems in (12) is a string of CVCV- underlyingly, that is, having two vowels in their lexical representations. We focus on the irregular case in (11). The lexical representation of the irregular case is given in (13), using *varan-* 'to scold' as an example.

(13) The lexical representation of *varan-*: /varn-/

```
        a                    vowel tier
        |
    C   V   C   C-           category (root node) tier
    |       |   |
    v       r   n            consonant tier
```

Similar to the case of Group 1 where VRI rule applies here to insert a vowel root in the position between two consonants, e.g., between /r/ and /n/, which is incurred by syllabifivation. The same VRI rule applies here again simply because the structure descriptoin is satisfied in this case.

The results of VRI rule application is that, in a string CC(C) a vowel root V_R is inserted and the segments are syllabified with a vocalic nuclear,[16] as shown in (14).

---

[16] Due to space limitations, we will not go into the details about the onset and coda phonotactics in Wakhi. The phonotactics of segments at these positions are generally constrained by the Sonority Sequencing Principle (Clements 1990) and the Syllable Contact Law (Vennemann 1972). Violations of SSP are found to be word-peripheral and can be analysed by using extra-syllabicity,

(14)

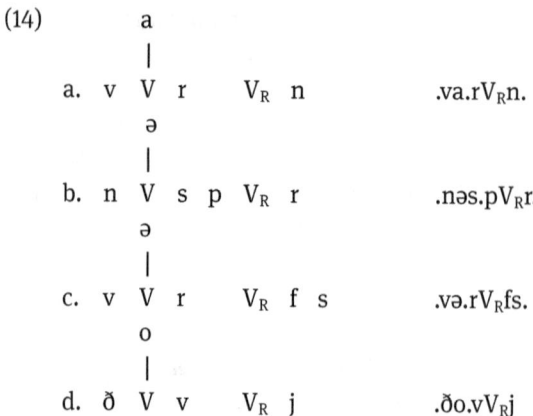

Subsequently, the only underlyingly fully specified vowel spreads to the inserted abstract V_R, turning the abstract V_R into a fully specified vowel, resulting in two identical vowels at the surface represnetation, as depicted in (15),

(15)   a
         ┌──────────
         │   ╲
    v   V   r V_R n   .va.ran.

The vowel that plays a role like this in the process of stem fomation and the stem formed in such a manner are referred to as *echo vowels* and *echo stems* respectively. Echo vowels and echo stems are also found in other languages, for instance in Yawelmany (Kenstowicz and Kisseberth 1979: 92–93). As a rule formulated here, the process of vowel spreading is given the name "echo vowel spreading'(EVS) rule, as given in (16) (V_E = echo vowel).

(16)   EVS rule: $V_R \to V_E / V_E C\_\_ C\#$

GV and EVS rules are two mechanisms operating for the phonetic realization of the inserted abstract vowel root incurred by syllabification. As for the order of rule application, we assume that GV rule applies prior to EVS rule, under Elsewhere Condition (Kiparsky 1982), since the structure description $CV_R j$ is a subset of the structure description $CV_R C$ of EVS rule.

---

as proposed by Clements and Keyser (1983). More importantly, vowels are the only class of segments that may map to the nuclear position of a syllable; segments other than vowels may not be nuclear segments, in Wakhi.

4 Regularity and Irregularity: The Derivation

Based on the data and the assumptions about representations and phonological mechanisms outlined above, we can construct tentatively a grammar of word stress placement in Wakhi. The hypothesis includes the following assumptions as stated in the following.

At the level of lexical representation, segments in a string constituting a stem morpheme are unsyllabified, and no word stress exists, in a lexical entry.

Word stress is assigned by WSA rule. The domain of stress assignment is morphologically defined. WSA rule assigns word stress to the rightmost vowel in the defined domain. After WSA rule has applied, that is, the rightmost vowel has been assigned with the word stress, VRI rule operates to syllabify the segments in the string, which is followed by alternative operations of GV and EVS rules, deriving the abstract vowel root into fully specified ones in different phonological environments. It is also hypothesized here that all the phonological operations assumed here take place in the lexicon of the language (Hou and Li 2020), similar as the classical lexical hypothesis in Kiparsky (1982).[17] The derivational procedure is demonstrated in (17).

(17) a. The UR of the stems CVCC- (including CVCj-) and CVCV-
b. WSA rule V → 'V/ __(C)] $_{\text{LEXICAL WORD / NON-FINITE VERB}}$ [18]
c. VRI rule ∅ → V_R / (C) C__C (C)#
d. GV rule /j/ → [i] /C__C#
e. EVS rule V_R → V_E/V_E C__C#

The derivation of a regular stress location is demonstrated in (18a), using tʃiˈlap-ov-d ('to spill-CAUS-PST'), ˈx-ak ('to do-INF') and diraw-ətˈk-ing ('to cut grass-Past Participle II') as examples. (18b) shows a derivation of the irregular stress loca-

---

17 We will not go into the details of the structure of the lexicon here, and future work will explore the morphological system of the language in more depth.
18 The application of WSA rule may not extend across the domain as defined. For instance,

[tʃingoˈl-ək]$_{\text{LEXICALWORD}}$ -iʃt
   rake DIM   PL
'rake-DIM-PL'
[ˈx-ak]$_{\text{NON-FINITE}}$ -ən =ək
  do-INF   ABL IPEV
'to do-INF-ABL=IPEV'

As for the question why non-finite verbs and derivative words (and mono-morphemic words as well) have the same effects upon stress placement, we leave it open for discussion.

tion, using ˈwəzi-t ('to come-PRS.3SG'), ˈvaran-d ('to scold-PRS.3SG') and ˈniviʃ-n ('to write-INF') as examples.

(18) a. Derivation of regular stress location

	'to spill-CAUS-PST'	'to do-INF'	'to cut grass-PstPII'
UR	[tʃilap]-ov-d#	[x-ak]#	[dɨraw-ətk-ɨng]#
WSA	[tʃiˈlap]-ov-d#	[ˈx-ak]#	[dɨraw-ətˈk-ɨng]#
VRI	n.a	n.a	n.a
GV	n.a	n.a	n.a
EVS	n.a	n.a	n.a
SR	tʃiˈlap-ov-d	ˈx-ak	dɨraw-ətˈk-ɨng

b. Derivation of irregular stress location

	'to come-PRS.3SG'	'to scold-PRS.3SG'	'to write-INF'
UR	[wəzj]-t#	[varn]-d#	[nivʃ-n]#
WSA	[ˈwəzj]-t#	[ˈvarn]-d#	[ˈnivʃ-n]#
VRI	ˈwəzV$_R$j-t#	ˈvarV$_R$n-d#	ˈnivV$_R$ʃ-n#
GV	ˈwəzi-t#	n.a	n.a
EVS	n.a	ˈvaran-d#	ˈniviʃ-n#
SR	ˈwəzi-t	ˈvaran-d	ˈniviʃ-n

As seen, the regular and irregular stress locations are derived by the same set of ordered rules. Crucially, WSA rule applies prior to the operation of VRI, assigning stress to the rightmost vowel in every domain properly defined, and the rules that follow WSA subsequently derive the regularly stressed ˈCVCC- into the form of superficial irregular location of stress ˈCVCVC-.

To generalize, irregular stress location as ˈCVCVC- at the surface representation results fundamentally from inserting into a consonantal cluster a vowel that is underlyingly absent in the domain of stress assignment.

5 Discussion and Concluding Remarks

Based on the description and analysis presented, we discuss the significance of word stress placement in Wakhi in an attempt to answer some of the questions about accent and stress as raised by many summarized in van der Hulst (2014: 6). Here we focus on stress against Wakhan background and ignore the distinction between stress and accent as discussed by the author.

a. *How do morphemes and complex words come to have their stress?*
   In Wakhi, as assumed and demonstrated, word stress is assigned by a Word Stress Assignment rule at an abstract representation in the lexicon of the language.
b. *Are stress locations unpredictable or predictable?*
   The location of word stress is unpredictable at the level of observation. However, at the level of lexical representation, the location of stress is predictable if the domain of stress assignment is properly defined on the morphological basis; the surface unpredictability is derived by a set of ordered phonological rules, as seen in Wakhi.
c. *What is the stress-bearing unit?*
   In Wakhi, Word Stress Assignment rule applies prior to syllabification, assigning stress to the rightmost vowel in the domain. Therefore, it is reasonable to assume that the vowel is the stress-bearing unit, as the vowel has already borne the assigned word stress before the syllable comes into existence, in the language. The syllable may function in parsing segments or do something else, but it is not a stress-bearer. Also importantly, as introduced, syllable structure and syllable weight play no role in determining the location of stress. This fact is consistent with our analysis based on the assumption that the irregularly stressed verbs are underlyingly CVCC- stems.
d. *What is the domain of stress?*
   In Wakhi, the domain of word stress placement is defined morphologically: word stress is located on the rightmost vowel in the lexical word and in the non-finite forms of verbs; elsewhere, word stress is located on the rightmost vowel in the base, to which inflectional (except non-finite verbal) suffixes are added.

To conclude, Wakhi is an example of languages in which (1) word stress placement is morphologically sensitive, or we may say that it is a morphological stress; (2) word stress is assigned at an abstract level of phonological representation; and (3) vowels, rather than syllables, bear word stress.

As for the question why the non-finite suffixes of verbs and the derivational suffixes behave similarly in attracting and bearing word stress, in Wakhi, we leave it open for discussion.

References

Anderson, John, Colin Ewen & Jørgen Staun. 1985. Phonological structure: Segmental, suprasegmental and extrasegmental. *Phonology Yearbook* 2. 203–224.
Bashir, Elena. 2009. Wakhi. In Gernot Windfuhr (ed.), *The Iranian Languages*, 825–862. London: Routledge.
Chomsky Noam & Morris Halle. 1968. *The Sound Pattern of English*. New York: Harper & Row.
Clements, George N. 1985. The geometry of phonological features. *Phonology Yearbook* 2. 225–252.
Clements, George N. 1990. The sonority circle in core syllabification. In J. Kinston & M. E. Beckman (eds.), *Papers in Laboratory Phonology, vol. 1: Between the Grammar and Physics of Speech*, 288–333. Cambridge: Cambridge University Press.
Clements, N. George & Samuel J. Keyser. 1983. *CV Phonology: A Generative Theory of the Syllable*. Cambridge, MA: MIT Press.
Harris, John. 1994. *English Sound Structure*. Oxford: Blackwell.
Hou, Dianfeng. 2020. Wahan Tajikeyu dongci yanjiu [A study of verbs in China's Wakhi]. Tianjin: Nankai University Ph.D. dissertation.
Hou, Dianfeng & Bing Li. 2020. Wahan Tajikeyu dongci cigen yuyin xingshi jiaoti. [The alternations of verb root morphemes in China's Wakhi]. *Minzu Yuwen* 3. 3–19.
Hu, Wei. 2017. Wahan Tajikeyu daicixing fuzhuo yusu yanjiu [A study of pronominal clitics in China's Wakhi]. Tianjin: Nankai University Ph.D. dissertation.
Hu, Wei & Bing Li. 2017. Wahan Tajikeyu daicixing fuzhuo yusu [Pronominal clitics in China's Wakhi]. *Minzu Yuwen* 6. 20–30.
Hulst, Harry van der. 2014. *Word Stress: Theoretical and Typological Issues*. New York: Cambridge University Press.
Hulst, Harry van der & Norval Smith. 1985. Vowel features and umlaut in Djingili, Nyangumarda and Warlpiri. *Phonology Yearbook* 2. 277–304.
Kenstowicz, Micheal & Charles Kisseberth. 1979. *Generative Phonology: Description and Analysis*. New York: Academic Press.
Kiparsky, Paul. 1982. Lexical phonology and morphology. In I. S. Yang (ed.), *Linguistics in the Morning Calm*, 3–91. Seoul: Hanshin.
Lapointe, Steven G. & Mark H. Feinstein. 1982. The role of vowel deletion and epenthesis in the assignment of syllable structure. In Harry van der Hulst & Norval Smith (eds.), *The Structure of Phonological Representations* (Part II), 69–120. Dordrecht: Foris Publications.
Li, Bing. 2016. Wahan Tajikeyu gaikuang [A general description of China's Wakhi]. *Minzu Yuwen* 1. 76–98.
Li, Bing & Dianfeng Hou. 2019. Wahan Tajikeyu budingshi [The infinitive in China's Wakhi]. *Minzu Yuwen* 2. 25–40.
Li, Bing, Wei Hu & Dianfeng Hou. 2016. Wahan Tajikeyu shuangyinjie cizhongyin shiyan yuyinxue baogao [An experimental phonetic report on word stress in disyllabic words in China's Wakhi]. *Nankai Linguistics* 2. 51–61.
Lorimer, D. L. R. 1958. *The Wakhi Language*, vols. 1 and 2. London: School of African and Oriental Studies, University of London.

Morgenstierne, Georg. 1938. *Indo-Iranian Frontier Languages, Vol. 2: Iranian Pamir Languages (Yidgha-Munji, Sanglechi-Ishkashmi and Wakhi)*. Oslo: H. Aschehoug & Co. (W. Nygaard).
Shaw, R. B. 1876. *On the Ghalchah Languages (Wakhí and Sariḳolí)*. [Reprinted from the Journal of the Asiatic Society of Bengal, for 1876]. Calcutta: C. B. Lewis, Baptist Mission Press.
Vennemann, Theo. 1972. On the theory of syllabic phonology. *Linguistiche Berichte* 18. 1–18.

Rob Goedemans and Jelena Prokic
Mining Metrical Data

Abstract: Since its inception in the early '90s, the StressTyp database (Goedemans, van der Hulst and Visch 1996) has been a valuable typological source for the testing of metrical theories against actual stress phenomena we find in the languages of the world. Grounded in the Primary Accent First-theory (van der Hulst 1984, 1996, 1997) we drew various quantitative analyses from the database to shed new light on metrical dependencies and metrical theory in general (e.g. Goedemans 2010a; 2010b; Goedemans and van der Hulst 2014). Since then, data from StressTyp has found its way to large-scale typological enterprises such as WALS (Haspelmath et. al. 2005) and the Typological Database System (Dimitriadis et al. 2009), but a marriage between StressTyp and the new methods and techniques that have become available since the dawn of the Digital Humanities has yet to take place. In this article we wish to present some exploratory work in this direction, in particular with respect to the continuum between left- and right-oriented stress systems we introduced for Arnhem Land languages in van der Hulst, Goedemans & Rice (2017). For this continuum, we would like to propose a computationally viable "distance scale" and visualize all the languages in StressTyp on that scale in an insightful way.

Keywords: StressTyp database, Australian languages, metrical phonology, stress parameters, Hamming distance, multidimensional scaling, clustering

1 Background

1.1 PAF Theory

The Primary Accent First theory (PAF: van der Hulst 1984, 1996, 1997) is different from other metrical theories by separating the descriptive parameters for primary and secondary stress, making it especially suitable for typological studies. The independent way in which PAF allows us to code locations for primary and secondary stress yields the descriptive power we need to capture the diversity in stress systems we encounter in the languages of the world. Let us just briefly recapitulate how PAF works.

Rob Goedemans and Jelena Prokic, Leiden University

A prototypical stress pattern is that of the Australian language Djambarrpuyngu, in which primary stress always falls on the first syllable, while secondary stresses are located on alternate syllables thereafter, as in ′lithan‚mara‚nhamirr 'dry CAUS+FOURTH+PROP'. To capture this pattern in PAF theory we need the parameters in (1).[1]

(1) Stress Domain: Left   Rhythm Direction: Left
     Stress if Both Light: Trochaic   Rhythm Type: Trochaic
     Stress EM: No   Rhythm Iterative: Yes
     Rhythm: Yes   Rhythm EM: No

| * . | (* .) (* .)
 σ σ   σ σ   σ σ

For main stress, **Stress Domain** places the primary stress window at the Left or Right side of the word. Alternatively, it covers the whole word in, so-called, "Unbounded" stress patterns. **Stress if Both Light** specifies what happens inside that domain in case no syllable weight is at play. In this case, a trochaic foot is placed there. Finally, **Stress Extrametricality** (EM) can be set to "Left/Right" if any element (specified in Stress EM_Unit in StressTyp, and for primary stress typically located at the edge of the Domain) should not be taken into account while deploying the pattern. For rhythm, we need to state, in the first parameter, whether there is rhythm in the first place, since many languages appear to do without it. **Rhythm Direction** then determines at what edge rhythmic alternation starts.[2] **Rhythm Type** specifies the foot type used in rhythmic parsing of the word, trochaic (* .) or iambic (. *) while **Rhythm Iterative** is set to "Yes" if feet are placed throughout the word, denoting persistent rhythmic stressing, while it is set to "No" if *only one foot* is built at the starting edge. Finally, **Rhythm EM** (and Rhythm EM_Unit) can be used to exclude units (usually syllables) at either edge of the word from rhythmic parsing. Thus, with the settings in (1), we derive the schematic representation of the Djambarrpuyngu stress pattern below the parameters.

---

[1] Symbols used: | = main stress domain boundary, ( ) = foot brackets, * = stressed syllable, . = unstressed syllable, σ = syllable. Below in (3) we also introduce "h" for heavy syllable and "l" for light syllable.

[2] In this brief recapitulation we will not go into the matter of whether the domains for Primary and Secondary stress overlap or not. The reader is referred to Goedemans, van der Hulst, and Visch (1996) for discussion.

Above, we already referred to syllable weight. Well documented is the metrical feature of Quantity Sensitivity, which signifies the ability of "heavy" syllables to influence stress locations. Scores of languages use it, and PAF accommodates it in parameters that state whether weight is relevant to stress assignment, and what happens in case there are two (or more) heavy syllables to choose from:

(2) **Stress Weight**: is set to "Yes" if stress location in the primary stress domain is dependent on syllable weight.

Stress if Both Heavy: specifies which syllable, Left or Right, gets the main stress if both syllables in the domain are heavy. If only one of them is heavy, it will be stressed, and if none of them is heavy, the default foot, specified in **Stress if Both Light**, applies.

Rhythm Weight: specifies whether heavy syllables in the rhythmic domain are stressed. They receive a foot of their own, after which parsing resumes with application of the default feet specified in **Rhythm Type**.

Note that PAF allows us to specify weight for primary and secondary stress separately. This is a great advantage, since we find many languages in which either one, but not the other, is Quantity Sensitive.[3] A language that stresses the final syllable if it contains a long vowel, and otherwise the penult, with secondary stresses on syllables with long vowels and the first of two consecutive light syllables, is schematically represented as in (3).

(3) Stress Domain: Right   Rhythm: Yes
    Stress Weight: Yes   Rhythm Direction: Right
    Stress if Both Light: Trochaic   Rhythm Type: Trochaic
    Stress if Both Heavy: Right Rhythm Weight: Yes
    Stress EM: No   Rhythm Iterative: Yes
                                 Rhythm EM: No

```
(* .) (* .)(*)| . *|              (* .)(* .)| * .|⁴
σ  σ  σ  σ  h  l  h              σ  σ  σ  σ  h  l
(* .)(*)(* .)| * .|              (*)(* .)(* .)| . *|⁵
σ  σ  h  σ  σ  l  l              h  σ  σ  σ  σ  h  h
```

---

3 See Goedemans and van der Hulst (2014).

This brief recapitulation of PAF hardly does justice to the theory. We have skimmed over some parameters, many theoretical issues and hot debates, but what we have shown here should suffice as a background for a small venture into the realm of metrical Data Mining.[6]

1.2 A Continuum of Stress Types

In Goedemans (2010b) and van der Hulst, Goedemans, and Rice (2017) we have discussed languages from a particularly interesting area with respect to Metrical Theory, and PAF in particular. It appears that the Australian languages near the boundary between the Pama-Nyungan and non-Pama-Nyungan families in the Northern Territory form a linguistic melting pot of stress types that are intermediate between prototypical Pama-Nyungan initial stress and a pocket of Non-Pama-Nyungan languages that exhibit penultimate stress. Considering the parameters PAF proposes to distinguish between left-oriented initial stress and right-oriented penultimate stress, we can find example languages in the area for many of the combinations one gets when flipping parameter settings in small steps from one pattern to the other. The overview in (4) exemplifies this (in this overview * indicates iterative foot assignment; changed settings in bold; tr=Trochee, ia=Iamb).

(4) **Primary | Rhythm   Description, language and example**

Left/tr | Left*/tr   Primary stress on the first syllable, secondary on alternates after it.
  Djambarrpuyngu   ˈlithanˌmaraˌnhamirr 'dry CAUS+FOURTH+PROP'

Left/tr | **Right***/tr   Primary stress on the first, but secondary on the penult and alternates before it.
  Nakara   ˈdiɟːaɽaˌbaga 'he emerges'

Left/tr | **Right**/tr   Primary stress on the first, but only one secondary stress at the right edge.
  Waanyi   ˈwabinbaraˌulu 'for turtles'

---

[4] Languages differ in what happens with the unparsed foot in this case. Some languages stress it, others leave it unstressed. This behaviour is captured in StressTyp by a parameter we will not consider here.

[5] The other heavy syllable in the primary stress domain *could* receive a rhythmic stress here. We leave it out for expositional purposes.

[6] Interested readers are referred to the literature cited above and references found there.

Left/Ø[7] | Right*/tr	Secondary stress on the penult and alternates before it. Primary stress on the first or second, depending on which of these receives a secondary stress.
	Ngankikurrungkurr
	ˈweriˌfepi 'cave' aˈnimpirrˌmire 'firefly'
none | Left*/tr	Secondary stress on the first and alternates after it. No primary stress.
	Rembarrnga ˌkamuˌnuŋku 'white ochre'
Left/tr | Right*/tr	Secondary stress on the penult and alternates before it *and* one secondary stress on the first (for which we use the primary stress domain).
	Anindilyakwa ˌningkwirriˌpwikwiˌrriwa 'you three'
Right/tr | Left*/tr	Secondary stress on the first and alternates after it *and* one secondary stress on the penult.
	Yanyuwa ˌmařuwaˌřala 'cousin'
none | Right*/tr	Secondary stress on the penult and alternates before it. No primary stress.
	Wardaman jaˌwarrga 'liver'
Right/tr | Left/tr	Primary stress on the penult, and only one secondary stress on the first.
	Umbugarla no example available
Right/tr | Left*/tr	Primary stress on the penult, secondary stress on the first and alternates after it.
	Nunggubuyu ˌrawuˌrrumuguˈrrumu plant species
Right/tr | Right*/tr	Primary stress on the penult, secondary stress on alternates before it.
	Limilngan ˌuruˌgalitjˈbagi 'bandicoot'

Of course, outside the Australian setting, in which iambs are virtually non-existent, one can imagine taking yet another step rightwards by assigning rhythmic iambs and an iamb for primary stress, deriving the pattern of Urubú-Kaapor

---

[7] The unspecified main stress domain allows main stress to end up on the first or second syllable, whichever one is made "strong" by iterative secondary stress assignment from right to left (see Goedemans, van der Hulst and Visch (1996) for a discussion of this unusual type of stress system, called a "count system"). In our view, count systems are hybrids situated well towards the center of the left-to-right spectrum.

(Kakumasu 1986) "primary stress is on the final syllable, and secondary stress on alternate syllables before it". It remains to be seen whether this type is the true prototypical right-hand side stress pattern, since the Limilngan penultimate type is found much more often on the right world-wide, but for the sake of our exposé, we will assume it is.

We consider this striking example of a "continuum" of languages ranging from left- to right-oriented to be the ideal springboard for a broader data-mining exercise in StressTyp. Just diving into the data and measuring haphazardly wherever and whatever we can is, in our view, not the right way to go about this. Exercises such as this one must be grounded in the theory and be based on well-motivated hypotheses. Therefore, based on the groundwork laid out in Goedemans (2010b) and van der Hulst, Goedemans and Rice (2017), we propose to look at the StressTyp data from the angle of a scale (or continuum) with languages like Djambarrpuyngu on the left and Urubú-Kaapor/Limilngan on the right as the extremes. The languages of the world can be plotted on this scale if we devise a means to calculate the "difference" between them and either one of the extremes. Below we will propose a way to do this by assigning weights to the individual stress parameters. The total weight then determines how left-oriented or right-oriented a particular language is. Using this foundation, we will show which parameters play key roles in the discrimination between languages. After that, reminiscent of the tasks we undertook for the World Atlas of Language Structures (Haspelmath et al. 2005), we can then plot the languages on a map, the crucial difference now being that we can do this based on *actual calculations* instead of categorisation by hand. Moreover, we can show their position on the scale we introduced, using a colour coding. We will finish the chapter with some examples of how this works.

The comparison of the Australian languages we discussed above, which was not based on actual difference calculations, was already rather time consuming. It is not difficult to imagine that comparison on a world-wide scale for hundreds of languages on the basis of assigned weights would be a daunting task. This is where we need computers. In the next section we will explain how we approach this problem using methods and techniques from the realm of the Digital Humanities.

2 Method

The StressTyp database contains a large number of parameters and text entry fields to capture the great wealth of metrical systems we encounter in the languages of the world. It is not possible, at this point, to try to incorporate all that data in the current study. For many of the languages in StressTyp, the values for non-core parameters have been left blank, due to the fact that information to fill them was not present in the sources. This sparsity of data makes it too great a challenge for quantitative approaches to generate sensible output. Therefore, we decided to limit ourselves to the parameters we introduced in Section 1. In the future, larger studies can expand on this one and incorporate other data.

To calculate distances between each pair of two languages in our data, we could simply count the number of parameter settings in which they differ. However, in order to include measurements of how "remote" they are from the two prototypical patterns we introduced in 1, we assigned weights to the respective parameters, depending on their influence on the general pattern. Creating such a weight scheme could largely be a matter of intuition. Metrical phonologists know, through their experience with these systems, which parameters should be assigned more weight. Almost 30 years of working on metrical systems and storing them in databases should count for something. Based on what we know of metrical typology, we came up with the scheme in (5). We propose a scale from 0 to 100, placing prototypical "leftmost" trochaic (Djamburrpuyngu) at 0 and prototypical "rightmost" iambic (Urubú Kaapor) at 100.[8] Each change in parameter settings that makes leftmost a little more right adds a scale point, while each change making the rightmost more left subtracts a point. We divided an absolute maximum of 100 over the available parameter settings, making sure we could not end up above 100 or below 0. Parameter settings that contribute, in our view, more movement towards the opposite edge, receive a higher percentage. Thus we end up with:[9]

(5) *Prototypical Left Trochaic*   *Prototypical Right Iambic*
    Domain   **Domain**
    Left   0   Right   100
    Stress_l_l   **Stress_l_l**
    trochaic   0   trochaic   −10
    iambic   10   iambic   0

---

[8] Additionally, we assigned 50 points to *all* unbounded systems, defining the unbounded domain as the natural mid-point between utmost left and utmost right domains. And we subtracted or added percentages if Stress if Both light (15), Stress if Both Heavy (10), Rhythm Type (20), Rhythm Direction (20) or Rhythm EM (5) made the system more left or right-oriented, respectively.

[9] For reasons of space, Stress if Both Heavy and Stress if Both Light (see 1–3) are transcribed here and below as Stress_h_h and Stress_l_l, respectively.

Stress Weight			**Stress Weight**	
No	0		No	0
Yes	10		Yes	−10
Stress_h_h			**Stress_h_h**	
Left	5		Left	−10
Right	10		Right	5
Stress_EM			**Stress_EM**	
No	0		No	0
Left	10		Right	−10
Rhythm			**Rhythm**	
Yes	0		Yes	0
No	5		No	−5
Rhythm Type			**Rhythm Type**	
Trochaic	0		Trochaic	−15
Iambic	15		Iambic	0
Rhythm Direction			**Rhythm Direction**	
Left	0		Left	−15
Right	15		Right	0
Rhythm Iterative			**Rhythm Iterative**	
Yes	0		Yes	0
No	10		No	−10
Rhythm Weight			**Rhythm Weight**	
Yes	5		Yes	−5
No	0		No	0
Rhythm_EM			**Rhythm_EM**	
Left	5		Left	0
Right	0		Right	−5

3 Language Comparison

In order to compare languages based on the eleven parameters and their settings, we calculated relative weighted Hamming distance between all pairs of languages in the database. We counted the number of parameters for which two languages have different settings and divided this number by the number of compared parameters between them. We calculated relative distance between the languages since, due to missing values for some parameters, the number of compared parameters is different for each pair of languages. Additionally, we introduced a weight for each of the parameters (Table 1) based on the scheme presented in (5):[10]

Table 1: Weights for the eleven parameters.

Parameter	Weight
Domain, Rhythm Direction, Rhythm Type	3
Stress_EM, Stress Weight, Stress_h_h, Sress_l_l, Rhythm Iterative	2
Rhythm, Rhythm_EM, Rhythm Weight	1

To illustrate this, in Table 2 we show parameter values for the languages Kongo and Dyirbal. These two languages have different values only for one parameter, namely 'Rhythm Direction', the weight of which is 3, making the distance between these two languages:

$$1/9*3 = 0.33$$

Features 'Stress_h_h' and 'Rhythm Iterative' are omitted from the comparison of these two languages due to missing values for the parameters for these languages.

Table 2: Feature values for Kongo and Dyirbal languages. Symbol '-' is used for missing values.

Lang.	Dom	S_EM	S_W	S_hh	S_ll	Rh.	Rh_D	Rh_EM	Rh_I	Rh_T	Rh_W
Kongo	Left	No	No	-	Tr	Yes	Right	No	-	Tr	No
Dyirbal	Left	No	No	-	Tr	Yes	Left	No	Yes	Tr	No

The distances between each pair of languages in our dataset were calculated in the same fashion and the obtained distances were analyzed using multidimensional scaling and clustering.

3.1 Data Analysis

Multidimensional scaling is a dimensionality reduction technique of which the main objective is to represent dissimilarities between the points as distances in

---

[10] With the exception of the Domain parameter, weights for all parameters are extracted from the scheme in (5), by calculating the range between min and max values for Prototypical Left and Prototypical Right languages for each parameter and dividing it by 10. The resulting weights have values 1, 2 and 3. We assign weight 3 to the Domain feature, which is the highest value in our weighting scheme.

a low dimensional space such that the distances correspond as closely as possible to the dissimilarities. While Black (1976) introduced multidimensional scaling (MDS) to areal linguistics, Embleton (1993) applied the technique specifically to dialectometry. By plotting points in two dimensions, we can graphically represent the relationships between the points and reveal the structure of a data set. Since in hierarchical clustering the number of groups to be retrieved has to be given to the algorithm, we used a plot of the first two MDS dimensions as a first step to determine if there are any clearly defined groups in the data, and how many. We use metric MDS as implemented in Python sklearn library. Metric MDS deals with numeric distances where there is exactly one distance value between each pair of items, which matches our data. The plot of the first two MDS-dimensions from our data set can be seen in Figure 1a.

The MDS plot reveals that there are five clearly separated groups of languages in our data. In the next step, we rely on hierarchical clustering (HC), an unsupervised machine learning technique, to identify these five groups and look in more detail into relationships among the identified clusters of languages. Among several tested HC algorithms, Ward's clustering algorithm (Ward 1963) was the most accurate in retrieving the five groups (Figure 1b).[11] The results of clustering can be represented in the form of a dendrogram, which shows the hierarchical relationship between objects. The height at which any two objects are joined together shows the distance between them. In Figure 2 we show the dendrogram produced from the same distance matrix used for the MDS analysis and colour 3 (left) and 5 (right) clusters that can be detected by a cut-off at 8.0 for three clusters and at 5.0. for five clusters.

On the left-hand side, we see that clustering has identified three groups of languages that can further be split into five groups presented in the dendrogram on the right. We calculated the homogeneity score (HS) for both 3- and 5-way divisions and compared them against each of the eleven parameters in order to check whether these divisions correspond well with any of the parameter settings. A clustering result receives a maximal homogeneity score of 1 if all of its clusters contain only data points that are members of a single class and a score of 0 if each

---

[11] Next to Ward's clustering algorithm, we tested average linkage, complete linkage and weighted average hierarchical clustering algorithms. Unlike Ward's clustering algorithm, none of these was successful in retrieving groups of languages identified by MDS that are completely homogeneous.

An anonymous reviewer noted that Unbounded systems seem to occupy a strange position here, being more extreme on the weight dimension than the other groups. This, however, is simply the result of the way be deal with Unbounded systems in StressTyp, in which true Quantity-Insensitive Unbounded systems do not exist.

Mining Metrical Data — **143**

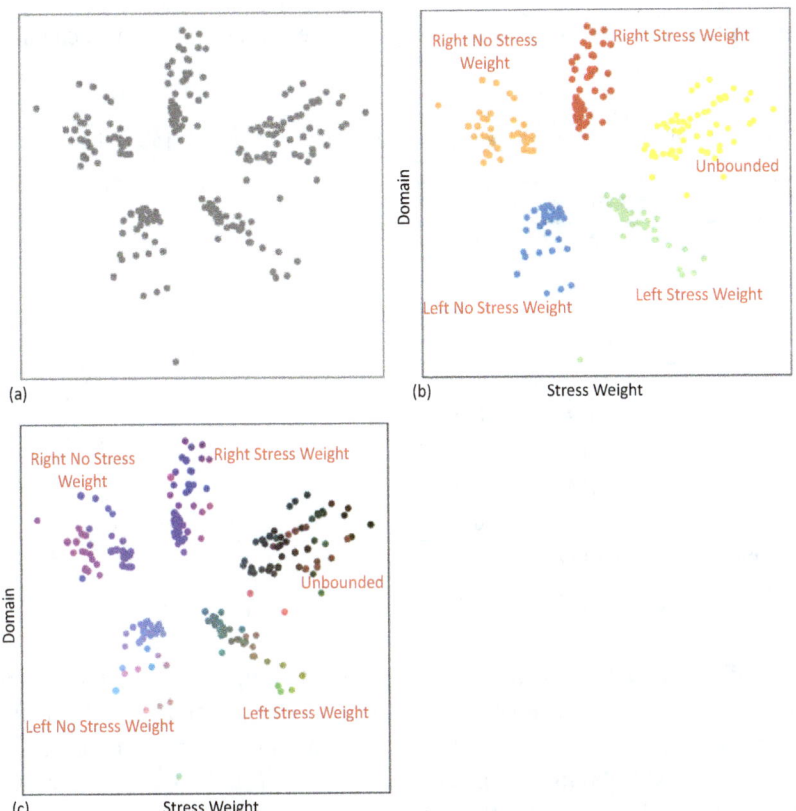

Figure 1: a) MDS plot of the first two dimensions shows five separate groups b) five groups identified by Ward's clustering algorithm c) MDS plot with dots for which the colour is based on the values for the first three MDS dimensions.

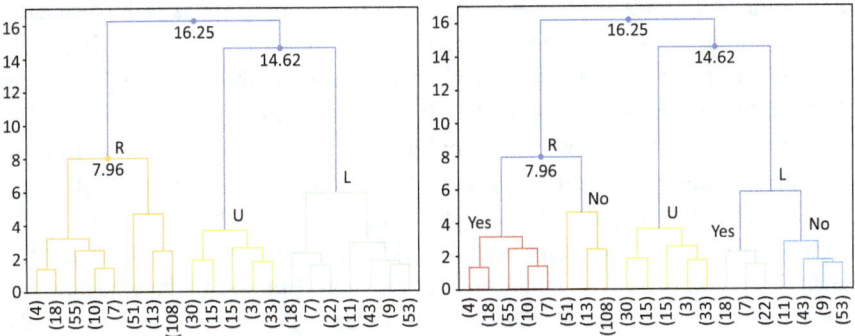

Figure 2: Dendrogram with three groups that correspond to Domain parameter (a) and five detected groups that correspond both to Domain and Stress Weight parameters (b).

cluster contains points belonging to multiple classes and members of each class are assigned to multiple clusters.

Table 3: Homogeneity score for 3 and 5 groups detected by Ward's clustering algorithm.

	HS 3 groups	HS 5 groups
Domain	**1.0**	**1.0**
Stress_EM	0.0592	0.0915
Stress_Weight	0.2093	**0.9363**
Stress_h_h	0.1471	0.5658
Stress _l_l	0.1003	0.1616
Rhythm	0.0335	0.0357
Rhythm_Direction	0.0781	0.0847
Rhythm_EM	0.474	0.0643
Rhythm Iterative	0.0363	0.0417
Rhythm Type	0.0497	0.0620
Rhythm_Weight	0.0362	0.0727

Homogeneity scoring reveals that the three detected groups are formed based on the Domain feature and they hold Right (R), Unbounded (U) and Left (L) domain languages, which we annotated in the dendrogram on the left. Lengths of the branches show that Unbounded languages are closer to Left than to Right-domain languages. Next to Domain, the other important feature detected by clustering is Stress Weight that further splits languages into five groups. Right and Left-domain languages are split into two groups, with and without Stress Weight, and together with Unbounded languages form five groups. We note that in the five-way clustering the Stress_h_h feature receives a high score, but that is caused by the fact that all languages without Stress Weight have no values for the Stress_h_h parameter. Of particular interest here is the low contribution of Stress_l_l and Rhythm Type. We gave these parameters high weight scores based on the common knowledge that foot type is universally thought to be omnipotent in metrical phonology. The computational results, however, do not justify our choice in that respect. Even though feet clearly have Left or Right dominance themselves, the results obtained here indicate that they do not come into play when we determine how "Left or Right-edge oriented" languages are. We did not come across this issue for our Australian examples, since iambs do not exist there, but we can imagine how foot type "has a mind of its own" when we consider all the languages in StressTyp. We already noted, for instance, in Section 1.2 that trochees, and not iambs, constitute the predominant foot type at the right-hand side of the word. All this means that we may have to reconsider our approach to the proposed scale. Exactly how to fit in foot type, which should really play a bigger role in calculations concerning metrical issues than it currently does, is one of the tasks we need to set for ourselves on the road of computational explorations in stress, on which we have only taken a few small steps in this article.

In order to check if there is a pattern in geographical distribution of Domain and Stress Weight features detected by clustering, we plotted the five groups of languages on a map (Figure 3).

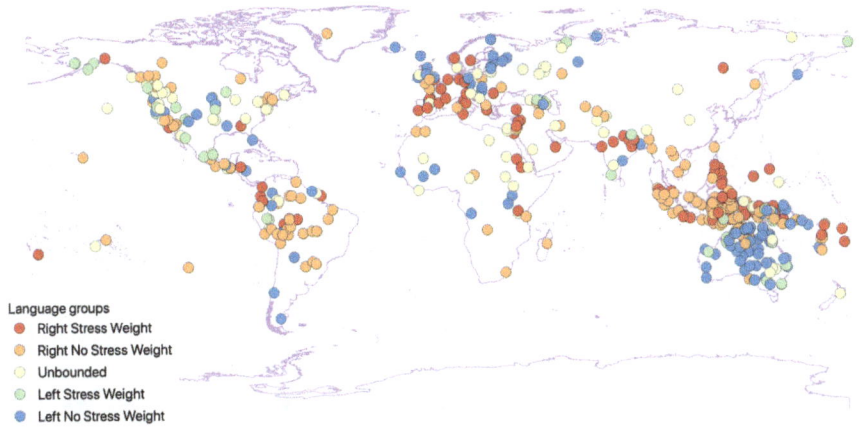

Figure 3: Geographical distribution of five groups of languages detected by Ward's clustering algorithm.

Unsurprisingly, we see that three areas in the southern hemisphere are very homogeneous, with South America and Southeast Asia (with the exception of Papua New Guinea) dominated by Right-domain languages (red and orange dots), and Australia dominated by Left-domain languages (green and blue dots). This confirms the observations we made in the WALS-publications. Areas in the northern hemisphere, however, are much more heterogeneous, with no areas that show dominance of one of the detected clusters. In North America we see presence of all five groups with a lot of mixing. A similar pattern that shows no geographical cohesion is also present in Europe, which is not in line with the observations we made in the WALS-publications. This, however, is due to the fact that we conflated two of the WALS-maps (those for fixed and variable stress) into one. When these are separated, Europe shows a more homogeneous pattern. The takeaway here is that, even when conflated, the three areas mentioned above, South America, Southeast Asia and Australia, remain rather homogeneous.

Present in the WALS-data, but never commented on previously, is a striking geographical distribution of Left-domain languages in Australia. Note that languages with Stress Weight are found only in the coastal areas (green dots in Figure 4).

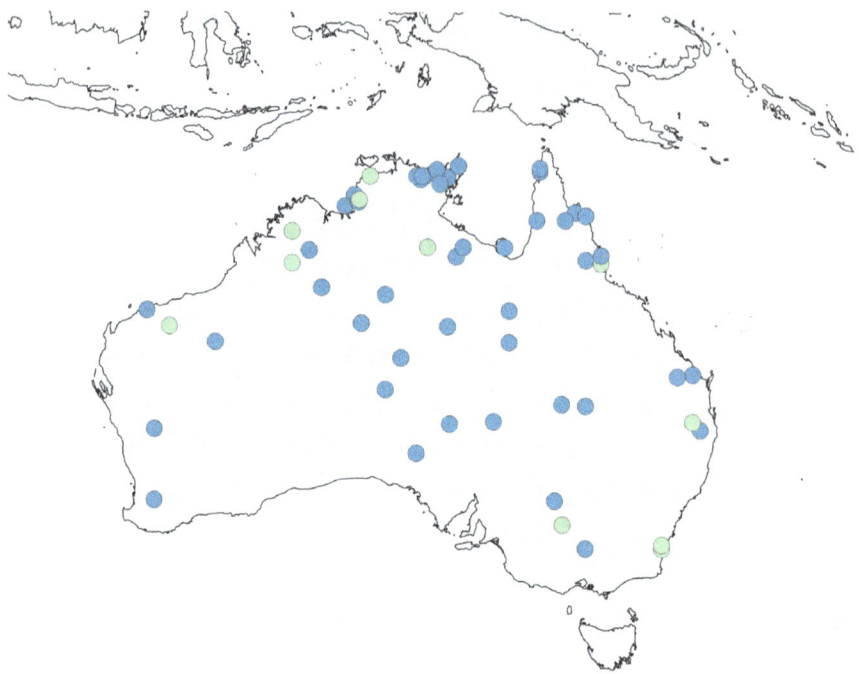

Figure 4: Distribution of Left-domain languages in Australia. Blue dots mark languages without Stress Weight. Green dots, found in the coastal areas, mark languages with Stress Weight.

Given the discussion in Goedemans (2010b) and van der Hulst, Goedemans, and Rice (2017) concerning the direction of change (towards, or away from, initial stress) we can add this piece of evidence to our argumentation. The distribution above strengthens our belief that the Djambarrpuyngu-pattern is the prototypical Australian pattern and that all other patterns, such as Penultimate stress or stress weight on the left, are innovations from outside.

In order to further visualise distances between the clusters, we used a colouring technique developed in dialectometry that relies on the MDS analysis (Nerbonne, Heeringa, and Kleiweg 1999). We extracted the first three MDS dimensions, converted them into RGB colours and assigned each dot a corresponding RGB value (see Figure 1c). In this way each dot received a colour that corresponds to the first three MDS dimensions.¹² As a result, dots are assigned colour in such a way that the smaller the distance between the points, the more similar their colour will be.

This visualisation technique allows us to see that there is a gradual change of colour between Left-domain languages with no Stress Weight and Right-domain languages. At the same time, Left-domain languages with Stress Weight form a group with Unbounded languages, shaded green. The transition between two groups of Left-domain languages is less smooth, which indicates that Left domain languages are less coherent than Right-domain languages. The similarity of Unbounded languages to Left-domain ones ties in with the fact that unbounded languages are typologically skewed towards having a default at the left edge. This observation, and the specific geographical distribution of Left-domain languages, deserves further study, but we leave that for future work.

Now that we have established the visualisations with the gradient colour changes, we can conclude our exposé with a revisit of the Northern Australian languages we started out with. The map in Figure 5 shows the relevant area, in which the languages are indicated using the colour codes introduced in Figure 1c.

Compared to the map we presented in van der Hulst, Goedemans, and Rice (2017) the difference is quite clear.¹³ Various colour shadings show deviations from the two basic patterns, thus indicating *and* categorising the hybrid languages at the same time. Thus, this computational method can assist linguists, saving them a lot of painstaking work, whether they want to reveal gradient differences in neighbouring languages or lump them together in a few discrete categories, like we have done for these Australian languages previously.¹⁴ We can repeat this for any domain, area, and parameter set we choose to. All that is left to do is go out there and find promising candidates for similar areal patterns.

---

12 Note that the position of dots in the plot is based on the first two MDS dimensions, while the colors are based on the first three MDS dimensions.
13 Map 7.1 on page 192 in van der Hulst, Goedemans, and Rice (2017) only indicates location of the languages and whether they have Initial stress, Penultimate stress, or show a "hybrid" pattern that is in between these two basic patterns.
14 Since the focus of this article is the introduction of a computational method instead of linguistic details, we will not go further into the nitty-gritty of the hybrid Australian languages here. The interested reader is referred to Goedemans (2010b) and van der Hulst, Goedemans, and Rice (2017).

Figure 5: Northern Australian languages with MDS-colour coding (blue: Initial stress; purple: Penultimate stress).

4 Conclusion

The explorations in this chapter constitute only the first steps of a long journey that we could undertake to fully apply digital techniques that have become quite common in the world of Digital Humanities since we started gathering data to build a database of stress phenomena in the early 1990s. We have barely scratched the surface, and yet, we hope to have shown how computational methods can be used to form solid foundations for enterprises that were based on manual, and sometimes necessarily more arbitrary, typological categorisations in the past. Concretely, we have shown that we can recreate the kind of maps that were made for the World Atlas of Language Structures (Haspelmath et al. 2005) based on calculated differences between the various stress types we find in the languages of the world. Along the way, we revealed characteristics of the complete StressTyp dataset, and specifics of the contribution the various stress parameters make towards discrimination of clusters of similar languages. As such, these computational tools can be of invaluable help to typologists, widening the field of exploration, much like the way in which we opened up new levels of discovery after we entered stress data in the computer for the first time, calculated frequencies and checked for dependencies between parameters. We expect these methods will be helpful to reveal linguistic treasures still hidden in StressTyp as well as many other Typological Databases, a few of which were represented along with StressTyp in WALS.

We must be careful, though. Typological databases like StressTyp are an invaluable source of information, but a major caveat in this type of exploration is formed by missing data. We have hinted at this problem above, and it continues to be a headache for those attempting similar computational approaches. In many cases, the problem is insoluble, since the necessary data to determine the parameter settings is not available in the grammars and never will be. All we can do is endeavour to be as complete as possible. Once these databases have more extensive coverage, the possibilities for applying computational approaches will grow rapidly. In the meantime, we plan to undertake a new exploration, using a subset of StressTyp-languages for which the data is as complete as we may expect, hoping to draw from that set some sharp analyses that are not hampered by missing parameter values.

Finally, a possible objection to the method we applied to generate different types of visualisations and maps above might be that we defined the weight scheme ourselves, based on the linguist's intuition. Although we feel the scheme we used is justified, we admit that some of the arbitrariness in categorisation we wished to eliminate still remains. Therefore, we plan further research in which we will devise a means to calculate the assigned weights intrinsically, using only the available data. Once we can do this, we are well and true on our way towards the creation of a Typological Artificial Intelligence module for linguistic research. The joy of hypothesising and interpretation of the results will be ours, while we can leave the tedious number crunching entirely to computers.

References

Black, Paul. 1976. Multidimensional scaling applied to linguistic relationships. *Cahiers de l'Institut de Linguistique de Louvain* 3. 43–92.

Dimitriadis, Alexis, Menzo A. Windhouwer, Adam G. Saulwick, Rob W. N. Goedemans & Támas Bíró. 2009. How to integrate databases without starting a typology war: The Typological Database System. In Martin Everaert, Simon Musgrave & Alexis Dimitriadis (eds.), *The Use of Databases in Cross-Linguistic Studies*, 155–207. Berlin/New York: Mouton de Gruyter.

Embleton, Sheila. 1993. Multidimensional scaling as a dialectometric technique: Outline of a research project. In Reinhard Köhler & Burghard Rieger (eds.), *Contributions to Quantitative Linguistics*, 267–276. Dordrecht: Kluwer.

Goedemans, Rob W. N. 2010a. A typology of stress patterns. In Harry G. van der Hulst, Rob W. N. Goedemans & Ellen A. van Zanten-Wervelman (eds.), *A Survey of Word Accentual Patterns in the Languages of the World*, 647–666. Berlin: Mouton de Gruyter.

Goedemans, Rob W. N. 2010b. An overview of word stress in Australian Aboriginal languages. In Harry G. van der Hulst, Rob W. N. Goedemans & Ellen A. van Zanten-Wervelman (eds.), *A Survey of Word Accentual Patterns in the Languages of the World*, 55–85. Berlin: Mouton de Gruyter.

Goedemans, Rob W. N. & Harry G. van der Hulst. 2014. The separation of accent and rhythm: Evidence from StressTyp. In Harry G. van der Hulst (ed.), *Word Stress: Theoretical and Typological Issues*, 119–148. Cambridge: Cambridge University Press.

Goedemans, Rob W. N., Harry G. van der Hulst & Ellis A. M. Visch (eds.). 1996. *Stress Patterns of the World*. (HIL Publications 2). The Hague: Holland Academic Graphics. And: http://st2.ullet.net/.

Haspelmath, Martin, Matthew S. Dryer, David Gil & Bernard Comrie (eds.). 2005. *World Atlas of Language Structures*. Oxford: Oxford University Press. And https://wals.info/.

Hulst, Harry G. van der. 1984. *Syllable Structure and Stress in Dutch*. Dordrecht: Foris.

Hulst, Harry G. van der. 1996. Separating primary accent and secondary accent. In Rob W. N. Goedemans, Harry G. van der Hulst & Ellis A. M. Visch (eds.), *Stress Patterns of the World. Part I*, 1–26. (HIL Publications 2). The Hague: Holland Academic Graphics.

Hulst, Harry G. van der. 1997. Primary accent is non-metrical. *Rivista di Linguistica* 9(1). 99–127.

Hulst, Harry G. van der, Rob W. N. Goedemans & Keren Rice. 2017. Word Prominence and Areal Linguistics. In Raymond Hickey (ed.), *The Cambridge Handbook of Areal Linguistics*, 161–203. Cambridge: Cambridge University Press.

Kakumasu, James. 1986. Urubu-Kaapor. In Desmond C. Derbyshire & Geoffrey K. Pullum (eds.), *Handbook of Amazonian Languages 1*, 326–403. Berlin: Mouton de Gruyter.

Nerbonne, John, Wilbert Heeringa & Peter Kleiweg. 1999. Edit distance and dialect proximity. In David Sankoff & Joseph Kruskal (eds.), *Time Warps, String Edits and Macromolecules: The Theory and Practice of Sequence Comparison*, v–xv. Stanford: CSLI.

Ward, Joe H., Jr. 1963. Hierarchical Grouping to Optimize an Objective Function. *Journal of the American Statistical Association* 58. 236–244.

Ana Lívia Agostinho and Larry M. Hyman
Interpreting Non-Canonical Word Prosody in Afro-European Contact

Abstract: In this paper we consider two non-canonical prosodic systems resulting from Afro-European contact: Lung'Ie (Principense) and Central African French. After establishing criteria for "tone" and "stress", we show that neither system meets the canonical properties of either: Lung'Ie restricts words to at most one ("culminative") high tone, but also allows toneless words, while Central African French assigns one and only one ("culminative and obligatory") high tone to the final syllable of each word, suggesting an accentual analysis, non-high syllables, instead of having interpolated pitch, are clearly realized with an output low target, thus making the language "feel like tone". Our study again shows that not all word-prosodic systems fit neatly into predefined typological "boxes". In these (and other cited) cases, the "non-canonical" systems show that Afro-European contact between tone and stress/accent can have quite different effects.

Keywords: tone, stress, accent, Lung'Ie, Central African French, contact

1 Introduction

"It is striking how elusive the conceptualization of a relatively simple prosodic system can be" (Hyman and Kobepa 2013: 307). Thus begins a discussion of Mee, a Wissel Lakes Papuan language, whose word prosodic system had been variously characterized as "stress", "pitch-accent", and "tone and stress". Although the above authors ultimately show that the "simple" contrast reduces to whether a H(igh) to L(ow) pitch drop will occur after the first vs. second mora of the word, e.g. [káìyà] 'where' vs. [káídò] 'Jew's harp', it is at this point that the problem of interpretation arises. Should these and both shorter and longer words be distinguished by the placement of an "accentual" mark (/ka⁺iya/ vs. /kai⁺do/) or by a prelinked /H/ tone (/káiya/ vs. /kaído/)? Is the first syllable also the head of a metrical stress foot? The Hyman and Kobepa quote underscores a major problem that arises in word prosodic systems where the pitch contrasts are either obligatory (e.g a word has to have a H tone), culminative (a word can have only one H

Ana Lívia Agostinho, Universidade Federal de Santa Catarina
Larry M. Hyman, University of California, Berkeley

https://doi.org/10.1515/9783110730081-008

tone), or both. Since the tonal vs. accentual analyses of Mee are completely equivalent, the choice that the analyst is forced to make is often one of taste.

In this paper we address the interpretation of such limited pitch contrasts that arise in the Afro-European contact situation, where the problem is particularly acute. While much more research is needed, the descriptions that exist are often at odds with each other, the same author even changing their mind whether a system is "tonal" or "accentual". There is good reason for this. The Afro-European contact situation is one where the stress system of the European language meets various African speech communities whose languages not only fail to mark stress in the ways familiar from English, Dutch, Portuguese etc., but which instead distinguish much greater tonal contrasts than the one just summarized in Mee. This raises two logically independent questions: First, what happens when such different prosodic systems meet in the Afro-European context? Second, how should the resulting systems be interpreted, i.e. analyzed? In the following sections we will first briefly present a short summary of word-prosodic typology, followed by discussion of two languages resulting from Afro-European contact. The first is Lung'Ie or Principense (ISO 639-3 code: [pre]), a highly endangered Portuguese-lexifier creole spoken in the Island of Príncipe, in São Tomé and Príncipe, located in the Gulf of Guinea. The second is Central African French, spoken in the Central African Republic, as recently described by Steien and Yakpo (2020). We end with some final observations concerning the study of prosodic systems in Afro-European contact.[1,2]

---

[1] We are especially pleased to dedicate this chapter to Harry van der Hulst who, among many other things, has contributed so much to our understanding of word prosody, particularly accentual systems. In his many publications, he has provided a lively forum for the sharing of ideas and results concerning the diverse word-prosodic systems attested in the world's languages. The extent to which he has stimulated the field is seen both through his own authored works as well as those of his colleagues, many of which appear as chapters in his edited volumes on word prosody. We salute Harry and thank him for making word-prosodic typology an exciting place to be!

[2] We are grateful to both Kofi Yakpo and Guri Bordal Steien for a stimulating e-mail exchange on the issues discussed in this chapter. While we outline a different analysis of their CAF material, we greatly appreciated the opportunity to share ideas and get their feedback. We also thank Bob Ladd and the audience at the *Berkeley Phonetics and Phonology Forum Talk Series 2020* for fruitful discussion on the issues we raise here and Jeroen de Weijer and Keith Snider for helpful comments on the original submission. Research by the first author was supported by the Brazilian National Council for Scientific and Technological Development (CNPq), grant 200519/2019-0.

2 Word-Prosodic Typology

In this section we briefly outline the terms and prosodic types we will be using in evaluating our two test cases. The first concerns tone. While there are various uses of this term in actual practice and systems that lie on the edges, we will assume the following definition of a tone system (Hyman 2006, 2011; Welmers 1959, 1973):

(1) A language with tone is one in which pitch is a contrastive feature of at least some morphemes.

The crucial word in this definition is "morphemes". Contrastive pitches that come in at the phrase level as a "pitch-accent" spellout of prominent stress, as a boundary tone, or as an intonational melody do not meet the definition. Although also often characterized as Hs and Ls in "intonation-only" languages, such phrasal tones can also exist alongside lexically contrastive pitch, i.e. in prosodic systems that meet the definition in (1). The crucial requirement is that the Hs and Ls (and other contrastive pitches) be properties at the word level. This includes cases where they are additional exponents of (lexical or grammatical) segmental morphemes, e.g. Basaá [bas] (Bantu; Cameroon) **só** 'escape' vs. **sɔ́** 'wash', or exert an effect through realizational rules, e.g. Noni [nhu] (Bantoid; Cameroon) **bìè** 'fish', plural **bíé**.

Turning to word stress or stress-accent, a working definition is given in (2) (Hyman 2006: 231):

(2) A language with stress-accent is one in which there is word-level metrical structure meeting the following two central criteria:
  a. *obligatoriness*: every lexical word has at least one syllable marked for the highest degree of metrical prominence
  b. *culminativity*: every lexical word has at most one syllable marked for the highest degree of metrical prominence.

Taken together, this means that there will be one and only one primary stress per word. If a language has stress, a "word" without primary stress is not a word (e.g. the English indefinite article in the phrase **a ˈbook**), and a "word" with two primary stress is two words (e.g. the co-compound **ˈmother-ˈdaughter**). The phonetic and phonological effects of stress can be quite varied, affecting consonants, vowels and even tones. Phrasal and intonational "pitch-accents" are often aligned with the most prominent stress(es) in an utterance.

Word-prosodic typology would be quite simple if all systems exclusively met the criteria in either (1) or (2), but not both, as once believed. However, we have known for some time that tone and stress are not mutually exclusive.[3] Thus, Swedish has a tonal contrast only on a stressed syllable (Riad 2018), hence many syllables lack a tone. In addition, there are languages without stress, but with severely restricted tonal contrasts meeting either the obligatory criterion in (2a), e.g. at least one H per word in Ekoti [eko] (Bantu; Mozambique) (Schadeberg 1986, 2000), the culminativity criterion in (2b), e.g. at most one H to L pitch drop per word in Tokyo Japanese (Kubozono 2008), or both the obligatory and culminativity criteria, e.g. one and only one H tone per word in Nubi (Gussenhoven 2006). In fact, we opened with one such language, Mee, and pointed out the availability of multiple analyses – another being that one of the patterns has a /H/ tone, while the other is underlyingly toneless. Despite their obvious differences, many have been tempted to group Swedish, Tokyo Japanese, Nubi and other languages into a third category of "pitch-accent" systems, a grab-bag for any type of system where there are "significant constraints on the pitch patterns for words" (Bybee et al. 1998: 277).

Because there is no one criterion (or "prototype") for systems with sparse tonal contrasts (Hyman 2009), we are left with the ambiguity of analysis referred to above – and we haven't yet mentioned the possibility of some languages having neither tone nor stress, another controversy: "As a working hypothesis, we might assume that all languages have accent" (Goedemans and van der Hulst 2009: 238). Of course all of this presupposes that each prosodic system will neatly fall into a "type", a problem we will encounter in discussing our two test cases in the next section. In fact, we will show that, while evoking elements of both, the prosodic systems of Lung'Ie and Central African French fail to meet the definitional criteria of either stress or tone.

3 Two Case Studies

In this section, we present the word-prosodic systems of Lung'Ie and Central African French. Lung'Ie is the result of the contact of a stress-accent superstrate (Portuguese) with African substrates/adstrates during the formation of a heavily restructured creole language: Edoid tone languages, which are fully specified for tones, and Bantu H/Ø privative tone systems. On the other hand, Central African French is the result of a less extreme and more recent contact of a non-tone superstrate (French) with fully specified tone languages adstrates (Sango, which is a Ngbandi-lexifier creole, and Ubangian languages).

---

3 Some recent examples are Uspanteko (Bennett and Henderson 2013), Iquito (Michael 2011), and Kuikuro (Becker et al. 2020).

3.1 Lung'Ie

This section summarizes the findings of Agostinho and Hyman (2021), based on extensive fieldwork data[4] collected by the first author in Príncipe, in which we argued that Lung'Ie presents a culminative non-obligatory /H/ tone system, with an unusual "weight-to-tone" requirement.[5]

The islands of the Gulf of Guinea were uninhabited before the arrival of the Portuguese in the late 15th century. The Island of São Tomé was first populated by enslaved people mainly from the Niger Delta, and, later, primarily from Congo and Angola (Caldeira 2008, 2013: 67–72; Seibert 2013: 66–67, 2014: 46). A creole language emerged from the contact between the Portuguese and African populations in this multilingual scenario during the fifteenth and sixteenth centuries in São Tomé. During the early to mid-16th century, the speakers of this language, the Proto-Creole of the Gulf of Guinea (henceforth PGG) (Bandeira 2017; Ferraz 1979; Hagemeijer 2011), were geographically separated into the other islands which contributed to the speciation that resulted in the four languages spoken today: Santome or Forro [cri] and Angolar [aoa] in São Tomé; Lung'Ie in Príncipe and Fa d'Ambô [fab] in Annobón. The main African substrate of PGG are the languages from the Niger Delta, particularly Edoid languages, which are fully specified for tone. Bantu languages, such as Kikongo and Kimbundu, which are H/Ø privative systems, played a secondary role (Hagemeijer 2011; see also Ladhams 2012; Agostinho, Araujo, and Santos 2019). Contrary to São Tomé and Annobón, Príncipe ceased to receive enslaved people from the Bantu zone after the separation of the PGG speakers and continued to receive a slave contingent from the Niger Delta region.[6]

Lung'Ie has a restrictive privative H/Ø tone system, in which the /H/ is culminative, but non-obligatory, and the tone-bearing unit is the (vocalic) mora. In the Portuguese origin words, the H tone is generally linked to the vocalic mora of the syllable that had stress in Portuguese through diachronic stress-to-tone alignment (via PGG). As seen in (3), nouns can bear one H or be all-Ø, i. e., have no phonological tone.

---

[4] The data consists of 517 lexical items (nouns, verbs and ideophones) recorded in isolation and in 18 syntactic frames with five speakers.
[5] The Lung'Ie word-prosodic system has been analyzed in several different ways in previous work: as a fully-specified tone language with H, L and R tones (Günther 1973); a free "pitch-accent" language with obligatory H (Traill and Ferraz 1981); a fully-specified tone language with H and L tones (Maurer 2009) and a mixed system of stress and tone (Agostinho 2015, 2016). Maurer (2009: 27) briefly mentions stress, but does not consider it in his discussion.
[6] Consequently, Lung'Ie has the lowest percentage of Bantu words and the highest percentage of Edo words compared to the other Gulf of Guinea creoles (Ladhams 2012).

(3) Lung'Ie tone patterns

		One H	*All-Ø*
a.	V	/dó/ 'pain'	/ibi/ 'coal'
		/káʃi/ 'house'	/maNpata/ 'palm oil residue'
		/kasó/ 'dog'	/ug͡bododo/ 'precipice'
	VV	/fɔ́ɔsa/ 'strength'	/baana/ 'banana'
		/tɛɛ́la/ 'star'	/ig͡bee/ 'room'[7]
b.	V	/víka/ 'to come'[8]	/sɛ/ 'to roast'
			/dumu/ 'to grind'
			/kidita/ 'to believe'
	VV	–	/fii/ 'to hurt'
			/fɔɔsa/ 'to force'
c.	V	/pí/ ideophone of 'shut up'; ideophone of 'black'	/diN/ ideophone of 'blue'
			/rarara/ ideophone of 'red'
			/pɔtɔpɔtɔ/ ideophone of 'wet'
	VV	–	–

Monosyllables must bear a H and words with more than one syllable can be all-Ø. Nouns show a weight-to-tone requirement in which long vowels and syllables with codas must have a H and, with very few exceptions, there are no final long vowels. The H can be in any syllable and the tone pattern is synchronically unpredictable in light-syllable words (see 3a). Verbs are generally toneless, with very few exceptions. Long vowels are allowed in monosyllabic verbs and in the penultimate syllable of a disyllabic verb (see 3b). Ideophones are toneless (with one exception) and of African origin (see 3c).

Lung'Ie presents a unique result of the contact of languages with different word prosody systems that has not previously been reported in the literature. The data shows that 87% of the nouns with a H are of Portuguese origin while 92% of all-Ø nouns are of African origin. Another way to look at it is that 97% of Portuguese origin nouns bear a H, whereas 70% of African origin nouns are all-Ø. This shows a clear correlation between word origin and tone pattern in Lung'Ie. A similar link is found in other creoles analyzed as having "split" systems, e.g. Nigerian Pidgin English (Faraclas 1984), Saramaccan (Good 2004), and Pichi (Yakpo 2009, although for a reanalysis, see Yakpo 2019). However, the "split" in these

---

[7] Within a lexicon of 383 nouns, /baana/ and /ig͡bee/ are the only examples of all-Ø nouns with a long vowel.
[8] There are only five H-Ø verbs in the data (out of 111).

languages is between H "accent" and fully specified tonal lexemes, not between culminative H "accent" and Ø. Moreover, it is quite surprising that 70% of the African-origin words are (i) adapted in the same way and (ii) adapted as all-Ø.

As previously reported by Traill and Ferraz (1981), long vowels can be either phonetically rising [LH] or falling [HL].[9] Both contours derive from the loss of liquids from Portuguese (via PGG) with compensatory lengthening of the adjacent V, as seen in (4a,b).

(4) Minimal pairs with [LH] and [HL] contours on long vowels

		Portuguese	Lung'Ie	Phonetic realization
a.		ˈpreto 'black'	/pɛɛ́.tu/	[pɛ̌:tu]
		ˈprata 'silver'	/paá.ta/	[pǎ:ta]
b.		ˈpɛrto 'close'	/pɛ́ɛ.tu/	[pɛ̂:tu]
		ˈmarka 'mark'	/máa.ka/	[mâ:ka]
c.		ˈpata 'duck (fem.)'	/pá.ta/	[páta]
		ˈmaka 'stretcher'	/má.ka/	[máka]

If a liquid in a 2nd position of a complex onset is lost, as in (4a), the result is a rising contour. On the other hand, if a liquid coda is lost, as in (4b), the result is a falling contour.[10] In our data, these results are very consistent and we found no exceptions. The examples in (4c) form a minimal pair of /H/ with [LH] and [HL] in (4b) and (4c), respectively. Since CVV́ and CV́V are contrastive and synchronically unpredictable, the location of the H tone must be marked underlyingly, independent of whether such words also have stress or not.

Even though tone indications are obviously needed, Lung'Ie presents an unusual "stress-like" weight-to-tone requirement, such that syllables with a coda or a long vowel require a H. This raises the question of whether H tone syllables are also "stressed". In order to argue against the need for stress, we present the following arguments reported in more detail in Agostinho and Hyman (2021):

a. There is no greater number of contrasting vowels or consonants in H tone syllables vs. Ø tone syllables, or in the case of all Ø words, in final syllable vs. preceding syllables.

---

9 Long vowels cannot be all H, and only two H nouns have been found with a long toneless vowel: /maakíta/ '*malagueta* pepper' and /paagɛ́/ 'parrot'. Since they are toneless in Lung'Ie, it is possible for a long toneless vowel to exist in verbs, e.g. /fii/ 'to hurt', /fɔɔsa/ 'to force'.
10 Fa d'Ambô shows the same realizations for long vowels, such as [pɛ̌:tu] and [pɛ̂:tu] (Agostinho and Araujo 2021).

b. H tone syllables potentially have increased amplitude[11] and slightly greater length, although not consistently.[12]
c. There is no clash resolution for adjacent H tones as would be expected with two adjacent stressed syllables in stress-accent languages (Kenstowicz 1994), and H tones are not protected from elision in external vowel sandhi processes.[13]
d. There might be more than one H in a phonological word (by a H insertion rule), e.g. /óroko kasó/ → [óʁokó kasɔ̨] 'the dog's mouse', or in a compound, e. g. /ufí kumíN/ 'road' (lit. 'thread way').
e. There is no phonetic or phonological difference between a final Ø syllable in a H word and a Ø syllable in an all-Ø word, i. e. both can undergo final reduction.

Unsurprisingly, the culminative H tone is perceptually "salient" in Lung'Ie. Besides its prominent pitch, H is accessible as a target in a language game (Agostinho 2015, 2016; Agostinho and Araujo 2021). This ludling consists of inserting a CV syllable with [p] as the onset and a copied vowel as the nucleus (i) after the first mora of the syllable bearing a H in the base and/or (ii) word-finally (the only option for all-Ø words):

(5) Ludling in Lung'Ie

	base	*ludling*		*gloss*	*rules*
a.	/fólogo/	fo**pó**logo	fologo**po**	'breath'	(i), (ii)
	/áriba/	a**pá**riba	ariba**pa**	'herb'	(i), (ii)
b.	/idíNti/	idi**pí**ntʃi**pi**		'teeth'	(i) and (ii)
	/pɛ́sugu/	pɛ**pɛ́**sugu**pu**		'peach'	(i) and (ii)

---

11 Even though greater intensity may be a reflection of stress, it also generally correlates with higher pitch (cf. Zee 1978). On this matter, Odden (1999: 191) argued that "work on tone languages has noticed a correlation between tone and amplitude, with higher pitched vowels having a higher amplitude than analogous lower pitched vowels. (...) It is likely that (...) amplitude could be shown not to be a reliable phonetic diagnostic of stress versus tone."
12 The average increase is 5%, whereas in Brazilian Portuguese it is around 25% (calculated from the data from Seara (2000) in Cristófaro Silva et al. (2019: 123)), in Santomean Portuguese it is 32% and in Principense Portuguese it is 30% (calculated from the data in Balduino 2022).
13 When a sandhi process occurs between two H tones, the first vowel is deleted and a H tone remains (on the second mora if there are two), e. g. /upá úsuda/ → [(u)pǔ:suda]; [(u)púsuda] 'a type of pepper plant'. If the first vowel bears a H and the second is toneless, the first vowel is deleted and the H tone is then associated with another mora (the first if there are two), e. g. /upá ukjɛbu/ [upû:kyɛbu]; [upúkjɛbu] 'okra tree'.

c. /péɛtu/   pɛpéɛtu   'close'   (i)
   /paátu/   papaátu   'plate'   (i)
d. /mutaNbu/ mutambu**pu** 'trap'   (ii)
   /akara/   akara**pa**   'fried banana' (ii)

The examples in (5a) show each rule applied by itself, while (5b) shows both rules applied concomitantly. The examples in (5c) show evidence of synchronic weight-to-tone and culminativity in long vowels.[14] The examples in (5d) show that only rule (ii) can apply in all-Ø words. The fact that rule (ii) can apply to H words does not support the argument that all-Ø words have final prominence (i.e. "stress"), as claimed in previous works (Agostinho 2015, 2016; Maurer 2009: 27).[15]

Regarding all-Ø words, there are no consistent phonetic correlates of stress (such as higher pitch, greater intensity and longer duration), nor is there any phonological evidence for accented syllables (van der Hulst 2010, 9). Also, the final Ø syllable can undergo reduction in all-Ø words just as in words with a (non-final) H. There is no difference in syllable structure or segment inventory between initial, medial, or final syllables in all-Ø words, nor stronger vs. weaker realization of consonants and vowels other than final reduction.

If we consider Lung'Ie as a mixed system of tone and stress with the more usual "weight-to-stress" requirement, toneless words would also have to have a stressed syllable since every word must have a stress in a stress-accent system (recall (2a)). Of course, if every H syllable were claimed also to be stressed, we could maintain weight-to-stress accompanied by stress-to-tone, in other words, a system with weight-to-stress-to-tone. Since the tone needs to be marked underlyingly and "stress", if existing, would be predictable from tone, we propose to analyze the requirement simply as weight-to-tone.[16] In our analysis, Lung'Ie has a culminative /H/ tone system that just happens to care about weight. Since Portuguese stress is (at least to some extent) sensitive to weight and words with heavy syllables are 86% of Portuguese origin, the sensitivity to weight in Lung'Ie is not surprising. While the resulting privative tone system is reminiscent of Bantu privative H tone languages such as Kikongo and Kimbundu and the non-contrastive

---

14 If one alternatively analyzed the [LH] realization as disyllabic and the [HL] as the only H pattern on a long vowel, we would expect /pa.átu/ 'plate' to come out as *paapátu rather than the correct **papaátu** in (5c). Such an interpretation would still not account for the toneless and stressless content words within the system.

15 The argument for final stress in all-Ø words in Agostinho (2015, 2016) are the examples in (5d), since the examples in (5a) and (5b) in which rule (ii) applies had not been identified.

16 Odden (1999: 21) mentions that although "uncommon, weight-related tone attraction is also attested". See also Newman (1981).

verb system shows a similarity with Edoid languages, it is clear that the culminativity emerged because of Portuguese.

On the other hand, the reason why the non-obligatoriness is linked to the African origin vocabulary remains unknown. We can speculate that earlier speakers of PGG might have had a different system for such words, e.g. a fully specified tone system, that was later generalized as all-Ø with the development of a culminative constraint on tone assignment. Another hypothesis is that the all-Ø words are a sort of clash resolution between the different prosodic systems of the Edoid and Bantu strata.[17] Applying McWhorter (2011: 104), Lung'Ie culminativity-without-obligatoriness and weight-to-tone may represent "a compromise between tonal systems spoken natively by its creators and the stress-based ones of the lexifier language".

3.2 Central African French

The second case study is Central African French (CAF), a variety of French spoken in the Central African Republic (CAR), which Bordal (2013, 2015) and Steien and Yakpo (2020) analyze as a "tone language" with a /H/ vs. /L/ contrast. Their analysis is based on spontaneous speech by speakers from Bangui, the capital of CAR.

The presence of CAF in the CAR is linked to the European invasion and French colonial period that began in the late 19th century. CAF is in close contact with Sango [sag], an Ngbandi-lexifier creole widely spoken in the CAR as a *lingua franca* that contrasts H, M and L tones (Samarin 2012). According to Samarin (2012: 13), Sango emerged during the last decades of the 19th century in Bangui. During the colonial times, French was spoken only by a small portion of CAR population as the language of daily communication and it remains spoken by fewer people than autochthonous languages today (Steien and Yakpo 2020: 7, 8). Currently, French is transmitted by people who acquired it locally and are not speakers of the European varieties (Steien and Yakpo 2020: 8). Both Sango and French are official languages of the CAR, but CAF is the language of education, formal settings, and media (Samarin 2012). Bordal (2013, 2015) argues that the tonal system of CAF is influenced by the phonological tone system of Sango to a great extent.

The prosodic system of CAF is quite simple, the general rule being that every word receives a H tone on its final syllable. The examples in (6) show the tone patterns for content and function words. Content words are analyzed with an obligatory and culminative final H, while monosyllabic function "words" contrast a H

---

[17] Similarly, McWhorter (2018: 23) argues that "the differences in tonal systems tend to cancel tone out", although this may not always be the case (cf. Downing 2017).

vs. L pattern on the surface. The fact that these grammatical morphemes contrast surface [H] and [L] is what makes the authors analyze CAF as fitting the criteria in (1), hence with underlying /H/ vs. /L/.[18]

(6) CAF patterns in Steien and Yakpo (2020: 15)

Syntactic Categories	Tone patterns		Examples
Content words	1	/(L)H/ monosyllables polysyllables	*père* /H/ 'father', *peux* /H/ '(I) can' *sentir* /LH/ 'feel' *phénomène* /LLH/ 'phenomenon' *instituteur* /LLLH/ 'teacher'
Function words	2	/L/ monosyllables	*je* /L/ '1SG.SBJ', *le* /L/ 'DEF.SG.M'
	3	/H/ monosyllables	*tu* /H/ '2SG.SBJ', *mon* /H/ '1SG.POSS.M'
	1	/(L)H/ polysyllables	*devant* /LH/ 'in front of', *après* /LH/ 'after'

As seen in (6), CAF differs from Standard European French (SEF) in three critical ways. First, while SEF assigns pitch within the larger "accentual phrase" (Jun and Fougeron 2000, 2002), CAF assigns a H tone to the last syllable of every word. Second, CAF (apparently) has only this one word-level pitch assignment vs. SEF which assigns more than one intonational pitch accent (Steien and Yakpo 2020: 9, 28 citing Jun and Fougeron 2000, 2002 and Delais-Roussarie et al. 2015). Third, like other "intonation-only" systems, SEF interpolates pitch between pitch-accents, while non-H syllables are produced with a relatively uniform L pitch in CAF (Steien and Yakpo 2020: 15).[19] This latter fact means that iterating sequences of a L function word + L-H lexical word, i.e. L-L-H-L-L-H, will sound like the alternating L and H tones of an unambiguous /L, H/ system where both tones are clearly activated and participate in phonological processes. If the Hs were phrase-level pitch accents and the Ls were underlyingly unspecified as in SEF, we would expect the pitches of latter to be interpolated on the basis of the /H/ tones.

---

18 Steien and Yakpo propose a similar analysis for Equatorial Guinean Spanish in which content words have /(L)H(L)/ patterns, i.e., culminative and obligatory H, aligned to the stressed syllable of Standard Spanish. Unlike CAF, the placement of the H is unpredictable. Function words can additionally be /((L)L)L/.

19 They state that "[s]yllables without H tones, we argue, are associated with L tones rather than being toneless. CAF utterances give an undulating and pulsating auditory impression that stands in stark contrast to the gradual pitch transitions of SEF intonational tunes. This is caused by abrupt transitions between adjacent H and L tones. If all or some of the syllables between two H tones were toneless rather than L-toned, we would expect interpolation, a gradual fall after a H over the span of several syllables before the next H".

While these three differences at first suggest a tonal interpretation of CAF, each of these properties is attested in a stress language. First, unlike most stress languages, Cairene Arabic (Hellmuth 2005: 108) and Santomean Portuguese (Braga and Fernandes-Svartman 2019: 29), spoken in the Island of São Tomé (in contact with Santome and Angolar), assign an intonational pitch-accent associated with the stress of every phonological word of an intonational contour. Second, concerning intonational melodies, some stress languages have relatively little intonational variation in terms of pitch-accents, such as Unangan, an Eastern Aleut language (Gussenhoven 2007: 254 citing Taff 1999) and Finnish (Arhold 2014), while some tone languages have lots of it, like Hausa (Inkelas and Leben 1990). Concerning the third difference, the relatively stable L pitches are a phonetic fact, arguably not necessarily due to an underlying /H/ vs. /L/ contrast, rather to phonetic implementation. In other words, the underlying system could have been set up as privative /H/ vs. Ø or, as we shall now show, without any indication of tone at all.

As mentioned, unlike SEF, every lexical word in CAF receives a H on its final syllable, e.g. **sentír** 'to feel', **phenoméne** 'phenomenon'. The one complication is that there are contrasts between [H] and [L] functional elements, e.g. L tone **je** '1SG.SBJ', **le** 'DEF.SG.M' vs. H tone **úne** 'INDF.SG.F', **tú** '2SG.SBJ'. There even are minimal pairs, as seen in (7).

(7) CAF tonal minimal pairs in Steien and Yakpo (2020: 16)

Word	Tone	Gloss	Word	Tone	Gloss
ce	H	'this/that'(ADJ)	ce	L	'it/that'(PRON)
nous	H	'1PL.SBJ'	nous	L	'1PL.OBJ'
vous	H	'2PL.SBJ'	vous	L	'2PL.OBJ'
ils	H	'3PL.SBJ.M'	il	L	'3SG.SBJ.M'
elles	H	'3PL.SBJ.F'	elle	L	'3SG.SBJ.F'

On the basis of this surface contrast, Steien and Yakpo assume that CAF meets the Welmers-Hyman definition of tone in (1), which they cite (2020: 5). However, if the L functional morphemes are analyzed as proclitics, as Hualde (2009) proposes for unstressed function words in Spanish, then /L/ would not be needed.[20] Instead, a single final /H/ would predictably occur on the last syllable of every word (with possible proclitic), and no underlying indication of pitch would be needed at all.

---

[20] The same can be argued for Equatorial Guinean Spanish. Diverging from CAF, Steien and Yakpo hold that Equatorial Guinean Spanish has a H-tone spreading rule, but this could also be a result of spilling over in the phonetic implementation (2020: 18).

We show this in (8), where we have manufactured the examples, extrapolating from Steien and Yakpo's description:

(8) Competing analyses of Central African French

	Steien & Yakpo	**Our analysis**	*Gloss*
a.	íls párlent H H	ils parlent → íls párlent H H	'they speak'
b.	ìl párle L H	il=parle → il=párle H	'he speaks'

As seen, Steien and Yakpo begin with underlying /H/ and /L/ identical to their realization in the (broad) phonetic outputs [íl párl] 'they speak' and [ìl párl] 'he speaks'. In our analysis the output Hs and Ls are totally predictable: Assign a H to the last syllable of a prosodic word, which maximally consists of a proclitic + lexical word. As further evidence of our analysis, we note that all of the object pronouns are proclitics (see (9) below). Since these occur closer to the verb (**íls me párlent** 'they (m.) speak to me' etc.), this is as expected: all of the function words that receive an output H tone are independent prosodic words which stand outside those that we analyze as proclitics, e.g. **je**, **il** and **elle**.[21]

(9) CAF personal pronouns in Steien and Yakpo (2020: 28)

	Subject (L- or H-toned)	*Object (L-toned)*	*Emphatic (H-toned)*
1SG	je /L/	me	moi
2SG	tu /H/	te	toi
3SG	il, elle /L/; on /H/	le, la, lui	lui, elle
1PL	nous /H/; on /H/	nous	nous
2PL	vous /H/	vous	vous
3PL	ils, elles /H/	les, lur	eux

---

[21] Re our proposal to divide the functional morphemes into words and proclitics, Kofi Yakpo (pers.comm.) expressed concern that the whole paradigm of, say, subject pronouns, are not clitics, as might be expected from their syntactic function. However, our definition of clitic is the traditional phonological one: a phrasal element that "leans" prosodically on a host. While we have to stipulate that it is only **je**= '1sg', **il**= '3sg.m' and **elle**= '3sg.f' that are subject proclitics on the verb, it is interesting to us that they are all singular, **je**= has a schwa vowel, and **il**= and **elle**= contrast with the plural subject pronouns **ils** '3pl.m.' and **elles** '3pl.f.'. That a marked category such as plurality would be more likely to be accented or, as we see here, be independent words, is reminiscent of the contrast in Guyanese and certain other English-lexifier creoles between the affirmative L pitch modal **kyan** 'can' vs. the corresponding H tone negative **kyáan** 'cannot' (Devonish 1989b: 90, 127). This produces contrasts such as **mi kyan gó** 'I can go' vs. **mi kyáan gó** 'I can't go' (Devonish 1989a).

In this view, the system would be closer to a fixed stress-accent system with the H tone taking the place of demarcative word-final stress. The fact that speakers of tone languages are more sensitive to pitch alternations than other phonetic cues is not at all surprising. It is in fact not the underlying system, but the output of discrete omnisyllabic Hs and Ls that makes CAF "feel" like tone.

4 Conclusion

In the preceding sections we have seen two different results when different word-prosodic systems meet in Afro-European contact. As seen, the result in our first case study was the "conversion" of the word-obligatoriness of the Portuguese stress system and African tone systems into a word-culminative (but not obligatory) /H/ in Lung'Ie. The Lung'Ie system thus meets the definition for tone in (1), but not the obligatoriness stress requirement in (2b). In our second case study, we saw that the phrasal assignment of pitch-accents in SEF has been "narrowed" to a single word-final /H/ that is totally predictable in CAF. Although Steien and Yakpo (2020) consider CAF to have a tone system, in our reanalysis the predictable one-H-per-word fails to meet the definition of tone in (1), but does meet the criteria for stress-accent in (2). In other words, Lung'Ie has gone from the contact of stress and tone to tone,[22] while CAF has established a word-accentual system, where the obligatory "accent" is realized as a H tone.

Of course, the above conclusions are based to a large extent on interpretation. While we have only found evidence for a culminative /H/ tone in Lung'Ie, there is nothing stopping other researchers from claiming that syllables with /H/ are also stressed, and that toneless words also have a stress on some syllable – but how can we tell which? At the same time, Steien and Yakpo's analysis with marginally contrastive input /H/ and /L/ would require us to say that CAF has a tone system which also meets the criteria for stress-accent. Whether to call a culminative or obligatory H tone a "(pitch-)accent" would hopefully not simply be a matter of taste. The issue seems to rest on two problems.

First, we know that there are systems that do not easily fall into one box vs. another, where the boxes are defined by "canonical" properties and prototypes (Hyman 2015). The most unambiguous two-height tone system is one where /H/

---

[22] If we look at it this issue from a superstratist perspective, we can consider Lung'Ie a case of tonogenesis by contact and phonological changes (i.e. the loss of Portuguese liquids). However, in a substratist view, we would have a simplification of the Niger Delta languages tone system and the introduction of culminativity and weight sensitivity from Portuguese.

and /L/ contrast on every syllable, such that a bisyllabic word would distinguish the four patterns: H-H, H-L, L-H, L-L, and a trisyllabic word would distinguish eight (etc.). The most unambiguous stress-accent system is one where there is a single most prominent syllable per word that is detectable from more than one phonetic and phonological property. Both of these "prototypes" predetermine our exceptions in two ways. One is that the study of prosodic systems has long been plagued by a bias of European language speakers to expect, seek, and hear word-stress when analyzing a non-European language (Ladd 2017). Thus, the potential of "stress ghosting" occurs when speakers of a language with stress misread stress into a language that does not have stress (Tabain, Fletcher, and Butcher 2014). This includes attributing stress to syllables with H tone, as claimed for Lung'Ie in previous work (Agostinho 2015, 2016; Maurer 2009: 27). Yet, according to Ladd (2017: 1), "there is increasing recognition that stress may not be a useful concept in describing many non-European languages".

In addition to the tendency to identify sparse H tones with accent, a similar stress-ghosting can occur with words that are analyzed as all-L or all-Ø. In many unambiguous tone systems, all L tone sequences tend to lower in pitch, hence starting higher and ending lower, typically with a quite noticeable prepausal fall. These phonetic pitch realizations can be responsible for stress-ghosting, where the first or last L is claimed to be stressed. In Lung'Ie, all-Ø words can be realized as a level [L] throughout or show declination or final lowering, which may contribute to the "ghosting" of final "stress".

The second preconception concerns our awareness and expectations concerning "tone". In this case we wonder if there isn't a more recent tendency to overcompensate with "tone ghosting", a temptation to interpret as tonal word-prosodic systems that assign predictable pitches differently from what we are used to in canonical stress-accent systems. Having had some exposure to the French spoken in Francophone Africa, the crucial difference between it and SEF may not only be the domain within which the Hs are assigned (word-finally in CAF, accentual-phrase-finally in SEF). A second difference reported by Steien and Yakpo is that non-H syllables are assigned L output pitch targets in CAF rather than gradually interpolating their pitch from the Hs. Certainly languages differ in this way, and the fixed L targets are attributable to the fact that CAF speakers also speak tone languages. However, even if this makes CAF "feel like tone", this shouldn't change the basic PHONOLOGICAL typology, which must be based on well-defined criteria such as those in (1) and (2).

Another potential issue mentioned by Agostinho and Hyman (2021) is that not all descriptions and analyses of word-prosody systems of pidgins, creoles and other contact languages include African origin words and that the "unexpected" systems are precisely the ones that take the African input into account. In creoles, there might be a correlation between origin and prosodic pattern (Agostinho 2022), as seen in Lung'Ie (Agostinho and Hyman 2021), Nigerian Pidgin English (Faraclas 1984), Saramaccan (Good 2004), and Yakpo's original analysis of Pichi (2009). Likewise, how loanwords from tone languages are adapted by bilingual and monolingual speakers of contact varieties like CAF should equally be taken into account when describing such systems.[23]

As we pointed out in our introduction, in contact studies it is quite common to have more than one interpretation of word-prosodic systems. This is particularly common in creoles, such as Papiamentu, Kabuverdianu, Kriyol/Guineense, Palenquero, Saramaccan, Sranan, Nigerian Pidgin English, Pichi, Lung'Ie and even CAF! However, we need to extrapolate away from the limitations and biases we have as scholars, whether these tempt us into stress ghosting or tone ghosting – and also recognize that not all languages fit neatly into boxes. After all, the goal is to typologize prosodic systems, not linguists (Hyman 2006: 230).

References

Agostinho, Ana Lívia. 2015. *Fonologia e método pedagógico do lung'Ie*. São Paulo: Universidade de São Paulo. Doctoral thesis.
Agostinho, Ana Lívia. 2016. *Fonologia do lung'Ie*. Munich: LINCOM.
Agostinho, Ana Lívia. 2022. Word prosody of African vs. European-origin words in Afro-European creoles. To appear in *Linguistic Typology*.
Agostinho, Ana Lívia & Gabriel Antunes de Araujo. 2021. Playing with language: Three language games in the Gulf of Guinea. *Language Documentation & Conservation* 15. 219–238.
Agostinho, Ana Lívia, Gabriel Antunes de Araujo & Eduardo Ferreira dos Santos. 2019. Interrogative particle and phrasal pitch-accent in polar questions in Fa d'Ambô. *Boletim do Museu Paraense Emílio Goeldi Ciências Humanas* 14(3). 1–16.
Agostinho, Ana Lívia & Larry M. Hyman. 2021. Word prosody in Lung'Ie: One system or two? *Probus* 33(1). 57–93.
Arhold, Anja. 2014. Finnish prosody: Studies in intonation and phrasing. Frankfurt: Johann Wolfgang Goethe-Universität. Doctoral dissertation.
Balduino, Amanda Macedo. 2022. "Fonologia do português de São Tomé e Príncipe." São Paulo: Universidade de São Paulo. Doctoral thesis.
Bandeira, Manuele. 2017. *Reconstrução fonológica e lexical do protocrioulo do Golfo da Guiné*. São Paulo: Universidade de São Paulo. Doctoral thesis.
Becker, Michael, Bruna Franchetto, Arawa Didi Kuikuro, Yanapa Mehinaku Kuikuro & Andrija Petrovic. 2020. "The incoherent stress of Kuikuro." *Talk at the Annual Meeting on Phonology*. University of California, Santa Cruz.

---

[23] According to Kang (2010: 2308) "the closer the contact between the two languages, the greater the possibility of the preservation of input suprasegmental prominence".

Bennett, Ryan & Robert Henderson. 2013. Accent in Uspanteko. *Natural Language & Linguistic Theory* 31(3). 589–645.
Bordal, Guri. 2013. Le français Centrafricain: Un français à tons lexicaux. *Revue française de linguistique appliquée* 18(2). 91–102.
Bordal, Guri. 2015. Traces of the lexical tone system of Sango in Central African French. In E. Delais-Roussarie, M. Avanzi & S. Herment (eds.), *Prosody and Language in Contact*, 29–49. (Prosody, Phonology and Phonetics). Berlin/Heidelberg: Springer.
Braga, Gabriela & Flaviane Romani Fernandes-Svartman. 2019. Associação de eventos tonais em português de São Tomé. *Diacrítica* 33. 19–40.
Bybee, Joan, Paromita Chakraborti, Dagmar Jung & Joanne Scheibman. 1998. Prosody and segmental effect: Some paths of evolution for word stress. *Studies in Language* 22. 267–314.
Caldeira, Arlindo Manuel. 2008. Tráfico de escravos e conflitualidade. O arquipélago de São Tomé e Príncipe e o Reino do Congo durante o século XVI. *Revista Ciências e Letras* 44. 55–76.
Caldeira, Arlindo Manuel. 2013. *Escravos e traficantes no império português*. Lisboa: Esfera do Livro.
Cristófaro Silva, Thaís, Izabel Seara, Adelaide Silva, Andréia Rauber & Maria Cantoni. 2019. *Fonética acústica: Os sons do português brasileiro*. São Paulo: Contexto.
Devonish, Hubert. 1989a. On the reinterpretation of stress as tone in Afro-European creole languages. *Talk at Phonology Workshop*.
Devonish, Hubert. 1989b. *Talking in Tones: A Study of Tone in Afro-European Creole Languages*. Barbados: Caribbean Academic Publications.
Downing, Laura J. 2017. Convergence of prosody under contact: Two African case studies. In Andrea Castro, Anton Granvik, Ester Fernández Incógnito, Sara Lindbladh, Andrea Romeborn & Katharina Vajta (eds.), *Språkens Magi: Festskrift for Ingmar Söhrman*, 29–40. Göteborg: Göteborgs Universitet, Institutionen för Språk och Litterarturer.
Faraclas, Nicholas. 1984. Rivers Pidgin English: Tone, stress, or pitch-accent language? *Studies in the Linguistic Sciences* 14(2). 67–76.
Ferraz, Luiz. 1979. *The Creole of São Tomé*. Johannesburg: Witwatersrand University Press.
Goedemans, Rob & Harry van der Hulst. 2009. StressTyp: A database for word accentual patterns in the world's languages. In Martin Everaert & Simon Musgrave (eds.), *The Use of Databases in Cross-Linguistics Research*, 235–282. New York/Berlin: Mouton de Gruyter.
Good, Jeff. 2004. Tone and accent in Saramaccan: Charting a deep split in the phonology of a language. *Lingua* 114(5). 575–619.
Günther, Wilfried. 1973. *Das portugiesische Kreolisch der Ilha do Príncipe*. Marburg an der Lahn: Im Selbstverlag.
Gussenhoven, Carlos. 2006. Between stress and tone in Nubi word prosody. *Phonology* 23(2). 193–223.
Gussenhoven, Carlos. 2007. Intonation. In Paul de Lacy (ed.), *The Cambridge Handbook of Phonology*, 253–280. Cambridge: Cambridge University Press.
Hagemeijer, Tjerk. 2011. The Gulf of Guinea creoles: Genetic and typological relations. *Journal of Pidgin and Creole Languages* 26(1). 111–154.
Hellmuth, Sam. 2005. No deaccenting in (or of) phrases: Evidence from Arabic for cross-linguistic and cross-dialectal prosodic variation. In Sónia Frota, Marina Vigário & Maria João Freitas (eds.), *Prosodies: With Special Reference to Iberian Languages*, 99–121. Berlin: Mouton de Gruyter.

Hualde, José Ignacio. 2009. Unstressed words in Spanish. *Language Sciences* 31(2–3). 199–212.
Hulst, Harry van der. 2010. Word accent: Terms, typologies and theories. In Harry van der Hulst, Rob Goedemans & Ellen van Zanten (eds.), *A Survey of Word Accentual Patterns in the Languages of the World*, 3–53. Berlin/New York: Mouton De Gruyter.
Hyman, Larry M. 2006. Word-prosodic typology. *Phonology* 23(2). 225–257.
Hyman, Larry M. 2009. How (not) to do phonological typology: The case of pitch-accent. *Language Sciences* 31. 213–238.
Hyman, Larry M. 2011. Tone: Is it different? In John Goldsmith, Jason Riggle & Alan C. L. Yu (eds.), *The Handbook of Phonological Theory*, 483–528. Malden: Wiley-Blackwell.
Hyman, Larry M. 2015. Towards a canonical typology of prosodic systems. In *Tono, accento y estructuras métricas en lenguas Mexicanas*, 13–38. Mexico City: El Colegio de México.
Hyman, Larry M. & Niko Kobepa. 2013. On the analysis of tone in Mee (Ekari, Ekagi, Kapauku). *Oceanic Linguistics* 52(2). 307–317.
Inkelas, Sharon & William R. Leben. 1990. Where phonology and phonetics intersect: The case of Hausa intonation. In G. N. Clements, John Kingston & Mary Beckman (eds.), *Papers in Laboratory Phonology*, vol. 1: *Between the Grammar and Physics of Speech*, 14–34. Cambridge: Cambridge University Press.
Jun, Sun-Ah & Cécile Fougeron. 2000. A phonological model of French intonation. In A. Botinis (ed.), *Intonation*. (Text, Speech and Language Technology 15), 209–242. Dordrecht: Springer.
Jun, Sun-Ah & Cécile Fougeron. 2002. Realizations of accentual phrase in French intonation. *Probus* 14(1). 147–172.
Kang, Yoonjung. 2010. Tutorial overview: Suprasegmental adaptation in loanwords. *Lingua* 120(9). 2295–2310. DOI: http://dx.doi.org/10.1016/j.lingua.2010.02.015.
Kenstowicz, Michael. 1994. *Phonology in Generative Grammar*. Oxford: Blackwell.
Kubozono, Haruo. 2008. Japanese accent. In Shigeru Miyagawa & Mamoru Saito (eds.), *Handbook of Japanese Linguistics*, 165–191. Oxford: Oxford University Press.
Ladd, D. Robert. 2017. Practical introduction to stress, accent and tone: Course materials – Part two. 23rd ABRALIN Summer Institute, UFF Niterói, March 2017.
Ladhams, John. 2012. Article agglutination and the African contribution to the Portuguese-based creoles. In Angela Bartens & Philip Baker (eds.), *Black through White*, 31–50. London: Battlebridge.
Maurer, Philippe. 2009. *Principense (Lung'Ie)*. London: Battlebridge.
McWhorter, John H. 2011. Tying up loose ends: The creole prototype after all. *Diachronica* 28(1). 82–117.
McWhorter, John H. 2018. *The Creole Debate*. Cambridge: Cambridge University Press.
Michael, Lev. 2011. The interaction of tone and stress in the prosodic system of Iquito (Zaparoan). *Amerindia* 35. 53–74.
Newman, Paul. 1981. Syllable weight and tone. *Linguistic Inquiry* 12(4). 670–673.
Odden, David. 1999. Typological issues in tone and stress in Bantu. In Shegeki Kaji (ed.), *Cross-Linguistic Studies of Tonal Phenomena: Tonogenesis, Typology, and Related Topics*, 187–215. Tokyo: ILCAA.
Riad, Tomas. 2018. The phonological typology of north Germanic accent. In Larry M. Hyman & Frans Plank (eds.), *Phonological Typology*, 341–388. Berlin/Boston: De Gruyter Mouton.

Samarin, William J. 2012. Sango. In Susanne Maria Michaelis, Philippe Maurer, Martin Haspelmath & Magnus Huber (eds.), *The Survey of Pidgin and Creole Languages*, 13–24. Oxford: Oxford University Press.

Schadeberg, Thilo C. 1986. Tone cases in Umbundu. *Africana Linguistica* 10(1). 423–447.

Schadeberg, Thilo C. 2000. The tonal system of Ekoti nouns. In Rainer Vossen, Angelika Mietzner & Antje Meissner (eds.), *Mehr Als Nur Worte*, 597–612. Cologne: Rüdiger Köppe Verlag.

Seibert, Gerhard. 2013. São Tomé and Príncipe: The first plantation economy in the tropics. In Robin Law, Suzanne Schwarz & Silke Strickrodt (eds.), *Commercial Agriculture, the Slave Trade and Slavery in Atlantic Africa*, 54–78. Woodbridge, Suffolk: Boydell & Brewer.

Seibert, Gerhard. 2014. Crioulização em Cabo Verde e São Tomé e Príncipe: Divergências históricas e identitárias. *Afro-Ásia* 49. 41–70.

Steien, Guri Bordal & Kofi Yakpo. 2020. Romancing with tone: On the outcomes of prosodic contact. *Language* 96(1). 1–41.

Tabain, Marija, Janet Fletcher & Andrew Butcher. 2014. Lexical stress in Pitjantjatjara. *Journal of Phonetics* 42(1). 52–66.

Taff, Alice. 1999. Phonetics and phonology of phonetics and phonology of Unangan (Eastern Aleut) intonation. Seattle: University of Washington Dissertation.

Traill, Anthony & Luiz Ferraz. 1981. The interpretation of tone in Principense creole. *Studies in African Linguistics* 12(2). 205–215.

Welmers, William E. 1959. Tonemics, morphotonemics, and tonal morphemes. *General Linguistics* 4. 1–9.

Welmers, William E. 1973. *African Language Structures*. Berkeley, CA: University of California Press.

Yakpo, Kofi. 2009. *A Grammar of Pichi*. Berlin/Accra: Isimu Media.

Yakpo, Kofi. 2019. *A Grammar of Pichi*. Berlin: Language Science Press.

Zee, Eric. 1978. Duration and intensity as correlates of F0. *Journal of Phonetics* 6(3). 213–220.

Matthew Gordon
The Phonetic Basis for Tone-Stress Interactions: A Cross-Linguistic Study

Abstract: Cross-linguistic research over the last half century has demonstrated a number of phonological dimensions that are relevant in predicting stress. One property that interacts with stress is lexical tone, which, in some languages, is positionally constrained by stress, but, in other languages, influences the location of stress. This paper explores the latter type of relationship involving tone-driven stress. Evidence is presented that intrinsic phonetic features of tone, both acoustic and perceptual, offer an explanation for the propensity for high tone to attract stress in many languages. Results of a cross-linguistic acoustic study of tone show that vowels associated with a high tone have intrinsically greater intensity and often greater duration than low-toned vowels. These findings are consistent with the hypothesis that tone-driven stress has the same phonetic underpinnings as the better studied phenomenon of weight-sensitive stress.

Keywords: stress, tone, tone-driven stress, intensity, duration

1 Introduction

The study of stress has been a productive area of research from both a theoretical and typological perspective for over a half century. Cross-linguistic research has demonstrated a number of dimensions along which stress systems may vary, including the degree of predictability, the location of stress, the presence of secondary stress, the role of syllable weight in conditioning stress, and the relationship between stress and other prosodic and morphosyntactic properties (see Gordon and van der Hulst 2020 for a recent survey). One property that has been increasingly shown to interact with stress is lexical tone, which, in some languages, is positionally constrained by stress, but, in other languages, influences the location of stress.

This paper explores the latter type of relationship, presenting evidence that intrinsic phonetic features of tone, both acoustic and perceptual, account for recur-

---

Note: The author gratefully acknowledges the helpful comments of Bert Remijsen and Alex Vaxman on an earlier draft of this paper.

Matthew Gordon, UC Santa Barbara

https://doi.org/10.1515/9783110730081-009

ring typological patterns in tone-driven stress systems. The structure of the paper is as follows. Section 2 provides an overview of the typology of associations between phonological stress and lexical tone. Section 3 summarizes formal treatments of tone-driven stress, while Sections 4 and 5 examine the acoustic and phonological correlates of stress, respectively, in tone languages. Section 6 introduces the hypothesis that tone-driven stress is attributed to intrinsic phonetic features of tone and Section 7 tests this hypothesis against acoustic data from several languages. Section 8 discusses the results of the acoustic study and perceptual factors in the context of the interpretation of tone-driven stress, while Section 9 concludes the paper.

2 The Relationship between Stress and Tone

The expanding database on tone-stress relationships has revealed different types of relationships between tone and stress, although comprehensive examination of the interaction between stress and tone within the same language is relatively sparse. There are three types of associations that are observed typologically: orthogonal tone and stress (Section 2.1), stress systems sensitive to tone (Section 2.2), and tone systems governed by stress (Section 2.3). In other languages, the nature of the relationship between stress and tone is less clear (Section 2.4). Across languages, typological surveys suggest an affinity between higher tones and stress (Section 2.5).

2.1 Orthogonal Tone and Stress

One possibility is for languages to possess orthogonal tone and stress systems, as in Pirahã (Everett and Everett 1984; Everett 1986, 1988), in which there is a contrast between high and low tone while stress is a function of syllable weight. Stress falls on the rightmost syllable that is heaviest according to the weight hierarchy KVV > GVV > VV > KV > GV (where K is a voiceless consonant, G a voiced consonant, and VV is a long vowel or diphthong) within a three-syllable window at the right edge of a word (1). Note that low tone is unmarked and high tone is marked with an acute accent; in the case of diphthongs, tone contrasts in its location on the first or the second element of the diphthong.

(1) Pirahã stress
KVV > GVV: 'hoa.gái 'come', 'kaa.gaí 'word', 'kai.baí 'monkey'
GVV > VV: poː.'gáí.hi.aí 'banana', ho.aː.'gai 'type of fruit', 'gao.i: 'proper name'
VV > KV: pia.hao.gi.so.'ai.pi 'cooking banana', ho.'aí.pi 'type of fish', pí.'ai 'also'

KV > GV: ˈʔa.ba.gi 'toucan', ti.ˈpo.gi 'bird species', ˈʔí.bo.gi 'milk'
Rightmost in case of tie: paó.hoa.ˈhai 'anaconda', bai.tói.ˈsái 'wildcat'

As comparison of the initial syllable in forms like pí.ˈai 'also' and ˈʔí.bo.gi 'milk' show, it is possible for high tone to either be stressed or unstressed. Conversely, low tone may either co-occur with stress, as in the first syllable of ˈhoa.gái 'come', or may not, as in the final syllable of ˈgao.ii 'proper name'.

2.2 Tone-Driven Stress

In other languages, tone and stress exhibit a dependency that falls into one of two broad categories explored by De Lacy (2002). In one set of languages instantiating "tone-driven stress" in De Lacy's (2002) terms, stress is predictable from tone. In these languages, certain tones preferentially attract stress over other tones. For example, stress in Golin (Bunn and Bunn 1970) falls on the rightmost high-toned syllable, otherwise on the rightmost syllable (2).

(2) Stress in Golin (Bunn and Bunn 1970: 5)
Stress on rightmost high tone
ˈHLL   ˈákòlà   'wild fig tree'
LˈHL   gòˈmágì   'type of sweet potato'
HˈHL   síˈbágì   'sweet potato type'
LHˈH   ògáˈlá   'woven hat'
HLˈH   éndèˈrín   'fire'
HHˈH   ówáˈré   'bat'

Otherwise, stress on rightmost syllable
LLˈL   kàwlìˈgì   'post'

2.3 Stress-Driven Tone

In other languages, those with "stress-driven tone", tonal contrasts are restricted to metrically strong syllables, a pattern found in Swedish (Riad 2014), Curaçao Papiamentu (Remijsen and van Heuven 2005), and Lamba (Bickmore 1995). For example, in Curaçao Papiamentu, lexical tone contrasts, analyzed by Remijsen and van Heuven (2005) as a distinction between a HL sequence vs. a lack of tone, are limited to stressed (penultimate) syllables and distinguish verbs from non-verbs (3). Stress is contrastive and can also fall on the final syllable, but there are no tone contrasts in this position.

(3) Tone in Curaçao Papiamentu (Remijsen and van Heuven 2005: 210)
ˈlora 'parrot' ˈlôra 'to turn'
ˈbaba 'dribble (noun)' ˈbâba 'to dribble'
ˈsala 'living room' ˈsâla 'to salt'

2.4 Ambiguous Tone-Stress Relationships

In many languages, the directionality of the relationship between stress and tone is ambiguous and hinges on one's assumptions about the definitional characteristics distinguishing stress and tone. This indeterminacy is particularly evident in languages, such as Lithuanian (Dogil 1999; Blevins 1993) and Nubi (Gussenhoven 2006), that possess a binary distinction between high and low tone in which one of the tones, typically the high one, occurs once and only once per word. This distribution, often falling under the heading of "pitch accent" (see van der Hulst 2011), displays two characteristics that are hallmarks of stress systems: obligatoriness, the requirement that every word have a stress, and culminativity, the constraint that every word has one prominence that is stronger than others. The ambiguity surrounding the relationship between tone and stress in certain languages reflects a more general uncertainty about the empirical grounding of the taxonomy of tone-stress interactions (see Hyman 2006 and Agostinho and Hyman this volume for discussion).

2.5 Statistical Distribution of Tone-Stress Interactions

Although lexical tone is widespread in languages of the world, estimated by Yip (2002) to occur in 60–70% of the world's languages, it rarely co-occurs with stress in the same language. Of the 75 languages in Gordon and Roettger's (2017) survey of stress correlates, only 13 possess lexical tone. Of these, the majority (eight) employ only a simple tone system (Maddieson 2013) involving a binary contrast either between high or low tone or between a single marked tone and lack of tone, as in Curaçao Papiamentu. The remaining five surveyed languages possess more than a binary tone contrast.

Although the nature of the interaction between tone and stress varies across languages, there are certain recurring patterns characterizing their relationship. One of these is the affinity between high tonal targets and stress. This mutual attraction is bidirectional. In certain languages, tones containing a high target, either a level high tone, as in Goizueta Basque (Hualde, Lujanbio, and Torreira 2008), or a bitonal sequence containing a high element, as in Curaçao Papiamentu (Remijsen and van Heuven 2005), are restricted to stress syllables. In other languages, high tones preferentially attract stress over other tones, as in Golin (Bunn and Bunn 1970) and Fore (Nicholson and Nicholson 1962). In still others, e.g. Lithuanian (Dogil 1999; Blevins 1993), the directionality of the relationship is ambiguous. Further evidence for the link between high tone and stress comes from language contact situations in which stress from one language is borrowed as a high tone in a borrowing language with lexical tone (see Agostinho and Hyman this volume).

The mutual attraction of high tone and stress is typologically robust although the sample on which this generalization is based is relatively small. In Gordon's (1999/2006) genetically-balanced survey of approximately 400 languages, stress location is at least partially a function of tone in nine languages, in all of which high-toned syllable preferentially receive stress over other tones (2006: 20). De Lacy (2002) discusses several additional languages in which either high tones attract stress or stress attracts high tone. I am aware of one language, Minto Tanana (Tuttle 1998), in which low tone attracts stress, an exception which is plausibly attributed to the fact that the only phonologically active tone is low.

The surveys in Gordon (1999/2006) and De Lacy (2002) reveal some additional nuances in the relationship between high tone and stress. First, in certain languages, high tone can be a secondary attractor of stress in addition to syllable weight. For example, in the variety of Tibetan described by Meredith (1990), stress in nouns falls on the most prominent of the first two syllables where prominence is a function primarily of the structure of the syllable rime and secondarily of a syllable's tone. A heavy syllable (CVV, CVC) attracts stress over a light syllable regardless of tone but in words with two light (CV) syllables, high tone triumphs over low tone.

Second, the small set of languages with both stress and more than a binary tone distinction displays a more finely grained relationship between stress and tone whereby a mid tone attracts stress over a low tone, as in Bobo (Le Bris and Prost 1981) and Ayutla Mixtec (Pankratz and Pike 1967).

Finally, in certain Mixtec languages (but not to the best of my knowledge in languages outside this family), the syllable immediately following a high tone is reported to impact stress placement. For example, in Ayutla Mixtec (Pankratz and Pike 1967), a high tone before a low tone in the immediately following syllable preferentially attracts stress over a high tone not followed by a low tone.

3 Formal Treatment of Tone-Stress Relationships

Various analyses of interactions between stress and tone have been proposed in the literature. The more challenging cases are those involving tone-driven stress, where certain tones, notably those associated with a high target, display a propensity to attract stress much like heavy syllables attract stress in quantity-sensitive stress systems.

Hayes (1995) seizes upon the parallel between syllable weight and high tone by proposing a separate prominence grid projected, in the case of tone-driven stress, by tone level: more prominent tones are associated with more grid marks than less prominent tones. Stress docks on the syllable with the greater number of grid marks, where ties are resolved by the parametric application of the End Rule. For example, in the Golin (Bunn and Bunn 1970) case considered earlier, low tones are associated with grid marks (represented as *) on only the lowest prominence tier while high tones also carry a grid mark on a higher tier. Stress (represented as x) docks on the rightmost syllable with two grid marks and on the rightmost syllable if all syllables have only a single grid mark (4).

(4) Golin tone-driven stress using prominence grids (Hayes 1995)

```
    Word with high tone(s)            Word with only low tones
    (    x   )                        (         x)
    σ    σ   σ                        σ    σ    σ
    |    |   |                        |    |    |
    L   'H   L                        L    L   'L
    *    *   *                        *    *    *
         *
    gò'mágì 'type of sweet potato'    kàw lì' gì 'post'
```

In stress systems sensitive to both syllable weight and tone, e.g. Tibetan (Meredith 1990), only syllables that are in metrically strong positions by virtue of their weight are eligible to receive grid marks based on tone, a restriction that captures the primacy of syllable weight over tone in these languages.

De Lacy (2002) adopts an analysis similar in spirit to Hayes (1995) but couched within an Optimality-theoretic framework. In his account, a series of constraints governs the mapping between metrical heads, i.e. accented or stressed syllables, and tones, where constraints banning associations between heads and lower tones are ranked above those prohibiting associations between heads and higher tones, a universal ranking that captures the mutual attraction of stress and higher tones. Taking the Golin example, a constraint banning low tones in the head syllable of a word, *HD/L, outranks a constraint prohibiting high tones in the head syllable, *HD/H. Another constraint, formulated here as ALLHDRIGHT,[1] ensures that stress falls on the rightmost syllable in case of a tonal tie (5).

---

[1] De Lacy (2002) formalizes these edge-sensitive constraints with reference to metrical feet.

(5) Golin stress using head prominence constraints (De Lacy 2002)

síbágì 'sweet potato type'	*HD/L	ALLHDRIGHT	*HD/H
✓ sí'bágì		*	*
síbá'gì	*!		
'síbágì		**!	*
kàwlìgì 'post'	*HD/L	ALLHDRIGHT	*HD/H
✓ kàwlì'gì	*		
'kàwlìgì	*	*!*	

In parallel to these constraints on heads, De Lacy postulates constraints that ban tones on different types of non-heads, where associations between higher tones and non-heads are banned before those linking lower tones with non-heads. The combination of these two families of constraints offers a unified approach to both the gravitation of higher tones toward stress, as in stress-driven tone systems, and to the preferential attraction of stress by high tone, as in tone-driven stress. Under the assumption that the stressed syllable belongs to a binary foot, a foot binarity constraint requiring that feet contain two syllables captures the preferential attraction of stress by high tone (or mid tone) immediately followed by a low tone over a high (or mid) tone not followed by a low tone, as in Ayutla Mixtec.

Whether couched with a rule-based or a constraint-based paradigm, a formal analysis capturing the affinity between high tone and stress is intuitively appealing since it encodes the inherent perceived prominence of high tones. This link between high tone and stress parallels the mutual attraction of stress and vowel length whereby long vowels are stressed in many languages and stressed vowels commonly lengthen. The empirical basis for tone-sensitive stress, however, is typologically less robust than the grounding of weight-sensitive stress.

4 Acoustic Correlates of Stress in Tone Languages

Phonetic evidence for stress in tone languages is largely limited to languages with either orthogonal tone and stress systems or languages that restrict (at least under one plausible analysis) tone on the basis of stress, e.g. Ma'ya (Remijsen 2002), Curaçao Papiamentu (Remijsen and van Heuven 2005), Swedish (Barbosa, Eriksson, and Åkesson 2013), Thai (Potisuk, Gandour, and Harper 1996), Pirahã (Everett 1998). In the Gordon and Roettger (2017) survey, only two of the thirteen tone languages that have demonstrable acoustic correlates of stress fall into the category of tone-driven stress. In Fort Ware Sekani (Hargus 2005), high tone preferentially attracts stress over low tone but tone is only one of four factors, including morphology, vowel quality, and position, that is predictive of stress. Hargus finds that stressed high toned vowels are longer and have greater intensity relative to the following unstressed vowel than their stressed low toned counterparts in the same position although no values for duration or intensity are reported. The genetically related language Minto Tanana also counts tone as one among multiple predictors of stress, but because the acoustic study of stress in Tuttle (1998) does not directly compare stressed and unstressed lexical tones, the phonetic interaction between tone and stress is uncertain. All of the other languages cited in Gordon and Roettger (2017) either have orthogonal tone and stress systems (five languages), or stress-driven tone under one plausible interpretation (six languages).

5 Phonological Evidence for Stress in Tone Languages

Descriptions offering independent phonological evidence for stress in tone languages are also skewed toward languages with either orthogonal tone and stress or those with stress-driven tone. In languages with both stress and tone, the evidence for stress characteristically comes from distributional restrictions on the number of contrasts, either segmental or suprasegmental, where syllables licensing a richer set of contrasts are often assumed to be stressed. In Na-Dene languages, for example, the stem is associated with a greater density of tonal and segmental contrasts than syllables outside of the stem (Rice and Hargus 2005), a pattern that may be taken as an argument in favor of the attraction of stress by the stem. Similarly, the attraction of tone to certain syllables and the confinement of vowel length in many Bantu languages to certain syllables may also be attributed to stress (Goldsmith 1987; Hyman 1989; Downing 2010), although it is interesting to note that different diagnostics, e.g. richness of segmental contrasts, may suggest different assumptions about the location of stress (see Hyman 1989). Pankratz and Pike (1967) suggest a probabilistic relationship between both syncope and vowel devoicing in Ayutla Mixtec but, based on the limited data they present, it is unclear whether either phenomenon is a reliable diagnostic of stress as opposed to being predictable from phrasal and/or segmental context.

6 Phonetic Conditioning of Tone-Driven Stress

Given that research suggests a phonetic basis for weight-sensitive stress (e.g. Gordon 2002, 2005; Ryan 2014), one might also ask whether similar phonetic grounding is present for tone-driven stress, in particular, the tendency for higher tones to preferentially attract stress over lower tones. On a more fundamental level, it is possible that phonetic prominence might even underlie descriptions of tone-sensitive stress for which there is a cross-linguistic paucity of both acoustic evidence and phonological support. We examine now the intrinsic features of tone and their acoustic and perceptual analogs that might contribute to the patterns of tone-sensitive stress reported in the literature.

The relationship between fundamental frequency (f0), the physical analog of tone, and the phonetic properties of intensity and duration is well documented both in the acoustic and perceptual domains. First, it is well known that f0 is positively correlated with intensity (Hirano, Ohala, and Vennard 1969; Zee 1978; Titze 1994), a common acoustic marker of stress whether averaged across frequencies as in many studies or in a spectrally-sensitive manner weighted toward certain (higher) frequencies (Sluijter and van Heuven 1996). The link between intensity and f0 has a physiological and aerodynamic basis related to vocal fold configuration and subglottal pressure but has also been shown to be under conscious control by speakers adopting particular articulatory settings to convey features such as phrasal prominence (Tilsen 2016).

Duration also has a close relationship with f0 albeit a more complex one that is examined by Yu (2010). High-toned vowels acoustically tend to be shorter than low-toned ones but are perceived as longer than low tones. Yu (2010) explains this apparent paradox as a perceptual compensation effect whereby lower tones are lengthened by speakers to achieve perceptual equivalence with high tones in the duration domain. In practice, in the expression of prominence, high f0 is often employed synergistically with increased acoustic duration, an effect that would presumably be enhanced in the perceptual domain given the link between high tone and greater perceived duration. In speech production, the combination of raised f0, greater intensity and longer duration gives rise to a three-way positive correlation between these parameters in stressed syllables (Alain 1993). Although the correlation between duration and both f0 and intensity is confined to stressed syllables, the link between f0 and intensity is observed even in unstressed syllables (Alain 1993), suggesting a closer association between f0 and intensity than between f0 and duration.

The particularly close relationship between f0 and intensity raises the possibility that these two properties synergistically conspire to increase the perceptual prominence of high-toned syllables. Duration might also play a secondary role in enhancing the prominence of high-toned syllables, at least if the duration of high-toned syllables is not substantially shorter than that of their low-toned counterparts. In fact, cross-linguistic support for the generalization that low tones are longer than high tones is relatively scant (see, for example, Zee (1978) who reports that high-toned vowels are longer than low-toned vowels in Taiwanese), so it is unclear whether the paradox between production and perception discussed by Yu (2010) is widespread in practice. Rather, the mutual attraction of high tone and other phonetic correlates of prominence, including both increased intensity and duration, is robustly evidenced in stress languages in the form of phrasal pitch accents docking on stressed syllables. These pitch accents are typically cued by a cluster of phonetic properties that includes increased intensity and duration in addition to f0 correlates, which are biased both across and within languages to contain a high f0 target (see Jun 2005 for typology).

Although the affinity between high tone and perceived prominence is abundantly evident, there are different interpretations of this relationship. One possibility is that high tone truly attracts phonological stress, in which case formal mechanisms such as prominence projections or constraints governing the relationship between tone and metrical (non-)heads are needed. Another possibility, though, is that perceived prominence on high-toned syllable is simply an auditory artifact of the high tone, which researchers might be predisposed to analyze as stress. Indirect evidence for this latter interpretation comes from the typology of reported cases of tone-driven stress cited by De Lacy (2002). In nine of the eleven cases he mentions, stress docks on the leftmost high tone in case there are multiple high tones and on the initial syllable in words lacking a high tone. The strong typological bias in favor of leftward orientation of tone-driven stress is consistent with a phonetic rather than phonological interpretation given the natural tendency for declination, whereby fundamental frequency and intensity decline over the course of an utterance. The declination trend would likely bolster the perceived prominence of high tones occurring earlier in a word but would not necessarily be expected if the attraction of stress by high tones were a phonological effect, though the latter possibility could not be definitively excluded.

The prospect for reanalyzing stress-driven tone as a perceptual artifact rather than a true phonological property belongs to a broader realm of uncertainty surrounding various other elements of the commonly assumed stress typology that have recently either been called into question or re-analyzed in different terms, including the presence of stress on final syllables (Hayes 1995; Lunden 2019), default-to-opposite stress (Gordon 2000), the typological scope of rhythmic stress (Newlin-Łukowicz 2012; Tabain, Fletcher, and Butcher 2014; Bowern, Alpher, and Round 2013), and stress based on vowel sonority (Shih 2018). For all of these types of stress systems, closer inspection of particular languages, often accompanied by instrumental analyses, have failed to provide verification of the described stress patterns in one or more languages, a finding that raises the possibility that analytic or perceptual biases have influenced researchers' phonological descriptions. On a typological level, the specter of widespread re-analyses raises questions about the empirical foundation of at least certain aspects of metrical stress theory.

7 The Phonetic Link between High Tone and Stress: A Cross-Linguistic Acoustic Study

Although typological and phonetic observations suggest that tone-driven stress or descriptions thereof may be rooted in acoustic and/or perceptual factors, a stronger argument for this grounding would be adduced from a demonstration of a robust cross-linguistic link between high tone and increased intensity and/or duration, the two most prevalent non-f0-based acoustic correlates of stress (Gordon and Roettger 2017). If such a relationship existed, it would support the view that high tone is intrinsically more prominent than other tones acoustically and (all else being equal) perceptually and that this perceptual prominence underlies reports of tone-driven stress in the literature.

Given the impracticality of conducting in-depth studies of all languages reported to have tone-driven stress, a phonetic sampling approach is adopted here whereby a set of languages is studied to determine whether the claimed phonetic precursors to a phonological phenomenon are universally (or nearly so) present across languages (see Gordon 2002; Zhang 2002; and Moreton 2008 for similar approaches to other phonological properties). Crucially, the scope of this evaluation includes languages in which the phenomenon under consideration is *not* present; such languages serve as experimental controls in the sense that the targeted phonetic property, if observed in that language, cannot reasonably be ascribed to the phonological manifestation of that property. For example, in the present study, a language without tone-driven stress serves as a control for examining the extent to which high tone and the acoustic parameters of duration and intensity are related across languages. A robust correlation between high tone and duration and/or intensity observed in languages without tone-driven stress would support the hypothesis that tone-driven stress (or reports of tone-driven stress) is phonetically-grounded.

7.1 Methodology

Data for the present study is drawn from eight languages with lexical tone that have not, to the best of my knowledge, been demonstrated to also have word stress. For each of the eight languages, both high and low tones were targeted for examination. Also investigated, if present in the corpus for a given language, were mid tones and/or falling tones, both of which have been claimed to impact stress placement in certain languages (see Section 2.5). For one of the languages, Angami, all four level tones were measured. The eight languages (and their genetic affiliations), the measured tones for each, and the number of tokens of each tone appear in Table 1.[2]

Table 1: Languages and their measured tones in the phonetic study.

Language	Genetic Affiliation	Tones (Number of tokens)
Angami	Sino-Tibetan	High (4), Low (4), Mid (4), Superhigh (4)
Defaka	Niger-Congo	High (26), Low (15)
Efik	Niger-Congo	High (10), Low (10), HL (=Falling) (6)
Hausa	Afro-Asiatic	High (5), Low (5)
Ibibio	Niger-Congo	High (10), Low (22)
Tee	Niger-Congo	High (19), Mid (18), Low (13)
Yoruba	Niger-Congo	High (9), Low (7), Mid (7)
Western Apache	Na-Dene	High (4), Low (4)

For each of the languages, measured data came from words in isolation uttered by a single speaker either once or twice depending on the language. The reliance on isolation words potentially introduces a confound in the form of phrasal prosody but the possible impact is minimized by the fact that the measured tones occurred in the same position relative to phrase edges. The locus of the measurement was a

---

[2] Data is from the UCLA Phonetics Archive: http://archive.phonetics.ucla.edu/. The following recordings were used for the analysis: Angami: http://archive.phonetics.ucla.edu/Language/NJM/njm.html (njm_word-list_1992_03); Defaka: http://archive.phonetics.ucla.edu/Language/AFN/afn.html (afn_word-list_1994_01); Efik: http://archive.phonetics.ucla.edu/Language/EFI/efi.html (efi_word-list_1964_01); Hausa: http://archive.phonetics.ucla.edu/Language/HAU/hau.html (hau_word-list_1962_01); Ibibio: http://archive.phonetics.ucla.edu/Language/IBB/ibb.html (ibb_word-list_1984_07); Tee: http://archive.phonetics.ucla.edu/Language/TKQ/tkq.html (tkq_word-list_1994_01, tkq_word-list_1994_02); Yoruba: http://archive.phonetics.ucla.edu/Language/YOR/yor.html (yor_word-list_1960_01; yor_word-list_1962_01); Western Apache: http://archive.phonetics.ucla.edu/Language/APW/apw.html (apw_word-list_1980_01).

vowel in all of the languages and the position and quality of the vowel were balanced across tones within languages in order to control for intrinsic differences in duration and intensity based on vowel quality or position in the word. For each measured segment, the duration and mean intensity values were collected using a Praat (Boersma and Weenink 2020) script and resulting values were processed for graphical presentation in R (R Core Team 2020).

7.2 Results

Results for intensity (left plot for each language) and duration (right plot for each language) of the target tones in each of the languages appear in boxplots in Figure 1, where boxes span the interquartile range (data encompassed within the middle 50% of the distribution), the dark line represents the median, and the whiskers encode the upper and lower bounds of the distribution 1.5 times beyond the interquartile range. Outliers falling outside of the whiskers are represented as open circles.

To assess the statistical robustness of the patterns (albeit tentatively given the small sample sizes), analyses of variance were conducted for each of the languages with tone as an independent variable and duration and intensity as dependent variables. For those analyses yielding a significant main effect, Tukey posthoc tests (equivalent to the main effect in languages with two tone levels) were conducted to compare differences between tone levels. Results are summarized in Table 2 (intensity) and Table 3 (duration).

Looking first at the intensity plots, all the examined languages show the same pattern whereby intensity is greater in high-toned vowels than in low-toned ones. This result is statistically reliable in even the small sample sizes for all languages except Ibibio. In languages with a second tone containing a high component, the superhigh tone in Angami and the falling tone in Efik, this other tone has similar intensity values to those associated with high tone. The intensity of mid tone diverges among the three languages possessing a mid tone. In Angami and Yoruba, the mid tone parallels high tone in intensity, whereas in Tee, it patterns together with low tone.

Turning to duration, the trend in half the languages is for high tone to be longer than low tone: languages showing this pattern include Angami, Hausa, Ibibio, and Tee, although only in Angami and Ibibio is this result statistically robust. In other languages, there is not a robust difference between the high and low tone in duration. In no language are low tones longer than high tones. Mid tones are also not reliably longer than either high or low tones in languages with a mid tone. Super high is associated with duration values similar to high tone in Angami, while falling tone in Efik is not durationally distinct from either high or low tone.

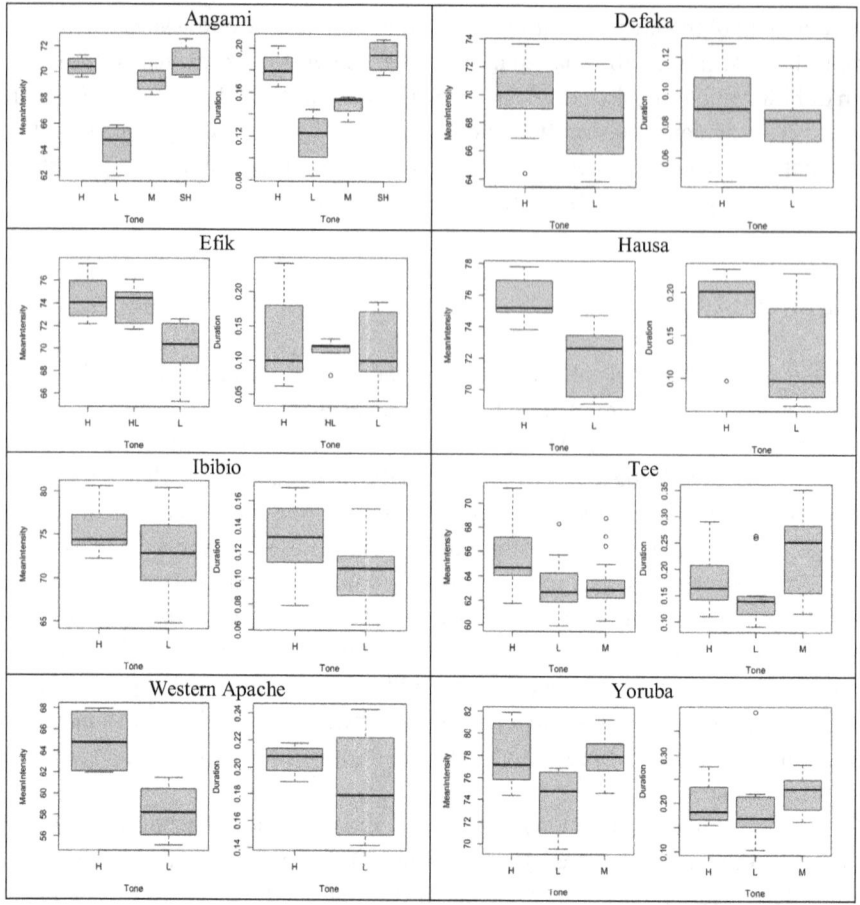

Figure 1: Intensity (in decibels) and duration (in seconds) values for different tones in eight languages.

Table 2: Results of ANOVAs and posthoc tests for intensity. Shaded cells are contrasts absent from a language. n.s. = non-significant.

	Angami	Defaka	Efik	Hausa	Ibibio	Tee	Apache	Yoruba
ANOVA	$F_{3,12}=$ 22.366 p<.0001	$F_{1,39}=$ 7.821 p<.001	$F_{2,23}=$ 13.267 p<.001	$F_{1,8}=$ 8.4704 p<.05	$F_{2,31}=$ 1.8064 n.s.	$F_{2,47}=$ 6.3808 p<.01	$F_{1,6}=$ 9.7633 p<.05	$F_{2,20}=$ 5.56 p<.05
Posthocs								
L vs. H	p<.0001	p<.001	p<.001	p<.05	n.s.	p<.01	p<.05	p<.05
L vs. M	p<.0001					n.s.		p<.05

Table 2 (continued)

	Angami	Defaka	Efik	Hausa	Ibibio	Tee	Apache	Yoruba
L vs. HL			p<.01					
L vs. SH	p<.0001							
M vs. H	n.s.					p<.05		n.s.
M vs. HL								
M vs. SH	n.s.							
H vs. HL			n.s.					
H vs. SH	n.s.							

Table 3: Results of ANOVAs and posthoc tests for duration. Shaded cells are contrasts absent from a language. n.s. = non-significant, n.a. = test not run due to lack of a significant main effect.

	Angami	Defaka	Efik	Hausa	Ibibio	Tee	Apache	Yoruba
ANOVA	$F_{3,12}=$ 14.758 p<.0001	$F_{1,39}=$ 1.818 n.s.	$F_{2,23}=$ 0.4096 n.s.	$F_{1,8}=$ 1.8827 n.s.	$F_{2,31}=$ 8.5258 p<.01	$F_{2,47}=$ 7.0394 p<.01	$F_{1,6}=$ 0.7165 n.s.	$F_{2,20}=$ 0.2479 n.s.
Posthocs								
L vs. H	p<.01	n.s.	n.a.	n.s.	p<.01	n.s.	n.s.	n.a.
L vs. M	n.s.					p<.01		n.a.
L vs. HL			n.a.					
L vs. SH	p<.001							
M vs. H	n.s.					p<.05		n.a.
M vs. HL								
M vs. SH	p<.05							
H vs. HL			n.a.					
H vs. SH	n.s.							

Summing up the results for both intensity and duration, high tones are consistently associated with greater intensity than low tones. Duration also displays a propensity to be greater for high tones relative to low tones, though this tendency is not as strong as the bias in favor of greater intensity on high-toned vowels. On the other hand, the perceptual difference in duration between high and low tones may be greater than the acoustic difference given the tendency for higher tones to be judged longer than lower tones (see Section 6). Other tones with a high element, either superhigh or falling, pattern together with high tone with respect to intensity but not consistently in duration. Mid tones vary between languages in their phonetic properties, behaving either like high tone or low tone.

8 Discussion

In summary, the eight-language sample examined in this study suggests a consistent relationship between high tone and low tone with respect to intensity: intensity is greater for vowels carrying high tone than those associated with low tone. This pattern mirrors results for languages like English in which pitch differences are used for intonational purposes rather than distinguishing lexical contrasts, suggesting that the positive association between high tone and increased intensity may be a candidate for universal status. Of course, the plausibility of this being a consistent link would be strengthened through verification over a considerably larger data set than the one examined here.

The observed link between high tone and increased intensity (and, to a lesser degree, increased duration), to the extent that it reflects a broader cross-linguistic pattern, is consistent with the observed link between higher tones and stress. Given the temporal integration of intensity by the auditory system (see Moore (2013) for an overview of temporal summation of loudness and Gordon (2002) for its potential role in stress systems), any additional duration would likely further enhance the perceptual prominence of high tone, especially in light of the independent bias toward longer perceived duration for high tone (Yu 2010). It may also be noted that the tendency in the examined data for higher tones to be longer, or at least not shorter, than lower tones casts doubt on the universality of the hypothesized association between low tone and increased duration.

The relationship between f0 and both intensity and duration is less consistent in the case of tones other than high and low in the data examined here. Looking first at mid tone, only in Angami does mid tone occupy an intermediate position in intensity between high and low tone, a pattern that mirrors that found by Zee (1978) for Taiwanese. In the other two languages with mid tone, Yoruba and Tee, it is not distinguished from either high or low tone (or both) in intensity. Similarly, falling tone patterns together phonetically with high tone with respect to intensity in the one surveyed language, Efik, with both high and falling tones that were measured.

Given the overall paucity of stress systems reported to be sensitive to a distinction beyond a binary one between high and low, only Bobo (Le Bris and Prost 1981) and Ayutla Mixtec (Pankratz and Pike 1967) in the survey in Section 2.5, it is unclear how to interpret the relationship between the phonetic results presented here and the phonological behavior of mid and contour tones with respect to stress. It is conceivable that these tones are more variable across languages in their phonetic characteristics and that this variability makes them less likely to be exploited in the positioning of stress, especially given the more robust phonetic division between tones containing a high element (either level or contour) and other tones. In any case, it is unclear how much of the rarity of stress systems sensitive to tones other than high and low is merely an artifact of the independent sparseness of stress in languages with more than a binary tone distinction.

Assuming that tone-sensitive stress is a robust phenomenon (rather than a perceptual artifact), the demonstrated link between high f0 and greater intensity observed in the present study raises the possibility of extending Gordon's (2002, 2005, 2006) model of weight-sensitive stress to tone-sensitive stress. Under this account, the attraction of stress by heavy syllables is attributed to the greater perceptual loudness of their rimes, which in turn is a function of their intensity integrated over time. Syllables thus are heavy if they are longer and/or more intense than other syllables. The "heavy" status of high tones in tone-driven stress systems would fall out from the same phonetic precursors conditioning weight at the segmental level, namely, greater intensity coupled in some languages with greater duration. In this account of tone-driven stress, the preferential stress-attracting ability of high tone would not be due directly to the higher fundamental frequency that is definitional for high tone; rather, it would be the indirect effect of higher tone on intensity that would be driving tone-sensitive stress. This collateral type of effect would be similar to the one claimed by Gordon (2005) to motivate onset weight effects in stress systems – heavier onsets, those that are voiceless or complex, increase the perceptual prominence of a syllable not directly but rather through the auditory boost they provide to the following rime.

9 Conclusions

Typological inspection indicates a link between high tone and stress, although the phonological and acoustic evidence for the phenomenon of tone-driven stress is less robust than support for stress based on syllable weight. Whether tone-sensitive stress is a genuine phonological feature or an artifact of perceptual biases, results of the present phonetic survey suggest that the association between high tone and increased intensity and, to a lesser extent, greater duration accounts for reports of high tone attracting stress. This finding points to the viability of a unified approach to tone- and weight-driven stress grounded in the same phonetic precursor of integrated loudness.

References

Alain, Claude. 1993. The relationship among fundamental frequency, intensity, and duration varies with accentuation. *Journal of the Acoustical Society of America* 94(4). 2434–2436. DOI: 10.1121/1.407464.

Barbosa, Plínio, Anders Eriksson & Joel Åkesson. 2013. Cross-linguistic similarities and differences of lexical stress realisation in Swedish and Brazilian Portuguese. In E. L. Asu and Pärtel Lippus (eds.), *Nordic Prosody: Proceedings of the 6th Conference, Tartu 2012*, 97–106. Frankfurt am Main: Peter Lang.

Bickmore, Lee. 1995. Tone and stress in Lamba. *Phonology* 12. 307–341.

Blevins, Juliette. 1993. A tonal analysis of Lithuanian nominal accent. *Language* 69. 237–273. DOI: https://doi.org/10.2307/416534.

Boersma, Paul & David Weenink. 2020. Praat: Doing phonetics by computer (version 6.1.33) (www.praat.org).

Bowern, Claire, Barry Alpher & Erich Round. 2013. Yidiny stress, length, and truncation revisited. Poster presented at Northeast Linguistics Society.

Bunn, Gordon & Ruth Bunn.1970. Golin phonology. *Pacific Linguistics* A23. 1–7.

De Lacy, Paul. 2002. The interaction of tone and stress in Optimality Theory. *Phonology* 19. 1–32. DOI: https://doi.org/10.1017/S0952675702004220.

Dogil, Grzegorz. 1999. The phonetic manifestation of word stress in Lithuanian, Polish, German and Spanish. In Harry van der Hulst (ed.), *Word Prosodic Systems in the Languages of Europe*, 273–310. New York: Mouton de Gruyter.

Downing, Laura J. 2010. Accent in African languages. In Harry van der Hulst, Rob Goedemans & Ellen van Zanten (eds.), *A Survey of Word Accentual Patterns in the Languages of the World*, 381–427. New York: Mouton de Gruyter.

Everett, Daniel. 1986. Pirahã. In Desmond Derbyshire & Geoffrey Pullum (eds.), *Handbook of Amazonian Languages* 1, 200–325. Berlin: Mouton de Gruyter.

Everett, Daniel. 1988. On metrical constituent structure in Pirahã. *Natural Language and Linguistic Theory* 6. 207–246.

Everett, Keren. 1998. The acoustic correlates of stress in Pirahã. *Journal of Amazonian Languages* 1(2). 104–162.

Everett, Daniel & Keren Everett. 1984. On the relevance of syllable onsets to stress placement. *Linguistic Inquiry* 15. 705–711.

Goldsmith, John. 1987. Tone and accent and getting the two together. *Berkeley Linguistics Society* 13. 88–104.

Gordon, Matthew. 1999/2006. *Syllable weight: Phonetics, phonology, typology*. Los Angeles: UCLA Ph.D. dissertation. (Published in 2006 by Routledge.)

Gordon, Matthew. 2000. Re-examining default-to-opposite stress. *Berkeley Linguistics Society* 26. 101–112.

Gordon, Matthew. 2002. A phonetically-driven account of syllable weight. *Language* 78. 51–80.

Gordon, Matthew. 2005. A perceptually-driven account of onset-sensitive stress. *Natural Language and Linguistic Theory* 23. 595–653. DOI: https://doi.org/10.1007/s11049-004-8874-9.

Gordon, Matthew & Harry van der Hulst. 2020. Word stress. In Carlos Gussenhoven & Aoju Chen (eds.), *The Oxford Handbook of Language Prosody*, 66–77. Oxford: Oxford University Press.

Gordon, Matthew & Timo Roettger. 2017. Acoustic correlates of word stress: A cross-linguistic survey. *Linguistics Vanguard* 3(1). DOI: 10.1515/lingvan-2017-0007.

Gussenhoven, Carlos. 2006. Between stress and tone in Nubi word prosody. *Phonology* 23. 192–223. DOI: 10.1017/S0952675706000881.

Hargus, Sharon. 2005. Prosody in two Athabaskan languages of Northern British Columbia. In Sharon Hargus & Keren Rice (eds.), *Athabaskan Prosody*, 393–423. Amsterdam: John Benjamins.

Hayes, Bruce. 1995. *Metrical Stress Theory: Principles and Case Studies.* Chicago: University of Chicago Press.

Hirano, Minuro, John Ohala & William Vennard. 1969. The function of laryngeal muscles in regulating fundamental frequency and intensity of phonation. *Journal of Speech Language and Hearing Research* 12(3). 616–628. DOI: https://doi.org/10.1044/jshr.1203.616.

Hualde, José Ignacio, Oihana Lujanbio & Francisco Torreira. 2008. Lexical tone and stress in Goizueta Basque. *Journal of the International Phonetic Association* 38. 1–24. DOI: https://doi.org/10.1017/S0025100308003241.

Hulst, Harry van der. 2011. Pitch accent systems. In Marc van Oostendorp, Colin Ewen, Elizabeth Hume & Keren Rice (eds.), *The Blackwell Companion to Phonology*, vol. 2, 1003–1027. West Sussex, UK: Wiley-Blackwell.

Hyman, Larry. 1989. Accent in Bantu: An appraisal. *Studies in the Linguistic Sciences* 19. 115–134.

Hyman, Larry. 2006. Word-prosodic typology. *Phonology* 23. 225–257. DOI: https://doi.org/10.1017/S0952675706000893.

Jun, Sun-Ah. 2005. Prosodic typology. In Sun-Ah Jun (ed.), *Prosodic Typology: The Phonology of Intonation and Phrasing*, 430–458. New York: Oxford University Press.

Le Bris, Pierre & André Prost. 1981. *Dictionnaire bobo-français, précédé d'une introduction grammaticale et suivi d'un lexique français-bobo.* Paris: Société d'Études Linguistiques et Anthropologiques de France.

Lunden, Anya. 2019. Explaining word-final stress lapse. In Rob Goedemans, Jeffrey Heinz & Harry van der Hulst (eds.), *The Study of Word Stress and Accent: Theories, Methods and Data*, 76–101. Cambridge: Cambridge University Press.

Maddieson, Ian. 2013. Tone. In Matthew S. Dryer & Martin Haspelmath (eds.), *The World Atlas of Language Structures Online*. Leipzig: Max Planck Institute for Evolutionary Anthropology. (Available online at http://wals.info/chapter/13, Accessed on 2021-03-05).

Meredith, Scott. 1990. *Issues in the phonology of prominence.* Cambridge, MA: MIT Ph.D. dissertation.

Moore, Brian. 2013. *An Introduction to the Psychology of Hearing.* Leiden: Brill.

Moreton, Elliott. 2008. Analytic bias and phonological typology. *Phonology* 25. 83–127. DOI: https://doi.org/10.1017/S0952675708001413.

Newlin-Łukowicz, Luiza. 2012. Polish stress: Looking for evidence of a bidirectional system. *Phonology* 29. 271–329. DOI: https://doi.org/10.1017/S0952675712000139.

Nicholson, Ruth & Ray Nicholson. 1962. Fore phonemes and their interpretation. In James C. Dean (ed.), *Studies in New Guinea Linguistics by Members of the Summer Institute of Linguistics*, 128–148. Sydney: University of Sydney.

Pankratz, Leo & Eunice Pike. 1967. Phonology and morphotonemics of Ayutla Mixtec. *International Journal of American Linguistics* 33. 287–299. DOI: https://doi.org/10.1086/464980.

Potisuk, Siripong, Jackson Gandour & Mary P. Harper. 1996. Acoustic correlates of stress in Thai. *Phonetica* 53. 200–220. DOI: 10.1159/000262201.
R Core Team. 2020. R: A language and environment for statistical computing. R Foundation for Statistical Computing, Vienna, Austria. URL: https://www.R-project.org/.
Remijsen, Bert. 2002. Lexically contrastive stress accent and lexical tone in Ma`ya. In Carlos Gussenhoven & Natasha Warner (eds.), *Laboratory Phonology VII*, 585–614. Berlin: Mouton de Gruyter.
Remijsen, Bert & Vincent J. van Heuven. 2005. Stress, tone, and discourse prominence in the Curaçao dialect of Papiamentu. *Phonology* 22. 205–235. DOI: https://doi.org/10.1017/S0952675705000540.
Riad, Tomas. 2014. *The Phonology of Swedish*. Oxford: Oxford University Press.
Rice, Keren & Sharon Hargus. 2005. Introduction. In Sharon Hargus & Keren Rice (eds.), *Athabaskan Prosody*, 1–45. Amsterdam: John Benjamins.
Ryan, Kevin. 2014. Onsets contribute to syllable weight: Statistical evidence from stress and meter. *Language* 90. 309–341.
Shih, Shu-hao. 2018. On the existence of sonority-driven stress in Gujarati. *Phonology* 35. 327–364. DOI: https://doi.org/10.1017/S0952675718000064.
Sluijter, Agaath M. C. & Vincent J. van Heuven. 1996. Spectral balance as an acoustic correlate of linguistic stress. *Journal of the Acoustical Society of America* 100. 2471–2485. DOI: 10.1121/1.417955.
Tabain, Marija, Janet Fletcher & Andrew Butcher. 2014. Lexical stress in Pitjantjatjara. *Journal of Phonetics* 42. 52–66. DOI: https://doi.org/10.1016/j.wocn.2013.11.005.
Tilsen, Sam. 2016. A shared control parameter for F0 and intensity. *Speech Prosody 2016*, 1066–1070.
Titze, Ingo. 1994. *Principles of Voice Production*. Englewood Cliffs, NJ: Prentice Hall.
Tuttle, Siri. 1998. *Metrical and tonal structures in Tanana Athabaskan*. Seattle: University of Washington Ph.D. dissertation.
Yip, Moira. 2002. *Tone*. Cambridge: Cambridge University Press.
Yu, Alan. 2010. Tonal effects on perceived vowel duration. In Cécile Fougeron, Barbara Kühnert, Mariapaola D'Imperio & Nathalie Vallée (eds.), *Laboratory Phonology X*, 151–168. New York: De Gruyter Mouton. DOI: https://doi.org/10.1515/9783110224917.2.151.
Zee, Eric. 1978. Duration and intensity as correlates of F0. *Journal of Phonetics* 6. 213–220.
Zhang, Jie. 2002. *The Effects of Duration and Sonority on Contour Tone Distribution: Typological Survey and Formal Analysis*. New York: Routledge.

B. Elan Dresher and Aditi Lahiri
Some Applications of the Primary Accent First Parameter

Abstract: We demonstrate two applications of Primary Accent First, a proposal by Harry van der Hulst that a main stress can be put down at a word edge independently of metrical structure that may be set up later. First, we show how Primary Accent First solves a problem in assigning metrical structure in Old English and other West Germanic languages. In these languages, which have trochaic feet, main stress is assigned to a word-initial syllable (apart from some prefixes) whether it is heavy (H) or light (L). The problem, however, is that a legal trochee cannot be constructed in a word whose first two syllables are L H. Primary Accent First allows us to assign a stress to the first L without constructing a foot; subsequently, this initial L can be resolved with a following L or H in an extended trochee in which the foot head is associated with at least two moras. We show how our analysis extends to West Germanic Gemination and Sievers's Law. Second, we show how Primary Accent First contributes to an improved learnability model for metrical stress by enabling learners to benefit from a fixed main stress which acts as a Trubetzkoyan boundary signal.

Keywords: Primary Accent First, Old English, resolved trochee, West Germanic Gemination, Sievers's Law, learnability, boundary signal

1 Introduction

Harry van der Hulst has contributed to virtually every area of phonology, including segmental structure, syllable structure, metrical structure, prosody, sign language phonology, and the history of phonology.[1] In this paper we focus on

---

[1] We are pleased to be able to participate in this volume in honour of Harry van der Hulst, a star among phonologists and a superb colleague and friend to both of us. Aditi and Harry go back three and a half decades, including projects together, arguments on metrical feet, schwas, train timetables, and Dutch eating habits, and have enjoyed many hours of talking about phonology! Elan has been working with Harry since the 1990s, when we collaborated on papers on acquisition and head-dependent asymmetries at workshops in the Netherlands, and continuing to

B. Elan Dresher, University of Toronto
Aditi Lahiri, University of Oxford

https://doi.org/10.1515/9783110730081-010

one of his contributions to the study of accentual systems and foot typology. In a number of publications (van der Hulst 1984, 1996, 1997, 2009, 2010, 2012; Lahiri and van der Hulst 1987; Goedemans and van der Hulst 2014), he has argued that there are stress systems that have 'Primary Accent First'. In such systems, a main stress is put down at a word edge, independently of metrical structure that may be set up later.[2]

In this paper we call attention to two different applications of this idea. In Section 2, building on Lahiri and van der Hulst (1987), we show how Primary Accent First applies to the metrical structure of West Germanic. In Section 3, we propose that Primary Accent First can help solve a conundrum in the learnability of metrical structure.

2 Primary Accent First in West Germanic

Quantity-sensitive (QS) languages with fixed initial stress, including on light syllables, pose a problem for moraic trochees as proposed in Hayes (1986). Under a strict moraic trochee analysis, LH words (where L represents a light syllable and H a heavy syllable) cannot be stressed on the initial light syllable, unlike HL words. In particular, the initial L of an LH word cannot be parsed into a moraic trochee, as neither (L H) nor (L) (H) are possible parses. We thus expect initial LH to be parsed as in (1a), where stress would be expected to fall on the second syllable. Unfortunately, Germanic languages, from reconstructed West Germanic to Gothic, Old English, and Old High German, all show fixed initial stress (excluding certain unstressed prefixes), no matter the type of syllable.

---

the present day, co-editing a new history of phonology (Dresher and van der Hulst 2022). Harry was also instrumental in the founding of the University of Toronto Linguistics Department band.

Aditi Lahiri gratefully acknowledges the funding from the European Research Council (ERC), Advanced Grant 695481. We would like to thank Jeroen van de Weijer and an anonymous reader for insightful comments on an earlier draft.

2 In the cited publications, van der Hulst proposes that Primary Accent First is the default mode that characterizes most stress systems except certain types, such as 'count systems' in which all the feet of a word must be calculated before main stress can be assigned. In this paper we take the conservative position that Primary Accent First applies *at least* in the cases where the main stress is fixed on a particular edge syllable; see further Section 3 for a proposal of how Primary Accent First might co-exist with the more metrically integrated main stress parameter.

(1) a. Expected moraic trochee   b. With ambisyllabic mora (based on Lahiri and van der Hulst 1987)

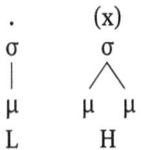
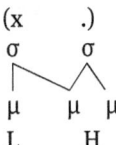

An important principle proposed by Harry van der Hulst is that primary stress could be assigned first, before assigning feet to the rest of the word (Primary Accent First; see also in this volume Bogomolets; Goedemans and Prokic; Revithiadou; and Vaxman). In a paper on foot typology, Lahiri and van der Hulst (1987) showed that one set of problems could be resolved for LH words by allowing a stress to first be assigned to an initial L, and then assuming that the first mora can be supported by a following mora, which becomes ambisyllabic. That is, a mora from the H syllable of an LH word could be subsumed into the first syllable, and this would still make up a moraic trochee, as shown in (1b).

In this section we revisit the Germanic data, reiterating the fact that the moraic trochee alone does not cover the facts of Germanic, unlike what has often been claimed (Keyser and O'Neil 1985; Halle, O'Neil, and Vergnaud 1993; Idsardi 1994; Hutton 1998; Bermúdez-Otero and Hogg 2003; Bermúdez-Otero 2005; Goering 2016a, 2016b), and even allowing for the ambisyllabic mora. We will show that van der Hulst's notion of Primary Accent First and mora borrowing holds; however, we still need the trochee to be an asymmetric one, allowing for at least a bimoraic head which can be maximally trimoraic and no more.

We show how the asymmetric trochee applies to Old English high vowel deletion, West Germanic gemination, and Sievers's Law. The crucial facts are discussed in the following sections.

2.1 Old English High Vowel Deletion

High vowel deletion (HVD) is observable in both Old English (OE) and Old High German (OHG). Our examples are from Old English. HVD deletes a high vowel *u* or *i* after a heavy syllable (either a long vowel, $\bar{V}$, or a syllable closed by a consonant, VC) or after a light syllable (ending in V) followed by another syllable. Lahiri and van der Hulst (1987) and Dresher and Lahiri (1991) showed that the moraic trochee is insufficient to account for the data in (2).

(2) Old English high vowel deletion (HVD)
    Gloss a. 'ship-NOM.PL' b. 'word-NOM.PL' c. 'head-GEN.SG'
    UR   /scip-u/   /word-u/   /hēafud-es/
    HVD   —   word   hēafdes

    Gloss d. 'head-DAT.SG' e. 'chicken-NOM.PL'
    UR   /hēafud-e/   /čicen-u/
    HVD   hēafde   —

If these words were parsed into moraic trochees where an unfooted [u] is deleted, we would have the derivations in (3); we obtain the wrong result in (3d), where the [u] cannot be deleted from *hēafude* since it is the head of a foot.

(3) OE HVD with a moraic trochee
            a. (x .)   b. (x) .   c. (x) . (x)
               sci pu   wor du   hēa fu des
    HVD   —   word   hēafdes

            d. (x) (x .) e. (x) (x .)
               hēa fu de   či ce nu
    HVD   *hēafude   —

A further problem occurs with words such as *wordum* 'word-DAT.PL' and *lofum* 'praise-DAT.PL' where the second syllable is heavy. These words are identical in the sense that neither lose their [u] and both are stressed on the initial syllable. Dresher and Lahiri (1986), an earlier iteration of their paper in (1991), had argued that all feet must have at least two moras. If the first syllable was light, a mora had to be borrowed from the second syllable (a process known in the study of metre as *resolution*). This was their 'sub-foot' analysis. Lahiri and van der Hulst (1987) accounted for this by assuming that the mora was borrowed from the second syllable. To allow a stress on a lone initial L in the first place, though, Lahiri and van der Hulst proposed that Primary Accent First creates a stress on a word-initial syllable, be it H or L.

The notion of stress assignment without foot construction can be expressed in terms of the simplified bracketed grid (SBG) theory of Idsardi (1992, 2009) and Halle and Idsardi (1995). In SBG, single unpaired brackets can be assigned to designated elements. In our case, we can specify that a left bracket is constructed at the left edge of the word, and that a stress is assigned to the first mora to the right of this bracket (4a). In a second step, metrical feet are created, with a second mora borrowed from the second syllable if necessary (4b).³ The only [u] which is not footed is in *wordu* and it is subject to HVD (indicated by underlining).

(4) Steps in stress assignment (based on Lahiri and van der Hulst 1987)
   a. Create initial stress on first syllable

```
(x       (x      (x        (x
μ  μμ    μ  μ    μμ   μ    μμ    μμ
lo fum   lo fu   wor  du   wor   dum
```

   b. Create metrical feet with an ambisyllabic mora when needed

```
(x    )   (x  )   (x ) .    (x )   (x )
 μ͡ μμ     μ͡ μ     μμ   μ     μμ     μμ
lo fum   lo fu   wor  du   wor    dum
```

Lahiri and van der Hulst's analysis had the added benefit that a moraic trochee analysis could be retained. Indeed, this was precisely the sort of analysis which Dresher and Lahiri (1991) had in mind when they argued in support of a resolved trochee. The resolved trochee is supported by two points: first, the initial syllable, which is the head of its foot, has to minimally have two moras; and second, the foot could branch. Thus, it could not be a strict moraic trochee. The resolved trochee could contain up to three moras in the head (one mora from an initial L + two from a following H) and a single mora as the weak branch of the foot. The crucial examples are words which have an initial heavy syllable followed by a [u] (*hēafude* > *hēafde*) or an initial light syllable followed by either a light or a heavy syllable and then a syllable with [u] (*fareldu* 'journey-NOM.PL' > *fareld*). The resolved trochee analysis is given in (5).

(5) Resolved trochee: μμ head labelled within square brackets

```
         a.  (x    )      b. (x    .)    c. (x    .)  (x)
             [μ͡ μ]           [μμ]  μ        [μμ]  μ   μμ
             sci pu          wor   du       hēa   fu  des
HVD           —               word            hēafdes

         d. (x    .) .    e. (x   .) .   f. (x         .)
             [μμ] μ  μ       [μμ]  μ μ       [μ͡ μμ]    μ
             hēa  fu de      čī    ce nu     fa  rel   du
HVD          hēafde            čīcenu          fareld
```

---

3 We do not attempt here an entire SBG analysis of OE stress. The device of assigning an initial bracket may have applications beyond Primary Accent First; see Dresher (2009) for an SBG analysis of Tiberian Hebrew.

Lahiri and van der Hulst's analysis correctly allows a L syllable to group together with a H syllable as well as with another L syllable (i.e. LX). But to argue that this is a strict moraic trochee would imply that HVD applies to a high vowel that is not part of a foot. HVD applies correctly to the first three words in (6) but not to the fourth one, where the u̱ which ought to be deleted is parsed as the head of a foot (in bold).

(6) HVD with moraic trochees with no weak branch
     a. (x   )   .   b. (x) (x .)   c. (x)   .   d. (x) (x .)
        μ͡ μμ   μ   μμ   μ μ   μμ   μ   μμ   μ μ
HVD   fa rel du̱   cī   ce nu   wor   du̱   *hēa fu de

Under this analysis, the unfooted final u̱ would be deleted for both *wordu* and *fareldu*. Note that the final [u] in *cīcenu* is retained correctly but the u̱ in *hēafude* should delete and cannot. The rule of HVD applies only to the underlined [u]s in the weak branch of the foot, as shown in (5).

The ambisyllabic mora indeed is the right idea for the head of the foot – viz. that it ought to be resolved so that LX=H; but it is also the case that the foot has to be asymmetric and branching to allow for all the facts.

2.2 West Germanic Gemination and the Resolved Trochee

Gemination in West Germanic affected all consonants except /r/. Stem-final consonants geminated when followed by /j/, which could be a suffix or a stem extension. However, gemination was only permissible if the stem was 'light'.[4] Here, too, we see that the LX resolved sequence patterns with H. The underlying glide /j/ was absorbed in the process of gemination; when there was no gemination, it became an /i/ if followed by a vowel or at the end of a word. The high vowel so produced was subject to HVD or lowered to *e* at the end of the derivation. The resolved trochee (7) assumed by Dresher and Lahiri (1991) and later permits the analysis in (8) (see Lahiri 1982 for further discussion of these rules and derivations).

---

[4] Note that a CVC stem is considered to be 'light', even though CVC itself is a heavy syllable, because when inflected, typically by a vowel or glide, the stem-final C syllabifies as an onset to the following syllable, thus making the stem-initial syllable truly L; e.g., CVC+V is syllabified CV.CV.

(7) Resolved trochee: [x]= HEAD OF THE FOOT

	a. H L	b. L L L	c. L H L
Foot	(x .)	(x .)	(x .)
Head	[x]	[x]	[x]
Moras	μμ μ	μ͡μ μ	μ͡ μμ μ
Syllables	H L	L L L	L H L

(8) OE gemination and HVD

	UR	/STEM-j-GEN.SG/	/STEM-j-NOM.PL/	/STEM-j-NOM.SG/
a.	'race'	/cyn-j-es/	/cyn-j-u/	/cyn-j-Ø/
	Gemination	cynnes	cynn-u	cynn
	/j/ > vowel/___V	—	—	—
	HVD	—	cynn	—
	word-final /j/ > [i]	—	—	—
	word-final [i] > [e]	—	—	—
	Output	[cynnes]	[cynn]	[cynn]
b.	'piece'	/styċċ-j-es/	/styċċ-j-u/	/styċċ-j-Ø/
	Gemination	—	—	—
	/j/ > vowel/___V	styċċies	styċċiu	—
	HVD	styċċes	styċċu	—
	word-final /j/ > [i]	—	—	styċċi
	word-final [i] > [e]	—	—	styċċe
	Output	[styċċes]	[styċċu]	[styċċe]
c.	'noble'	/æþel-j-es/	/æþel-j-u/	/æþel-j-Ø/
	Gemination	—	—	—
	/j/ > vowel/___V	æþelies	æþeliu	—
	HVD	æþeles	æþelu	—
	word-final /j/ > [i]	—	—	æþeli
	word-final [i] > [e]	—	—	æþele
	Output	[æþeles]	[æþelu]	[æþele]

The point to note is that gemination and HVD interact when the stem is L (8a), but gemination is blocked for H (8b) and LL (8c) stems. Finally, the /j/ glide is vocalized during syllabification if it is not word final. It survives to the very end, when it has to vocalize to survive and eventually becomes a schwa (written <e>) like all unstressed vowels. A summary of the interaction of gemination and HVD is given in (9).

(9) Interaction of gemination and HVD
   a. Gemination feeds HVD: *cynnu* > *cynn*.
   b. Gemination is blocked in stems of the form H (*styċċ*) and LL (*æþel*).
   c. HVD appears not to apply to the final *u* in the H (*styċċu*) and LL (*æþelu*) *ja*-nouns (unlike what occurs in the *a*-nouns).

In (10) we compare the light and heavy stems of the the *ja*-nouns with the *a*-nouns; the difference is that the *ja*-nouns have a /j/ stem extension.

(10) Comparing OE neuter *a*- and *ja*-nouns

		a. Neuter *a*-nouns		b. Neuter *ja*-nouns	
L stem		/lof-Ø/	/lof-u/	/cyn-j-Ø/	/cyn-j-u/
		[lof]	[lofu]	[cynn]	[cynn]
H stem		/word-Ø/	/word-u/	/styċċ-j-Ø/	/styċċ-j-u/
		[word]	[word]	[styċċe]	[styċċu]

On the surface it looks as if the H stems maintain the [u] in the *ja*-nouns but not in the *a*-nouns and that the L stems are exactly the opposite. The reason, of course, is the interaction of gemination and HVD as we saw in (8). We observe the following generalization about gemination:

(11) Generalization about WGmc gemination
Stem final C+j is geminated unless the HEAD of the foot would be trimoraic. If gemination leads to a trimoraic head, gemination is blocked.

The resolved trochee accounts for gemination and HVD as shown in (12).

(12) Derivations of L, H, and LL stems

   Footing → Gemination → j > i → HVD → Output
   a. 'race-DAT.SG'
      ([x])   ([x] .)
       μ μ   μμ   μ
       cy nje   cyn ne   —   —   cynne
      'race-NOM.PL'
      ([x])   ([x] .)   ([x])
       μ μ   μμ   μ   μμ
       cy nju   cyn nu   —   cynn   cynn

	Footing →	Gemination →	j > i →	HVD →	Output
b.	'punishment-GEN.SG'				
	([x]) (x)	([x]) (x)	([x] .) (x)	([x]) (x)	
	μμ μμ	*μμμ μμ	μμ μ μμ	μμ μμ	
	wī tjes	wīt tjes	wī ti es	wī tes	wītes
		BLOCKED			
	'punishment-NOM.PL'				
	([x] .)	([x] .)	([x] .) .	([x] .)	
	μμ μ	*μμμ μ	μμ μ μ	μμ μ	
	wī tju	wīt tju	wī ti u	wī tu	wītu
		BLOCKED			
c.	'noble-DAT.SG'				
	([x] .)	([x] .)	([x] .) .	([x] .)	
	μ͡μ μ	*μ͡μμ μ	μ͡μ μ μ	μ͡μ μ	
	æ þe lje	æ þel lje	æ þe li e	æ þe le	æþele
		BLOCKED			
	'noble-NOM.PL'				
	([x] .)	([x] .)	([x] .) .	([x] .)	
	μ͡μ μ	*μ͡μμ μ	μ͡μ μ μ	μ͡μ μ	
	æ þe lju	æ þel lju	æ þe li u	æ þe lu	æþelu
		BLOCKED			

Gemination is blocked in /æþel-j/ (12c) because the result of this process would not make the foot any heavier; instead it is the ambisyllabic mora of Lahiri and van der Hulst (1987) or the sub-foot of Dresher and Lahiri (1991) which would become heavier. In the case of /wīt-j/ (12b), gemination is blocked because the head syllable would become trimoraic. That, too, is not permitted.[5]

To summarize, gemination has the consequences and constraints shown in (13):

(13) Constraints on WGmc gemination
  a. Gemination occurs: Cj   >   C: CVCj   >   CVC:
  b. Gemination is blocked: CV:Cj   (*CV:CC) CV CVCj (*CV CVC:)

---

[5] In fact, a similar constraint is still valid in Level 1 English phonology: all stressed syllables can be maximally trimoraic (*wide, safe*) unless the coda ends with a coronal cluster such as *field, kind*.

2.3 Sievers's Law in Gothic

Sievers's Law, most clearly manifested in Gothic, is equally relevant for the resolved trochee. The main facts are as follows. The glide /j/ vocalizes when an /i/ follows, leading to a long vowel /iː/. However, the vocalization is blocked under certain conditions which are very similar to the constraints on gemination. The data (Lahiri 1982) is summarized in (14).

(14) Results of Sievers's Law (in orthography [iː] = <ei> in Gothic)

	STEM.2SG	Sievers's Law	Gloss	Stem type
a.	Light stems			
	nasjis	— (*nasiis)	'save.2SG'	CVC = L
	arjis	— (*ariis)	'plow.2SG'	VC = L
b.	Heavy stems			
	sookjis	sookiis	'plow.2SG'	CV:C = H
	namnjis	namniis	'name.2SG'	CVCC = H
c.	Polylsyllabic stems			
	sipoonjis	sipooniis	'be a disciple.2SG'	CV CV:C = LH = H
	mikiljis	mikiliis	'glorify.2SG'	CV CVC = LL = H

As before, LH, LL, and H stems behave like a single category. Building the resolved trochee on these forms (15), we find that Sievers's Law and gemination have very similar constraints (16). Both gemination and Sievers's Law are blocked if the foot HEAD becomes trimoraic. This analysis again crucially hinges on being able to assign the first (x in (15a, c) by Primary Accent First.

(15) Resolved trochee and Sievers's Law

	a. Light stems	b. Heavy stems	c. Polysyllabic stems
Foot	(x)	(x) (x)	(x) (x)
μμ head	[x]	[x] x	[x] x
	μ͡ μμ	μμ μμ	μ͡ μ μμ
	na sjis	soo kjis	mi ki ljis
	nasjis	sookiis	mikiliis

(16) Sievers's Law
/ji/ > [iː] iff the HEAD of the foot does not gain an additional mora.

Van der Hulst's intuition that the initial syllable must be assigned a stress by Primary Accent First remains supported, as does the notion that a mora is 'borrowed' from the next syllable. What is necessary in addition is that the foot type must be an asymmetric trochee, i.e. a branching trochee with a bimoraic or trimoraic head. Mora borrowing alone does not solve all the problems.

3 Primary Accent First and the Learnability of Metrical Structure

In this section we consider the way that Primary Accent First can help solve an incongruity that arises in the learning model for metrical stress developed by Dresher and Kaye (1990) and continued in Dresher (1994, 1999, 2016). This model assumes that the acquisition of the grammar of stress involves setting a number of parameters to their correct values. Parameter setting proceeds in an order set by Universal Grammar that largely reflects inherent dependencies between parameters. That is, if setting a parameter Q depends on having correctly set parameter P, then the acquisition of P must precede that of Q.

For example, in order to determine what sort of metrical feet a language has, it is necessary to know if the language distinguishes light from heavy syllables, and if it does, it is necessary to know which syllables are light and which are heavy. The parameter order proposed by Dresher and Kaye (1990) is given in (17):[6]

(17) Dresher and Kaye (1990) order for setting metrical parameters
  a. Syllable Quantity: The language {does not/does} distinguish between light and heavy syllables (a heavy syllable may not be a dependent in a foot).
  b. Extrametricality: A syllable on the {right/left} {is not/is} extrametrical.
  c. Bounded constituent construction: Line 0 constituents {are not/are} bounded.
  d. Main stress: Project the {left/right}-most element of the line 1 constituent.
  e. Headedness and directionality of feet: {Left/right}-headed feet are constructed from the {left/right}.
  f. Destressing: {Various types of} feet are destressed in {various situations}.

---

[6] The grid lines 0 and 1 mentioned in (17) have been conflated in the grids in this paper: a mark on line 0 that is not projected to line 1 is indicated by a dot, and a line 0 mark that is projected to line 1 is indicated by x.

The parameters in (17) presuppose a metrical theory in which main stress is the result of promoting either the leftmost or rightmost metrical foot in a word. As the ordering of (17) indicates, to find where the main stress is it is not necessary to know whether feet are left- or right-headed, or whether they are constructed from the left or from the right. But in order to know if main stress falls within the leftmost or rightmost foot, one has to know how large a foot is.

For example, the main stress rule of Present Day English (PDE) nouns assigns the main stress to the penultimate syllable if it is heavy, and otherwise to the antepenultimate (18).

(18) PDE main stress rule (nouns)
Main stress falls on the penultimate syllable, if heavy, or if the word contains no more than two syllables; otherwise, stress falls on the antepenult.

In order to locate the PDE main stress in terms of metrical structures, one must know that the final syllable is extrametrical and that feet are binary and QS, with long vowels and syllables closed by a consonant both counting as heavy. If one does not know this, one could be misled by words like *álgebra* (19a), where the stress appears on the leftmost syllable. A word like *agénda* (19b), with a heavy penult, is highly ambiguous as to the location of main stress if one does not know about quantity, foot size and headedness, and extrametricality. Of the words in (19), only *Mànitóba* (19c) reveals in a straightforward manner that main stress is on the rightmost foot.

(19) PDE main stress on the rightmost foot
```
     a.   x              b.     x         c.            x
          (x   .)  <.>        .  (x)  <.>       (x  .)  (x)  <.>
          al  ge   bra          a  gen  da       Ma  ni  to:  ba
```

In other types of stress systems the location of main stress can be even more difficult to perceive at first appearances. Selkup, for example, has the stress system in (20) and sample words as in (21) (Halle and Clements 1983; Dresher 1999).

(20) Selkup main stress rule
Main stress falls on the rightmost long vowel; if there is no long vowel, stress falls on the initial syllable.

(21) Selkup words
qúmmin 'human being (GEN)' kanaŋmí: 'our dog'
qummí: 'our friend' qól⁽ʸ⁾cimpati 'found'
ámirna 'eats' u:cikkó:qɪ 'they two are working'
qumó:qɪ 'two human beings' qumo:qlɪlí: 'your two friends'

As is evident from (21), in Selkup stress can fall anywhere in the word, depending on the distribution of heavy syllables (long vowels). It is only after one has discovered that Selkup feet are unbounded that one can analyze a word like *qól⁽ʸ⁾cimpati* as being consistent with main stress being on the right. Moreover, in the absence of secondary stress one cannot perceive a main stress following a secondary stress, as in English *Mànitóba*; in Selkup, secondary stresses are theoretical as in (22), but not perceived in the signal.

(22) Selkup main stress on the rightmost foot (secondary stresses not realized phonetically)

a.   x   b.   x   c.   x
   (x . . .)   (x .) (x)   (x) (x .) (x)
   qol⁽ʸ⁾ cim pa ti   ka naŋ mí: qu mo:q lɪ lí:

In languages such as English and Selkup, it makes sense for a learner not to rush to conclusions in determing the location of main stress. However, in many languages the location of main stress is very easy to find: it is fixed on a certain syllable or mora of the word relative to the left or right edge. An example is Old English, which, as discussed above, always has main stress on the initial syllable of a word (barring certain unstressed prefixes), no matter the weight of the initial syllable. It is a counterintuitive result of the learning path in (17) that a learner must first determine a number of less self-evident parameters before being able to locate the main stress in such languages. Indeed, Trubetzkoy (1939: 245) has identified the main stress in such languages as a *Grenzsignal* ('boundary signal'), a marker that indicates to speakers the relationship of the stressed syllable or mora to a word boundary. One might suppose that such markers would be useful to language learners in acquiring the prosodic structure of their language, but only if they are able to identify them relatively early in the learning path.

It is one thing to observe that the position of main stress in some languages is very easy to find; it is another matter to incorporate this observation into the learning path in (17), or some learning path like it, while still allowing the learner to successfully find the main stress in languages like English and Selkup. To this problem van der Hulst's notion of Primary Accent First provides a simple solution, which is to split the main stress parameter in (17) into two separate parameters, as in (23).

(23) Revised order for setting metrical parameters
    a.   Primary Accent First: A main stress is consistently observed on a fixed syllable.

    b–d. Syllable quantity, extrametricality, bounded constituents

    e.   Main stress: Project the {left/right}-most element of the line 1 constituent.

    f–g. Headedness and directionality of feet and destressing.

That is, very early in the learning path the learner checks to see if main stress appears on a fixed syllable. If it does, then the learner assigns an accent, either by putting down a bracket or by putting a mark on line 1 of the grid, as the particular form of the theory requires. As van der Hulst has proposed, this accent is 'non-metrical' in the sense that it exists independently of any other metrical structure, and does not depend even on knowledge of QS. If learners do not find a fixed accent, then they move on to set the rest of the parameters, eventually arriving at the main stress parameter in (23e).

As listed in (23), Primary Accent First appears to be *hors système*, as if tacked on to an otherwise cohesive metrical system. However, in the revision of the learning path proposed by Dresher (2016), it can be seen to be better integrated into the model than appears in (23). Dresher (2016) observes that the cue for QS proposed by Dresher and Kaye (1990), shown in (24), does not directly address syllable quantity, whose metrical manifestation is characterized in (25).

(24) Cue for syllable quantity (Dresher and Kaye 1990: 190)
    a.   Parameter: The language {does not/does} distinguish between light and heavy syllables.

    b.   Default: Assume all syllables have the same status; i.e., that they are quantity insensitive (QI).

    c.   Cue: Detect words of n syllables with conflicting stress contours (QS).

(25) QS in metrical theory
    In a QS system, a heavy syllable may not be a dependent in a foot. Depending on the theory, heavy syllables are assigned a left or right bracket on line 0, or a mark on line 1.

There is an obvious disconnect between what QS practically means in metrical theory (25) and the cue for QS in (24c). The rationale for (24c) is that in a QI language, all syllables are equal as far as the metrical system goes; therefore, it follows that every word of *n* syllables is metrically indistinguishable from every other word of *n* syllables. Thus, all three-syllable words should have the same stress, and the same for words of any other length. Dresher (2016) points out that Dresher and Kaye (1990) were primarily interested in the distinction between QI and QS systems, and if we restrict stress systems to those two types, the cue makes sense.

However, there are reasons other than QS for a language to have different stress contours on words of a given number of syllables. A language could have lexical accent, which is lexically assigned and not determined by syllable structure. Russian, for example, has words like *golová* 'head-NOM.SG', *gólovu* 'head-ACC.SG', and *koróva* 'cow-NOM.SG', *koróvu* 'cow-ACC.SG', where the stress is determined by the distribution of lexically-accented roots and affixes, and not by syllable quantity. Another way for a language to show stress differences unrelated to syllable structure is if there is influence from the morphology. English, for example, has noun ~ verb stress doublets such as *pérmit* (NOUN) ~ *permít* (VERB), and similarly *rébel ~ rebél, récord ~ recórd, cónvict ~ convíct,* etc.

Dresher (2016) observes that the cue in (24c) is not actually a cue for QS, but is part of a more general principle of contrast:

(26) Principle of contrast (Dresher 2016: 20)
      Do not make more distinctions than are required.
      Or more positively:
      Create only as many distinctions as are required.

Learners following the principle of contrast will start out assuming that there are no contrasts based on stress, and that all words are equal with respect to the metrical system. This necessarily implies that there are no distinctions based on syllable weight, lexical accent, or morphology: that is, a QI system with no further complications. While it is correct to assume QI if one does not find any contrasts based on stress, it does not hold that the finding of contrasts demonstrates that the language is QS. Rather, the existence of stress contrasts could have a number of sources, and it is up to the learner to determine if the cause is QS, or lexical accent, or morphology. Dresher (2016: 27) concludes that 'we can now understand the learning model of Dresher and Kaye (1990) and the variation of it proposed here as containing two types of cues: cues for discovering how many contrasting elements there are, and cues for identifying specific bits of structure that may be parametrically present or absent'.

Primary Accent First has a clear connection to contrast, or rather its absence: it is detected just in case the language does not show contrasts in the position of main stress. It is thus a restricted version of the cue in (24c) that is used to detect or rule out simple QI. Whereas (24c) looks for n syllables with conflicting stress contours, including both main and secondary stresses, Primary Accent First is triggered if main stress occurs on the same syllable (measured from the edge) in every word.

4 Conclusion

Primary Accent First instantiates Harry van der Hulst's correct intuition that in some stress systems, the main stress is not derived by calculating which of the metrical feet in a word is the strongest, but rather is identified at a relatively early stage independently of the other metrical parameters that may be relevant in the given language. We have looked at two different ways that Primary Accent First contributes to phonological theory.

In the analysis of a language like Old English it gives us a way to assign the main stress to a word-initial syllable even when it is light, in apparent defiance of metrical foot typology. This initial assignment then forces an adjustment in the form of mora borrowing from the next syllable (resolution) to bring the first foot into compliance with the requirement that it be associated with a minimum of two moras.

We have also shown that separating out stress systems with Primary Accent First from those where main stress is more integrated into metrical structure also results in a more intuitive learning path, and provides a theoretical justification for having two types of main stress parameter. On this model, main stress can serve as a Trubetzkoyan boundary signal in those languages with Primary Accent First without interfering with the acquisition of main stress in languages where it is dependent on the successful setting of other metrical parameters.

References

Bermúdez-Otero, Ricardo. 2005. A-stem nouns in West Saxon: Synchrony. Chapter 4 of *The life cycle of constraint rankings: Studies in early English morphophonology*. Ms. http://www.bermudez-otero.com/lifecycle_chapter4.pdf

Bermúdez-Otero, Ricardo & Richard M. Hogg. 2003. The actuation problem in Optimality Theory: Phonologization, rule inversion, and rule loss. In D. Eric Holt (ed.), *Optimality Theory and language change*, 91–120. Dordrecht: Kluwer Academic Publishers.

Dresher, B. Elan. 1994. Acquiring stress systems. In Eric Sven Ristad (ed.), *Language computations (DIMACS Series in Discrete Mathematics and Theoretical Computer Science, v. 17)*, 71–92. Providence, RI: AMS.

Dresher, B. Elan. 1999. Charting the learning path: Cues to parameter setting. *Linguistic Inquiry* 30(1). 27–67.

Dresher, B. Elan. 2009. Stress assignment in Tiberian Hebrew. In Charles Cairns & Eric Raimy (eds.), *Contemporary views on architecture and representations in phonology*, 213–224. Cambridge, MA: MIT Press.

Dresher, B. Elan. 2016. Covert representations, contrast, and the acquisition of lexical accent. In Jeffrey Heinz, Rob Goedemans, & Harry van der Hulst (eds.), *Dimensions of phonological stress*, 231–262. Cambridge: Cambridge University Press.

Dresher, B. Elan & Harry van der Hulst (eds.). 2022. *The Oxford history of phonology*. Oxford: Oxford University Press.

Dresher, B. Elan & Jonathan D. Kaye. 1990. A computational learning model for metrical phonology. *Cognition* 34(2). 137–195.

Dresher, B. Elan & Aditi Lahiri. 1986. On the metrical equivalence of H and L L in Germanic. Presented at the 61st annual meeting of the Linguistic Society of America, New York City, December 1986.

Dresher, B. Elan & Aditi Lahiri. 1991. The Germanic Foot: Metrical coherence in Old English. *Linguistic Inquiry* 22(2). 251–286.

Goedemans, Rob & Harry van der Hulst. 2014. The separation of accent and rhythm: Evidence from StressTyp. In Harry van der Hulst (ed.), *Word stress: Theoretical and typological issues*, 119–146. Cambridge: Cambridge University Press.

Goering, Nelson. 2016a. Early Old English foot structure. *Transactions of the Philological Society* 114(2). 171–197.

Goering, Nelson. 2016b. The linguistic elements of Old Germanic metre: Phonology, metrical theory, and the development of alliterative verse. D.Phil thesis, University of Oxford.

Halle, Morris & G. N. Clements. 1983. *Problem book in phonology*. Cambridge, MA: MIT Press.

Halle, Morris & William J. Idsardi. 1995. General properties of stress and metrical structure. In John Goldsmith (ed.), *The handbook of phonological theory*, 403–443. Cambridge, MA: Blackwell.

Halle, Morris, Wayne O'Neil, & Jean-Roger Vergnaud. 1993. Metrical coherence in Old English without the Germanic Foot. *Linguistic Inquiry* 24(3). 529–539.

Hayes, Bruce. 1986. A revised parametric metrical theory. *North East Linguistics Society*, Vol. 17: Article 18. Available at: https://scholarworks.umass.edu/nels/vol17/iss1/18

Hulst, Harry van der. 1984. *Syllable structure and stress in Dutch*. Dordrecht: Foris Publications.

Hulst, Harry van der. 1996. Separating primary accent and secondary accent. In Rob Goedemans, Harry van der Hulst, & Ellis Visch (eds.), *Stress patterns of the world*, 1–26. The Hague: Holland Academic Graphics.

Hulst, Harry van der. 1997. Primary accent is non-metrical. *Rivista di Linguistica* 9: 99–127.

Hulst, Harry van der. 2009. Brackets and grid marks or theories of primary accent and rhythm. In Charles Cairns & Eric Raimy (eds.), *Contemporary views on architecture and representations in phonology*, 225–245. Cambridge, MA: MIT Press.

Hulst, Harry van der. 2010. Representing accent. *Phonological Studies* 13: 117–128.

Hulst, Harry van der. 2012. Deconstructing stress. *Lingua* 122(13). 1494–1521.

Hutton, John. 1998. The development of secondary stress in Old English. In Linda van Bergen & Richard M. Hogg (eds.), *Historical Linguistics 1995: Volume 2: Germanic linguistics*, 115–130. Amsterdam: John Benjamins.
Idsardi, William J. 1992. The computation of prosody. Doctoral dissertation, MIT, Cambridge, MA.
Idsardi, William J. 1994. Open and closed feet in Old English. *Linguistic Inquiry* 25(3). 522–533.
Idsardi, William J. 2009. Calculating metrical structure. In Charles Cairns & Eric Raimy (eds.), *Contemporary views on architecture and representations in phonology*, 191–211. Cambridge, MA: MIT Press.
Keyser, Samuel Jay & Wayne O'Neil. 1985. *Rule generalization and optionality in language change*. Dordrecht: Foris Publications.
Lahiri, Aditi. 1982. Theoretical implications of phonological change: Evidence from Germanic languages. Doctoral dissertation, Brown University, Providence, RI.
Lahiri, Aditi & Harry van der Hulst. 1987. On foot typology. *North East Linguistics Society*, Vol. 18: Iss. 3, Article 2. Available at: https://scholarworks.umass.edu/nels/vol18/iss3/2
Trubetzkoy, N. S. 1939. *Grundzüge der Phonologie. Traveaux du cercle linguistique de Prague 7.* 2nd edn. Göttingen: Vandenhoek & Ruprecht, 1958.

Anthi Revithiadou
Accent as Autosegment: A Unified Account of Lexical Accent and Lexical Stress Systems

Abstract: In this chapter, we put forward an accent-based analysis of stress and tone in the so-called lexical stress and lexical accent systems, respectively. Although such systems are not good candidates for tone and stress prototypicality (Hyman 2001, 2006, et seq.), their shared features and common prosodic behavior provide a good basis for treating them on a par. Following van der Hulst (1984, 1996 et seq.), we propose that they both share an abstract prosodic autosegment (Spahr 2016), called the *accent*, which can be phonetically realized as tone or stress, depending on the language. On the basis of empirical evidence, we show that accents can be either linked or floating. They may also differ with respect to their inherent strength, called *activity level* (Smolensky and Goldrick 2016), a property that decisively interacts with phonological edgemost effects and the morphological and/or lexical conditions that control the resolution of accentual conflicts. The chapter concludes with a *Gradient Harmonic Grammar* (Smolensky and Goldrick 2016) analysis of some intriguing patterns of accentuation from Lithuanian.

Keywords: accent, activity level, dominance, gradient strength, Gradient Harmonic Grammar, lexical accent/stress systems, pitch-accent, π-node autosegment

1 Introduction

In his seminal work on word prosody, Hyman (2001, 2006, 2009, 2014; see also Agostinho and Hyman, this volume) argues that, while there is consensus that certain properties are used to identify two prototypes – tone and stress – some languages do not exhibit a minimum of properties that would allow them to be designated as canonical stress or tone systems.[1] He makes explicit reference

---
[1] For the relation between tone and stress, see Gordon, this volume.

Note: I wish to thank the two anonymous reviewers and the editor of the volume for their insightful comments and suggestions. I also thank Ksenia Bogomolets for her valuable feedback. All errors are of course my own.

Anthi Revithiadou, Department of Linguistics, School of Philology, Aristotle University of Thessaloniki

to *pitch-accent* languages, which he proposes should be treated as defective or 'restricted tone systems' (Voorhoeve 1973) because their tone is subject to specific constraints such as obligatoriness, culminativity and/or privativity (Hyman 2009: 220). Obligatoriness and culminativity are clearly prototypical properties of stress systems because they refer to the fact that every lexical word has at least one and at most one prominent syllable, respectively. For instance, some pitch-accent systems display an obligatory and culminative H tone in the domain of the word (see, e.g., Nubi, Gussenhoven 2006; Kinga, Schadeberg 1973, among others). Privativity refers to the absence of tonal contrasts in pitch-accent languages, i.e., the restriction of contrastive tone to /H/ vs. /∅/ (or, more rarely, /L/ vs. /∅/), as opposed to prototype tonal systems, which distinguish among three or more tone levels. In conclusion, Hyman refutes the necessity of the notion accent as a prosodic type. He holds that pitch-accent is essentially a label that refers to a system with a very reduced tone inventory (see also Yip 2002; Gussenhoven 2004) which displays only a fraction of the properties attested in prototypical tone systems.

On the other hand, van der Hulst (2011) emphasizes the abundance of typological surveys that identify pitch-accent as a distinct prosodic type, discussing systems in which the distributional properties of pitch-accents are very similar to the properties of accents that are phonetically manifested as stress in other languages, widely known as *stress-accent systems*. Van der Hulst's observation leads him to conclude that tone in pitch-accent systems and stress in stress-accent systems should be treated alike, i.e. in terms of an abstract entity called *accent* (van der Hulst 1996, 1999, 2011). Van der Hulst follows the Abercrombian tradition (Abercrombie 1991 [1976]: 82–83; see also Fox 2000) which distinguishes accent from its phonetic realization. For him, accent is an abstract phonological entity that is part of the lexically-specified information in the entry of some morphological exponent. Formally, it is encoded as a (pre-specified) metrical head[2] that can be realized as either stress or pitch, depending on the language. When accents are not underlyingly present (and obligatoriness holds in a pitch-accent system), the position of primary accent is decided on a predictable location by the

---

[2] There are several views in the literature regarding the nature and the representation of accent. For Halle and Vergnaud (1987b), Idsardi (1992), Halle and Idsardi (1995), among others, the specification of accent is cast in the same terms as foot structure, which is enforced by a morpheme-specific parsing algorithm. For Alderete (1999, 2001a, 2001b) and Revithiadou (1999) it is an autosegmental element, for van der Hulst (1999) and Vaxman (2016; see also Vaxman, this volume) it is a special 'weight diacritic', whereas for Inkelas (1999) it takes the form of a pre-assigned trochaic foot. See also Bogomolets (2020) for a recent view on the topic.

language-specific default.[3] Van der Hulst nonetheless acknowledges that, under a more liberal interpretation of accent, obligatoriness may be lifted and accentual systems may allow unaccented words to surface (van der Hulst 2011: 1018).

In light of van der Hulst's (2011, 2014b) view on accent, well-known pitch-accent systems, like Nubi and Kinga, can be analyzed as 'accent systems'. Instead of postulating that one syllable in every word has an H pitch, the special syllable can be treated as being pre-specified with an accent that is phonetically realized as an H tone (an analysis that has been advanced, for instance, by Goldsmith 1976 for Kinga). Nevertheless, van der Hulst (2011, 2014b) admits, that it is not always crucial whether languages like Nubi or Kinga are labelled as restricted tone (see, Hyman 2001, 2006, et seq.) or as pitch-accent systems. However, the existence of floating elements might drive one to decide in favor of the tonal analysis, given that floating tones exist but floating accents are questionable. The same analysis should also be preferred when tonal spreading processes are attested in a system. Conversely, an accentual analysis may be favored in cases in which clash resolution affects the realization of neighboring accents.

We conclude from the above that pitch-accent and stress-accent systems share certain similarities that will go unnoticed if they are not treated in the same way. Indeed, some pitch-accent and stress-accent systems, broadly known as *lexical accent* (LA) and *lexical stress systems* (LS), respectively, display astounding similarities with each other. The first reason for our conclusion is that the assignment of tone and stress in languages with lexical accent or stress (e.g., (Ancient) Greek, Russian, Lithuanian, Tokyo Japanese, Sanskrit) is not predictable (see also discussion on Wakhi stress in Li, this volume). Most morphological elements (e.g., roots, affixes) come with their own lexically-specified tone/stress, one of which is selected to be pronounced and become a property of the whole word (culminativity). Secondly, in these languages lexical tone/stress shows migration effects, in the sense that tone/stress can be realized on a close – or, more rarely, distant – syllable of a morpheme other than the one which sponsors it. Thirdly, lexical tone/stress may be erased under certain circumstances, in which case the word either receives the unmarked tone (binary tone system) or is assigned a tone (privative

---

[3] Van der Hulst introduces a non-rhythmic account for primary accentuation, known as *Accent-First Theory*, advocated extensively in several of his works (e.g., van der Hulst 1984, 1996, 1999, 2010, 2012, 2014a, 2014b; Goedemans and van der Hulst 2014; see also Dresher and Lahiri, this volume and Vaxman, this volume). The theory formally separates the representation of primary accent from the representation of rhythmically prominent syllables: primary accent is assigned first, whereas predictable secondary prominence is computed later on by a different – i.e. a grid-based – mechanism that is kept separate from accent, even in languages where it is analytically possible to unify the two phenomena (see Bogomolets, this volume).

tone system, provided obligatoriness holds) or stress by the default algorithm.[4] To describe these languages either as hybrid systems with mixed 'tonal' and 'stress' properties or as tonal systems with severe restrictions on the distribution of tones, as Hyman (2006, 2009 et seq.) suggests, conceals some important generalizations concerning the typology of accents and their patterns of interaction. Therefore, following van der Hulst (2011, 2014b), we propose that LA and LS systems should be offered a unified account in terms of the notion accent. More specifically, in line with Spahr (2016), we identify the accent as an autosegment of prosodic nature and, more importantly, we assert that accents have different degrees of strength (see Smolensky and Goldrick 2016). This difference in strength explains their curious behavior in relation to other accents in certain systems.

The remainder of this chapter is organized as follows: In Section 2, we briefly review autosegmental approaches to stress and pitch-accent and adopt Spahr's (2016) notion of prosodic autosegment for the representation of accents. In Section 3, we discuss the typology of accents and address issues that reveal differences in their inherent strength. In Section 4, we use empirical data from Lithuanian and Tokyo Japanese to explore patterns of interaction between accents. We also construct a formal analysis of representative examples within the *Gradient Harmonic Grammar* framework (Smolensky and Goldrick 2016). In Section 5 we conclude the chapter.

2 An Autosegmental Approach to Lexical Stress and Pitch-Accent

Due to its clearly tonal nature, an autosegmental analysis of a system like Japanese is anticipated (see, e.g., Haraguchi 1977, 1991, 2017; McCawley 1968, 1977, 1978; Poser 1984; Pierrehumbert and Beckman 1988, among others); an autosegmental approach to stress, however, is less conventional. Interestingly, an analysis of stress as an autosegment of a different nature than tone has been offered by Hagberg (1993, 2006).[5] In Hagberg's view of metrical theory, stress differs from tone in domain and phonetic realization, but not in principles of operation: the foot is the domain of stress while the word is the domain of tone. Feet are inherently headless and stress is assigned to feet based on the principles of autosegmen-

---

[4] Not all LA systems allow obligatoriness (see, e.g., Tokyo Japanese). For reasons of space, we refrain from addressing here issues of obligatoriness and culminativity in such systems.
[5] Hagberg (2006: 58–59) cites Halle and Vergnaud (1987a) who, following Liberman (1975), adopt a slightly autosegmental perspective on stress by assuming that stressed elements (called 'stressed phonemes') exist in a separate autosegmental plane than the sequence of phonemes.

tal theory (Goldsmith 1976, 1990). Some of the advantages of Hagberg's proposal become evident in the analysis of lexical accent in Tagalog in (1). The exponent of the Tagalog suffix that derives adjectives from nouns is argued to consist solely of a floating *-autosegment, i.e. /-*/ (Hagberg 2006: 179). The surface effect of this 'affixation' is a stress shift from the initial to the final syllable. An analysis along the same lines is also assumed for the exponent of the 3SG preterite in Spanish, e.g., *habló* 'he spoke' (cf. *háblo* 'I speak', Hagberg 2006: 48).[6]

(1) *Affix as floating stress autosegment in Tagalog*
    a. bí:his   'way of dressing' bihís 'dressed up'
    b. gú:tom 'hunger'   gutóm 'hungry'
    c. bú:tas   'hole'   butás   'punctured'
    d. bí:lang 'number'   biláng 'counted'

The autosegmental treatment of stress naturally raises a question as to whether or not stress can spread like other autosegments do. Hagberg's (2006: 192) answer is straightforward: Spreading within the foot is generally attested[7] but stress (as prominence) does not spread because that would be incompatible with its primary function, which is to signal out one element as more prominent than all others. Therefore, lack of spreading must be treated as an idiosyncratic property of the stress autosegment, just as downstep is treated as an idiosyncratic property of tone.

Alas, by being designed strictly for stress systems, the *-autosegmental primitive does not allow us to develop a unified model for the representation of accent in both LA and LS systems. This problem aside, however, Hagberg's attempt to analyze stress systems using autosegmental principles, as is the case in tonal systems, is a step in the right direction.

The characteristics of stress in Belarusian led Dubina (2012) to the same hypothesis as Hagberg, namely that accent is autosegmental in nature which takes the form of an H tone (Dubina 2012: 113–115). Essentially, H is a 'super-autosegment' the phonetics of which are decided on a language-specific basis. In an LA system, such as Lithuanian, H is phonetically implemented as pitch movements, whereas in an LS system, like Russian and Belarusian, it is realized as stress prominence. Dubina's proposal builds on Lockwood's (1983) insight that pitch is not the only possible phonetic expression of tone. Tonal entities may be realized with several phonetic properties beyond pitch, such as laryngealization,

---

6 For the reader's convenience, stress is indicated with an acute accent '´' on the stressed vowel.
7 Hagberg (2006: 191–192) reports on two cases of spreading within the foot: tonal spread in Capanahua (Loos 1969) and [+nasal] spreading in Applegross Gaelic and in Guaraní, which are discussed in more detail by van der Hulst and Smith (1982).

duration and intensity, the latter two of which are prototypically associated with stress. There is, however, one important difference between Dubina's and Lockwood's perspective on tone: For Lockwood tone cannot be culminative, which precludes the possibility for both pitch-accent and stress-accent systems to be analyzed as tonal. On the other hand, Dubina's analysis of Belarusian operates under the assumption that tone is culminative.

Spahr (2016) makes an intriguing contribution in the debate on the nature of accent. He too posits that accent is an autosegment, but one that can receive a wide range of interpretations, depending on the particular grammar. There is therefore no reason to consider it inherently tonal, as suggested by Dubina. More specifically, Spahr proposes that phonological systems operate on a single formal autosegment that represents a prosodic root node, called the π-*node*. Such π-nodes have language-specific phonetic realizations. The phonological representations of π for privative H tone and stress-accent languages are given in (2a–b). (The 'x' signifies a tier of segmental root nodes.)

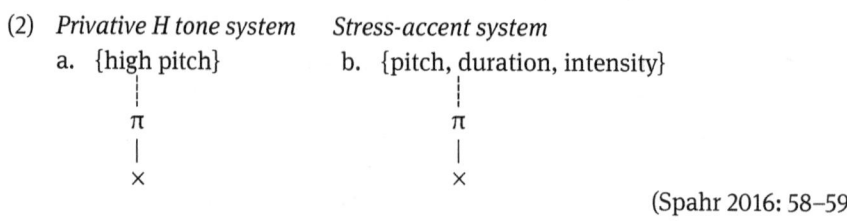

(Spahr 2016: 58–59)

For Spahr, the primary difference between a privative tone language and a stress-accent one is in the phonetic realization of π. For instance, a tone system with a H/Ø tonal distinction will include a featureless π-node, like the one depicted in (2a). In this language, the π accent will be phonetically realized with high pitch. The same featureless π-node in a stress-accent system, (2b), however, will be phonetically interpreted with pitch, duration and intensity, i.e. the phonetic correlates of stress. Formally, therefore, there is no distinction between the π-nodes in (2a) and (2b) since both represent the same phonological entity. Moreover, as autosegments, they ought to exhibit the same phonological behavior; for instance, they could both spread. It is undeniable, however, that the absence of stress spreading phenomena in languages of type-(2b) accents is still puzzling. A possible explanation for this absence could be that, when processed by the component responsible for phonetic implementation, the relevant representations will crash as stress is impossible to sustain over a greater number of syllables.

In a binary tone system, say H/L, the π-node of will be specified with the contrastive feature [±H]. Each representation in (3) implements different tone heights according to the featural specification of π.

(3) *Binary tone language*
   a. [+H]   b. [−H]
      | |
      π   π
      | |
      ×   ×

(Spahr 2016: 59)

To conclude, Spahr's π-node as an autosegment is similar to Hagberg's (1993, 2006) *-autosegment and Dubina's (2012) H tone but, at the same time, it is pivotally different from these phonological entities because, by being formally abstract, it bears no information on its phonetic implementation. In this respect it is much closer to van der Hulst's (1984, 1996, et seq.) definition of accent. In the following section we explore the descriptive and theoretical efficiency of Spahr's π-autosegment with empirical data from LA (Sanskrit, Lithuanian, Tokyo Japanese) and LS (Greek, Russian) systems (see also discussion on lexical stress in Wakhi in Li, this volume).

3 Typology of Accents and Gradience

In this section, we establish, on the basis of empirical evidence from a group of LA and LS systems, that accents as autosegments come in different shapes and forms: some are linked, whereas others are floating. We also propose that accents have a gradient degree of strength, in the sense that certain accents may be inherently stronger than others (Revithiadou 1999; see also Smolensky and Goldrick 2016 for phonological elements with *gradient* strength and, for a different view on strength, Vaxman, this volume). We also show that the degree of strength of an accent has important implications for *dominance*, that is, the particular edgemost or morphological and/or lexical factors that determine which accent will be pronounced in a string of multiple underlying accents and which accents will be silenced. The issue of dominance is addressed in more detail in Section 4.

Although the majority of accents are lexically linked to a specific position of a root or an affix, LA and LS systems often display instances of so-called *migrating accents*. These accents are sponsored by a specific morphological exponent but are realized in different positions within the word.[8] Migrating accents constitute the

---

[8] The accent is realized as stress (amplitude and duration) in Russian (Jones and Ward 1969) and in Greek (Arvaniti 2007). It is realized as an H tone in Sanskrit (Macdonell 1910: 77–78), in Lithuanian (Kushnir (2019: 37–38), who also adds intensity and length to its phonetic manifestation)

most robust argument in support of the autosegmental treatment of accents. The examples in (4) are telling. The accent, introduced by the suffixal element, overrides the accent of the base (if any) and is realized on some syllable of the root or on the inflection,[9] giving the surface effect of pre-/post-accentuation. (Floating accents are indicated with a superscript π, '^π', next to the sponsoring exponent. Linked accents are represented for convenience with an acute accent on the sponsoring vowel: V́.)

(4) *Floating accents in LA and LS systems*
    a. /purukuts-^{π}i/   Páurukutsi   'Purukutsa-NMZ,[10] son of P.'   Skr
    b. /kaːr-áj-^{π}itum/   káːrajitum   'make-CAUS-INF'
    c. /pad-^{π}am/   páːdam   'foot-SG.ACC'
    d. /o^π-susí/   osúsi   'HON-sushi'   TJ
    e. /úra-^{π}ke/   uráke   'Ura family/household'
    f. /eláð-ik^π-os/   elaðikós   'Greece-ADJZ-SG.NOM'   Gr

The data in (5) involve inputs with multiple accented syllables. All accents here are local, i.e. linked to the morpheme by which they are introduced. It is the leftmost accent, introduced by the root/stem, which is phonetically realized when followed by an accented suffix. Some representative examples from the languages under examination are given in (5).

(5) *Accentual conflict resolution*
    a. /kaféð-ón/   kaféðon   'coffee-PL.GEN'   Gr
    b. /bolót-á/   bolóta   'swamp-PL.NOM'   Ru
    c. /ráth-ám/   rátham   'chariot-SG.ACC'   Skr
    d. /várn-aá/   várnaa   'crow-SG.ACC'   Lith
    e. /jorokób-éba/   jorokóbeba   'be pleased-COND'   TJ

---

and in Tokyo Japanese (Kawahara 2015; cf. H*L proposed by Pierrehumbert and Beckman (1988), Gussenhoven (2004), and HL proposed by Haraguchi (2017)).

9 The data in the chapter are culled from the following sources: Revithiadou (1999, 2007) and Revithiadou and Spyropoulos (2016) for Greek; Poser (1984), Haraguchi (1977, 1991, 2017), Kawahara (2015) for Japanese; Kushnir (2019) for Lithuanian; Melvold (1989), Alderete (1999, 2001b) for Russian; Kiparsky (1984), Halle and Vergnaud (1987a), Macdonell (1910), Whitney (1993) for Sanskrit.

10 The following abbreviated glosses are used in this chapter: ADJZ: adjectivizer, CAUS: causative, COND: conditional, DAT: dative, DIM: diminutive, F: feminine, GEN: genitive, HON: honorific, INF: infinitive, M: masculine, NMZ: nominalizer, NOM: nominative, NPAST: non past, PL: plural, SG: singular.

Interestingly, Kushnir (2019) observes that certain roots and inflections in Lithuanian seem to have 'stronger' underlying accents (indicated with an acute and an underscore). The examples in (6) are informative in this respect. We observe that in (6a–b) the leftmost accent, that is, the one on the root, prevails over the accent of the inflection. In contrast, in (6c–d), the root accent outweighs the accent of the SG.ACC suffix (6c) but loses to the accent of the PL.GEN exponent (6d). Kushnir clarifies that the accent in roots like /vaĩk-/ must be underlying and not assigned by the default because the accent is not anchored to the absolute left edge of the word. As suggested by examples like *vilk̃-aa* 'wolf-SG.ACC, *kam̃bar-ii* 'room-SG. ACC', *nuostaáb-uu* 'wonderful-M.ACC.SG', it can show up anywhere in the moraic skeleton of the root, which confirms its lexically pre-specified status.

(6) *Strong and weak accents in Lithuanian*
 a. /vár̲n-aá/ várnaa 'crow-SG.ACC'
 b. /vár̲n-uú̲/ várnuu 'crow-PL.GEN'
 c. /vaík-aá/ vaíkaa 'child-SG.ACC'.
 d. /vaík-uú̲/ vaikuú 'child-PL.GEN' (Kushnir 2019: 10–11)

On the basis of the above examples, one could argue that the realization of the PL.GEN accent results from the idiosyncratic specification of the exponent /-uú/ as dominant inflection. This lexical property would allow the inflection to impose its accent on the whole word. However, the proposed solution fails to explain why the same inflection is accentually inactive with roots like /várn-/ (6b). An alternative explanation would be to attribute the observed asymmetry to the inherent strength of the accent located on the root. Under this assumption, the accent in /vaík-/ appears to be weaker compared to the accent in /várn-/, and this difference in strength has important consequences for its realization.[11] Weak accents are not totally inert because they can successfully compete with other weak accents, such as those sponsored by weakly accented inflections, like /-aá/ in example (6c), as well as by such accentually non-dominant derivational suffixes as those discussed in the following paragraph.

A handful of derivational suffixes in Lithuanian, while never accented themselves, fix accent on the base they attach to regardless of what comes after them (Kushnir 2019: 112–113). This pattern is particularly interesting in weakly accented roots, such as the root /vaík-/ in (7b). In both examples in (7), it is the leftmost

---

[11] Kushnir (2019: 11–12) provides further empirical evidence in support of the distinction between weak and strong underlying accents in Lithuanian from an accent shift process known as *Saussure's Law* (Blevins 1993).

accent which is phonetically realized. Especially intriguing here is the fact that the accent of the root /vaĭk-/, which loses to the strongly accented inflection /-uú̲/ (6d), prevails over the suffixal accent /-íʃk/ in (7b). What causes the accentual prevalence of this root?

(7) Latent weak accents in Lithuanian
    a. /bro̲ol-íʃk-uú̲/   bróoliʃkuu 'brother-ADJZ-PL.GEN, brotherly'
    b. /vaĭk-íʃk-uú̲/   vaĭkisʃkuu 'child-ADJZ-PL.GEN, childish' (cf. 6d)

Kushnir (2019: 111–112) claims that the originally feeble accent of the root /vaĭk-/ is enhanced with the help of an equally weak and somehow latent accent that is sponsored by the adjectivizer *-išk* /-íʃk/. We will see exactly how this is accomplished in Section 4. What is important to establish here is that, first, accents in Lithuanian have a *gradient degree of strength* (Smolensky and Goldrick 2016) in the sense that some are stronger than others, e.g. accent(*vár̥n-*) > accent(*vaĭk-*), accent(*-uú̲*) > accent(*-aá*) and, second, accents of low strength cannot surface unless they are somehow enhanced by a neighboring accent (see Vaxman, this volume, for a different approach on strength scales).

Further empirical support for the existence of weak accents can be found in a group of suffixes in Tokyo Japanese. According to Kawakami (1974) and Poser (1984: 83–86), deverbal nouns formed with the suffix /-í/ involve what Poser calls *dependent accents*. Such accents manage to surface only when there is at least one underlying accent elsewhere in the UR of the complex form, as illustrated in examples (8c–d). With accentless bases, like those in (8a–b), the affixal accent remains mute. Recall that obligatoriness does not apply to Tokyo Japanese accentuation (see fn 4), hence, unaccented words are grammatical outputs. We realize that the nominalizing suffix /-í/ is dominant when its accent meets the requirements that allow it to surface, as shown in (8c–d). In these examples both roots are accented, and it is exactly the presence of their accent that somehow initiates the activation of the suffixal accent. A similar behavior is also displayed by the pre-accenting suffix /-mono/ 'thing' (see Kawahara 2015: 469 for examples).

(8) Dependent accents in Tokyo Japanese
    a. kariru   'borrow'   kari   'borrowing'
    b. kasu   'lend'   kasi   'lending'
    c. hajíru   'be ashamed'   hají   'shame'
    d. kaségu   'work, toil'   kasegí   'labor, work'

As suggested by the examples in (8), the accent of /-í/ is activated by the accent of the base. We believe that this happens because, as in Lithuanian above, the accent of the base merges with the accent of the nominalizer into a strong autosegment that is eventually realized onto the suffix. The two languages differ in which element acts as a 'charger' and provides extra strength: in Lithuanian the adjectival suffix fills this role, in Tokyo Japanese the root accent is the 'charger'.

The question that arises at this point is why an accent should depend on another accent in order to be realized? Under the premise that accents are autosegmental entities, the answer is simple: neighboring weak accents have the option to coalesce into a strong autosegment, as depicted in (9). Once the accent is strong enough, depending on the language, some edgemost principle or the specifics of dominance, which, as mentioned above, are either lexically or morphologically controlled, will eventually determine where the fused accent is realized: on the (derivational) suffix or on the root.

(9) *Accent coalescence*

Smolensky and Goldrick's (2016, henceforth S&G) *Gradient Symbolic Representations / GSR*[12] model allows us to capture the gradient strength of accents in a clear and straightforward manner. In traditional analyses, phonological elements (segments, autosegments, syllables, etc.) are assumed to be either present or absent in an input and/or an output form. S&G change this view by proposing that a phonological element's degree of presence in a given linguistic representation is gradient (S&G 2016: 2). That is, a phonological entity may be stored as part of a vocabulary item with a varying degree of strength, which is called *activity level* and is represented numerically with a value that ranges from 0 to 1. Only elements with activity equal to 1 are pronounced; those with activity lower than 1 are partially active and thus more likely to change during phonological computation than are high activation elements. Depending on the language-specific grammar, weak elements may either delete (in violation of Max) or fuse with others (in violation of Unif(ormity)), or even get the required activity that will allow them to be pronounced from the Grammar (in violation of Dep).

---

[12] For an analysis of accentuation within this framework, see Zimmermann (2017) for Moses Columbian Salish; Rosen (2018, 2019) for Japanese compounds; Revithiadou (2018) for Ancient Greek; Kushnir (2019) for Lithuanian, among others.

Obviously, S&G's take on the structure of URs has serious implications on how Eval computes the violations incurred by different candidates. More specifically, in an analysis that is cast within the weighted constraints framework of *Harmonic Grammar* (HG, Legendre, Miyata, and Smolensky 1990a, 1990b; see also Goldsmith 1993a, 1993b; Smolensky and Legendre 2006), the difference in activity is implemented as a higher penalty score for the candidate that most violates the respective faithfulness constraint. For instance, if an input has an accent π of 0.6 activity, it must be provided the extra 0.4 activity by the Grammar in violation of DEP[π]. This implies that the realization of a 0.6 accent will be more costly for the Grammar compared to the realization of an accent, say, with an input activity 1 if, in that Grammar, violation of DEP[π] is deemed as more serious than violation of MAX[π]. On the other hand, deletion of the low activity accent in the same Grammar will automatically be rendered less costly than the loss of a stronger accent because it would entail a lower violation of MAX[π]. The formal details of the analysis are discussed in Section 4.

Central to this discussion is the fact that accents, as autosegments, are specified to have gradient activity. The level of activity is an idiosyncratic property of each accent. Strong accents have activity 1, whereas weak accents have an activity below 1. There is a whole range of activity values that a weak accent can possibly take. For Japanese and Lithuanian, this activity is proposed here to be 0.5. The representations in (10) depict the types of linked accents that theoretically can be found in LS and LA systems. Floating π-nodes may also be strong or weak, but due to space limitations they are not included in (10). Since the LA systems under investigation are all privative, only the representations in (10a–b) are of interest to our analysis. (The activity of a phonological element is indicated with a subscript number at its right side.)

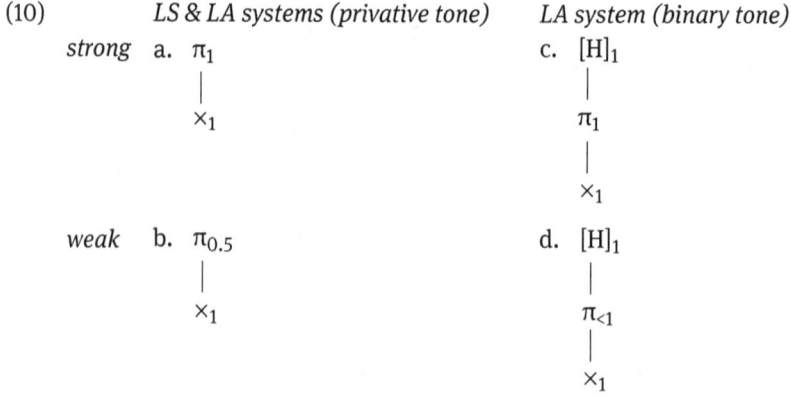

In summary, in this section we have shown that floating accents are common to both LA and LS systems, lending support to our hypothesis that accents are autosegmental in nature. We have also argued that certain LA systems have accents with gradient activity level and discussed cases in which weak accents are fortified via coalescence. Finally, we proposed that degree of strength can be formally expressed within S&G's (2016) GSR model.

4 A Gradient Harmonic Grammar Analysis of Strong and Weak Accents

Following our presentation of accent typology, we are ready to construct a *Gradient Harmonic Grammar* (GHG, S&G 2016) analysis of the data at hand, with emphasis on the Lithuanian accentual patterns discussed above. Our analysis integrates both the relative strength of accents, expressed as activity, and the relative strength of morphemes, expressed as dominance. HG has the same Gen-cum-Eval architecture as classical Optimality Theory (Prince and Smolensky 1993; McCarthy and Prince 1993a, 1993b), but substitutes the constraint ranking with a system of numerical weights; each constraint is assigned a specific *weight* (w) that reflects its relative strength. (In the tableau, constraint weights are given as positive integers placed below the constraint names.) Because constraint violations constitute penalties, they are indicated with negative integers ($-n$ for n number of violations). The loss, for instance, of an input π-node with 0.6 activity in the output incurs a violation of MAX[π]. The penalty score for MAX[π] results by multiplying the number of violations incurred by the candidate output which deleted the π with the weight of the constraint ($-n \times w$). Assuming that the weight of MAX[π] is, for instance, 10, then the penalty for deleting $π_{0.6}$ is $-0.6 \times 10 = -6$, which is indicated in the relevant cell of the tableau. Similarly, an input π-node with 0.6 activity, which acquires the missing 0.4 activity from Grammar, causes a -0.4 violation of DEP[π]. With a constraint weight of, say, 5, the penalty score is -2 ($-0.4 \times 5 = -2$). In HG, violations are cumulative, meaning that the violations of all constraints, even of the low-ranking ones, add up to a total penalty score called *harmony* (H; stated in the rightmost column of the tableau). In non-probabilistic versions of HG, the optimum is the candidate with the lowest cumulative penalty score or, more accurately, the candidate with the highest H.

At this point we are equipped to examine the way in which the accentual patterns under investigation may be accounted for within the GHG model. Here we construct the grammar of Lithuanian which demonstrates the split between strong and weak accents as discussed in Section 3. We assume that weak accents have activity 0.5, as opposed to strong ones, which have activity 1. Among accents of equal activity, the leftmost one prevails (see examples in (6)). The grammar responsible for this relation includes the following constraints and their respective weights:

(11) a. MAX[π], *w 20*: Any amount of underlying activity of the autosegmental π-node has a correspondent amount of activity in the output.
b. LEFTMOST[π], *w 8*: Align the left edge of the π-node with the left edge of the phonological word.
c. DEP[π], *w 10*: Any amount of activity of the autosegmental π-node in the output has a correspondent amount of underlying activity.

The constraint LEFTMOST in (11b) is a reincarnation of the *Basic Accentuation Principle* (Kiparsky 1984; Halle and Vergnaud 1987a, 1987b) which, all things being equal, promotes the realization of the leftmost accent in the word. The constraints MAX[π] and DEP[π] are violated when an input accent deletes or is added epenthetic activity, respectively. The first tableau in (12) demonstrates that the most harmonic output is the one which realizes the accent of the root (12a). Bear in mind that both accents in the input are of equal activity, but the grammar shows a bias for the preservation of the leftmost accent due to the cumulativity in constraint evaluation that characterizes HGs. The situation, however, is reversed in the tableau in (13), where the candidate with the accented inflection is selected as the optimum. We observe that the 0.5 activity of the root accent has detrimental effects on its survival during evaluation.[13] Candidate (13a) incurs a −5 penalty score on DEP[π], which is added to the −20 penalty caused by the deletion of the inflectional accent. The sum of these penalties, expressed as H, is lower than the total penalty score, i.e. −18, triggered by candidate (13b), which chooses not to realize the weak accent of the root. Obviously, because the deleted accent is of low activity, its obliteration is deemed less costly by this particular grammar.[14]

---

[13] Merging the weak accent of the root with the accent of the suffix entails a violation of UNIF that penalizes the sharing of π by two ×'s. Due to lack of space, we have not included in these tableaux outputs with merged accents. Accent coalescence, however, is crucial in accounting for certain cases of accent resolution when multiple accents are underlyingly present in linearized string of morphemes; thus the effects of UNIF are fleshed out below.

[14] The evaluation of inputs with two weak accents, as in /vaĩk-aá/ *vaíkaa* (6c), is not discussed here due to space limitations. Since both accents are equally weak, the grammar will opt for the output that enhances the leftmost accent with epenthetic activity.

(12)

π₁Root π₁Infl /×₁Root-×₁Infl/	MAX[π] w: 20	LEFTMOST[π] w: 8	DEP[π] w: 10	H
☞ a. π₁R | ×₁R-×₁I	−20			−20
b. π₁I | ×₁R-×₁I	−20	−8		−28

(13)

π₀.₅Root π₁Infl /×₁Root-×₁Infl/	MAX[π] w: 20	LEFTMOST[π] w: 8	DEP[π] w: 10	H
a. π₁R | ×₁R-×₁I	−20		−5	−25
☞ b. π₁I | ×₁R-×₁I	−10	−8		−18

The following crosslinguistic examples demonstrate cases where the derivational suffix accent prevails over any other accent, regardless of its strength (see 14f).

(14) *Dominance in accented derived words*
    a. /sapun-á₁ð-ó₁n/   sapunáðon   'bubble-NMZ.FEM-PL.GEN'   *Gr*
    b. /gó₁rl-á₁st-á₁/   gorlásta   'throat-ADJZ-F.SG.NOM,'   *Ru*
    c. /rá₁th-í₁n-é₁/   rathíne   'chariot-NMZ-SG.DAT, charioteer'   *Skr*
    d. /netú₁-ppó₁-i/   netuppói   'fever-ADJZ-NPAST, feverish'   *TJ*
    e. /bró₁ol-εέ₁l-iuú₁/   broolεέliuu   'brother-DIM-PL.GEN'   *Lith*
    f. /vaí₀.₅k-εέ₁l-iuú₁/   vaikεέliuu   'kid-DIM-PL.GEN'

Certain affixes have been argued either to be lexically specified as dominant (e.g., Melvold 1989; Alderete 1999) or to acquire this property from a position they occupy in a given structure (e.g., Revithiadou 1999). Gouskova and Linzen (2015) claim that, possibly depending on their structural relation to their complements and, specifically, whether they are spelled out in the same cycle as the root or not, most derivational suffixes come with a particular *morphological regularization factor* that targets a specific constraint via indexing. With the appropriate value, this regularization factor manipulates the evaluation of the constraint it is indexed to with dramatic effects on the phonological behavior of the root.

Although Gouskova and Linzen (2015) follow a different line of research than the one taken here,[15] we believe that their assumption on affixation being associated with a particular scaling factor is on the right track. Following their lead, we postulate that affixation introduces a *scaling factor*, s (Coetzee and Pater 2011; Coetzee and Kawahara 2013), which is indexed to MAX[π]. As a result, the scalar constraint becomes more punitive because the number of its violations is multiplied by the constraint weight and the s introduced by the suffix (–n × w × s; see McPherson and Hayes 2016). When a candidate contains, for instance, the dominant suffix /-ppó/ in Japanese or /-εέl/ in Lithuanian, with s equal to 2, satisfaction of MAX[π] becomes mightily significant, and deletion of the scaled / dominant suffix is eventually blocked. In Lithuanian, for instance, failure to realize the strong accent of /-εέ¹l/, would yield a ((–1 × 20w) × 2s=) –40 penalty for MAX[π]. In this approach, non-dominant affixes are associated with a scaling factor of 1, thus, exercising practically no effect on the evaluation of MAX[π].

The tableau in (15) illustrates with an abstract example the effect a dominant suffix has on output evaluation. All accents in the input are assumed to have activity 1, but, because MAX[π] is scaled by the derivational suffix, non-pronunciation of its accent doubles the penalty score of MAX[π] in candidates (15b–c) raising their harmony score. By doubling the weight of MAX[π], via scaling, deletion of the dominant affix accent is much more costly than deletion of any other accent in the string. The cost of pronouncing a non-leftmost accent is low, given the weight of LEFTMOST[π], and obviously it cannot block the selection of (15a) as the most harmonic output. Although the grammar constructed here is tailored to meet the requirements of Lithuanian accentuation, it can apply (with certain modifications on the constraint weights) to other LA and LS systems as well.

---

15 In the MaxEnt grammar analysis (Goldwater and Johnson 2003; Hayes and Wilson 2008) Gouskova and Linzen (2015) develop for Russian lexical stress, the grammar computes the same constraints differently depending on whether or not a morpheme in an input introduces a scaling factor for a specific constraint, which, in turn, is added to the constraint's weight.

(15)

$\pi_{1R}\ \pi_{1D}\ \pi_{1I}$ | | | /x_{1R}-x_{1D}-x_{1I}/	MAX[π] w: 20, s: 2	LEFTMOST[π] w: 8	DEP[π] w: 10	H
a. ☞	π_{1D} | x_{1R}-x_{1D}-x_{1I}	−40 (−1$_R$ × 20w) + (−1$_I$ × 20w)	−8		−48
b.	π_{1R} | x_{1R}-x_{1D}-x_{1I}	−60 ((−1$_D$ × 20w) × 2s) + (−1$_I$ × 20w)			−60
c.	π_{1I} | x_{1R}-x_{1D}-x_{1I}	−60 ((−1$_R$ × 20w) × 2s) + (−1$_I$ × 20w)	−16		−76

We now turn to the analysis of the Lithuanian examples in (7), formed with the non-dominant suffix *-išk*. Keep in mind that the accent of the PL.GEN suffix /-uú/ prevails over the weakly (0.5 activity) accented root, *vaikuú* /vaí$^{0.5}$k-uú^1/ (6d, see tableau (13)), but not when *-išk* intervenes between the root and the inflection; in this case, the weak accent of the root surfaces instead (e.g., *vaíkisʃkuu* /vaí$^{0.5}$k-í$^?$ʃk-uú^1/ (7b)). The key to understanding the accentual pattern of the above word pairs lies in determining the activity of the adjectival suffix *-išk*. In Section 3, we suggested, based on Kushnir (2019), that *-išk* is accented itself, albeit with a latent weak accent of 0.5 activity: /-í$^{0.5}$ʃk/. When weak accents are adjacent in a string of morphemes, as in the input /vaí$^{0.5}$k-í$^{0.5}$ʃk-uú^1/, a perfect situation is created because neighboring π-nodes can combine their below 1 activities – via merge – into a strong π-node of activity 1 (see Kushnir 2019: 112).

To account for the above set of Lithuanian data, our grammar must be enriched with the anti-coalescence constraint UNIF, stated in (16). This constraint should have a weight that would prevent coalescence from blindly or excessively taking place among accents in the language. We set its weight to 12 in the proposed grammar.

(16) UNIF[π], *w 12*: No π-node in the output has multiple correspondents in the input.

The tableau in (17) illustrates how our grammar evaluates candidate outputs. Candidates (17a–b) choose to coalesce the accent of the root with the accent of the derivational affix at the expense of UNIF. This move proves more cost-effective than the alternative, i.e., to insert epenthetic activity to either weak accent in violation of DEP[π], illustrated by candidates (17d–e). The lower harmony score of these candidate outputs is anticipated given the difference in weight between the two faithfulness constraints.[16] LEFTMOST[π] is the constraint that decides that the coalesced accent will be located on the root (17a). Realizing the strong accent of the inflection (17c) causes multiple violations of LEFTMOST[π], thus raising the harmony score of the candidate.

(17)

		$π_{0.5R}\ π_{0.5D}\ π_{1I}$ | | | /×$_{1R}$ -×$_{1D}$ -×$_{1I}$/	MAX[π] w: 20, s: 1	DEP[π] w: 10	UNIF[π] w: 12	LEFTMOST[π] w: 8	H
☞	a.	$π_{1R+D}$ | ×$_{1R}$-×$_{1D}$-×$_{1I}$	−20		−12		−32
	b.	$π_{1R+D}$ | ×$_{1R}$-×$_{1D}$-×1I	−20		−12	−8	−40
	c.	$π_{1I}$ | ×$_{1R}$-×$_{1D}$-×$_{1I}$	−20			−16	−36
	d.	$π_{1D}$ | ×$_{1R}$-×$_{1D}$-×$_{1I}$	−30	−5		−8	−43
	e.	$π_{1R}$ | ×$_{1R}$-×$_{1D}$-×$_{1I}$	−30	−5			−35

The dependent accents of Tokyo Japanese can be analyzed along the same lines with two important modifications. First, because obligatoriness of accent within the word is not enforced in the language, unaccented outputs should be selected as more harmonic than accented ones. This entails that the weight of the constraint *ACCENT must be rather high in the system. Second, the correlation wDEP[π] > wMAX[π] must hold here as well, given that this particular grammar also opts to leave weak accents unpronounced rather than to enhance them by inserting epenthetic activity. Consider the examples in (8a–b) where, with accentless bases, the

---

[16] This difference will also cause a low activity dominant accent to first seek to unite with another accent and, if such option is not possible, then to get epenthetic activity.

weak accent of the dominant suffix /-í/ is not phonetically realized, as opposed to the examples in (8c–d), where the suffixal accent surfaces only when coalescing with a neighboring accent in the base. Unfortunately, due to space restrictions, a full-fledged analysis of Tokyo Japanese cannot be developed here.

5 Conclusions

In this chapter we put forward an accent-based analysis of stress and tone in LS and LA systems, respectively. Although we agree with Hyman's proposal (2001, 2006, et seq.) that such systems are not good candidates for tone and stress prototypicality, we do believe that their shared features and common prosodic behavior provide sufficient ground to be treated on their own terms. Besides, most of Hyman's arguments in favor of a pick-and-choose approach to the idiosyncrasies of LS and LA systems are founded on prosodic characteristics that pertain primarily to pitch-accent systems (obligatoriness, culminativity, privativity) and much less to lexical stress languages. On the other hand, van der Hulst's (1984, 1996 et seq.) take on accentuation (via the Accent-First Theory, see fn 2) acquires a more global perspective on the study of LA and LS systems by means of the notion of accent. In order to further establish the distinct phonological reality of accent, we boldly proposed that it has an autosegmental status. For this reason, after reviewing autosegmental approaches to lexical stress and tone, we concluded that Spahr's π-node autosegment is best-suited to capture the accentual versatility that the systems at hand display.

A short cross-linguistic survey confirmed that accents behave like other autosegments since they can come in linked as well as in floating forms. More significantly, our typological investigation revealed that accents may also differ in their inherent strength, a property that interferes in a determinative way with phonological edgemost effects and the morphological and/or lexical conditions that control the resolution of accentual conflicts, known as dominance. The discussion revealed that a low-activity accent usually runs the risk of losing to any higher activity accent in the word, unless the grammar increases its activity (e.g., via coalescence or epenthesis of activity). Despite their marginality, gradient patterns of accent manifestation are typologically attested and need to be appropriately accounted for. We constructed a GHG analysis of Lithuanian – which with some adjustments can be easily adopted to other LA and LS systems – that hopefully highlights the diversity of accents and provides some important insights on their interaction with morphological structure.

Future research should focus more on the typological study of these systems in order to help us acquire a better understanding of the properties that bring them together and of those that set them apart.

References

Abercrombie, David. 1976. Stress and some other terms. *Work in Progress. Department of Linguistics, University of Edinburgh* 9. 51–53 [Reprinted in Abercrombie, D. 1991. *Fifty Years in Phonetics*. Edinburgh: Edinburgh University Press].

Alderete, John D. 1999. *Morphologically-governed accent in Optimality Theory*. Amherst, MA: University of Massachusetts, Amherst Doctoral dissertation.

Alderete, John D. 2001a. Dominance effects as transderivational anti-faithfulness. *Phonology* 18. 201–253. https://doi.org/10.1017/S0952675701004067.

Alderete, John D. 2001b. *Morphologically-Governed Accent in Optimality Theory*. (Outstanding Dissertations in Linguistics.) New York/London: Routledge.

Arvaniti, Amalia. 2007. Greek phonetics: The state of the art. *Journal of Greek Linguistics* 8. 97–208. https://doi.org/10.1075/jgl.8.08arv.

Blevins, Juliette. 1993. A tonal analysis of Lithuanian nominal accent. *Language* 69, 237– 273. https://doi.org/10.2307/416534.

Bogomolets, Ksenia. 2020. *Lexical accent in languages with complex morphology*. Storrs, CT: University of Connecticut Doctoral dissertation.

Coetzee, Andries W. & Shigeto Kawahara. 2013. Frequency biases in phonological variation. *Natural Language & Linguistic Theory* 31. 47–89. https://doi.org/10.1007/s11049-012-9179-z.

Coetzee, Andries & Joe Pater. 2011. The place of variation in phonological theory. In John Goldsmith, Jason Riggle & Alan Yu (eds.), *The Handbook of Phonological Theory*, 2nd edn, 401–434. Oxford: Blackwell.

Dubina, Andrei. 2012. *Towards a tonal analysis of free stress*. Nijmegen: Radboud Universiteit Nijmegen Doctoral dissertation.

Fox, Anthony. 2000. *Prosodic Features and Prosodic Structure*. Oxford: Oxford University Press.

Goedemans, Rob & Harry G. van der Hulst. 2014. The separation of accent and rhythm: Evidence from StressTyp. In Harry G. van der Hulst (ed.), *Word Stress: Theoretical and Typological Issues*, 119–146. Cambridge: Cambridge University Press. https://doi.org/10.1017/CBO9781139600408.006.

Goldsmith, John A. 1976. *Autosegmental phonology*. Cambridge, MA: MIT Doctoral dissertation.

Goldsmith, John A. 1990. *Autosegmental and Metrical Phonology*. Oxford/Cambridge, MA: Blackwell.

Goldsmith, John A. 1993a. Introduction. In John Goldsmith (ed.), *The Last Phonological Rule: Reflections on Constraints and Derivations*, 1–20. Chicago: University of Chicago Press.

Goldsmith, John A. 1993b. Harmonic phonology. In John A. Goldsmith (ed.), *The Last Phonological Rule*, 21–60. Chicago: University of Chicago Press.

Goldwater, Sharon & Mark Johnson. 2003. Learning OT constraint rankings using a maximum entropy model. In Jennifer Spenader, Anders Eriksson & Östen Dahl (eds.), *Proceedings*

of the Stockholm Workshop on Variation within Optimality Theory, 111–120. Stockholm: Stockholm University.
Gouskova, Maria & Tal Linzen. 2015. Morphological conditioning of phonological regularization. *The Linguistic Review* 32. 427–473. https://doi.org/10.1515/tlr-2014-0027.
Gussenhoven, Carlos. 2004. *The Phonology of Tone and Intonation*. Cambridge: Cambridge University Press.
Gussenhoven, Carlos. 2006. Between stress and tone in Nubi word prosody. *Phonology* 23. 193–223. https://doi.org/10.1017/S0952675706000881.
Hagberg, Lawrence Raymond. 1993. *An autosegmental theory of stress*. Tucson, AZ: University of Arizona Doctoral dissertation.
Hagberg, Lawrence Raymond. 2006. *An Autosegmental Theory of Stress*. SIL e-Book.
Halle, Morris & William Idsardi. 1995. General properties of stress and metrical structure. In John A. Goldsmith (ed.), *The Handbook of Phonological Theory*, 403–443. Cambridge, MA/Oxford: Blackwell.
Halle, Morris & Jean-Roger Vergnaud. 1987a. Stress and the cycle. *Linguistic Inquiry* 18. 45–84.
Halle, Morris & Jean-Roger Vergnaud. 1987b. *An Essay on Stress*. Cambridge, MA: MIT Press.
Haraguchi, Shosuke. 1977. *The Tone Pattern of Japanese: An Autosegmental Theory of Tonology*. Tokyo: Kaitakusha.
Haraguchi, Shosuke. 1991. *A Theory of Stress and Accent*. Dordrecht: Foris.
Haraguchi, Shosuke. 2017. Accent. In Natsuko Tsujimura (ed.), *The Handbook of Japanese Linguistics*, 1–30. Malden, MA/Oxford: Blackwell. https://doi.org/10.1002/9781405166225.ch1.
Hayes, Bruce & Colin Wilson. 2008. A maximum entropy model of phonotactics and phonotactic learning. *Linguistic Inquiry* 39. 379–440. https://doi.org/10.1162/ling.2008.39.3.379.
Hulst, Harry G. van der. 1984. *Syllable Structure and Stress in Dutch*. Dordrecht: Foris.
Hulst, Harry G. van der. 1996. Separating primary accent and secondary accent. In Rob Goedemans, Harry van der Hulst & Ellis Visch (eds.), *Stress Patterns of the World. Part I*, 1–26. (HIL Publications 2). The Hague: Holland Academic Graphics.
Hulst, Harry G. van der. 1999. Word accent. In Harry G. van der Hulst (ed.), *Word Prosodic Systems in the Languages of Europe*, 3–115. (Eurotyp: Typology of Languages in Europe 4). Berlin/New York: Mouton de Gruyter.
Hulst, Harry G. van der. 2010. Word accent: Terms, typologies and theories. In Harry G. van der Hulst, Rob W. N. Goedemans & Ellis A. M. Visch (eds.), *A Survey of Word Accentual Patterns in the Languages of the World*, 3–54. Berlin/Boston: De Gruyter Mouton. https://doi.org/10.1515/9783110198966.1.3.
Hulst, Harry G. van der. 2011. Pitch accent systems. In Marc van Oostendorp, Colin J. Ewen, Elizabeth Hume & Keren Rice (eds.), *The Blackwell Companion to Phonology*, 1003–1027. Chichester, UK/Malden, MA: Wiley-Blackwell. https://doi.org/10.1002/9781444335262.wbctp0042.
Hulst, Harry G. van der. 2012. Deconstructing stress. In SI: Varieties of Pitch Accent Systems, [special issue], *Lingua* 122. 1494–1521. https://doi.org/10.1016/j.lingua.2012.08.011.
Hulst, Harry G. van der. 2014a. The study of word accent and stress: Past, present, and future. In Harry G. van der Hulst (ed.), *Word Stress: Theoretical and Typological Issues*, 3–55. Cambridge: Cambridge University Press. https://doi.org/10.1017/CBO9781139600408.003.

Hulst, Harry G. van der. 2014b. Representing rhythm. In Harry G. van der Hulst (ed.), *Word Stress: Theoretical and Typological Issues*, 325–365. Cambridge: Cambridge University Press. https://doi.org/10.1017/CBO9781139600408.015.

Hulst, Harry G. van der & Norval S. H. Smith. 1982. Prosodic domains and opaque segments in autosegmental theory. In Harry G. van der Hulst & Norval S. H. Smith (eds.), *The Structure of Phonological Representations (Part II)*, 311–336. Dordrecht: Foris.

Hyman, Larry M. 2001. Privative tone in Bantu. In Shigeki Kaji (ed.), *Cross-linguistic Studies of Tonal Phenomena*, 237–257. Tokyo: Institute for the Study of Languages and Cultures.

Hyman, Larry M. 2006. Word-prosodic typology. *Phonology* 23. 225–257. https://doi.org/10.1017/S0952675706000893.

Hyman, Larry M. 2009. How (not) to do phonological typology: The case of pitch-accent. *Language Sciences* (Data and Theory: Papers in Phonology in Celebration of Charles W. Kisseberth) 31. 213–238. https://doi.org/10.1016/j.langsci.2008.12.007.

Hyman, Larry M. 2014. Do all languages have word accent? In Harry G. van der Hulst (ed.), *Word Stress: Theoretical and Typological Issues*, 56–82. Cambridge: Cambridge University Press. https://doi.org/10.1017/CBO9781139600408.004.

Idsardi, William. 1992. *The computation of prosody*. Cambridge, MA: MIT Doctoral dissertation.

Inkelas, Sharon. 1999. Exceptional stress-attracting suffixes in Turkish: Representations versus the grammar. In Harry G. van der Hulst, René Kager & Wim Zonneveld (eds.), *The Prosody-Morphology Interface*, 134–187. Cambridge: Cambridge University Press. https://doi.org/10.1017/CBO9780511627729.006.

Jones, Daniel & Dennis Ward. 1969. *The Phonetics of Russian*. Cambridge: Cambridge University Press.

Kawahara, Shigeto. 2015. The phonology of Japanese accent. In Haruo Kubozono (ed.), *Handbook of Japanese Phonetics and Phonology*, 445–492. Berlin/Munich/Boston: De Gruyter Mouton. https://doi.org/10.1515/9781614511984.445.

Kawakami, Shin. 1974. Nihongo onsuuritu no saikentoo [Re-examination of the rhythm of Japanese verse]. In *Onisi hakuri kiju kinen onseigaku sekai ronbunshu* [Worldwide anthology of papers in phonetics in honor of Dr. Onishi's sixtieth birthday], 665–671. Tokyo: Phonetic Society of Japan.

Kiparsky, Paul. 1984. A compositional approach to Vedic word accent. In S. D. Joshi (ed.), *Amrtadhara: R.N. Dandekar Felicitation Volume*, 201–210. Delhi: Ajanta Publications.

Kushnir, Yuriy. 2019. *Prosodic patterns in Lithuanian morphology*. Leipzig: Leipzig University Doctoral dissertation.

Legendre, Géraldine, Yoshiro Miyata & Paul Smolensky. 1990a. Harmonic grammar – a formal multi-level connectionist theory of linguistic wellformedness: An application. In *Proceedings of the Twelfth Annual Conference of the Cognitive Science Society*, 884–891. Mahwah, NJ: Lawrence Erlbaum.

Legendre, Geraldine, Yoshiro Miyata & Paul Smolensky. 1990b. Harmonic grammar – a formal multi-level connectionist theory of linguistic well-formedness: Theoretical foundations. In *Proceedings of the Twelfth Annual Conference of the Cognitive Science Society*, 388–395. Mahwah, NJ: Lawrence Erlbaum Associates.

Liberman, Mark. 1975. *The intonational system of English*. Cambridge, MA: MIT Doctoral dissertation.

Lockwood, David. 1983. Tone in a non-substantive theory of language. *Lacus Forum* 10. 131–140.

Loos, Eugene E. 1969. *The Phonology of Capanahua and Its Grammatical Basis*. (Summer Institute of Linguistics Publications in Linguistics and Related Fields 20). Norman, OK: SIL/University of Oklahoma.

Macdonell, Arthur Anthony. 1910. *Vedic Grammar*. Strassburg: Verlag von Karl J. Trübner.
McCarthy, John J. & Alan S. Prince. 1993a. Prosodic morphology I: Constraint interaction and satisfaction. Technical Report #3, Rutgers University Center for Cognitive Science 3. New Brunswick: University of Massachusetts, Amherst, and Rutgers University.
McCarthy, John J. & Alan S. Prince. 1993b. Generalized alignment. In Geert Booij & Jaap van Marle (eds.), *Yearbook of Morphology 1993*, 79–153. Dordrecht: Springer.
McCawley, James D. 1968. *The Phonological Component of a Grammar of Japanese*. The Hague: Mouton.
McCawley, James D. 1977. Accent in Japanese. In Larry M. Hyman (ed.), *Studies in Stress and Accent*, 261–302. Los Angeles: University of Southern California.
McCawley, James D. 1978. What is a tone language? In Victoria Fromkin (ed.), *Tone: A Linguistic Survey*, 113–131. New York: Academic Press.
McPherson, Laura & Bruce Hayes. 2016. Relating application frequency to morphological structure: The case of Tommo So vowel harmony. *Phonology* 33. 125–167. https://doi.org/10.1017/S0952675716000051.
Melvold, Janis Leanne. 1989. *Structure and stress in the phonology of Russian*. Cambridge, MA: MIT Doctoral dissertation.
Pierrehumbert, Janet & Mary Beckman. 1988. *Japanese Tone Structure*. Cambridge, MA: MIT Press.
Poser, William J. 1984. *The phonetics and phonology of tone and intonation in Japanese*. Cambridge, MA: MIT Doctoral dissertation.
Prince, Alan S. & Paul Smolensky. 1993. *Optimality Theory: Constraint Interaction in Generative Grammar*. (RuCCS-TR-2; CU-CS-696-93). Malden, MA/Oxford: Blackwell.
Revithiadou, Anthi. 1999. *Headmost Accent Wins: Head Dominance and Ideal Prosodic Form in Lexical Accent Systems*. (LOT Dissertation Series 15) (HIL/Leiden Universiteit). The Hague: Holland Academic Graphics.
Revithiadou, Anthi. 2007. Colored turbid accents and containment: A case study from lexical stress. In Sylvia Blaho, Patrik Bye, and Martin Krämer (eds.), *Freedom of Analysis?*, 149–174. Berlin/New York: Mouton de Gruyter.
Revithiadou, Anthi. 2018. Ancient Greek pitch accent: Extending tonal antepenultimacy to enclitics and the σωτῆρα words. In Ryan Bennett, Andrew Angeles, Adrian Brasoveanu, Dhyana Buckley, Nick Kalivoda, Shigeto Kawahara, Grant McGuire & Jaye Padgett, *Hana-bana (花々): A Festschrift for Junko Itô and Armin Mester*. https://cpb-us-e1.wpmucdn.com/sites.ucsc.edu/dist/3/529/files/2017/12/Revithiadou2018-Ancient-Greek-Pitch-Accent-1zd9dbm.pdf.
Revithiadou, Anthi & Vassilios Spyropoulos. 2016. Stress at the interface: Phases, accents and dominance. *Linguistic Analysis* 41. 3–74.
Rosen, Eric R. 2018. Predicting semi-regular patterns in morphologically complex words. *Linguistics Vanguard* 4. 20170037. https://doi.org/doi:10.1515/lingvan-2017-0037.
Rosen, Eric R. 2019. Weak elements make strong predictions: Evidence for gradient input features from Sino-Japanese compound accent. In *Supplemental Proceedings of the Annual Meeting on Phonology*. https://doi.org/10.3765/amp.v9i0.4918.
Schadeberg, Thilo C. 1973. Kinga: A restricted tone language. *Studies in African Linguistics* 4. 23–48.
Smolensky, Paul & Matthew Goldrick. 2016. Gradient symbolic representations in grammar: The case of French liaison. Ms. Johns Hopkins University & Northwestern University. [ROA 1552].

Smolensky, Paul & Géraldine Legendre. 2006. *The Harmonic Mind: From Neural Computation to Optimality-Theoretic Grammar*. Cambridge, MA: MIT Press.

Spahr, Christopher E. 2016. *Contrastive representations in non-segmental phonology*. Toronto: University of Toronto Doctoral dissertation.

Vaxman, Alexandre. 2016. *How to beat without feet: Weight scales and parameter dependencies in the computation of word accent*. Storrs, CT: University of Connecticut Doctoral dissertation.

Voorhoeve, Jan. 1973. Safwa as restricted tone system. *Studies in African Linguistics* 4. 1–22.

Whitney, W. D. 1993. *Sanskrit Grammar*. Cambridge, MA: Harvard University Press.

Yip, Moira. 2002. *Tone*. Cambridge: Cambridge University Press.

Zimmermann, Eva. 2017. Being (slightly) stronger: Lexical stress in Moses Columbian Salish. Paper presented at the workshop Strength in Grammar, Leipzig, Leipzig University, November 11, 2017.

Vincent J. van Heuven
Stress Deaf and Color Blind: Native Language Background and Perceptual Categories

Abstract: This chapter argues that phenomena like 'stress deafness' and 'tone deafness' are not principally different from other manifestations of loss of sensitivity to differences between sounds due to the acquisition of one's native language. Moreover, I argue that the inability to perceive differences between sound categories in a foreign or unknown language exemplify the same type of problem that is experienced by members of a linguistic community with different (especially fewer) basic color distinctions in the lexicon, if they are asked to discriminate between colors that have no name in their native lexicon.

Keywords: Stress deafness, tone deafness, Native Language Perceptual Magnet Theory, Categorical Perception, Perceptual identification, Perceptual discrimination, Sapir-Whorf hypothesis, Visual color perception

1 Introduction

In recent literature is has become fashionable to coin catchy terms for the description of interference phenomena in second language acquisition. Since the late 90s of the previous century, the notion of *stress deafness* has been used to describe the phenomenon that native speakers of a language that does not use stress contrastively at the word level, i.e., speakers of a language with fixed stress such as Finnish or French, perceive differences in stress position (in other languages) less accurately and less quickly than speakers of a native language with contrastive lexical stress (e.g., Dupoux et al. 1997). More recently, we have seen the rise in phonetics and phonology of the term *tone deafness*, which refers to the reduced accuracy and speed shown by speakers of a non-tone language when asked to discriminate between lexical tones in a non-native language (e.g., Rahmani, Rietveld, and Gussenhoven 2015).

The relative insensitivity to non-native sound contrasts has been observed on many earlier occasions in the literature on second and foreign language acqui-

---

Vincent J. van Heuven, Leiden University Centre for Linguistics, Leiden, The Netherlands and Doctoral School of Multilingualism, University of Pannonia, Veszprém, Hungary

sition. A range of theories have been developed to account for the observation that mismatches between the sounds of the native language (L1) and the target language (L2) yield incorrect perception and production of the L2 sounds. A non-exhaustive list includes Transfer Theory (Lado 1957), the Speech Learning Model (SLM, Flege 1987, 1995), SLM-r (Flege and Bohn 2020), the Perceptual Assimilation Model (PAM, Best 1995; Best, McRoberts, and Goodell 2001), PAM-L2 (Best and Tyler 2007), the Second Language Linguistic Perception model (L2LP, Escudero 2005), and the Markedness Differential Hypothesis (Eckman 1977, 1985). These theories generally concentrate on predicting learning difficulties in the segmental domain, i.e., the perception and production of vowels, consonants and consonant clusters, but they have recently been extended to account for prosodic phenomena as well (e.g., So and Best 2010; Best 2019). Yet, no-one has suggested that we should refer to the difficulty experienced by, for instance, Japanese learners of English to discriminate between /l/ and /r/ as liquid deafness. I would like to argue that the 'deafness' phenomena identified above and the more classical cases of second-language learners' difficulties with the unfamiliar sounds of a target language, are manifestations of the same learning problem.

Moreover, I will argue that the learning problem is not limited to the acquisition of a non-native sound system but that the relative inability to distinguish between phenomena in a non-native way is also seen in the perception of non-speech sounds, and even in the perception of visual phenomena. In all the domains we will examine, I will (try to) show, however, that the relative insensitivity to unfamiliar distinctions is caused by properties of the learner's native language.

2 Categories

No two objects in nature are exactly the same but some objects are more alike than others. The human response to cope with the endless diversity of objects in the real world is to sort them into categories and to communicate about their experiences in terms of these categories. An important role of language is to enable the members of a social group, a linguistic community, to refer to objects in the outside world by means of categories that are understood by all members of the community. It is also a fact of life that no two human languages are the same (they are different by definition), and the way one language carves up reality differs from that of the next.

The object we sit on is called *chair*. For an object to be categorized as a chair (in English) it must have a backrest. Without a backrest we would categorize it as a *stool* (which would be the typical sound shape in German and Dutch denoting a regular chair). Differences within and between categories can additionally be expressed by naming their properties, e.g., adjectives such as *big* vs *small*, *round* vs *square* and *hot* vs *cold*. These distinguishing properties constitute categories by themselves. The names of objects and of their properties are the content words in the language of the community. The number of basic words (morphemes) in any human language is finite, say somewhere around 15,000.[1] The words in human languages are objects with properties by themselves. Just like a chair is composed of smaller parts such as its legs, bottom and backrest, words are composed of smaller parts which we call speech sounds. The sounds have distinguishing properties such as sonorant vs obstruent or voiced vs voiceless.[2] This system is basic to any human language and has evolved in order to allow us to have some 15,000 different sound shapes.

3 Native Language Magnet Theory

Learning how to carve up reality into categories is one of the most important tasks of the infant. Its is an essential part of language learning. The native language magnet (NLM) theory (e.g., Kuhl 1991; Kuhl and Iverson 1995) argues that human infants in the first 6 to 9 months of their lives set up prototypes of the speech sounds they hear in their environment. The prototype would be the ideal realization of a sound in its category, located at the largest possible distance away from the prototypes of competing categories in the same sound space. Human infants are born with pre-wired auditory categories, which are subdivisions of the auditory space represented somewhere on the cortex, where each category is an area within which differences between sounds are (relatively) difficult to

---

[1] For Dutch we developed a morphological parser for text-to-speech conversion of unrestricted text, i.e., which would be able to decompose any Dutch word into its constituent morphemes (Heemskerk and van Heuven 1993). The number of morphemes we needed in the lexicon was 13,000 (some 300 of which were function words, derivational affixes or inflections). I would expect other Indo-European languages to have morpheme inventories of similar size. Mandarin (and other Chinese languages/dialects) is written with a morpheme-based writing system using one character per morpheme. The number of different characters is said to be roughly 8,000 for an educated Chinese speaker, and 12,500 to cover all the words in a comprehensive present-day Chinese dictionary (https://studycli.org/chinese-characters/number-of-characters-in-chinese/).
[2] These properties are often described as dichotomies of some multidimensional continuous space. For instance, the distinction between voiced and voiceless sounds rests on a boundary in a space of some ten acoustic parameters most of which are in a trading relationship (Slis and Cohen 1969; Lisker and Abramson 1971).

perceive and which is bounded by corridors of high sensitivity to auditory differences, so-called natural boundaries. As a first approximation to category formation, the infant sorts the incoming sounds into the pre-wired categories (Kuhl 1988). Within the categories the infant then notices that the distribution of the category members is not uniform but gravitates towards one specific spot somewhere central within the category. This gravitational point corresponds to the category prototype. Prototypical exemplars of a category are easier to categorize, easier to remember and are preferred over other instances of the same category. The basic tenet of the NLM model is that sounds are more difficult to discriminate from each other as they are closer to the prototype. It is as if the prototype draws similar sounds towards it, and that the magnetic pull gets stronger as the sounds are closer to the prototype. It follows from this account that two sounds that find themselves halfway between two competing prototypes (i.e., adjacent categories), are relatively easy to discriminate (see Figure 1A, dotted line).

Within the first year of its life the infant learns to set up the prototypes of the ambient language. It also discovers that some (or many, depending on the language) of the natural boundaries that make up its genetic endowment are irrelevant, and drops these ('unlearns' them). Under the influence of subsequent language input in the next few years the remaining boundaries are sharpened and/or shifted so as to optimally separate the categories on either side of the boundary.[3]

4 Categorical Perception

The phenomenon of categorical perception (CP) is that a stimulus continuum from one category prototype to the prototype of an adjacent category that is sampled in a number of physically equidistant steps, is not continuously perceived. The ultimate shape of CP is that all tokens sampled from the continuum on one side of the category boundary cannot be discriminated from one another, while the same goes for the tokens on the other side of the boundary. However, whenever two tokens are sampled from opposite sides of the boundary they are easily discriminated, even if they are separated from each other by just one step along the continuum (Figure 1A–B, solid lines).

---

[3] Shifting a natural boundary would come at a special cost. The listener would have to become insensitive at locations where high sensitivity is part of our genetic predisposition, while a naturally insensitive area should be made highly sensitive. Alternatively, shifted boundaries should always remain less categorical than natural boundaries. Also, unlearned natural boundaries might be reinstated at relatively low cost.

The hallmark of CP is that the discrimination function is at (or close to) chance level performance for stimulus pairs on one side of the category boundary but shows a sharp peak (close to 100% correct discrimination) for stimulus pairs straddling the boundary. The Haskins formula (Cutting 1982) predicts how well two tokens sampled from the continuum will be discriminated given the identification scores of the tokens concerned: $D_{pred} = 0.5 \times [1 + (P_1 - P_2)^2]$. The better the correlation between the actual discrimination scores and the predicted scores, the more categorical the perception is. However, I am not aware of a threshold value for the correlation coefficient that demarcates categorical from continuous perception. Van Heuven and Kirsner (2004) tested a hybrid continuum (between L% final lowering and H% final boundary tone) across two boundaries, i.e., one separating statement from non-statement melody, and a second boundary between question and no-question.[4] We argued that the former division was linguistic and categorical whereas the latter one was paralinguistic and continuous. The Haskins correlation coefficients were .95 and .71, respectively, suggesting that the threshold between categorical and continuous perception should lie somewhere between these values.

It was assumed in the 1950s that CP was exclusive to human speech perception and applied to the perception of consonants only (e.g., Liberman et al. 1957). It soon transpired that CP was also found for vowel perception. More recently, it was demonstrated that suprasegmental contrasts can also be categorically perceived (see below). Moreover, CP turned out not to be unique to speech perception. Any contrast in sounds that is highly familiar to the listener can be perceived in categorical fashion. Cutting and Rosner (1974) showed that the category boundary between the English voiceless affricate and fricative was identical to the boundary value for the difference between plucked and bowed violin strings. The contrast between a major and a minor three-note chord was perceived categorically by trained musicians but not by lay listeners (Locke and Kellar 1973; Howard, Rosen, and Broad 1992). However, some form of CP was also found for non-humans, viz. chinchillas (Kuhl 1987), and other animals – ranging from birds to primates (e.g., Green, Brandley, and Nowicki 2020). It would seem reasonable, therefore, to assume that humans share their auditory apparatus with other species, and have some form of innate boundaries that allow newborn individuals of a species to sort sounds into categories. With sufficient exposure and experience the boundaries between relevant categories are sharpened, while others get lost.

---

4 The intermediate category, i.e., neither statement/command nor question, would signal continuation.

An important question here is what happens in second language acquisition. Is it possible to learn new sound categories, defined by new prototypes and new boundaries? Or will the new categories always be less clearly defined in the L2 speaker's mental representation of L2 sound system?

From the description given, NLM and CP seem to provide parallel accounts of roughly the same phenomena. It should be noted, however, that there are non-trivial differences between the accounts. NLM says that discrimination between sounds gets poorer as they are closer to the category prototype. On a continuum between two adjacent category prototypes, discrimination is poor in the vicinity of each prototype and gets better as the sounds are farther away from the competing prototypes. Discrimination will be optimal for two sounds that find themselves in the middle of the continuum, i.e., midway between the prototypes. However, there is no suggestion that there is a sharp local peak in the discrimination function at the category boundary (Figure 1A, dotted line). CP, on the other hand, claims a sharp peak in the discrimination function exactly at the category boundary but poor discrimination between any two sounds on one side of the boundary; for CP it does not matter whether the two sounds are close to the category prototype or not, as long as they find themselves on the same side of the boundary (Figure 1A, sold lines).

5 Stress 'Deafness'

It has been shown by Dupoux and co-workers that speakers of a language that does not use stress to discriminate between lexical words are less accurate and relatively slow when asked to discriminate between stimuli that are segmentally identical but differ in the position of the word stress. This was found, for instance, for French listeners who responded to minimal stress triplets in trisyllabic Spanish nonwords. The same stimuli were discriminated faster and more accurately by Spanish listeners. Dupoux et al. (1997) called the poorer task performance of the French listeners *stress deafness*.[5] The inability to discriminate quickly and accu-

---

[5] The term *stress deafness* was used before in an informal setting to refer to the phenomenon that quite a few Dutch native speakers are unable to point out which syllable in a polysyllabic Dutch word carries the stress, even though the same persons realize the words with the correct stress pattern. It is unclear why stress position is not part of the metalinguistic knowledge of these language users. We would need to establish whether it is purely a matter of being unable to label the stress position. We do not know at this time if such a stress-deaf person is able to tell the difference between correct and incorrect stress patterns when realized on the same word, or indeed, whether the person is able to discriminate between two different stress patterns on the

rately between minimal stress pairs has been attested for other groups of speakers of fixed-stress languages as well, including Finnish, Turkish, Hungarian, Polish, and Persian (Dupoux et al. 1997; Lukyanchenko, Idsardi, and Jiang 2011; Peperkamp and Dupoux 2002; Peperkamp, Vendelin, and Dupoux 2010).

The stress 'deafness' can be overcome (to some extent) by training. Carpenter (2015) trained francophones on stress discrimination of nonsense trisyllables (same as used by Dupoux et al. 1997) and found that her participants responded faster and more accurately after training (from 30% error down to 19%, and from 981 down to 835 ms) – but still not as accurate as native English participants with 15% error (and no significant learning effect).[6]

It has been argued that stress 'deafness' is caused by the absence of a marking of the stress position in the lexicon of speakers whose native language does not use stress contrastively (e.g., Peperkamp and Dupoux 2002; Rahmani, Rietveld, and Gussenhoven 2015). The mental lexicon does not have to specify stress when stress is fixed on one syllable position for all the words in the lexicon, such as in Hungarian, Finnish (initial) or in French, Turkish and Persian (final). Also, languages that do not use stress at all would have no need for a lexical marking of stress position. The prediction would then be that speakers of pure tone languages such as Yoruba or Akan, where high and low tones may occur on any syllable within a word without ever making one syllable stand out from its neighbors, would also show the stress deafness symptoms. There are indications that speakers of non-stress languages experience fewer difficulties learning English (or Dutch) stress patterns than speakers with a fixed-stress L1 – but I have not (yet) seen the relative advantage of non-stress L1 in terms of stress discrimination tasks that involve some form of lexical recoding.

It has been pointed out repeatedly, by Dupoux and colleagues (as well as by Rahmani et al.) that the idea of stress 'deafness' does not mean the listener is unable

---

same word (i.e., the same sequence of segments). Wolf (2019) brings up the problem and suggests pedagogical tricks to increase the stress-deaf student's metalinguistic awareness – but it remains to be seen if the suggestions would work. The same labeling problem has come up in connection with the term *tone deaf*. About 4 percent of the population suffers from *congenital amusia*; these persons are unable to label the difference in pitch between two sounds as either a rise or a fall. Their pitch discrimination is normal, so the problem must reside in the labeling. Peretz et al. (2009: 1277) write: "the amusic brain is equipped with the essential neural circuitry to perceive fine-grained pitch differences. What distinguishes the amusic from the normal brain is the limited awareness of this ability and the lack of responsiveness to the semitone changes that violate musical keys. These findings suggest that, in the amusic brain, the neural pitch representation cannot make contact with musical pitch knowledge along the auditory-frontal neural pathway."
6 Somewhat surprisingly, the native English participants, though faster than the francophones before training (824 ms), were slower after training (932 ms).

to hear the difference between, for instance, identical sound sequences with stress on the first or on the last syllable. Therefore, Dupoux and co-workers always use the term 'deafness' between quote marks, indicating that the listeners are not really deaf. The 'deafness' will not appear when the listener performs experimental tasks that rely solely on auditory memory. The difficulties are observed only when the experimental task requires the listener to keep a sequence of stimulus sounds in memory for a longer period of time. When the listener has the possibility to recode the short-term auditory image into a representation that can be held in memory for more than, say, one second, the distinguishing properties of the items in the sequence can still be retrieved. However, when the listener has no possibility to recode the auditory stimulus property into something more abstract, performance rapidly deteriorates.

6 Tone 'Deafness'

Speakers of a tone language have a lexical representation that specifies the type of word tone. It would appear that languages belong to one of two types of word prosodic system, i.e., they either have stress or lexical tone. To be true, there are so-called restricted tone languages such as Norwegian and Swedish, and even some (Franconian) dialects of Germanic languages, that exploit different tones but these always occur on the stressed syllable of the word (e.g., van der Hulst 2010).

Languages that allow different tones in both stressed and unstressed syllables are highly exceptional. If a listener's native language does not exploit lexical tone, the prediction follows that a native speaker of a non-tone language who learns a tone language after the critical age (say, after puberty), will not be able to perceive the lexical tones in the L2 categorically, i.e., will not be able to recode the tone category to some more abstract and longer-lasting memory trace. In this situation tone 'deafness' is expected when the learner has to fulfill tone discrimination tasks over longer time intervals than can be covered by the immediate auditory representation, just as in the case of stress 'deafness'. Indeed, tonal distinctions that involve pitch movement are perceived in categorical fashion by native speakers of tone languages (Hallé, Chang, and Best 2004; Xu, Gandour, and Francis 2006; Peng et al. 2010). Rather more continuous tone perception was found for non-tone language speakers, e.g., Dutch (Leather 1987), English (Xu et al. 2006), French (Hallé, Chang, and Best 2004, DiCanio 2012) and German (Peng et al. 2010). Again, it has been suggested that the non-tone listeners process the tonal differences in an acoustic (or psychophysical) mode, which affords high sensitivity to small tonal differences as long as the time span during which the stimuli have to be kept in auditory memory is short (as was the case in the above studies). The tone-language listeners, however, processed the stimuli in a linguistic mode, recoding the tones to categories known to them, thereby ignoring small acoustic differences between them (Jongman and Tremblay 2020).

Advanced learners of a tone language with a non-tone background, e.g., English L1 learners of Thai (Wayland and Guion 2003) or Mandarin (Guion and Pederson 2007), still discriminate less accurately between target tone categories than native Thai or Mandarin listeners, but do clearly better than English listeners with no exposure to the target languages. Tone (Mandarin L1) and non-tone (English L1) learners benefitted equally from a 10-hour training on Cantonese tones, although the English participants primarily used the mean pitch differences to distinguish the Cantonese tones while Mandarin participants gave equal weight to mean pitch and direction of pitch change (rise, fall or a combination, see Francis et al. 2008). Overall, previous experience with lexical tones, in one's native language or in an acquired non-native language, has some form of positive transfer to the acquisition of a new lexical tone system (Qin and Jongman 2006; Jongman and Tremblay 2020). It is not clear from the available evidence whether tone 'deafness', even if in mitigated form, can still be demonstrated for the advanced learner of a tone language with a non-tone L1 background.

A general problem with the comparison of the various domains is that there is an obvious lack of systematicity in the establishing of CP. Complete diagnostics of CP are generally given in the segmental literature, i.e., on CP of specific contrasts involving consonants and vowels. Full diagnostics can also be found in a number of studies on lexical tone perception (e.g., Hallé, Chang, and Best 2004 for Mandarin tones).[7] Full diagnostics, i.e., sharply defined cross-over from one category to the other, coinciding with a peak in the discrimination function at the cross-over, are only rarely given in the case of prosodic contrasts at the sentence level. Remijsen and van Heuven (2003) gave full diagnostics for the L%-H% boundary tone contrast in Dutch. However, it soon transpired that this is not a contrast between adjacent categories on the continuum. Van Heuven and Kirsner (2004) showed that the continuum should be divided into three categories, L%, %, H%, where only the contrast between L% and % is perceived categorically (with full diagnostics), while the % – H% continuum is perceived in gradient (paralinguistic) manner. Ladd and Morton (1997) ran full diagnostics on the English contrast between a normal H*L accent versus an emphatic ^H*L

---

[7] Recently, Gussenhoven and van de Ven (2020) ran full CP diagnostics on the perception of Zhumadian Mandarin lexical tones and on the signaling of sentence mode (statement vs question) as cued by early and late aligned rises and falls (7-step continua). Zhumadian L1 listeners showed CP for the lexical tones but not for the boundary tones. Indonesians showed no CP effects at all.

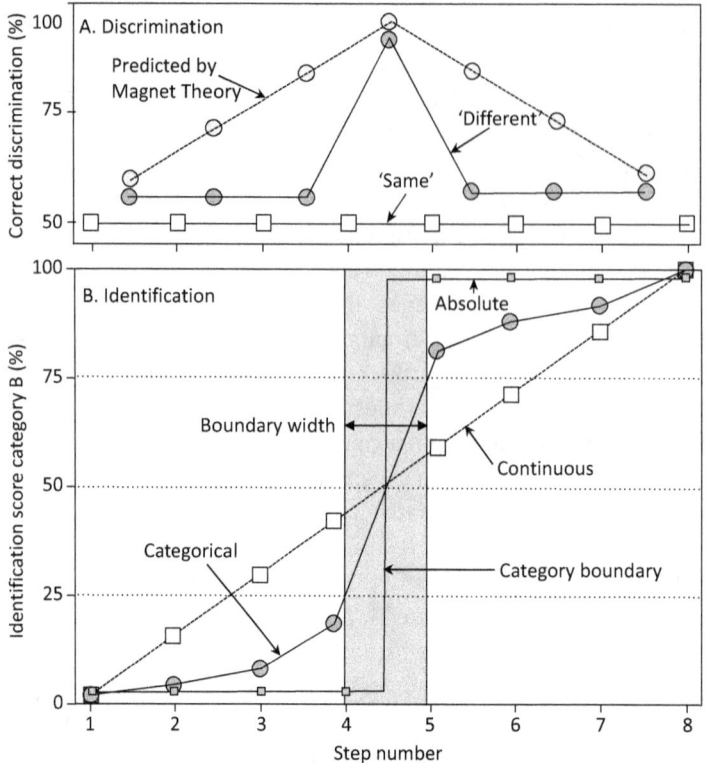

Figure 1: Panel A. Hypothetical discrimination function for physically same and different pairs of stimuli (one-step difference) reflecting predictions of categorical perception (solid lines and markers) and of Native Language Magnet theory (dotted lines and markers). Panel B. Hypothetical identification as predicted by continuous (squares) versus categorical (circles) perception in the identification and discrimination paradigm. The thin line with small squares represents the ideal step function that should be obtained when categorical perception is absolute. Category boundary and boundary width are indicated. (Adapted from Remijsen and van Heuven 2003: 228).

accent. The results showed a sharp cross-over but no peak in the discrimination curve – so that the conclusion follows that the contrast between normal and emphatic accents is paralinguistic rather than linguistic. These are possible CP effects on intonational morphemes, i.e., configurations of tones that are part of the sentence melody and that affect the interpretation of a speaker's communicative intentions at the discourse level, e.g., the marking of clause, sentence and paragraph boundaries, focus, clause type, expectations and possibly also affect (attitude and emotion, although these may also be seen as paralinguistic – and therefore non-categorical – components).

I have not seen classical full CP diagnostics on word stress. Relevant studies typically report the results for either the identification curve or for the discrimination function but not both – which would be a prerequisite to test the presence of an identification peak coinciding with the cross-over point in the identification curve. A large number of studies have been done on the identification of stress patterns (for a summary see van Heuven 2018) in di- and trisyllabic words (and nonwords).[8] Manipulation of duration and shifting the location of a pitch change yield well defined cross-overs but this by itself is not definitive proof of CP; none of these studies, however, included discrimination tasks. It can probably be argued, however, that the stress 'deafness' studies basically test discrimination of stress differences, using a different procedure (i.e., sequence recall) indicating that listeners with stress 'deafness' cannot perceive stress differences categorically.

7 Color Blindness: Categories in the Visual World

Perception is not limited to hearing and sound. There would be no reason, a priori, to doubt that contrasts in other sensory domains exist, and can be perceived categorically if the human has sufficient experience with the categories. Probably, the sensory domain most amenable to experimentation would be vision. Indeed, a lot of research has been done on the perception of color. The color we perceive depends primarily on the frequencies of the light wave that strikes our eyes. The frequency of the electromagnetic waves causing our eyes to perceive differences in color are continuously variable, between 430 and 750 THz. We have three types of color receptor cells, called cones, which are sensitive to high frequencies (650–750 THz, blue-violet), middle frequencies (540–580 THz, green) and low frequencies (430–480 THz, red). A visual color space can be set up as a two-dimensional plane, rather like the auditory vowel space.

There is a substantial literature on categorical perception of color contrasts. One would expect categorical effects, i.e., a sharp cross-over in the identification curve and a local peak in the discrimination function that coincides with the cross-over point, in the visual color domain. CP for color is manifest in that

---

8 In addition, Hermes (1997) tested the effect of time-shifting a pitch movement on the perception of stress on Dutch pentasyllabic nonwords. Well-defined cross-overs were found but no discrimination performance was tested. Similarly, Amir, Ben-Chemo, and Silber-Varod (2015) tested the effect of changes in syllable duration on the perception of initial versus final stress in Hebrew minimal stress pairs. The study reports complete and sharp cross-overs but did not test discrimination.

discrimination of stimuli (Laws, Davies, and Andrews 1995) and same-different judgments (Bornstein and Korda 1984) are faster and more accurate across than within categories with similar effects in memory when there is a delay between the presentation of the stimuli to be matched (Boynton et al. 1989; Uchikawa and Shinoda 1996). Prototype-magnet effects were found for stimuli from the center of color categories, which are matched and classified faster than those at or close to category edges (Bornstein and Monroe 1980).

Also, many studies have been done on the possible effect of linguistic categories on the way humans process visual information on color. The phenomena concerned have been used in support of the Sapir-Whorf hypothesis, which – crudely – says that the lexical distinctions made in our native language determine (to some extent) the way we perceive and categorize objects and their properties in the real world. It has been observed that the way members of a linguistic community process visual color information is affected by the number and physical definition of the words in the lexicon denoting basic colors. English has a rather large number of basic color terms, i.e., *red*, *blue*, *green*, *yellow*, *brown*, *pink*, and three more terms that do not so much address chromaticity but intensity, i.e., *white*, *grey* and *black*. Note that these words are monosyllabic and of Germanic ancestry.[9] They are high-frequency words acquired early in life. Moreover, these color terms are not derived from some object with the same name or color, such as *orange*, *indigo*, *salmon*, *olive* or *lilac*.

Other languages may have a larger number of basic color words, such as French, which adds *beige* to the inventory. Other languages may have fewer basic color words. Ova-Himba, for instance, spoken in Northern Namibia, has four basic color terms (Roberson et al. 2006), Baramba, spoken in Mali, has three, and Bassa (Liberia, Sierra Leone) has two (McNeil 2008). Pirahã, an Amazonian language, is claimed to be the only known human language that has no words denoting color (Kay 2007).[10]

When a language has fewer color terms, the color spectrum is divided up differently than in English, by lumping adjacent color categories together and shifting boundaries between categories, in a way that is strongly reminiscent of how languages divide up the vowel space differently depending on the number of

---

9 *Yellow* would be an exception to this definition. The cognate forms in other Germanic languages, however, are monosyllabic, e.g., Dutch *geel* /ɣel/, German *gelb* /gɛlb/, Frisian *giel* /giəl/, Danish *gul* /gul/, etc.

10 Pirahã is a rather elusive language. It is said to be a tone language in which parents can have a meaningful conversation using humming as a secret language not accessible to children (Dan Everett, personal communication). It has also been advanced as the only living language in which syllable weight (attracting stress) is determined by the onset (Everett 1988; Goedemans 1998) but this claim was later shown to be untenable (Gordon 2005; Topintzi 2008).

vowels in the phoneme inventory. The hierarchical subdivision of the visual color space as suggested by Berlin and Kay (1969), and more recently by Kay and Maffi (2013), bears a remarkable similarity to the Liljencrants and Lindblom (1972) dispersion theory for the subdivision of the vowel space depending on the number of vowels in a language.

When a particular color contrast is not made in a language, there is no boundary and hence no CP. This is what was found by, for instance, Roberson, Davies, and Davidoff (2000), who obtained clear CP with native speakers of Berinmo (spoken in Papua) between two Berinmo color categories that do not exist in English, and with English participants on a green-blue continuum (which colors are not lexically distinguished in Berinmo). The study used the two-alternative forced choice paradigm (2-AFC or X-AB) to establish the discrimination function. The participant sees a colored patch (X) for a short duration, which then disappears. After 30 seconds the original patch and a distractor, which differs from the original by one step along the color continuum, are displayed side-by-side. The participant then has to indicate which of the two patches (A or B) is the same as the original (X). Results show, as predicted, that the proportion of correct decisions is relatively high (79%) when the original and the distractor belong to differently named color categories in the participant's native vocabulary, i.e., when they straddle the color category boundary. The proportion of correct decisions is significantly smaller when original and distractor lie on the same side of the color boundary (64%). This is what was found for Berinmo participants, while the English participants did not show any discrimination peak for stimulus pairs straddling the Berinmo category boundary (72–74% correct). Conversely, the English participants did significantly better on color shades straddling the blue-green boundary (84% correct) than to equally different shades on the same side of the boundary (71% correct). The boundary effect was not seen for the Berinmo participants, because blue and green are not differentiated in the Berinmo vocabulary. The procedure was repeated with the Berinmo participants in a separate experiment, in which the time interval between X and A-B was reduced from 30s to 5s. The CP effect persisted but discrimination was 13 percentage points better. The results of these experiments are summarized in Figure 2.[11]

---

[11] There are discrepancies between the numerical values mentioned in Table 11 and in the summary Figure 10 in Roberson, Davies, and Davidoff (2000). I assume that the graphic results are correct as they fit the verbal discussion of the results best. The present Figure 2 shows the corrected values.

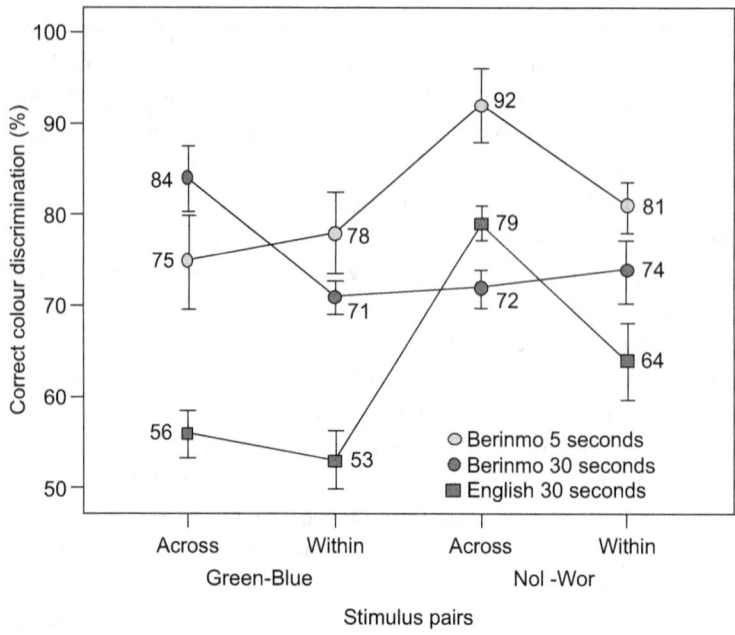

Figure 2: Correct color discrimination (%) within and across category boundaries by Berinmo speakers for green-blue and nol-wor stimuli with a 5-s retention interval and for Berinmo and English speakers with a 30-s retention interval. (After Roberson, Davies, and Davidoff 2000: 393).

Put together, the evidence suggests that Categorical Perception shows the influence of language on perception. These results would indicate that linguistic experience can affect low-level perception as suggested by Goldstone (1994). However, more than that, the results uphold the view that the structure of linguistic categories distorts perception by stretching perceptual distances at category boundaries (Goldstone 1994, 1998; Hamad 1987; Kay and Kempton 1984). It would appear that the color space (Davidoff 1991) is not static; some distances within it are stretched or distorted by the influence of linguistic categories.

The idea is that being able to recode two colors as instances of two different lexical categories (i.e., each color has a different name) makes the discrimination task easier (faster execution and fewer errors, longer retention). Presumably, L2 speakers of English can learn to identify and discriminate between English basic colors, even if their native language has different and fewer color categories (and basic color terms), but their performance will be slower and less accurate than that of native English speakers. Exaggerating somewhat, these L2 learners of English are color blind.

8 Conclusion

The question we aimed to answer in this chapter is whether the phenomenon of stress 'deafness' or tone 'deafness' is or is not the same thing as the loss of sensitivity to some innate category boundary that is characteristically found as the cause of failure to differentiate in a nativelike fashion between sounds in a foreign language. Reviewing the evidence discussed above, it would appear that the 'deafness' phenomena are a recurrent feature of any type of perception task that forces the observer to sort phenomena into categories that are not part of the observer's cognitive system, i.e., the system of categories that the observer has learned from childhood onwards and which can be referred to by the words in the lexicon of the observer's native language. Such native categories are manifest by a number of functional characteristics. They are subject to the prototype magnet phenomenon, that says that the perceived distance between two physically equally different tokens of a category is smaller as the tokens are closer to the prototype. They are also the source of the categorical perception phenomenon, i.e., poorer discrimination for within-category tokens but better discrimination for physically equally different tokens that straddle the category boundary. When distinctions have to be made between properties of sound objects for which the observer has no familiar, native categories (identified or exemplified by explicit words in the native lexicon), 'deafness' results, whether the objects are vowels, consonants, stress patterns or lexical tones. The 'deafness' phenomenon is not limited to the perception of speech. It is also seen in the perception of non-speech sounds such as musical chords – as long as the observer is highly familiar with the categories (e.g., major vs minor chord, or happy vs sad melody). The evidence also suggests that, across the board, non-native categories can be learned after childhood but the 'deafness' will never completely disappear.

Moreover, the evidence reviewed shows that such acquired insensitivity is also seen in the visual domain (and probably in other sensory domains as well). Specifically, we discussed evidence from experiments on the perception of chromaticity (hue, color), which showed CP and prototype magnet effects for color categories that can be identified by basic color terms in the observer's native language. Color 'blindness' (although I have not seen the term used in this fashion) results when colors have to be sorted into categories for which the observer's native language has no words.

It would seem that studies on categorical perception and 'deafness' for non-native categorical distinctions pre-date similar studies in the visual domain. Interestingly, researchers of color perception refer to the speech studies but not vice versa. Nevertheless, it would seem that a generalization can be made that early experience in life shapes the way humans categorize phenomena both in their language and in the outside world. The automatized use of categories yields category prototypes with perceptual magnet effects and categorical perception. It also results in relatively inadequate processing of distinctions made in unfamiliar languages, leading to – among other things – stress and tone 'deafness' and color 'blindness'.

References

Amir, N., C. Ben-Chemo & V. Silber-Varod. 2015. Categorical perception of lexical stress: The effect of manipulated duration. *Proceedings of the 15th International Congress of Phonetics Sciences*, Glasgow. https://dblp.org/rec/conf/icphs/AmirCS15.html.
Berlin, B. & P. Kay. 1969. *Basic Color Terms: Their Universality and Evolution*. Berkeley/Los Angeles, CA: University of California Press.
Best, C. T. 1995. A direct realist perspective on cross-language speech perception. In W. Strange (ed.), *Speech Perception and Linguistic Experience: Theoretical and Methodological Issues in Cross-Language Speech Research*, 167–200. Timonium, MD: York Press.
Best, C. T. 2019. The diversity of tone languages and the roles of pitch variation in non-tone languages: Considerations for tone perception research. *Frontiers in Psychology* 10. 364. DOI: 10.3389/fpsyg.2019.00364.
Best, C. T., G. W. McRoberts & E. Goodell. 2001. Discrimination of non-native consonant contrasts varying in perceptual assimilation to the listener's native phonological system. *Journal of the Acoustical Society of America* 109(2). 775–794. DOI: 10.1121/1.1332378.
Best, C. T. & M. D. Tyler. 2007. Nonnative and second-language speech perception: Commonalities and complementarities. In M. J. Munro & O.-S. Bohn (eds.), *Language Experience in Second Language Speech Learning: In Honor of James Emil Flege*, 13–34. Amsterdam: John Benjamins. DOI: 10.1075/lllt.17.07bes; https://www.academia.edu/24865551/.
Bornstein, M. H. & N. O. Korda. 1984. Discrimination and matching within and between hues measured by reaction times: Some implications for categorical perception and levels of information processing. *Psychological Research* 46(3). 207–222. DOI: 10.1007/BF00308884.
Bornstein, M. H. & M. D. Monroe. 1980. Chromatic information processing: Rate depends on stimulus location in the category and psychological complexity. *Psychological Research* 42(3). 213–225. DOI: 10.1007/BF00308529.
Boynton, R. M., L. Fargo, C. X. Olson & H.S. Smallman. 1989. Category effects in color memory. *Color Research and Application* 14(5). 229–234. DOI: 10.1002/col.5080140505.
Carpenter, A. 2015. Phonetic training significantly mitigates the stress 'deafness' of French speakers. *International Journal of Linguistics* 7(3). 94–108. DOI: 10.5296/ijl.v7i3.7661.
Cutting, J. E. 1982. Plucks and bows are categorically perceived (sometimes). *Perception and Psychophysics* 31(5). 462–476. DOI: 10.3758/BF03204856.
Cutting, J. E. & B. S. Rosner. 1974. Categories and boundaries in speech and music. *Perception and Psychophysics* 16(3). 564–570. DOI: 10.3758/BF03198588.
Davidoff, J. 1991. *Cognition through Color*. Cambridge, MA: MIT Press.

DiCanio, C. T. 2012. Cross-linguistic perception of Itunyoso Trique tone. *Journal of Phonetics* 40(5). 672–688. DOI: 10.1016/j.wocn.2012.05.003.

Dupoux, E., C. Pallier, N. Sebastián-Gallés & J. Mehler. 1997. A destressing 'deafness' in French? *Journal of Memory and Language* 36(3). 406–421. DOI: ff10.1006/jmla.1996.2500.

Eckman, F. R. 1977. Markedness and the contrastive analysis hypothesis. *Language Learning* 27(2). 315–330. DOI: 10.1111/j.1467-1770.1977.tb00124.x.

Eckman, F. R. 1985. Some theoretical and pedagogical implications of the markedness differential hypothesis. *Studies in Second Language Acquisition* 13(1). 23–41. DOI: 10.1017/S0272263100009700.

Escudero, P. 2005. *Linguistic Perception and Second Language Acquisition: Explaining the Attainment of Optimal Phonological Categorization*. (LOT Dissertation Series 113). Utrecht: LOT. https://www.lotpublications.nl/Documents/113_fulltext.pdf.

Everett, D. 1988. On metrical constituent structure in Pirahã phonology. *Natural Language and Linguistic Theory* 6. 207–246. DOI: 10.1007/BF00134230.

Flege, J. E. 1987. The production of 'new' and 'similar' phones in a foreign language: Evidence for the effect of equivalence classification. *Journal of Phonetics* 15(1). 47–65. DOI: 10.1016/S0095-4470(19)30537-6.

Flege, J. E. 1995. Second language speech learning: Theory, findings, and problems. In W. Strange (ed.), *Speech Perception and Linguistic Experience: Theoretical and Methodological Issues in Cross-Language Speech Research*, 233–277. Timonium, MD: York Press.

Flege, J. E. & O.-S. Bohn. 2020. The revised Speech Learning Model (SLM-r). In R. Wayland (ed.), *Second Language Speech Learning: Theoretical and Empirical Progress*, 3–83. Cambridge: Cambridge University Press. DOI: 10.1017/9781108886901.002.

Francis, A. L., V. Ciocca, L. Ma & K. Fenn. 2008. Perceptual learning of Cantonese lexical tones by tone and non-tone language speakers. *Journal of Phonetics* 36(2). 268–294. DOI: 10.1016/j.wocn.2007.06.005.

Goedemans, R. W. N. 1998. *Weightless Segments: A Phonetic and Phonological Study Concerning the Metrical Irrelevance of Syllable Onsets*. The Hague: Holland Academic Graphics.

Goldstone, R. 1994. Influences of categorization on perceptual discrimination. *Journal of Experimental Psychology: General* 123(2). 178–200. DOI: 10.1037/0096-3445.123.2.178.

Goldstone, R. L. 1998. Perceptual learning. *Annual Review of Psychology* 49(1). 585–612. DOI: 10.1146/annurev.psych.49.1.585.

Gordon, M. 2005. A perceptually-driven account of onset-sensitive stress. *Natural Language and Linguistic Theory* 23(3). 595–653. DOI: 10.1007/s11049-004-8874-9.

Green, P. A., N. C. Brandley & S. Nowicki. 2020. Categorical perception in animal communication and decision-making. *Behavioral Ecology* 31(4). 859–867. DOI: 10.1093/beheco/araa004.

Guion, S. G. & E. Pederson. 2007. Investigating the role of attention in phonetic learning. In O.-S. Bohn & M. J. Munro (eds.), *Language Experience in Second Language Speech Learning: In Honor of James Emil Flege*, 57–77. Amsterdam: John Benjamins. DOI: 10.1075/lllt.17.09gui.

Gussenhoven, C. & M. van de Ven. 2020. Categorical perception of lexical tone contrasts and gradient perception of the statement–question intonation contrast in Zhumadian Mandarin. *Language and Cognition* 12(4). 614–648. DOI: 10.1017/langcog.2020.14.

Hallé, P. A., Y.-C. Chang & C. T. Best. 2004. Identification and discrimination of Mandarin Chinese tones by Mandarin Chinese vs. French listeners. *Journal of Phonetics* 32(3). 395–421. DOI: 10.1016/S0095-4470(03)00016-0.

Hamad, S. 1987. Psychophysical and cognitive aspects of categorical perception: A critical overview. In S. Hamad (ed.), *Categorical Perception: The Groundwork of Cognition*, 535–565. Cambridge: Cambridge University Press. http://eprints.soton.ac.uk/id/eprint/250386.

Heemskerk, J. S. M. & V. J. van Heuven. 1993. MORPA, a morpheme lexicon based morphological parser. In V. J. van Heuven & L. C. W. Pols (eds.), *Analysis and Synthesis of Speech, Strategic Research towards High-Quality Text-to-Speech Generation*, 67–86. Berlin: Mouton de Gruyter. DOI: 10.1515/9783110879001.67.

Hermes, D. J. 1997. Timing of pitch movements and accentuation of syllables in Dutch. *Journal of the Acoustical Society of America* 102(4). 2390–2502. DOI: 10.1121/1.419623.

Heuven, V. J. van. 2018. Notes on the phonetics of word and sentence stress: A cross-linguistic (re-)view. In H. van der Hulst, J. Heinz & R. Goedemans (eds.), *The Study of Word Stress and Accent: Theories, Methods and Data*, 13–59. Cambridge: Cambridge University Press. DOI: 10.1017/9781316683101.002.

Heuven, V. J. van & R. S. Kirsner. 2004. Phonetic or phonological contrasts in Dutch boundary tones? In L. Cornips & J. Doetjes (eds.), *Linguistics in the Netherlands 2004*, 102–113. Amsterdam/Philadelphia: John Benjamins. DOI: 10.1075/avt.21.13heu.

Howard, D., S. Rosen & V. Broad. 1992. Major/minor triad identification and discrimination by musically trained and untrained listeners. *Music Perception* 10(2). 205–220. DOI: 10.2307/40285607.

Hulst, H. van der 2010. Word accent: Terms, typologies and theories. In H. van der Hulst, R. Goedemans & E. van Zanten (eds.), *A Survey of Word Accentual Patterns in the Languages of the World*, 3–53. Berlin/New York: Mouton de Gruyter. DOI: 10.1515/9783110198966.1.3.

Jongman, A. & A. Tremblay. 2020. Word prosody in second language acquisition. In C. Gussenhoven & A. Chen (eds.), *The Oxford Handbook of Linguistic Prosody*, 594–604. Oxford: Oxford University Press. DOI: 10.1093/oxfordhb/9780198832232.013.39.

Kay, P. 2007. Pirahã color terms. *Language Log*. http://itre.cis.upenn.edu/~myl/languagelog/archives/004399.html.

Kay, P. & W. Kempton. 1984. What is the Sapir-Whorf hypothesis? *American Anthropologist* 86(1). 65–78. http://www.jstor.org/stable/679389.

Kay, P. & L. Maffi. 2013. Number of basic colour categories. In M. S. Dryer & M. Haspelmath (eds.), *The World Atlas of Language Structures Online*. Leipzig: Max Planck Institute for Evolutionary Anthropology. http://wals.info/chapter/133.

Kuhl, P. K. 1987. The special-mechanisms debate in speech perception: Nonhuman species and nonspeech signals. In S. Harnad (ed.), *Categorical Perception: The Groundwork of Cognition*, 355–386. Cambridge: Cambridge University Press.

Kuhl, P. K. 1988. Auditory perception and the evolution of speech. *Human Evolution* 3(1–2). 19–43. DOI: 10.1007/BF02436589.

Kuhl, P. K. 1991. Human adults and human infants show a "perceptual magnet effect" for the prototypes of speech categories. *Perception and Psychophysics* 50(2). 93–107. DOI: 10.3758/BF03212211.

Kuhl, P. K. & P. Iverson. 1995. Linguistic experience and the 'perceptual magnet effect'. In W. Strange & J. J. Jenkins (eds.), *Speech Perception and Linguistic Experience: Issues in Cross-Language Research*, 121–154. Timonium MD: York Press.

Ladd, D. R. & R. Morton. 1997. The perception of intonational emphasis: Continuous or categorical? *Journal of Phonetics* 25(3). 313–342. DOI: 10.1006/JPHO.1997.0046.

Lado, R. 1957. *Languages across Cultures: Applied Linguistics for Language Teachers*. Ann Arbor, MI: University of Michigan Press.

Laws, G., I. Davies & C. Andrews. 1995. Linguistic structure and non-linguistic cognition: English and Russian blues compared. *Language and Cognitive Processes* 10(1). 59–94. DOI: 10.1080/01690969508407088.

Leather, J. 1987. F0 pattern inference in the perceptual acquisition of second language tone. In A. James & J. Leather (eds.), *Sound Patterns in Second Language Acquisition*, 59–81. Dordrecht: Foris.

Liberman, A. M., K. S. Harris, H. S. Hoffman & B. C. Griffith. 1957. The discrimination of speech sounds within and across phoneme boundaries. *Journal of Experimental Psychology* 54(5). 358–368. DOI: 10.1037/h0044417.

Liljencrants, J. & B. Lindblom. 1972. Numerical simulation of vowel quality systems: The role of perceptual contrast. *Language* 48(4). 839–862. DOI: 10.2307/411991.

Lisker, L. & A. S. Abramson. 1971. Distinctive features and laryngeal control. *Language* 47(4). 776–785. DOI: 10.2307/412155.

Locke, S. & L. Kellar. 1973. Categorical perception in a non-linguistic mode. *Cortex: A Journal Devoted to the Study of the Nervous System and Behavior* 9(4). 355–369. DOI: 10.1016/S0010-9452(73)80035-8.

Lukyanchenko, A., W. J. Idsardi & N. Jiang. 2011. Opening your ears: The role of L1 in processing of nonnative prosodic contrasts. In G. Granena, J. Koeth, S. Lee-Ellis, A. Lukyanchenko, G. Prieto Botana & E. Rhoades (eds.), *Selected Proceedings of the 2010 Second Language Research Forum*, 50–62. Somerville, MA: Cascadilla Proceedings Project. http://www.lingref.com/cpp/slrf/2010/paper2615.pdf.

McNeill, N. B. 2008. Colour and colour terminology. *Journal of Linguistics* 8(1). 21–33. DOI: 10.1017/S002222670000311X.

Peng, G., H.-Y. Zheng, T. Gong, R.-X. Yang, J.-P. Kong & W. S. Y. Wang. 2010. The influence of language experience on categorical perception of pitch contours. *Journal of Phonetics* 38(4). 616–624. DOI: 10.1016/j.wocn.2010.09.003.

Peperkamp, S. & E. Dupoux. 2002. A typological study of stress 'deafness'. In C. Gussenhoven & N. Warner (eds.), *Laboratory Phonology 7*, 203–240. Berlin: Mouton de Gruyter. DOI: 10.1515/9783110197105.203.

Peperkamp, S., I. Vendelin & E. Dupoux. 2010. Perception of predictable stress: A cross-linguistic investigation. *Journal of Phonetics* 38(3). 422–430. DOI: 10.1016/j.wocn.2010.04.001.

Peretz, I., E. Brattico, M. Järvenpää & M. Tervaniemi. 2009. The amusic brain: In tune, out of key, and unaware. *Brain* 132(5). 1277–1286. DOI: 10.1093/brain/awp055.

Qin, Z. & A. Jongman. 2016. Does second language experience modulate perception of tones in a third language? *Language and Speech* 59(3). 318–338. DOI: 10.1177/0023830915590191.

Rahmani, H., T. Rietveld & C. Gussenhoven. 2015. Stress 'deafness' reveals absence of lexical marking of stress or tone in the adult grammar. *PLoS ONE* 10(12). e0143968. DOI: 10.1371/journal.pone.0143968.

Remijsen, A. C. & V. J. van Heuven. 2003. On the categorical nature of intonational contrasts: An experiment on boundary tones in Dutch. In J. M. van de Weijer, V. J. van Heuven & H. van der Hulst (eds.), *The Phonological Spectrum*, volume 2, 225–246. Amsterdam: John Benjamins. DOI: 10.1075/cilt.234.15rem.

Roberson, D., J. Davidoff, I. R. L. Davies & L. R. Shapiro. 2006. Colour categories and category acquisition in Himba and English. In N. Pitchford & C. P. Biggam (eds.), *Progress in Colour Studies, vol. 2: Psychological Aspects*, 159–172. Amsterdam: John Benjamins. DOI: 10.1075/z.pics2.14rob.

Roberson, D., I. Davies & J. Davidoff. 2000. Color categories are not universal: Replications and new evidence from a stone-age culture. *Journal of Experimental Psychology: General* 129(3). 369–398. DOI: 10.1037/0096-3445.129.3.369.

Slis, I. H. & A. Cohen. 1969. On the complex regulating the voiced-voiceless distinction. *Language and Speech* 12(2). 80–102; 12(3). 137–155. DOI: 10.1177/002383096901200202; 10.1177/002383096901200301.

So, C. K.-L. & C. T. Best. 2010. Cross-language perception of non-native tonal contrasts: Effects of native phonological and phonetic influences. *Language and Speech* 53(2). 273–293. DOI: 10.1177/0023830909357156.

Topintzi, N. 2008. On the existence of moraic onset geminates. *Natural Language and Linguistic Theory* 26(1). 147–184. DOI: 10.1007/s11049-008-9034-4.

Uchikawa, K. & H. Shinoda. 1996. Influence of basic color categories on color memory discrimination. *Color Research and Application* 21(6). 430–439. DOI: 10.1002/(SICI)1520-6378(199612)21:6<430.

Wayland, R. P. & S. G. Guion. 2003. Perceptual discrimination of Thai tones by naive and experienced learners of Thai. *Applied Psycholinguistics* 24(1). 113–129. DOI: 10.1017/S0142716403000067.

Wolf, Henk. 2019. Hoe vind je de klemtoon in een woord? [How to find the stress in a word?]. *Neerlandistiek, online tijdschrift voor taal- en letterkunde* 19(6). https://neerlandistiek.nl/2019/06/hoe-vind-je-de-klemtoon-in-een-woord/.

Xu, Y., J. T. Gandour & A. L. Francis. 2006. Effects of language experience and stimulus complexity on the categorical perception of pitch direction. *Journal of the Acoustical Society of America* 120(4). 1063–1074. DOI: 10.1121/1.2213572.

Alexandre Vaxman
The Representation and Computation of Weight in Hybrid Accent Systems: The Case of Standard Eastern Mari

Abstract: This paper investigates accent assignment in "hybrid" accent systems, *i.e.* systems in which word accent location is not fully predictable on phonological grounds alone, but requires, in addition, reference to morphological information. The focus is here on the proper treatment of morpheme-specific exceptions in such systems. Following the Scales-and-Parameters theory (Vaxman 2016b, 2018a, 2019), I analyze the accent-attracting capacity of morphemes in terms of diacritic weight (rather than lexical accent). In hybrid systems, accent is assigned with reference *both* to syllable weight and to the diacritic weight of exceptional morphemes, ordered on a single weight scale. In this way, the accentual competition between the two is effectively captured. Based on this proposal, the theory is shown to account, in a uniform manner, for regular and exceptional accent patterns in the hybrid system of Standard Eastern Mari (Uralic).

Keywords: morpheme-specific exception, diacritic weight, hybrid weight scale, Weight Grid, accentual parameters, Scales-and-Parameters theory, Standard Eastern Mari

1 Introduction

When, as a beginner two decades ago, I discovered for myself the classic volumes of *Structure of Phonological Representations*, little could I gather that, years later, I would have the luck and honor to delve, under Prof. van der Hulst's guidance, into representational issues in phonology, with a special interest to word prosody.

In the present contribution, building on the "diacritic weight" notion proposed in van der Hulst (1999), we examine the role of weight representation and computation in accent assignment, focusing on word accent in the complex system of Standard Eastern Mari (henceforth, SEM) where, as will be argued, accent is assigned with reference to a weight scale that orders phonological and diacritic weight.

Alexandre Vaxman, Université de Tours (France)

https://doi.org/10.1515/9783110730081-013

We will show how this generalized approach to weight, augmented with a parameter system akin to that of the Primary Accent First theory (PAF) proposed by Harry van der Hulst in a number of publications (van der Hulst 1996, 2010, 2012, 2014), leads to a unified account of accentual regularities and morpheme-specific exceptions.

PAF is a non-metrical parametric theory that separates word accent ("primary stress") and rhythm ("non-primary stress"). (For empirical evidence, see van der Hulst 1996; Goedemans and van der Hulst 2014; McGarrity 2003). Accent and rhythm are assigned on separate planes, without using metrical constituents (van der Hulst 1996, 2010, 2012). We adopt these aspects of PAF in our approach. Importantly, with respect to phonological accent systems, the PAF parameter system and the modified version which we propose do not undergenerate (Vaxman 2016b, 2018b).

A broader goal of the current project is to determine the role and extent of morphology in accounting for phonological phenomena, including morpheme-specific phonological processes (such as those addressed here). As a point of departure, we adopt a null hypothesis that accentual phenomena may be accounted for without recourse to morphology. Only then, by letting in elements of morphology whenever this is unavoidable, it should become clear which elements are, in fact, indispensable and how they interact with phonology. In this way, we would be able to gain a better understanding of the precise place and contribution of morphology in accounting for phonological phenomena. In the case discussed in this paper, no reference to morphology turns out to be necessary.

The present paper is organized as follows. After introducing the basic concepts in Section 2, we turn to SEM. Section 3 describes the accent rule and the morpheme-specific exceptions. Section 4 puts forth the scale-based approach to accent assignment: it establishes the hybrid weight scale and the parameter settings for SEM, discusses weight representation and provides evidence that the proposed grammar correctly derives the SEM patterns discussed in Section 3. At the end, a conclusion sums up the results.

2 Basic Notions

2.1 Diacritic Weight

In a seminal work on accent and weight, van der Hulst (1999: 19) aptly notes that, since accent-attracting and accent-repelling capacities of individual morphemes in lexical accent systems parallel those of syllables in weight-sensitive systems, these capacities constitute a type of weight. Unlike syllable weight ("phonological weight"), morphemic weight is unpredictable and must, therefore, be assigned in the lexicon (hence, van der Hulst's term "diacritic weight"). Accordingly, we view accent-attracting morphemes as diacritically heavy and accent-repelling morphemes as diacritically light.

Extending this proposal, one may attempt to dispose of lexical accent altogether and reanalyze lexical accent systems as weight-sensitive systems with diacritic weight (Vaxman 2016b, 2018a, 2019).

2.2 Weight Scales

It is well known that, in certain phonological accent systems, accent is assigned with reference to a phonological weight scale, rather than a binary heavy/light distinction among syllables. Some examples of such scales (from Gordon 2006: 27) are given in (1).

(1) Klamath   CVV(C) > CVC > CV
     Fula   CVVC > CVV, CVC > CV
     Moro   CVC > full V > reduced V
     Chukchi   low V, mid V > high V > reduced V

Thus, phonological weight is ordinal.

At the same time, there is strong empirical evidence that diacritic weight is also ordinal: similar to phonological weight, it allows for weight scales (Vaxman 2016a, 2016b, 2018a, 2019). For example, the analysis of Uzbek accentual patterns shows that, in this language, morphemes fall into three classes according to their diacritic weight and that these three morpheme classes are ordered on the diacritic weight scale in (2) (Vaxman 2016b, 2018a).

(2) diacritically superheavy > diacritically heavy > diacritically light

Summarizing, diacritic weight and phonological weight both capture accent attraction and allow for weight scales, indicating that diacritic weight, on a par with phonological weight, is a weight type.

Now, since weight is ordinal and there exist two types of weight, phonological and diacritic, then it is predicted that there exists a language in which accent is assigned with reference to *both* weight types ordered on a single weight scale. I will call such scales "hybrid weight scales".

An example of a hybrid weight scale is given below.

(3) diacritically heavy > phonologically heavy > {diacritically light, phonologically light}

(The specifics of (3) will be clarified in Section 4.1.)

Evidently, the "diacritic weight" proposal developed in this paper raises the question about how weight differs from strength and, accordingly, weight scales from strength scales.

2.3 Weight vs. Strength

The concept of "scale" in accent assignment is not new. Several so-called "strength scales" have been proposed in the literature (Carlson 1989: 204–205; Montler 1986; Thompson and Thompson 1992; Czaykowska-Higgins and Kinkade 1998: 16; for discussion, see Czaykowska-Higgins 1993: 198; Dyck 2004: 10–11; Revithiadou 1999) where strength referred to the relative ability of a morpheme to win the word accent. However, unlike the weight scales which we propose, the strength scales played a purely descriptive role in capturing the accentual behavior of morphemes. The focus there was on accentual abilities, viewed as a degree of accentual strength, whereas the scales which we propose conceptualize accent-attraction as a degree of weight: morphemes are not accentually stronger/weaker but heavier/lighter.

Further, while strength scales are stated based on simple observation of accent patterns in the data, our approach requires demonstrating that the weight relation ("HEAVIER-THAN") defined on the set of morpheme classes has the formal properties of scales, i.e., it is irreflexive, transitive and antisymmetric.

An early principled scales proposal is found in the pioneering work by Garde (1965, 1968) who applies it mainly to Russian affixes. His scales resemble strength scales in that they order accents ("les accentuations"), rather than weight, and do not offer a means for accentual resolution. Unlike the latter, though, these scales play a formal role in accent assignment. Note that, like the strength scales approach, Garde's proposal appears to be limited to lexical accent systems. Nevertheless, it is regrettable that this insight was never elaborated into a full-fledged theory.

In Gradient Symbolic Representation (Smolensky and Goldrick 2016; Faust and Smolensky 2017), couched in the Harmonic Phonology framework (Legendre, Miyata, and Smolensky 1990), a theory actively developed by Eva Zimmermann (Zimmermann 2017a, 2017b, 2018, a.o.), strength is a continuous variable defined on the set of real numbers. Apparently, it may be associated, in the form of coefficients, with any kind of representational entity, both on the input and on the output candidates. In addition, as usual in Harmonic Grammar, (violable, unordered) constraints also carry weights, which are real numbers. In order to select the correct candidate, mathematical operations are performed on these values.

Thus construed, "strength" and "weight" crucially differ from the notion of "weight" in our approach. Indeed, we propose that, in some languages, morpheme classes, characterized by differences in accentual behavior, exhibit a scalar property, which we call "weight", that allows for an ordering over the set of these morpheme classes or the set of morpheme classes and syllable types, which we call a "diacritic weight scale" and a "hybrid weight scale", respectively. Importantly, to the best of our knowledge, all weight-sensitive systems (phonological, lexical and hybrid) involve a very small number of weight degrees, unlike the continuous "strength" of Gradient Symbolic Representation. In other words, the scale-based approach is conceptually and computationally simpler.

Next, turning to SEM, we will survey its accentual patterns, including systematic irregularities due to particular morphemes.

3 Description

3.1 The Background

SEM is the standardized dialect of Eastern Mari (Uralic, Russian Federation), also known in the literature as "Meadow Mari", formerly "Eastern Cheremis", the other major dialectal group being the less researched Western, or Hill, Mari. (In earlier publications, we referred to SEM as "Eastern Literary Mari".)

Accent in Eastern Mari has been an object of several important studies, in particular Sebeok and Ingemann (1961), Kiparsky (1973), Lehiste et al. (2005) and Vaysman (2009). Some of these, though, could not be used for the present description because they are devoted to non-standard dialects. In particular, Vaysman (2009), which includes a well-known study of Eastern Mari metrical structure, draws on her fieldwork on a regional dialect "spoken on the boarder of Nizhni Novgorod region and Mari El republic, in Russia" (Vaysman 2009: 60).

Accentual data in this paper come from Riese et al. (2012), Sebeok and Ingemann (1961), as well as the highly useful Mari-Russian dictionary by Vasil'jev and Učaev (2003) where accent is systematically marked.

According to the literature, SEM has the following vowel system:

(4) i y   u
     e ø   o
           ə
           a

In word-final position, all mid vowels (both full and schwa) undergo reduction (Riese et al. 2012); nevertheless, /ə/ remains phonetically central-mid. In support of qualitative reduction, an experimental investigation by Lehiste et al. (2005) has shown that, word-finally, full mid vowels are centralized towards schwa (but not neutralized).

3.2 Accentual Patterns

3.2.1 Regular Accentual Patterns

For the most part, accent location in SEM is phonologically predictable. However, as discussed in the next section, several morphemes systematically violate the phonological accent rule.

Regarding regular, phonologically predictable accent, SEM can be characterized as an unbounded weight-sensitive Last/First system with the accent rule in (5).

(5) *Accent falls on the rightmost heavy syllable; otherwise, accent is initial.*

In words with full vowels, accent generally falls on the last such vowel, as in (6).

(6) a. olˈma   'apple'
     b. izeˈmaʃ   'reduce'
     c. oˈza   'master'
     d. puʃkaˈta   'soft'

However, if the final syllable is open and contains a mid vowel, then this syllable repels accent, which shifts to the closest syllable with a (full) non-mid vowel.

(7) a. kopˈʃange 'beetle'
　　b. ˈjumo 'God'
　　c. ˈʃyrgø 'face'

However, mid vowels in word-final closed syllables receive the accent, as in (8).

(8) a. pajˈrem 'holiday'
　　b. køgørˈtʃen 'dove'
　　c. moˈtor 'pretty'
　　d. ikˈtør 'straight'
　　e. iziˈmør 'wild strawberry'

In words with full vowels schwa always repels the accent (even in closed syllables).

(9) a. ˈerək 'freedom'
　　b. ˈkalək 'nation'
　　c. ˈputʃəməʃ 'porridge'
　　d. ˈluʃkədələk 'slack'

In words with a final open syllable containing a mid vowel and preceded by schwa, both repel the accent, so it falls on the immediately preceding syllable.

(10) a. ˈkoləzo 'fisherman'
　　 b. ˈikʃəve 'child'
　　 c. ˈkørgəʃtø 'inside'

In words where all syllables contain schwa, as in (11), and words where it occurs in all but the last syllable, which has a mid vowel, as in (12), accent is initial, even though it falls on schwa.

(11) a. ˈpələʃ 'ear'
　　 b. ˈtʃələm 'phone receiver'

(12) a. ˈərəʃe 'stale'
　　 b. ˈʃəmləʃe 'researcher'
　　 c. ˈʃəmle 'seventy'

In other words, the default accent location is initial in this system.

Summarizing, in SEM, schwa and the mid vowels in an open word-final syllable count as light, while all other full vowels, non-final mid-vowels and final mid-vowels in closed syllables count as heavy.

3.2.2 Morpheme-Specific Accentual Exceptions

Several inflectional suffixes in SEM systematically violate phonological accent rule (5). They are productive; therefore, their exceptional behavior cannot be simply listed and requires a formal account.

In nouns marked with the comitative /-ge/, this case suffix always gets the accent (see Riese 2012: 97), even though the final open syllable containing a mid vowel is light in SEM.

(13) a. jo'tʃa   'child'
     b. jotʃa-'ge   'child-COMIT'

The first person plural possessive suffix [-na] also wins the accent in violation of the accent rule, witness (14), where it receives the accent when followed by a heavy syllable.

(14) pørt-'na-vlak   'house-1PL.POSS-PL'

Similarly, in negative gerunds formed with the suffix /-de/, accent falls on /-de/, thus violating the phonological accent rule.

(15) a. nal-aʃ   'take-INF'
        nal-'de   'take-NEG.GERUND'
     b. tunem-aʃ   'study-INF'
        tunem-'de   'study-NEG.GERUND'

In forms with more than one accent-attracting suffix occurs in a form, accent systematically falls on the rightmost one.

(16) a. jeʃ   'family'
        jeʃ-na-'ge   'family-1Pl.Poss-COMIT'
     b. tʃodra   'forest'
        tʃodra-na-'ge   'forest-1Pl.POSS-COMIT'

By contrast, certain affixes exhibit exceptional accent-repelling behavior. In particular, the suffix /-la/ is never accented (Riese et al. 2012: 127), even though it consists of an open syllable with a full non-mid vowel and can occur word-finally. Thus, when the root is suffixed with the 1Sg.Poss /-em/ or 2Sg. Poss /-et/ followed by /–la/, accent consistently falls on the possessive suffix, not on /-la/.

(17) a. ˈkajək   'bird'
       ˈkajək-la   'bird-COMPAR'
       tulˈʃol   'coal'
       tulˈʃol-la   'coal-COMPAR'
       tøˈʃak   'featherbed'
       tøˈʃak-la   'featherbed-COMPAR'
    b. pørt-ˈem-la   'house-1Sg.POSS-COMPAR'
       pørt-ˈet-la   'house-2Sg.POSS-COMPAR'

Similarly, the imperative suffix /-sa/ (2Pl.IMPER) is never accented word-finally:

(18) koˈd-aʃ   'stay-INF'
     ˈkod-sa   'stay-2PL.IMPER'

Summarizing, the phonological accent rule of SEM states that accent falls on the last heavy syllable; otherwise, accent is initial. At the same time, SEM exhibits systematic deviations from the regular pattern that are triggered by a small set of exceptional, morphologically productive morphemes. Note, though, that in forms with more than one exceptionally accent-attracting morpheme, it is the last such morpheme that receives the accent.

4 The Account

4.1 The Hybrid Weight Scale

In this section, we propose a single accent-assigning mechanism aimed at uniformly and accurately predicting accent location for both regular and exceptional patterns of SEM.

In this language, accent is assigned with reference to both phonological weight and the accent-affecting properties of individual suffixes, treated here in terms of diacritic weight. Below, it will be shown that, in SEM, there is a separate binary weight distinction for morphemes and for syllables, and that the resulting weight classes form a hybrid weight scale. To that end, the method of pairwise comparison of morphemes and/or syllables is used.

To begin with, from the accentual behavior of exceptional suffixes (Section 3.2.2), we conclude that SEM accent-affecting morphemes form two (non-intersecting) classes. *Class A* morphemes, including /-ge/ and /-de/, receive word accent in violation of the phonological accent rule, i.e. they win the accent over heavy syllables. Hence, they are diacritically heavy (with respect to syllables). *Class B* morphemes, including /-la/ and /-sa/, never receive word accent, even when this leads to a violation of the accent rule; in other words, they lose accent to light syllables. Hence, they are diacritically light (with respect to syllables).

We will now show that Class A and Class B are ordered so that there exists a HEAVIER-THAN relation holding over them, *viz.* Class A > Class B.

We must, then, look at forms which contain morphemes from both classes, such as (19). In these forms, reference is made not to the weight of the root *syllable*, but to the diacritic weight of the root as a *morpheme*: indeed, the root retains the accent under prefixation, even though its syllable is light, while the initial syllable is heavy.

(19) a. mo   'what'
        kö   'who'

    b. ni-'mo   'nothing'   c. *'ni-mo
       ni-'gö   'nobody'   *'ni-gö

We conclude that this morpheme class is heavier than the class of phonologically heavy syllables and, therefore, the roots in (19) are Class A. Now, note that, in (20), where the same roots as above are followed by the Class B suffix /-la/, accent falls on the root, rather than on the suffix.

(20) ni-'mo-la   'nothing-COMPAR'
     ni-'gö-la   'nobody-COMPAR'

Therefore, Class A > Class B.

Summarizing so far, diacritically heavy morphemes are heavier than diacritically light morphemes ($h_d > l_d$) and than phonologically heavy syllables ($h_d > h_p$).[1]

---

[1] For the sake of clarity, weight distinctions of type (phonological/diacritic) and degree (heavy/light) will be expressed using the following notation: the lower-case letter indicates weight degree (h, l), the subscript indicates weight type ($_p$, $_d$). In this way, "$h_p > l_p$" is short for "phonologically heavy syllables are heavier than phonologically light syllables".

Second, observe that the Class B suffix /-la/ in [ˈpørt-ʃə-la] ("house-3Sg. POSS-COMPAR") loses the accent to /pørt/. This implies that heavy syllables are heavier than the Class B morphemes ($h_p > l_d$).

Third, since the monomorphemic form in (21a) bears initial accent and the default initial accent is assigned to schwa-only forms, then accent assignment here makes reference to phonological, rather than diacritic, weight. However, the diacritically heavy suffix in (21b) attracts the accent.

(21) a. ˈpələʃ   'ear-NOM'
     b. pələʃ-ˈge 'ear-COMIT'

Therefore, Class A morphemes are heavier than phonologically light syllables ($h_d > l_p$).

Finally, the default initial accent in [ˈpələʃ-la] ("ear-COMPAR"), where the root consists of phonologically light syllables and the suffix is diacritically light (see above), reveals that light syllables and light morphemes have equal weight. Therefore, the two classes are mutually unordered ($\{l_d, l_p\}$). (But they are ordered with respect to the other classes, as already shown.)

These weight asymmetries together imply the following hybrid weight scale for SEM:

(22) $h_d > h_p > \{l_d, l_p\}$

One must add that, since accentually neutral morphemes respect the phonological accent rule, accent assignment does not make reference to those morphemes as such, but to syllables which these contain.

4.2 The Parameter System

In the spirit of the Primary Accent First theory (van der Hulst 1996, 2010, 2012), we have proposed the set of parameters in (23), some of which may be blocked by dependency relations defined on that set. This system has been empirically shown (based on StressTyp1 records revised by us) to accurately derive cross-linguistic variation with respect to phonological accent systems (Vaxman 2016b, 2018b).

(23) Domain Size (Bounded/Unbounded)
Domain Edge (Left/Right)
Weight (Yes/No)
Nonfinality (Yes/No)
Nonfinality Unit (Syllable/Segment)
Select (Left/Right)
Default (Left/Right)

The reader will note that (23) slightly differs from the parameter set in PAF (van der Hulst 1996, 2010, 2012). The main points of divergence are the replacement of extrametricality with nonfinality (instances of left-edge extrametricality being rare and dubious) and the splitting of PAF's Domain parameter into two binary parameters, Domain Size and Domain Edge.

Based on the description in Section 3.2, the parameter settings for SEM are as follows:

(24) Domain Size (Unbounded)
Domain Edge (blocked by a dependency)
Weight (Yes)
Nonfinality (No)
Nonfinality Unit (blocked by a dependency)
Select (Right)
Default (Left)

4.3 Weight Representation and Accent Assignment

We assume that word-level prominence involves a planar (arguably, modular) architecture: it is assigned on several dedicated planes. Thus, following PAF, separation of accent and rhythm is captured using distinct planes: the Accent Plane and the Rhythm Plane, where the former feeds accent locations onto the latter to serve as reference for rhythm assignment (performed by a separate mechanism, see van der Hulst 2014).

Crucially, we have proposed a Weight Plane containing the Weight Grid, a formal device for explicit representation and computation of weight (Vaxman 2016b). The weight of individual units is encoded on the Weight Grid. For example, in a weight-sensitive system with a binary weight distinction, heavy syllables are marked as "2" and light ones as "1" under the respective syllable. For a system with a weight scale, the weight degree of each unit is placed on the Weight Grid under the relevant unit. The Weight Projection Principle states that all, and only, the heaviest units in the form are projected onto the Accent Grid. In this way, the Weight Projection Principle serves as a filter on weights.

As an example, consider the phonological system of Latin, which has a heavy/light distinction. First, heavy syllables, marked with "2" on the Weight Grid, are projected onto the Accent Plane as gridmarks on line 1. Then, the final syllable is made extrametrical and the bounded domain is assigned near the right edge (modulo EM). Finally, the Select parameter, set to Right, chooses the rightmost gridmark in the accent domain on line 2, yielding accent on the penult (25 a). Light syllables, marked with "1" on the Weight Grid, are not projected (only heavy are); therefore, in all-light forms, the accent domain is empty. Then, the Default parameter supplies a gridmark on line 1, from which accent is read off. Thus, in (25b), Default (Left) assigns a gridmark to the leftmost syllable, yielding antepenultimate accent.

(25) a.
```
            *              Select (Right)
     (*    *)<*> ]         Weight Projection       Accent Grid
    ─────────────────────────────────────────
     h_p  h_p  h_p
      2    2    2                                  Weight Grid
     re:k'sis<tis>
```

b.
```
     (*  ) ]                Default (Left)         Accent Grid
    ─────────────────────────────────────────
     l_p l_p l_p
      1   1  1                                     Weight Grid
     'ani<ma>
```

This accent-assigning mechanism, illustrated above for a phonological system, is readily extended to systems where accent is unpredictable, entirely ("lexical accent systems") or partly ("hybrid accent systems"). In the former, it makes reference to a diacritic weight scale (in the absence of phonological weight); in the latter (such as SEM) to a hybrid weight scale. In the three types of system, the scale, together with the Weight Projection Principle, controls the selection of units (morphemes and/or syllables) on the Weight Grid for projection onto the Accent Grid, after which the parameter system assigns word accent.

4.4 Sample Derivations

Below, sample derivations are provided that illustrate how accent assignment works in SEM in different types of case.

i. Words with several heavy morphemes

Consider first the SEM form in (26). Based on the scale in (22), heavy morphemes are heavier than light syllables; therefore, the heavy suffixes are projected from the Weight Grid onto line 1 of the Accent Grid, while the heavy syllables are not. Select (Right) chooses the rightmost of the two gridmarks on line 1, yielding accent on the final syllable.

(26)
```
                    *              Select (Right)
         (      *   *   )          Weight Projection      Accent Grid
        ─────────────────────
         h_p  h_p  h_d  h_d                                Weight Grid
          2    2    3    3
         tʃodra- na- ge        [tʃodrana'ge]     'forest-1Pl.POSS-COMIT'
```

ii. Words with several heavy syllables, without heavy morphemes

The two syllables in the SEM form in (27) are equally heavy and there is no heavy affix. So, both syllables are projected onto line 1 of the Accent Grid. Select (Right) chooses the rightmost of the two gridmarks on line 1, yielding final accent.

(27)
```
              *             Select (Right)
          (*   *)            Weight Projection      Accent Grid
        ──────────────
          h_p  h_p                                   Weight Grid
           2    2
          pajrem             [paj'rem]     'holiday'
```

iii. Words with heavy morphemes and heavy syllables

Since the suffix /-ge/ is the heaviest unit in (28), it is projected from the Weight Grid onto line 1 of the Accent Grid, while syllables are not. Select (Right) (here, vacuously) chooses the line 1 gridmark, yielding final accent.

(28)
```
                  *              Select (Right)
          (        *)              Weight Projection      Accent Grid
        ─────────────────
          h_p  h_p  h_d                                    Weight Grid
           2    2    3
          pørt-em-ge           [pørtem'ge]     'house-1Sg.POSS-COMIT'
```

iv. Words with heavy morphemes and light syllables

Since the suffix /-ge/ is the heaviest unit in (29), it is projected onto line 1 of the Accent Grid, while the root *syllables* are not. Select (Right) chooses the line 1 gridmark, yielding final accent.

(29)
```
              *              Select (Right)
         (    * )             Weight Projection      Accent Grid
       ─────────────
         l_p  l_p  h_d                               Weight Grid
          1    1   3
         pələʃ-ge          [pələʃˈge]               'ear-COMIT'
```

v. Words with a light and a heavy morpheme

Based on (22), morphemes and heavy syllables are both lighter than heavy morphemes. Therefore, the suffix /-na/ in (30) is alone projected onto the Accent Grid. Select (Right) chooses the rightmost gridmark on line 1, yielding accent on [na].

(30)
```
              *              Select (Right)
         (    *  )            Weight Projection      Accent Grid
       ─────────────
         h_p   h_d   l_d                             Weight Grid
          2     3    1
         pørt-na-la        [pørtˈnala]              'house-1Pl.POSS-COMPAR'
```

vi. Words with a light morpheme and a heavy syllable

Based on (22), heavy syllables are heavier than light morphemes; therefore, in (31), the heavy syllable /pørt/ alone is projected onto the Accent Grid. Select (Right) chooses the line 1 gridmark over /pørt/, yielding initial accent.

(31)
```
          *                  Select (Right)
         ( *   )              Weight Projection      Accent Grid
       ─────────────
         h_p   l_d                                   Weight Grid
          2    1
         pørt-la           [ˈpørtla]                [ˈpørtla] 'house-COMPAR'
```

vii. Words with light morphemes and light syllables

Since light syllables and light morphemes are both light, nothing in (32) is projected from the Weight Grid onto the Accent Grid. As the accent domain remains empty, Default (Left) supplies a gridmark over the leftmost syllable in the accent domain on line 1, resulting in initial accent.

(32)

(*)	Default (Left)	Accent Grid
l_p l_p l_d		Weight Grid
1 1 1		
pələʃ-la	[ˈpələʃla]	'ear-COMPAR'

5 Conclusion

In this paper, we have presented a novel approach to accent and weight, building on the insight that, in addition to the phonological (predictable) weight of syllables, accent attraction may be a manifestation of the diacritic weight of morphemes (van der Hulst 1999: 19).

For hybrid accent systems, the combination of the two types of weight on a single scale captures accentual competition of syllables and exceptional morphemes. In the case of SEM, there are only four classes ordered on the hybrid weight scale (22).

This approach has the advantage of providing a uniform treatment of regular and exceptional accentual patterns. In particular, regular patterns and dominant exceptions in lexical accent systems are derived in the same manner, using a single mechanism.

Another advantage is that encoding both phonological and diacritic weight on the same dedicated representation (the Weight Grid) makes it possible to uniformly treat all types of accent system (phonological, lexical and hybrid) as weight-sensitive. Thus, systems apparently as different as, say, the phonological accent system of Latin, the lexical accent system of Uzbek (Vaxman 2016b, 2018a) and the hybrid accent system of SEM (Vaxman 2016a, 2016b, 2019) are all accounted for in essentially the same way.

References

Carlson, B. F. 1989. Reduplication and stress in Spokane. *International Journal of American Linguistics* 55. 204–213.

Czaykowska-Higgins, E. 1993. Cyclicity and stress in Moses-Columbia Salish (Nxa'amxcin). *Natural Language and Linguistic Theory* 11. 197–278.

Czaykowska-Higgins, E. & M. D. Kinkade 1998. Salish languages and linguistics. In E. Czaykowska-Higgins & M. D. Kinkade (eds.), *Salish Languages and Linguistics: Theoretical and Descriptive Perspectives*, 1–68. Berlin: Mouton.

Dyck, R. A. 2004. *Prosodic and morphological factors in Squamish (Skwxwú7mesh) stress assignment*. Victoria, BC: University of Victoria Doctoral dissertation.

Faust, N. & P. Smolensky. 2017. Activity as an alternative to autosegmental association. Paper presented at the 25th Manchester Phonology Meeting, Manchester, May 25, 2017.

Garde, P. 1965. Accentuation et morphologie. *La linguistique* 1(2). 25–39.

Garde, P. 1968. Les propriétés accentuelles des morphèmes dans les langues slaves. *Revue des études slaves* 47(1–4). 29–37.

Goedemans, R. & H. G. van der Hulst. 2014. The separation of accent and rhythm: Evidence from StressTyp. In H. G. van der Hulst (ed.), *Word Stress: Theoretical and Typological Issues*, 119–145. Cambridge/New York: Cambridge University Press.

Gordon, M. 2006. *Syllable Weight: Phonetics, Phonology, Typology*. New York/London: Routledge.

Hulst, H. G. van der. 1996. Separating primary and secondary accent. In R. Goedemans, H. G. van der Hulst & E. Visch (eds.), *Stress Patterns of the World. Part I*, 1–26. (HIL Publications 2). The Hague: Holland Academic Graphics.

Hulst, H. G. van der. 1999. Word accent. In H. G. van der Hulst (ed.), *Word Prosodic Systems in the Languages of Europe*, 3–116. Berlin/New York: Mouton de Gruyter.

Hulst, H. G. van der. 2010. Representing accent. *Phonological Studies* 13. 117–128.

Hulst, H. G. van der. 2012. Deconstructing stress. *Lingua* 122. 1494–1521.

Hulst, H. G. van der. 2014. Representing rhythm. In H. G. van der Hulst (ed.), *Word Stress: Theoretical and Typological Issues*, 325–365. Cambridge: Cambridge University Press.

Kiparsky, P. 1973. 'Elsewhere' in phonology. In S. Anderson & P. Kiparsky (eds.), *A Festschrift for Morris Halle*, 93–106. New York: Holt, Rinehart and Winston.

Legendre, G., Y. Miyata & P. Smolensky. 1990. Harmonic grammar – a formal multi-level connectionist theory of linguistic well-formedness: Theoretical foundations. *Proceedings of the 12th Annual Conference of the Cognitive Science Society*, 388–395.

Lehiste, I., P. Teras, T. Help, P. Lippus, E. Meister, K. Pajusalu & T.-R. Viitso. 2005. *Meadow Mari Prosody*. (Linguistica Uralica Supplementary Series 2). Tallinn: Teaduste Akadeemia Kirjastus.

McGarrity, L. W. 2003. *Constraints on patterns of primary and secondary stress*. Bloomington: Indiana University Doctoral dissertation.

Montler, T. 1986. An outline of the morphology and phonology of Saanich, North Straits Salish. *University of Montana Occasional Papers in Linguistics* 4. Missoula.

Revithiadou, A. 1999. *Headmost Accent Wins: Head Dominance and Ideal Prosodic Form in Lexical Accent Systems*. (HIL/LOT Dissertation 15). The Hague: Holland Academic Graphics.

Riese, T., J. Bradley, E. Yakimova & G. Krylova. 2012. *Оҥай марий йылме: A Comprehensive Introduction to the Mari language*. Department of Finno-Ugric Studies, University of Vienna.

Sebeok, T. A. & F. J. Ingemann. 1961. *An Eastern Cheremis Manual. Phonology, Grammar, Texts and Glossary*. Bloomington: Indiana University / The Hague: Mouton.

Smolensky, P. and M. Goldrick. 2016. Gradient symbolic representations in grammar: The case of French liaison. Ms. Johns Hopkins University and Northwestern University, ROA 1286.

Thompson, L. C. and M. T. Thompson. 1992. The Thompson Language. *University of Montana Occasional Papers in Linguistics* 8. Missoula.

Vasil'jev, V. M. and Z. V. Učaev. 2003. *Marijsko-russkij slovar'* [Mari-Russian dictionary]. Joškar-Ola: Marijskoe knižnoe izdatel'stvo.

Vaxman, A. 2016a. Diacritic weight in the Extended Accent First Theory. *University of Pennsylvania Working Papers in Linguistics* 22(1).

Vaxman, A. 2016b. *How to beat without feet: Weight scales and parameter dependencies in the computation of word accent*. Storrs, CT: University of Connecticut Doctoral dissertation.

Vaxman, A. 2018a. Accounting for dominance in Uzbek: A scale-based approach. In B. Erbasi, I. Mantenuto & S. Ozkan (eds.), *Proceedings of the 3rd Workshop on Turkish, Turkic and Languages of Turkey, UCLA Working Papers in Linguistics* 20.

Vaxman, A. 2018b. Parametric dependencies result in correct predictions about word accent typology. In K. Garvin, N. Hermalin, M. Lapierre, Y. Melguy, T. Scott & E. Wilbanks (eds.), *Proceedings of the 44th Annual Meeting of the Berkeley Linguistics Society*, 301–314.

Vaxman, A. 2019. The scales-and-parameters approach to morpheme-specific exceptions in accent assignment. In R. W. N. Goedemans, J. Heinz & H. G. van der Hulst (eds.), *The Study of Word Stress and Accent: Theories, Methods and Data*, 387–424. Cambridge: Cambridge University Press.

Vaysman, O. 2009. *Segmental alternations and metrical theory*. Cambridge, MA: MIT Doctoral dissertation.

Zimmermann, E. 2017a. Gradient symbolic representations in the output: A typology of lexical exceptions. Paper presented at the 48th Annual Meeting of the North East Linguistic Society, University of Iceland, October 29, 2017.

Zimmermann, E. 2017b. Being (slightly) stronger: Lexical stress in Moses Columbian Salish. Paper presented at the Strength in Grammar workshop, University of Leipzig, November 11, 2017.

Zimmermann, E. 2018. Gradient symbolic representations in the output: A case study from Moses Columbian Salishan stress. In S. Hucklebridge & M. Nelson (eds.), *Proceedings of the Forty-Eighth Annual Meeting of the North East Linguistic Society*, Amherst, 275–284.

Wendy Sandler
From Latent to Blatant: Unmasking Phonological Iconicity in Sign Language Theatre

Abstract: One of the most important breakthroughs in contemporary phonology was the discovery that the signs of sign languages are comprised of a finite list of formational units which recombine to create large vocabularies. It showed that the property of duality of patterning does not result from the nature of the vocal-auditory channel, but rather characterizes any natural human language, including manual-visual languages. However, sign languages are also unlike spoken languages. In sign languages, unlike spoken languages, form and meaning are closely linked, and iconicity permeates all levels of sign language grammar, including phonology. This chapter reveals the subtle interplay between the meaningless and the meaningful at the phonological level in sign languages, showing that a strict bifurcation is neither warranted nor explanatory. Instead, the ubiquity of iconicity in sign languages reveals the flexibility of human language, a flexibility that is heightened in artistic expression. Authentic examples from sign language theatre show how latent phonological iconicity can be blatantly exploited, becoming a potent aesthetic and communicative tool.

Keywords: sign language phonology, iconicity, duality of patterning, theatrical signing

Acknowledgements: The Ebisu Sign Language Theatre Laboratory was created as part of a larger project, called The Grammar of the Body, funded by European Research Council grant 340140. http://gramby.haifa.ac.il/ Thank you to Debi Menashe for modeling ISL signs and creating the drawings, and to Shai Davidi for images extracted from video. The ISL video dictionary was created by the Institute for the Advancement of Deaf People. Some of the research reported here was funded by the Israel Science Foundation, the U.S.-Israel Binational Science Foundation, and the U.S. National Institutes of Health. This analysis would not have been possible without the dedicated and creative work of the director, Atay Citron, grad student assistant, Gal Belsitzman, and the Ebisu actors: Shoval Ben Ze'ev, Lee Dan, Ella Okhotin, Alaa Sarsour, Nurit Shalom, Adis Tesffa Sibaht, Alon Zenou, and Golan Zino.

Wendy Sandler, University of Haifa

https://doi.org/10.1515/9783110730081-014

1 Introduction: Iconicity in Sign Language Phonology

The word 'iconic' is popularly used with a variety of meanings. Famous performers are sometimes called iconic, as are brand names and advertising symbols, and people representing particular opinions. In semiotics, according to the Random House Dictionary, an icon is 'a sign or representation that stands for its object [or action] by virtue of resemblance or analogy to it.' The signs of sign languages are often iconic in this sense: they look like what they mean, giving the impression that they are holistic icons.[1] For example, the sign TAKE in Israeli Sign Language (ISL) looks like gripping an object and moving it toward oneself (Figure 1).[2]

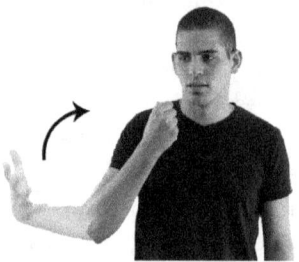

Figure 1: An iconic sign in ISL: TAKE.

While it is widely understood that many whole sign words are iconically motivated, and that there is also iconicity in the morphology (Aronoff, Meir, and Wendy Sandler 2005; Wilbur 2008), I focus here on iconicity in phonology, a level of structure that is taken to be mostly meaningless. The idea that sign languages are comprised of holistic iconic gestures, with no internal structure, was shattered by William Stokoe's (1960) groundbreaking research. He showed that, at the sublexical level corresponding to phonology in spoken language, there is a finite list of formational elements that combine to make signs, and that these correspond to the meaningless, contrastive phonological elements of spoken languages.

---

1 I follow earlier work in distinguishing iconicity from mimesis. In sign languages, "iconicity creates a likeness of an object or concept symbolically, through a configuration of the hands (or the mouth). It is to be contrasted with mimesis, which uses [the body] to replicate itself . . . . The distinction . . . reflects qualitatively different types of representation." (Sandler 2009: 251). Here the focus is on iconicity.
2 Unless otherwise indicated, examples in this chapter are from Israeli Sign Language (ISL), but they demonstrate general properties of sign languages.

Languages in the spoken modality are not entirely devoid of phonological iconicity. In recent years, research has uncovered a good deal more iconicity in the phonology of spoken languages than dreamt of in Saussure's philosophy,[3] to paraphrase Shakespeare's Hamlet. The spoken language literature includes phonological properties of ideophones in many languages, Japanese mimetics, and many other examples of phonological iconicity (see Perniss, Thompson, and Vigliocco (2010) and Dingemanse et al. (2015) for overviews). So, while both arbitrariness and iconicity can characterize phonology in any language modality, iconicity is far more common than arbitrariness in signed than in spoken languages, and vice versa.

Consider the Israeli Sign Language (ISL) sign EAT, which looks like the act of putting something into the mouth (Figure 2a). The fingertips-to-thumb Hand Configuration for holding an object moves in a straight (doubled) Movement path, toward the lower face Location.[4] This sign contrasts with the ISL sign BORING, shown in Figure 2b, on the basis of the Handshape only; the Location and Movement are identical in the two signs. Though BORING might have been iconically motivated by covering one's mouth when yawning, formally, it differs from EAT by only one formational parameter: Hand Configuration. Like the other major phonological categories, Movement and Location, the features of Hand Configuration belong to a finite list of formational elements that combine to make and to minimally distinguish signs.

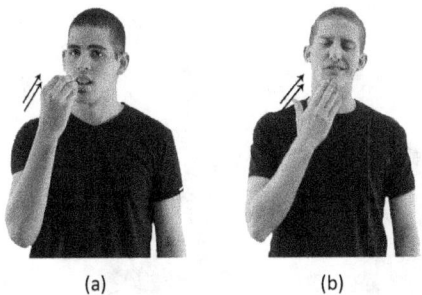

Figure 2: A minimal pair with contrastive, iconic sublexical units of handshape: (a) EAT, (b) BORING in ISL.

In addition, there are many phonological (and morphological) processes that refer only to the formational elements of signs, without regard for meaning (Bellugi and Klima 1979), some of which will be described below. So far so good: duality of

---

[3] The reference to Saussure is of course to his influential generalization that the relation between form and meaning in language is arbitrary (de Saussure 1959).
[4] This chapter assumes the Hand Tier model of phonological structure (Sandler 1989; Sandler and Lillo-Martin 2006).

patterning (Hockett 1960) characterizes sign languages too (de Boer, Sandler, and Kirby 2012), and can be considered a design feature of all human language.

Nevertheless, sublexical iconicity – a direct correspondence between form and meaning in phonological building blocks – is strikingly resilient in sign languages. Even those elements that make contrasts and that function in terms of form are often iconically motivated, and the motivation is discernible across the lexicon (Kegl 1985; Taub 2001; Fernald and Napoli 2000). Els van der Kooij (2002) developed the idea that iconicity is a property of phonology in Sign Language of the Netherlands, and her observations hold for other sign languages as well.

We see that iconicity is also exploited at the phonological level in Figure (3). The sign LEARN (Figure 3a) metaphorically extends the iconic notion of putting something somewhere – in this case, putting knowledge in the head.[5] The signs EAT and LEARN are a minimal pair, but the distinguishing features (lower and upper face Location Settings[6]) are not arbitrary; they are iconically motivated. In fact, many signs involving the mouth (like SPEAK, TASTE) are signed at the same lower face Location Setting; many signs involving mental processes are at the temple Location Setting, like LEARN (3a), e.g, THINK (3b), DREAM (3c). Similarly, many signs that involve gripping something are signed with the same "closed B" handshape (EAT, PUT, MOVE). We can call the result "dual duality of patterning", a level of structure with both meaningless and meaningful properties (Sandler 2018).

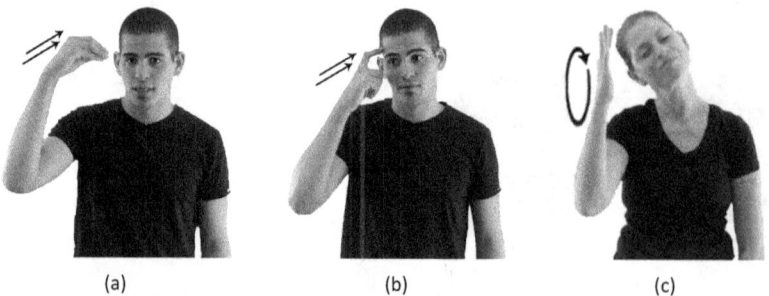

Figure 3: ISL signs with iconic Location Setting: the temple. (a) LEARN, (b) THINK, (c) DREAM.

---

5 Taub's 2001 book describes how metaphor is incorporated into iconic signs in ASL. But sign language iconicity has a constraining effect as well. If the intended metaphor does not correspond to aspects of an object or event ionically represented in a literal sign, the metaphor is blocked (Meir 2010).
6 In the Hand Tier model adopted here, Location refers to a major body area (e.g., head, torso, non-dominant hand), and Setting refers to a point on that Location, (e.g., hi, lo, lateral, contralateral, proximal, distal, etc.). According to Battison (1978), there is only one major body area per monomorphemic sign. In a canonical sign, the hand moves from one Setting to another on that Location.

All of the signs we have seen so far manifest the canonical form of a sign: a single Hand Configuration articulates a single path Movement from one Location Setting to another. The visual system can perceive these feature complexes simultaneously (Brentari 2002), so that there is little sequential structure within the sign. This, in turn, has led Harry van der Hulst (1993) to propose that signs are best represented underlyingly as single segments. Because of this relatively simple linear structure, there is typically little phonological alternation within signs. But we will see in the next section that when two signs are concatenated to form compounds, phonological processes based on form occur, obscuring the iconicity in the signs.

Can the iconicity in sign languages be integrated with strictly form-based structures and rules? To show that it can, I will begin in Section 2 with some examples of 'pure' phonology in sign languages, in which constraints and rules refer only to form and not to meaning. In Section 3, examples from the Ebisu Sign Language Theatre will demonstrate the resilience of phonological iconicity in artistic expression. We will see that strictly formational properties are involved in phonological operations related only to form, while latent iconic properties can become blatant when they are tapped for creative purposes.

2 Form-Based Phonology in Sign Language

The focus here will be on two physical attributes of sign languages that uniquely contribute to linguistic structure. One is the existence of two anatomically identical articulators in lexical signs: the two hands.[7] The other is the human face. While both articulators encode a wide variety of functions at morphological, syntactic, intonational, and discourse levels (see Sandler 2018) – these are all beyond the scope of this section, which focuses on phonology in the word.

2.1 Formal Properties of the Two Hands

Two constraints on the form and interaction of the two hands in lexical signs, formulated for ASL by Battison in 1978, have withstood the tests of time and of cross-linguistic research: the Dominance Condition and the Symmetry Condition.

---

[7] For phonological studies of the nondominant hand in sign languages, see Sandler (1993, 2006), Brentari and Goldsmith (1993), van der Hulst and Sandler (1994), Nespor and Sandler (1999), and Crasborn (2011).

The Dominance Condition states that when one hand is dominant (i.e, moves) in a two-handed sign, then the nondominant, static hand must either have the same shape as the non-dominant hand, or it must manifest one of a small number of unmarked handshapes. In such signs, the nondominant hand typically functions as the Location of the sign. We see this constraint instantiated in Figure 4 with the sign for EMPTY in three unrelated sign languages; American, Israeli, and Swedish (Lepic et al. 2016). These signs are iconically motivated, in that the nondominant hand represents a container or surface, and the dominant, moving hand indicates emptiness or bareness with respect to it. But the constraint on their form is purely phonological, with no direct relation to meaning. In the three sign languages, the dominant hand may have different shapes, including a marked shape in the ASL sign, but the static nondominant hand as a Location is configured in the least marked handshape – all fingers extended – obeying the Dominance Condition.

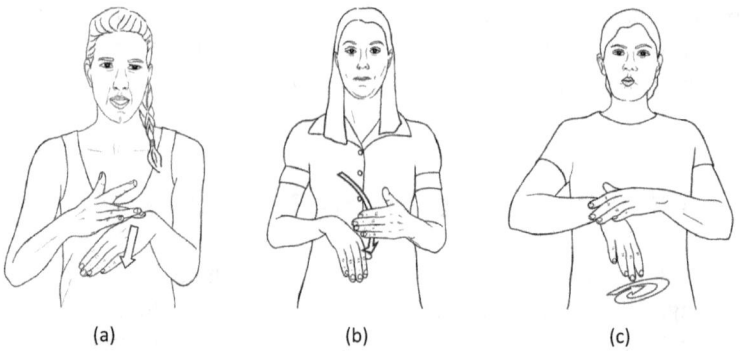

Figure 4: Iconic motivation in two-handed lexical signs. EMPTY in (a) American SL, (b) Swedish SL, and (c) Israeli SL. The Dominance Condition is revealed most clearly by ASL figure (a), which has a marked handshape on the dominant hand but an unmarked handshape on the nondominant hand.

The Symmetry Condition stipulates that if both hands move, they must have the same handshape, and perform the same Movement, at the same or symmetrical Locations. We see this in the signs for NEGOTIATE in two sign languages: Israeli Sign Language (Figure 5a) and Al-Sayyid Bedouin Sign Language (5b) (Sandler 2018). Here again, the iconic motivation is apparent – the two hands represent two sides to a negotiation, and the alternating Movement represents the give and take of negotiation. In the sign in each language, the two hands are symmetrical in Hand Configuration, Location, and Movement, as the formal constraint requires.

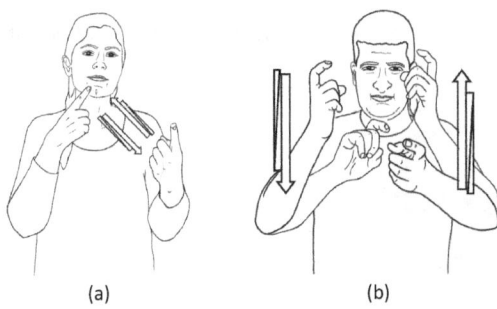

Figure 5: Iconic motivation and the Symmetry Condition in lexical signs: NEGOTIATE in (a) ISL, (b) Al-Sayyid Bedouin Sign Language.

As Figures 4 and 5 suggest, phonological constraints and iconicity are independent of one another, but they are not mutually exclusive, and there is a good deal of iconic motivation in the use of two hands in signs. Comparing four unrelated sign languages, Lepic et al. (2016) found that signs conveying concepts such as *interaction, location, dimension,* and *composition* are significantly more likely to be two-handed in any sign language than chance would predict. The authors subsume these properties under the broader category of *plurality*. Yet iconic two-handed signs like EMPTY (two-handed because they represent location) and NEGOTIATE (conveying interaction) also conform to strict constraints related to form and not meaning.

The Symmetry Condition is widespread across sign languages, and Kita, van Gijn, and van der Hulst (2014) have argued that it is a more general phonetic constraint that also applies to gestures. Be that as it may, the constraint is form-based, and in sign languages, it holds only on sign words. It is required neither by meaning nor by physiological limitations. In fact, it can be freely violated in sign language classifier constructions, which are complex expressions but not words. These constructions consist of a lexically listed classifier handshape standing for a class of concepts (humans, vehicles, small animals, flat objects, etc., Supalla 1986; Zwitserlood 2012) which combine post-lexically with gestural Locations and Movements (Sandler and Lillo-Martin 2006). In such constructions, the non-dominant hand can be configured in a marked shape that is different from that of the dominant hand (Figure 6a), violating the dominance condition, and both hands can move, symmetrically or asymmetrically, the latter violating the symmetry condition (Figure 6b), demonstrating multiple degrees of freedom in the interaction of the two hands (Aronoff et al. 2003).[8] It is only in the behavior of

---

[8] An asymmetrical classifier construction from the theatre performance illustrates the potential independence of the two hands in Figure 9.

the two hands in lexical signs that this freedom is significantly constrained, on formal grounds.

Figure 6: In classifier constructions, each hand functions as an independent nominal morpheme, so that constraints on two-handed lexical signs do not apply. (a) 'man approaches an airplane', the static hand is configured in a marked shape contra the dominance condition. (b) 'man drags dog', both hands move, configured in different shapes, contra the symmetry condition. (Aronoff et al. 2003).

Returning to lexical signs, these are subject to phonological constraints and undergo phonological processes. The best place to look for phonological alternations is in lexicalized compounds. The reason for this is that by concatenating two signs linearly, we get more sequential phonological complexity, competing with the monosyllabic form of the optimal prosodic word. While the canonical sign consists only of a single Hand Configuration and one (sometimes reduplicated) Movement from one Location Setting to another, as in all the illustrations thus far, compounds start out as a concatenation of two such signs. When these compounds are lexicalized, the members often merge in particular ways (Liddell and Johnson 1986) that reveal formal phonological primitives: Hand Configuration and Location categories, and the syllable (Sandler 1987, 1989, 1999). As we will see, the resulting lexical form of the compound also conforms to the Symmetry Condition.

The example I bring here is a compound in which the second member is two-handed. It consists of the signs THINK and STOP. On the widely accepted proposal that movement constitutes a syllable nucleus, THINK and STOP are each monosyllabic, each with its own lexical movement. The lexicalized compound means STUNNED. The two members and the lexicalized compound form are shown in Figure 7.

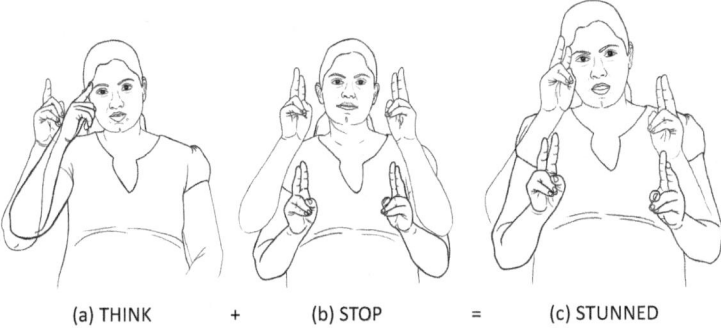

Figure 7: Truncation and assimilation in an ISL compound: (a) THINK, (b) STOP, (c) STUNNED.

The phonological processes at work in the compound are truncation and assimilation. The compound reduces the two syllables of the member signs to a single syllable, i.e., a single path Movement. A single Hand Configuration is assimilated regressively from the second member of the compound to characterize the whole compound word, and the Hand Configuration of the first member is lost. The second Location Setting of the first sign (on the temple) survives, as does the last Location Setting of the second sign (low in the space in front of the signer). The two interim Location Settings fall out, leaving a single path Movement, and the optimal monosyllabic form of the prosodic word (Sandler 1999). Since STOP is a two-handed symmetrical sign, after total regressive assimilation, the Hand Configuration for the lexicalized compound is also two-handed and symmetrical, indicating that Hand Configuration is a phonological feature category that includes features for number of hands, their shapes and orientations.[9] The Symmetry Condition requiring symmetrical Movement, Hand Configuration, and Location for two moving hands then holds over the whole compound.

There are two points to be made here. First, precisely these same processes of truncation and assimilation are typical in lexicalized compounds in both ISL, as cited above, and ASL (Sandler 2017). The processes are stated as generalizations in terms of formal categories in both languages, and not in terms of their meanings.[10] Second, and as a result, the iconic properties that motivated the individual members of the compound, such as pointing to the temple for THINK, are

---

[9] The behavior of hand orientation in such compounds is consistent; it assimilates together with the handshape but never alone, in either ASL or ISL. This is evidence that orientation is dominated by the Hand Configuration category in a feature geometry model (Sandler 1989). Formal representations of this process are found in Sandler (2012a, 2017).
[10] The question of why reduction and assimilation in two unrelated sign languages, ASL and ISL, are formally the same has yet to be addressed.

obscured in the lexicalized form, which has undergone purely formal phonological processes.

2.2 Lexically Specified Facial Expressions

One characteristic of sign language that immediately impresses even passing observers is salient and rapidly changing facial expressions. And indeed, the face is an abundantly rich source of different kinds of information in sign languages. Linguistic functions of the face in sign languages are myriad, though most of them are either morphological or intonational, characterizing syntactic or prosodic constituents, and not part of the lexical phonology.

The lower face systematically conveys adjectival and adverbial information, functioning morphologically (Liddell 1980). The upper face manifests a complex intonational system, obligatorily and distinctively accompanying polar questions, content questions, shared information, relative clauses, and conditionals in ASL and ISL (e.g., Dachkovsky and Sandler 2009; for overviews, see Sandler and Lillo-Martin 2006; Sandler et al. 2020). These intonational expressions might have originated in facial gestures shared with hearing people (such as raised brows for polar questions, see Janzen 1999), and in that sense might be considered to have mimetic – but not iconic – origins.[11]

One sublexical facial category is specified in certain individual signs, which are obligatorily accompanied by meaningless facial movements. Investigating British Sign Language, Woll (2014) labels these interesting elements 'echo phonology', since they echo the motion of the hands in the sign. She proposes an evolutionary relation between the hand and the mouth in human language generally. Echo facial elements are phonological, but not iconic in and of themselves.

A small number of lexical signs are obligatorily accompanied by facial expressions that are iconic, in particular, expressions made by the mouth. For example, Figure 8 shows the signs for FAT and SKINNY in ISL. For FAT the mouth and cheeks are puffed, and for SKINNY, the mouth and cheeks are sucked in.[12] Like other iconic forms, they are likely to have originated in a gestural system that

---

[11] The origin of intonational facial expressions is not iconic in the sense intended here, since they do not look like what they mean. They are mimetic of people expressing various emotions and attitudes, but do not look like the emotions and attitudes themselves, which do not have concrete physical forms.
[12] While some of the signs taken from the ISL video dictionary that are pictured here involve facial expressions, these are affective and idiosyncratic, and are not obligatorily part of the sign, unlike the mouth components for FAT and SKINNY.

enhances the images of the hands (see Sandler 2009). But some have made their way into the linguistic system, in the sense that they are lexically specified and obligatory for particular signs. On formal grounds, we might tentatively compare them to sporadic lexical tones. It appears that that these mouth components are rare in the lexicon – other signs in ISL that convey large or small size have no specified facial expression, nor do most other signs. Nevertheless, the mouth components pictured are formational components of signs. And, like other motivated formal elements described here, they reflect the latent iconic potential that comes to the fore in creative contexts, like theatre.

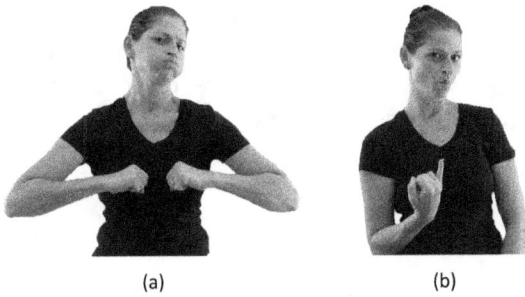

Figure 8: ISL signs with iconic lexical mouth features (a) FAT, (b) SKINNY.

3 Theatrical Signing: Retrieving Iconicity

Nearly 50 years ago, the Dutch scholar Bernard Tervoort observed that iconicity in sign language "is not a more or less accidental feature because it comes to the surface only once in a while, but a basically concomitant characteristic that is potentially present all the time" (Tervoort 1973: 357). This concomitant characteristic seems largely latent in the phonology of everyday signing. But in artistic use of sign language, latent phonological iconicity becomes a blatant and potent artistic tool.

It is not unusual to appeal to creative uses of language in order to illuminate internal linguistic structure. In spoken language, language games and poetry isolate such components as syllable onsets and rhymes. Here the creative vehicle is theatre, and the component is phonological iconicity.

In 2014, the Ebisu Sign Language Theatre Laboratory was founded as part of a broader research project.[13] The group is named after a Japanese Shinto god of prosperity – the only deaf god in the mythologies of the world. Eight signing actors, seven deaf or hard of hearing and one hearing, were selected by audition for this theatrical experiment. The theatre project had two goals, one artistic and the other linguistic. Guided by the director, Atay Citron, through exercises and improvisation, the artistic goal was to create theatrical productions that draw on sign language and physical theatre, and that would be accessible to deaf and hearing audiences alike, without interpreting.[14] Since the improvisations were created within this framework by deaf actors, the result was an expression of deaf culture in a visual world. The linguistic goal was to identify and study the elements of linguistic structure that lay dormant in everyday signing, waiting to be awakened in the process of artistic expression. For coherence, the focus here is primarily on the two hands, and on iconic mouth images.

3.1 Two Hands and Iconicity

We have seen that there are strict constraints on the interaction of the two hands in lexical two-handed signs, and that they behave like meaningless phonological elements in phonological processes of sign languages. At the same time, two-handed signs have a considerable degree of iconic motivation. The latent iconicity of the signs becomes blatant in theatrical signing.

The Ebisu actors were given an exercise in which they were asked to choose an ISL sign, and the only instruction was to keep repeating it, allowing it to take on new meanings, in a technique that director Citron calls, "Let the body lead the mind". Actress Nurit Shalom chose the sign for LEARN (see the citation form in Figure 3a above). In order to convey different shades of meaning and attitude, the actress altered the sign iconically throughout the exercise. She changed from being a passive recipient in the citation form of the sign (Figure 9a), to becoming an active agent, seeking and gaining knowledge. To convey this transformation, she introduced a grasping motion (observable in the lexical sign TAKE, in Figure 1), actively taking information and metaphorically putting it into her

---

13 The theatre project was one of five research directions included in the Grammar of the Body research project, funded by the European Research Council.
14 Links to trailers for the three theatre performances:
'It's Not About Ebisu' https://www.youtube.com/watch?v=YeS5Z3GQifo&feature=youtu.be;
'Their Language' https://www.youtube.com/watch?v=2gilwYRAbVM&feature=youtu.be;
'About Ebisu Theatre' https://www.youtube.com/watch?v=VqREpLKBb5g&feature=youtu.be.

head (9b). Eventually, the deluge of information overwhelms her, shown by using two hands and repeating the action. Here we see iconic simultaneous reduplication in the form of two hands, and linear reduplication of the sign (not pictured), to represent being taught more and more information (9c). Reduplication is often iconic in spoken languages as well, to represent more of something (Kouwenberg and LaCharité 2015). The body is also actively involved mimetically in interpreting the meanings conveyed. The change back from agent to recipient is conveyed by the direction of the action toward herself, and her reaction is portrayed mimetically, by turning her body away in (9c).

The actress recombines iconic elements that are latent in sign language: two hands for plurality (Lepic et al. 2017), reduplication for repeated action (Klima and Bellugi 1979), and closing handshape for active agency. In (9d), Nurit further deconstructs TAKE into its iconic components using only the open handshape on two hands, to indicate 'holding' that which is being taken in (a great deal of knowledge), and adds an iconic mouth gesture to convey 'huge' – too much knowledge to take in. We will return to the mouth in Section 3.2.

Figure 9: Decomposing iconic elements. (a) LEARN, (b) 'take-in-knowledge', (c) 'being-taught-too-much', (d) 'a-huge-amount-of-knowledge'.

In the show, *Their Language*, actor Golan Zino performs a poem that tells of communication difficulties between hearing and deaf people, despite grueling and often fruitless efforts on the part of deaf people. At the beginning of the poem, the actor's left hand represents a deaf person trying to sign with a hearing passer-by, as the hearing person, represented by his right hand, looks down on him (Figure 10). The actor exploits the iconic option of letting each hand stand for a different referent, and allowing them to be configured and to move independently, violating the Symmetry Constraint in artistic extension of intrinsic iconic properties.[15] Here each hand is configured for a lexical sign, LOOK-AT and SIGNING, so that this artistic expression is like neither either lexical signs nor classifier constructions – but exploits latent properties of the system.

Figure 10: Theatre: Each hand conveys a referent; no symmetry or dominance. Upper hand: LOOK-DOWN-ON, Lower hand: SIGNING.

Later in the poem, the actor manipulates the sign BROKEN, normally signed in neutral space in front of the signer (Figure 11a), adopting a different Location iconically – the ear (Belsitzman 2017). The expression conveys hearing people's distorted impression of deaf people as broken-ear people (11b). We saw that the Location can be iconic across the lexicon, for example, the head (temple) representing mental processes and the lower face representing the mouth in Figures 3 and 4. Here, the actor summons this latent iconic property, giving the ear Location iconic meaning, to blatantly confront the audience with a provocative image.

---

15 Crasborn (2006) describes a similar use of two hands to stand for two propositions simultaneously in a SLN poem by Wim Emmerik. Crasborn notes that he had not seen use of this device extended across a stretch of signing, an option that is exploited in the Ebisu theatrical narrative excerpted in Figure 10.

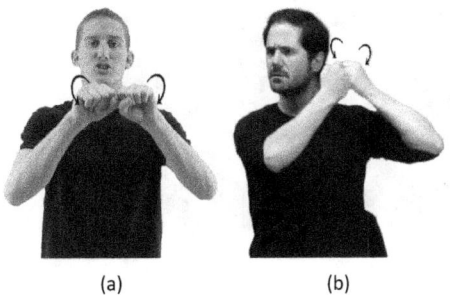

Figure 11: (a) The lexical sign BREAK. (b) Theatre: Isolating iconic location in the creative sign: 'broken ear'.

3.2 Enter the Face

As in everyday signing, the face is an abundant source of information in theatrical signing as well. Here I ignore the vast domains of linguistic and emotional facial expression, and focus on iconicity as defined here. In Section 2.2, Figure 7, we saw examples of iconic facial expressions that are obligatorily parts of the lexical signs FAT and THIN, and can therefore be considered phonological components comparable to lexical tones. These and many other such mouth shapes with gestural characteristics are independently exploited in creative signing, especially in descriptive narratives involving classifier constructions (Sandler 2009).[16] It is not surprising, then, that they are also summoned in theatrical performance. Let's look at two examples from the Ebisu theatre that exploit exactly the same iconically motivated mouth gestures as those lexically specified for FAT and THIN.

In the same production, Their Language, an actor tells the story of creation from the bible (only to be upstaged later by the rest of the company's Big Bang evolutionary account). In picturing the state of the world in the beginning, actor Alon Zenou describes the earth as without form and void. He accompanies his signing with a puckered mouth and cheeks expression (Figure 12a), enhancing the visual image of 'void'. In describing the waters rising and falling, bringing forth vegetation on the third day, the actor puffs out his mouth and cheeks to enhance description of the swelling of the waters. Alon makes use of iconic mouth images inherent in the language to convey a heightened visual image.

---

[16] Goldin-Meadow and Brentari (2017) propose that the study of language must include gesture, which compensates for some of the iconic imagery that is missing in spoken language.

Figure 12: Theatre: Iconic mouth gestures: (a) 'emptiness, void' with sucked in mouth and cheeks, (b) 'rising mass (water)' with puffed mouth and cheeks.

The same puffed mouth and cheek expression conveying swelling of the waters that we see in Figure 12b, motivated by iconicity, and lexically specified for the sign FAT, surfaced in Nurit Shalom's expression of a huge quantity (of knowledge) in Figure 9d above. This is no surprise. In both examples of artistic expression, the actors are reaching into the rich iconic repertoire of their language, a repertoire that has been only partly tamed by grammar.

4 Conclusion: Full Circle

Sign languages originate in gestures with a strong iconic base. Since the hands and the rest of the body are so pliable, and the visual system is so good at interpreting the visual iconic images they create, it would make no sense for sign languages to have arisen any other way. Yet within about three generations, these languages develop systematic linguistic form (Senghas and Coppola 2001; Aronoff et al 2008; Sandler 2012b). Even phonological structure, typically meaningless by definition, emerges over time, though gradually (Sandler et al. 2011), so that established sign languages are characterized by duality of patterning, a fundamental property of language. Nevertheless, iconicity persists at all levels, including the least likely level, phonology. This inherent iconicity is latent in everyday signing and can be recruited blatantly in creative signing.

By analyzing artistic use of sign language by deaf actors, we have seen here that iconic building blocks are psychologically real. Linguistic constraints on the two hands are relaxed so that the meaning inherent in the iconic shape and movement of each hand can be exploited. Iconic Locations can be independently manipulated to create novel poetic images. The images are intelligible because the latent iconicity of each Location is made blatant by artistic manipulation. Iconic mouth gestures that made their way sporadically into the lexicon are retrieved from the iconic base to enhance expressive visual images made by the hands. Artistic expression brings sign languages full circle – from iconic origins to linguistic structuring and back to sophisticated manipulation of the iconic base.

Sign languages are like spoken languages in important ways, and both systems are characterized by the universal design feature, duality of patterning. But the differences – such as the inverse contributions of arbitrariness and iconicity to language form – are just as real. Together, the two language systems reveal the remarkable flexibility and creativity of the whole human language.

References

Aronoff, Mark, Irit Meir, Carol Padden & Wendy Sandler. 2003. Classifier constructions and morphology in two sign languages. In Karen Emmorey (ed.), *Perspectives on Classifiers Constructions in Sign Languages*, 53–84. Mahwah, NJ: Lawrence Erlbaum.

Aronoff, Mark, Irit Meir, Carol Padden & Wendy Sandler. 2008. The roots of linguistic organization in a new language. In Derek Bickerton & Michael Arbib (eds.), *Holophrasis, Compositionality and Proto Language* [Special issue]. *Interaction Studies*, 133–149.

Aronoff, Mark, Irit Meir & Wendy Sandler. 2005. The paradox of sign language morphology. *Language* 81(2). 301–344.

Battison, Robbin. 1978. *Lexical Borrowing in American Sign Language*. Silver Spring, MD: Linstok Press.

Bellugi, Ursula & Edward Klima. 1979. Language: Perspectives from another modality. In Ciba Foundation Symposium 69, *Brain and Mind*. 99–128.

Belsitzman, Gal. 2017. The Ebisu tool kits: Realizing the potential of the expressive body. Paper presented at the GRAMBY Workshop, University of Haifa.

Boer, Bart de, Wendy Sandler & Simon Kirby. 2012. New perspectives on duality of patterning: Introduction to the special issue. *Language and Cognition* 4(4). 251–259.

Brentari, Diane. 2002. Modality differences in sign language phonology and morphophonemics. In Richard Meier, Kearsy Cormier & David Quinto-Pozos (eds.), *Modality and Structure in Signed and Spoken Languages*, 35–64. Cambridge: Cambridge University Press.

Brentari, Diane & John Goldsmith. 1993. Secondary licensing and the nondominant hand in ASL phonology. In Geoffrey Coulter and Stephen Anderson (eds.), *Current Issues in ASL Phonology: Phonetics and Phonology*, 19–41. San Diego: Academic Press.

Crasborn, Onno. 2006. A linguistic analysis of the use of two hands in sign language poetry. In Jeroen van de Weijer & Bettelou Los (eds.), *Linguistics in the Netherlands*, 65–77. Amsterdam: John Benjamins.

Crasborn, Onno. 2011. The other hand in sign language phonology. In Marc van Oostendorp, Colin J. Ewen, Elizabeth V. Hume & Keren Rice (eds.), *The Blackwell Companion to Phonology*, 223–240. Oxford: Wiley-Blackwell.

Dachkovsky, Svetlana & Wendy Sandler. 2009. Visual intonation in the prosody of a sign language. *Language and Speech* 52(2–3). 287–314.

Dingemanse, Mark, Damián E. Blasi, Gary Lupyan, Morton H. Christiansen & Padraic Monaghan. 2015. Arbitrariness, iconicity, and systematicity in language. *Trends in Cognitive Sciences* 19(10). 603–615.

Fernald, Theodore & Donna Jo Napoli. 2000. Exploitation of morphological possibilities in signed languages: Comparison of American Sign Language with English. *Sign Language & Linguistics* 3(1). 3–58.

Goldin-Meadow, Susan & Diane Brentari. 2017. Gesture, sign and language: Coming of age of sign language and gesture studies. *Behavioral and Brain Sciences* 40. 1–82.

Hockett, Charles D. 1960. The origin of speech. *Scientific American* 203. 89–96.

Hulst, Harry van der. 1993. Units in the analysis of signs. *Phonology* 10(2). 209–241.

Hulst, Harry van der & Wendy Sandler. 1994. Phonological theories meet sign language: Two theories of the two hands. *Toronto Working Papers in Linguistics* 13. 43–73.

Janzen, Terry. 1999. The grammaticization of topics in American Sign Language. *Studies in Language* 23(2). 21–306.

Kegl, Judy. 1985. *Locative relations in American Sign Language word formation*. Cambridge, MA: MIT PhD thesis.

Kita, Sotaro, Ingeborg van Gijn & Harry van der Hulst. 2014. The non-linguistic status of the Symmetry Condition in signed languages: Evidence from a comparison of signs and speech-accompanying representational gestures. *Sign Language & Linguistics* 17. 209–232.

Klima, Edward S. & Ursula Bellugi. 1979. *The Signs of Language*. Cambridge, MA: Harvard University Press.

Kooij, Els van der. 2002. *Phonological categories in sign language of the Netherlands: The role of phonetic implementation and iconicity*. PhD Dissertation. Utrecht: LOT.

Kouwenberg, Silvia & Darlene LaCharité. 2015. Arbitrariness and iconicity in total reduplication: Evidence from Caribbean Creoles. *Studies in Language* 39. 971–991.

Lepic, Ryan, Carl Börstell, Gal Belsitzman & Wendy Sandler. 2016. Taking meaning in hand. *Sign Language & Linguistics* 19(1). 37–81.

Liddell, Scott K. 1980. *American Sign Language Syntax*. The Hague: Mouton de Gruyter.

Liddell, Scott. K. & Robert E. Johnson. 1986. American Sign Language compound formation processes, lexicalization, and phonological remnants. *Natural Language & Linguistic Theory* 4(4). 445–513.

Meir, Irit. 2010. Iconicity and metaphor: Constraints on metaphorical use of iconic forms. *Language* 86(4). 865–896.

Nespor, Marina & Wendy Sandler. 1999. Prosodic phonology in Israeli Sign Language. *Language and Speech* 42(2–3). 143–176.

Perniss, Pamela, Robin L. Thompson & Gabriella Vigliocco. 2010. Iconicity as a general property of language: Evidence from spoken and signed languages. *Frontiers in Psychology* 1. DOI: 10.3389/fpsyg.2010.00227.

Sandler, Wendy. 1987. Assimilation and feature hierarchy ASL. *Chicago Linguistics Society Parasession on Autosegmental Phonology*, 266–278.

Sandler, Wendy. 1989. *Phonological Representation of the Sign: Linearity and Nonlinearity in American Sign Language*. Dordrecht: Foris.

Sandler, Wendy. 1993. Hand in hand: The roles of the nondominant hand in sign language phonology. *The Linguistic Review* 10. 337–390.

Sandler, Wendy. 1999. Cliticization and prosodic words in a sign language. In T. A. Hall & U. Kleinhenz (eds.), *Studies on the Phonological Word*, 223–254. Amsterdam: John Benjamins.
Sandler, Wendy. 2006. Phonology phonetics, and the nondominant hand. In L. Goldstein, D. H. Whalen & C. Best (eds.), *Papers in Laboratory Phonology: Varieties of Phonological Competence*, 185–212. Berlin: Mouton de Gruyter.
Sandler, Wendy. 2009. Symbiotic symbolization by hand and mouth in sign language. *Semiotica* 174(1–4). 241–275.
Sandler, Wendy. 2012a. Dedicated gestures in the emergence of sign language. *Gesture* 12(3). 265–307.
Sandler, Wendy. 2012b. The phonological organization of sign languages. *Language and Linguistics Compass* 6(3). 162–182.
Sandler, Wendy. 2017. The challenge of sign language phonology. *Annual Review of Linguistics* 3. 43–63.
Sandler, Wendy. 2018. The body as evidence for the nature of language. *Frontiers in Psychology*. DOI: doi.org/10.3389/fpsyg.2018.01782.
Sandler, Wendy, Mark Aronoff, Irit Meir & Carol Padden. 2011 The gradual emergence of phonological form in a new language. *Natural Language and Linguistic Theory* 29. 503–543.
Sandler, Wendy & Diane Lillo-Martin. 2006. *Sign Language and Linguistic Universals*. Cambridge: Cambridge University Press.
Sandler, Wendy, Diane Lillo-Martin, Svetlana Dachkovsky & Ronice Müller de Quadros. 2020. Sign language prosody. In Carlos Gussenhoven and Aoju Chen (eds.), *The Oxford Handbook of Language Prosody*, 104–122. Oxford: Oxford University Press.
Saussure, Ferdinand de, Charles Bally & Albert Sechehaye. 1959. *Course in General Linguistics*, trans. W. Baskin. New York: McGraw Hill.
Senghas, Ann & Marie Coppola. 2001. Children creating language: How Nicaraguan Sign Language acquired a spatial grammar. *Psychological Science* 12(4). 323–328. DOI: 10.1111/1467-9280.00359.
Stokoe, William C. 1960. *Sign Language Structure*. Silver Spring, MD: Linstock Press.
Supalla, Ted. 1986. The classifier system in American Sign Language. In Collette Greenberg Craig (ed.), *Noun Classes and Categorization*, 181–216. Amsterdam: John Benjamins.
Taub, Sara. 2001. *Language from the Body: Iconicity and Metaphor in American Sign Language*. Cambridge: Cambridge University Press.
Tervoort, Bernard. 1973. Could there be a human sign language? *Semiotica* 9. 347–382.
Wilbur, Ronnie B. 2008 Complex predicates involving events, time, and aspect: Is this why sign languages look so similar? In Josep Quer (ed.), *Theoretical Issues in Sign Language Research*, 217–250. Hamburg: Signum Press.
Woll, Bencie. 2014. Moving from hand to mouth: Echo phonology and the origins of language. *Frontiers in Psychology*. DOI: 10.3389/fpsyg.2014.00662.
Zwitserlood, Inge. 2012. Classifiers. In Roland Pfau, Markus Steinbach & Bencie Woll (eds.), *Sign Language: An International Handbook*, 158–185. Berlin/Boston: De Gruyter.

Rachel Channon
A New Feature Type: Functional Features in Sign Languages

Abstract: Features are the smallest phonological units of language. As originally understood in spoken languages, they are both meaningless and arbitrary. Crosslinguistic data from more than 40 sign languages demonstrate a new non-arbitrary feature type: functional features with two subtypes: production and perception. The signs are selected from our (van der Hulst and Channon) crosslinguistic SignTyp project and from Spread the Sign, a similar project. So far, four features have been found and described: synchronizing, supporting, unifying, and isolating. The synchronizing and supporting features assist the signer in production. An example is thumb grasp in many versions of BUTTERFLY, where the grasp synchronizes the motion of the hands. The unifying and isolating features assist the viewer in perception. These two are unusual because they also have featural meaning. An example of an isolating feature is seen in many versions of CLOTHES where signers grasp clothing to isolate it from the body and thus improve perception. The feature meaning is *isolation from the background*. Some minimal pairs may exist for these features, but the primary reason to believe they are phonological is because they are marked forms and cannot be predicted by simple physical or perceptual constraints.

Keywords: feature types, feature inventory, grasping, functional features, sign languages, crosslinguistic, SignTyp

---

Acknowledgements: My deepest gratitude is to Harry himself, whose support and interest has allowed me to continue my study of sign languages. I also thank the signers, their colleagues who helped me to find signers and who acted as intermediaries for many of the signers, and the transcribers. There are too many people to name here who helped in this project, but they are all listed in https://signtyp.uconn.edu/Credits/creditindex.html.

SignTyp is sponsored by the National Science Foundation and is made possible by grant 0544944 to Harry van der Hulst and Rachel Channon and grant BCS-1049510 to Harry van der Hulst. The primary subcontract on the second grant was to Sign Language Investigations LLC owned by Rachel Channon.

Rachel Channon, University of Connecticut

https://doi.org/10.1515/9783110730081-015

1 Introduction

This chapter describe four subtypes of a newly observed feature type, so far observed only in sign languages. Functional features are neither arbitrary nor iconic. Some are meaningful.

Two of the functional features are useful in sign production, by assisting the signer to synchronize actions or to support the arm. Two others are useful in sign perception, by assisting the viewer to isolate or unify other features. These last two also appear to have meaning at the featural level.

Each feature is described with examples, followed by a discussion that argues that the features are phonological not phonetic. A few minimal or near minimal pairs occur, but the primary claims to phonological status are that they are marked forms and cannot be derived from physical or perceptual constraints.

The chapter has the following sections:
- 2 Background
- 3 Functional Feature Descriptions
- 4 Phonological Features or Phonetic Characteristics?
- 5 Conclusion

2 Background

2.1 SignTyp

SignTyp is an ongoing crosslinguistic study of single sign videos. The 1000 prompts created for the project use photographs and a few drawings of picturable objects that are crosslinguistically understandable. The video responses are assumed to be primarily nouns, adjectives, or adverbs (because of the use of pictures).

The number of prompt responses varies by prompt, with most prompts having between 14 and 25 responses from signers around the world (one signer per country). Signers were compensated for their work and gave permission for their videos to be used in SignTyp. They are referred to here by the name of their country of origin, but some were recorded here in the United States.

A minority of the signers consider themselves or are named by others as native signers. For a similar project of sign responses to pictorial prompts for objects, Padden et al. (2013) note that between native and non-native ASL signers, they find "no reliable difference in their responses" and conclude that "for at least very familiar, everyday objects, native language ability is not a requirement."

The prompts, videos, transcriptions, and downloadable files are available at https://signtyp.uconn.edu/. Contacting the project to request permission for use is required.

In addition to SignTyp, a similar project, Spread the Sign (STS), is also referenced. Many of their signs, such as BUTTERFLY and WINDMILL, have the same glosses as the SignTyp videos. The site (https://www.spreadthesign.com/) is easy to search but does not provide direct hyperlinks to signs.[1]

Some pictures of example signs are included in the text, and an Appendix includes links to all of the mentioned sign videos from SignTyp.

2.2 Terms

A few terms used in the descriptions need explanation: *substitute*, *tracing*, and *exemplar*.

Substitute means that the handshape, orientation, action, or location iconically represent some aspect of the named entity. Substitutes are similar to Padden et al. (2015) *instrumental strategy*, Simper-Allen (2019) *substitutes*, and Nyst (2018) *embodiment*.

Examples are a flat handshape representing the wing of a BUTTERFLY or the vanes of a WINDMILL, an upright orientation representing an upright object such as a person, and a swooping action representing a butterfly's path.

Tracing occurs when the action does not represent a path but instead represents the outline of a shape drawn in the air, such as the shape of a tree, a fingernail, or a muzzle. Various authors discuss tracing (Schembri 1996; Cogill-Koez 2000; Padden et al. 2015; Napoli and Ferrara 2021). It has also been called *drawing* (Mandel 1977) or *sketching* (Streeck 2008).

Tracing actions have three variations: 1) with one finger (usually the index) for an object that is thought of as one-dimensional as in tracing the EYEBROW (many signers), 2) with the thumb and index when outlining something two dimensional with both length and width as in Kurdistan MINT or some versions of EYEBROW (Brazil, Portugal, Russia, Turkey) where the signer shows both length

---

[1] While SignTyp has the same signer for all videos for a given country, STS sometimes has different signers for the same country. For example, the USA signer for SKIN is a different signer from the USA signer for HAIR. A minor issue with STS is that some signers are listed twice producing the same sign, so that readers may notice the counts given here vary from the number listed on the site. This most often occurs with Belarus and India.

and width, and 3) with the thumb plus multiple fingers for three dimensional objects such as the muzzles in FOX (many signers) and WOLF (many signers).²

Exemplars are real world objects, such as clothing or the signer's body parts, which are used symbolically as an example of an entity. Examples: Pointing at the signer's eye as an example of EYE (most signers) or grasping and pulling at the signer's shirt as an example of CLOTHES (many signers).

Exemplars, substitutes, and tracing can combine. In ASL BRACELET, the signer shows a substitute for the bracelet but uses her own wrist as an exemplar for where it is located. FOX uses tracing plus an exemplar, and Kurdistan MINT uses tracing plus a substitute.

The difference between substitutes and exemplars can be subtle, but substitutes have some element of mismatch and an underlying metaphorical relationship: x is similar to y because of some characteristic, while exemplars have the underlying set relationship: x is a member of Y ($x \in Y$).

3 Functional Feature Descriptions

This section describes four functional feature types with examples. As it happens, almost all the examples involve a grasp, but this is probably an accidental result of my current interest in grasping signs. They were discovered serendipitously while pursuing other research objectives, so other functional features may await discovery.

Note that grasp is sometimes functional, but it can also be iconic or arbitrary. For example, CHAIN for most signers includes a grasp of the thumb and index which iconically shows how the links are connected. Arbitrary grasp occurs in FRIEND (USA), MAN (Nepal), and PATIENT (Kurdistan).³

---

2 Napoli and Ferrara observed that signers varied in whether they used one or two hands to trace one-dimensional objects. If the object is straightedged and bilaterally symmetrical, signers tend to use two hands, otherwise they use one hand. In the signs I am looking at, signers usually trace with one hand (and a varying number of fingers). The prompt objects are generally not straightedged, although they are usually bilaterally symmetrical.
3 While these grasps seem arbitrary, the iconic etymology is clear: a close relationship (FRIEND), a grasp of a mustache (MAN) and taking the pulse (PATIENT).

3.1 Production Feature Function 1: Synchronization

Example 1: Thumb grasp in BUTTERFLY and WINDMILL
BUTTERFLY (Figure 1) is highly iconic for all signers, with multiple characteristics of the butterfly imitated in the signs. Flat hands substitute for flat wings. Close together hand placement substitutes for the close together wing placement. The finger or hand flexing and the path of the hands substitutes for the opening and closing of the wings, and for the random directional path as the butterfly moves from place to place.

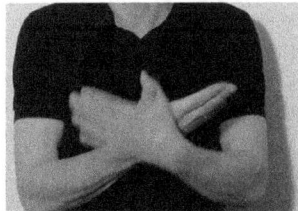

Figure 1: BUTTERFLY (Denmark).

As Table 1 shows, all 52[4] signers (44 different countries) in SignTyp and STS produce BUTTERFLY with a substitute flat handshape. All signers produce a substitute action for the wings opening and closing. Most signers (47) produce a close together placement of the hands to substitute for the close together location of the wings. Half the signers (26) also show the butterfly's directional movement from place to place. They add a second substitute action which uses the whole arm, moving up, down, circularly, diagonally, side to side, or toward the viewer, etc. as well as combinations of these directions. Signers differ in their directions (perhaps indirectly reflecting the random nature of a butterfly's flight).

The above characteristics are all iconic, but in 35 signers (the first row in the table), a functional feature also occurs: thumb cross/grasp with the hands crossed.[5] This feature holds the hands together, which makes it easier for the signer to synchronize the hand motions, especially if there is both opening and closing and directional motion. (Two other signers, the Romanian

---

[4] Although there are 52 signers, there are only 44 different countries because 9 SignTyp and STS countries overlap: Brazil, China, Denmark, Estonia, Germany Portugal Russia Turkey USA. Overlapping signers range from near identical (Portugal, USA) to quite dissimilar (China and Russia).

The STS signer from Romania produces a 3 part version: 1) hands together, thumbs crossed, opening, and closing in place, 2) hands separate from each other, moving directionally while opening and closing, 3) repeat part 1. The two different forms are counted separately in the table, so the total count is 53 instead of 52.

[5] Thumb crossing and thumb grasping may be distinct features but are conflated here. Thumb crossing occurs when the signer crosses the extended thumbs, thumb grasping occurs when the thumbs are flexed around each other. Thumb grasping is more likely to hold the hands together, but thumb crossing has some of the same effect, since the pads of the thumbs press against each other. The difference between them is not always clear. The grasping may be a more emphatic version of crossing.

and Slovakian, also cross their thumbs but without crossing the hands and with the palms oriented toward the viewer not the self. In this position, the thumbs do little to coordinate or synchronize the hands.)

Table 1: Characteristics that vary crosslinguistically for BUTTERFLY.

Hands relationship	hands crossed	thumbs contact	SignTyp	STS	Total
Together	Crossed	Crossed	11 Brazil Denmark Ethiopia Germany Kurdistan Nicaragua Philippine Portugal Turkey USA Honduras	24 Austria Brazil Bulgaria Cyprus Czech Denmark Finland France Germany Greece Iceland India Latvia Lithuania Poland Portugal Russia Spain Sweden Turkey Urdu UK USA Ukraine	35
Together	Crossed	No contact		1 China	1
Together	Uncrossed	Crossed		2 Romania Slovakia	2
Together	Uncrossed	Contact	5 China Egypt Estonia Haiti Nepal	4 Argentina Estonia Italy Japan	9
Far apart (separate at side of body)	Uncrossed	No contact	3 Lithuania Russia Rwanda	2 Croatia Romania	5
Touching at wrists	Crossed	No contact		1 Belarus	1
Total			19	34	53

Readers can verify that thumb crossing assists in production by experiment: Cross the hands with palms toward the self as in Figure 1, but without a thumb grasp. Move both hands randomly up and down or in a circle, while simultaneously bending and extending the fingers of both hands together. A tendency for the bending-extending action of one hand to be reduced or alternate with the other hand should be felt. Now try the same motions with the thumbs grasping each other. This makes it easier to synchronize the motion of the hands, so that both hands act simultaneously, and can perform complicated swooping, circling and directional movements on different axes while opening and closing the fingers.[6]

---

[6] Although only half of the signers performed any path action in this situation, I am certain that any of the signers who use thumb grasping can optionally include path action, in more elaborate versions.

It might be proposed that the thumb grasp is iconic and that the thumbs are substitutes for antenna. But this is unlikely since the thumb grasp makes them look less, not more, like antenna. Furthermore, thumb grasps also occur in WINDMILL where the grasp could not mean antenna. Five of 44 signers responding to WINDMILL (SignTyp: Denmark (Figure 2), Estonia, Lithuania, STS: Latvia, Sweden) use a thumb grasp and crossed hands similar to the most frequent form of BUTTERFLY (as well as flat hands and hand placement close together). The paths for WINDMILL differ from BUTTERFLY: circles or arcs.

There are two possible reasons why thumb grasp forms are not used as often for WINDMILL as they are for BUTTERFLY. First, signers who use the thumb-grasp BUTTERFLY may avoid using it for WINDMILL. Only the Danish signer uses thumb grasp for both signs, and his WINDMILL has both a different action and a different handshape (the extended index-middle instead of the whole flat hand). This avoids creating a minimal pair that would differ only in action.

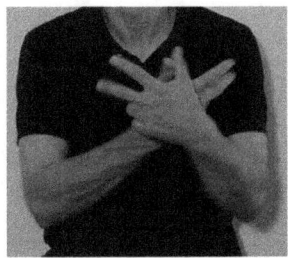

Figure 2: WINDMILL (Denmark).

Second, only BUTTERFLY has iconic reasons for two types of movement: path and hand internal opening-closing. Since windmill vanes do not open and close, the signers do not open and close the fingers. They use path motion only, and that motion is fixed: either a circle or side-to-side arcs showing the rotation of the windmill vanes. Table 2 shows that if there is path action in BUTTERFLY, 19 signers cross their thumbs. Without path action, 18 cross their thumbs. The difference is small, but it suggests that thumb grasps make it easier to open and close AND move along a path, especially since it is highly likely that the 18 signers without path action might easily add paths if circumstances prompted a more elaborate form of BUTTERFLY. Since WINDMILL has only path action, thumb grasps are less valuable for this sign and therefore less used.

Table 2: Thumb grasp and path action in BUTTERFLY for SignTyp and STS signers. All signers opened and closed their fingers.*

Path action occurs	No thumb grasp	Thumb grasp
No	33% (9)	67% (18)
Yes	27% (7)	73% (19)
Total	**30% (16)**	**70% (37)**

*Romanian signer counted twice because he has two different forms.

Example 2: FOX (Turkey)

The second example of thumb-grasp synchronization is Turkish FOX[7] (Figure 3). The signer uses his right flat spread hand as a substitute for the fox's plumy tail. His left fist is a substitute for the fox's body. The fist grasps the right thumb.

Figure 3: FOX (Turkey).

Why is the fist grasping the thumb? No iconic motivation is obvious. However, there are several possible functional reasons. First, the thumb grasp gets it out of the way, so the four fingers with their more similar lengths can represent the plumy tail. This gives the tail a more unified appearance. Secondly, the thumb grasp arranges the tail closer to the body. Thirdly, since the emphasis is on the waving tail, the thumb grasp allows the signer to wave the tail back and forth without losing contact with the body. In this case, the functional feature works to keep the two hands together and the thumb out of the way. The functions are slightly different than the synchronization function in BUTTERFLY but are close enough to group them together.

Example 3: SPIDER (Ethiopia)

The Ethiopian signer shows SPIDER by crossing her hands, palms down, with all fingers slightly curved to show the many legs of the spider (Figure 4). The two pinky fingers grasp each other. The pinky grasp functions to keep both hands together, so the hands move forward together. The viewer therefore sees all the fingers as legs belonging to one spider.

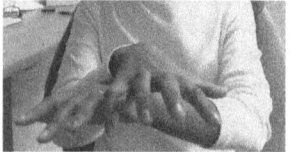

Figure 4: SPIDER (Ethiopia).

Interestingly, two other SignTyp signers (USA and Russia) demonstrate SPIDER with two hands. The American appears to lightly touch her two hands together at the thumbs. The appearance is ambiguous between one or two spiders. The Russian moves the hands toward the viewer with the hands about shoulder width apart from each other, so that an obvious interpretation is two

---

7 This signer's version of FOX is a sequence of three segments showing the tail, muzzle, and ears. The interest here is in the first segment only.

spiders. The other signers use only one hand, which less clearly demonstrates that there are eight legs. Only the Ethiopian has arrived at a sign that shows both a single spider and one of the special qualities of a spider – the many long legs.

No other SignTyp or STS signer uses this pinky crossing form. Some of the STS signers cross their hands without crossing the pinky and one signer (Japan) crosses his thumbs, with palms down. This version does not provide the unified appearance of the Ethiopian form.

Pinky grasp for SPIDER is rare because there is a cost to this solution: it is more difficult to set up than a simple one handed version, or even a two handed version without the grasp.

To summarize, there is little or no direct iconic value to the thumb or pinky grasp in these signs (BUTTERFLY, WINDMILL, FOX, SPIDER). The grasp does not represent an iconic action and is not a substitute for a shape. It has a function: to keep the hands together to allow for synchronized motion and/or a synchronized pictorial unit.

3.2 Production Feature Function 2: Support and Stabilization

Example: AMBULANCE

Most signers show AMBULANCE (Figure 5 and Table 3) by raising either one or both forearms perpendicular to the ground and then moving the wrist and/or fingers to show a flashing light.[8]

Using the non-dominant hand, the Nepal and American signers grasp the dominant arm when signing AMBULANCE. The Chinese signer appears to grasp the sleeve of the dominant arm. The Honduran and Egyptian signers touch the dominant forearm.

Figure 5: AMBULANCE (China).

Among the STS signers, there are 7 examples of support forms: France, Spain, Cyprus, Greece (3 signers, 3 different forms), India. All others use either non-supporting (20) or unrelated forms (9). Table 3 summarizes these numbers.

---

8 Vinson et al. (2015) mention that hearing raters gave flashing lights as the most salient characteristic of ambulance.

Table 3: AMBULANCE forms in SignTyp and STS.

Form	SignTyp	STS	Total
Flashing lights without supporting arm	11	20	31
Flashing lights with supporting arm	5	7	12
Unrelated forms	2	9	11
Total	18	36	54

These grasps or touches appear to be attempts to stabilize the forearm, and to keep them in the same location throughout the sign. The upright posture of the forearm is physically stressful if held for any length of time. Supporting it with the other hand reduces that stress.

It is possible that the Egyptian signer and some of the STS signers could be interpreted as establishing a base for the flashing light. Many signers establish base or ground lines for signs like TREE, so this is possible. The overall impression is of support and stabilization, not baselines, but this possible functional feature has the weakest evidence, because of the difficulty of separating out supporting hands from hands establishing a base line.

3.3 Perceptual Feature Function 1: Unifying

Consider the rightmost photo and leftmost drawing in Figure 6:

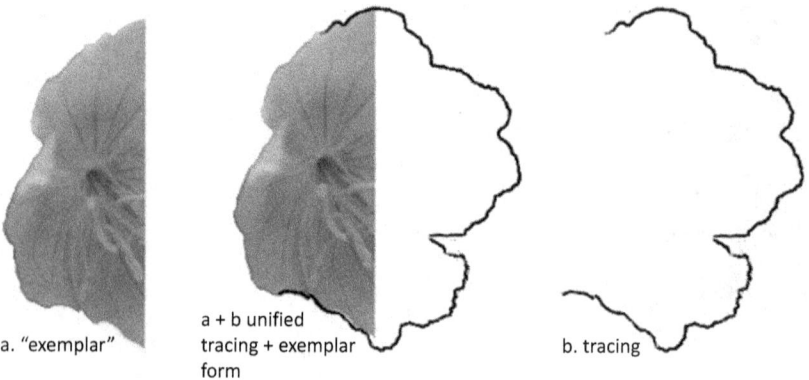

a. "exemplar"
a + b unified tracing + exemplar form
b. tracing

Figure 6: Exemplar + Tracing analogy.

The association between the photographic image of part of a flower (a), and the tracing of the edge of the flower (b) is not immediately clear. But if these two images are *unified* as shown in the center, the relationship becomes clearer. Note how the tracing overlaps the photographic image instead of simply butting up to it. This unification is analogous to how signers unify tracing: the object (substitute or exemplar) overlaps the tracing because the signer grasps the object and begins the tracing on the object instead of next to it. This unifying feature emphasizes that two apparently separate elements are parts of the same entity.

Example 1: Tracing plus substitute: MINT
The Kurdistan signer shows the stem of the mint leaf with a substitute – the extended left index finger (Figure 7). She grasps the sides of the stem/finger almost halfway down and then traces the shape of a mint leaf with her right thumb and index. The signer could have used her right hand to begin tracing the mint leaf at the tip of the left index, but instead she used an overlapping grasp.

Figure 7: MINT (Kurdistan).

The grasp plus the overlap suggest that the two sub-items (stem and leaf) are connected as part of a single unit MINT, even though the stem is shown using a substitute on one hand and the leaf is shown with the other hand using tracing.

Example 2: Tracing plus exemplar: FINGERNAIL
Several signers use similar signs for FINGERNAIL (Estonia in Figure 8, Lithuania, Russia, Turkey). They use the thumb and index to grasp the sides of a finger (the exemplar) and then trace the sides of an imaginary fingernail that begins on the finger and then moves out beyond the end of the finger. The signs show the fingernail being traced as though it extended over the edges of the finger, which is a non-iconic contradiction of the reality that fingernails are embedded within the backside of the finger. This suggests that the extension of the grasp below the tip of the fingernail is not iconic, but a functional feature which unifies the exemplar and tracing.

Figure 8: FINGERNAIL (Estonia).

Example 3: Tracing plus exemplar: FOX and WOLF

Eight signers include a grasping action on the face for FOX (Brazil in Figure 9, China, Estonia, Honduras, Nicaragua, Portugal, Turkey, Uganda) and 7 for WOLF (USA, Brazil, China, Estonia, Ethiopia, Honduras, Nicaragua). The signer's head is an exemplar for *head*, and the tracing shows the extended muzzle. Signers spread all the digits (or just the index middle and thumb) to grasp and contact the face, and then trace the muzzle out from the face. The grasp on the face is very slight, and quick, but it unifies the two different methods of exemplar and trace.[9]

Figure 9: FOX (Brazil).

These unification features have a meaning at the featural level: "the two elements of the symbol are one entity." But that meaning does not seem to carry up to the morphemic level, because the morpheme (sign) means *mint, fingernail, fox,* or *wolf*, not *unitary mint leaf and stem, finger plus fingernail, head plus muzzle,* etc.

3.4 Perceptual Feature Function 2: Isolation from Background

Example 1: Fabrics

SignTyp included at least 60 signs from 16 languages where signers grasp and pull out their clothing (usually their shirts) as in Figure 10. The meanings are related to clothing or fabric. Of these grasps, 2 are iconic.[10] The other 58 grasps are functional and are shown in Table 4. |The function is to separate the clothing from the body, to clarify that the signer is talking about the fabric and not the skin or body.

---

9 A substitute method of showing a muzzle (instead of tracing + exemplar) is much simpler: the signer holds up a hand with the index and pinky extended and the thumb contacting the flexed middle and ring. This shows the muzzle of an animal and the pricked ears. But only the Kurdistan signer produces a version of this for FOX and the Turkish signer for WOLF. It may be that this symbol is too generic and is used for many animals in a classifier predicate manner and therefore is not suitable as a name. It may also be that complex handshapes without other information are less perceptually salient than a larger more active sign made on the face.

10 In PREGNANT (Rwanda), the signer pulls out the shirt to show the swelling belly, in PEN (China) the signer grasps the edge of a shirt pocket to show a pen clipped to the pocket.

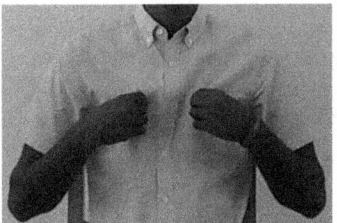

Figure 10: CLOTHES (Haiti).

Table 4: Fabric related signs using a grasp of clothing.

Country	Sign glosses
USA	FABRIC
Brazil	CLOTHES WASHER, CLOTHES
China	DOLL, STUFFED ANIMAL, JEANS, SHIRT, COTTON, SWEATER, CLOTHES
Denmark	LAUNDRY, CLOTHES
Egypt	CLOTHES DRYER
Estonia	FABRIC
Ethiopia	CLOTHES DRYER, WOOL, HOOK, LAUNDRY, CLOTHES WASHER, COTTON, HANGER
Honduras	LAUNDRY, FABRIC, HANGER
Haiti	CLOTHES DRYER, LAUNDRY, SHIRT, CLOTHES
Kurdistan	CLOTHES
Nepal	CLOTHES DRYER, SEWING MACHINE, PLAID, HOOK, LAUNDRY, SHIRT, CLOTHES WASHER, FABRIC, HANGER, CLOTHES
Philippines	LAUNDRY
Portugal	CLOTHES DRYER, CURTAIN, WOOL, TOWEL, LAUNDRY, COTTON, SWEATER, FABRIC, CLOTHES
Rwanda	CLOTHES DRYER, BUTTON, ZIPPER, HOOK, CLOTHES WASHER, HANGER
Uganda	FABRIC, CLOTHES
Venezuela	CLOTHES
Total signs	58

Examples 2 and 3: HAIR and SKIN

HAIR and SKIN use grasp in similar ways. In the most common form for HAIR, 21 of 51 signers grasp a lock or single strand of hair and pull it slightly away from the rest of the hair (Figure 11). The function is to separate the hair from the scalp and the head, and thus disambiguate which object is being named.

Grasping and pulling away is also seen in signs for SKIN, where 27 of 58 signers pull up on the skin of their cheeks, hands, or arm as in Figure 12. Some other signers grasp the skin but do not pull it up. Here, the functional grasp identifies the named object as *skin* not *body*.

Table 5 summarizes these actions for both sources and signs. Note that two signers (Kurdistan and Turkey) both grasped and rubbed for SKIN, so their signs are counted twice.

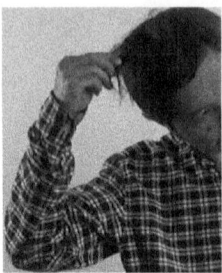

Figure 11: HAIR (China).

Figure 12: SKIN (Nepal).

Table 5: Grasps and other actions for HAIR and SKIN signs.

Action	HAIR	SKIN	Total
grasp and pull away	21 SignTyp: Brazil China Denmark Estonia Ethiopia Germany Nepal Turkey Uganda USA STS: Brazil China India Japan Latvia Poland Portugal Romania Slovakia Sweden Ukraine	27 SignTyp: Denmark Egypt Ethiopia Germany Haiti Honduras Nepal Philippines Turkey Uganda USA STS: Argentina Austria Chile China Estonia France Iceland India Italy Japan Latvia Lithuania Romania Turkey Ukraine Urdu-2	48
grasp without pulling away	6 SignTyp: Haiti Philippines Rwanda STS: Bulgaria Greece USA		6

Table 5 (continued)

Action	HAIR	SKIN	Total
Pseudo grasp	18 SignTyp: Lithuania Portugal Russia STS: Argentina Austria Czech Denmark Estonia France Germany Iceland Italy Lithuania Russia Spain Turkey UK Urdu	12 SignTyp: China Kurdistan Lithuania STS: Croatia Denmark Portugal Russia Spain Sweden-1 Sweden-2 UK USA	30
other	6 SignTyp: Egypt Honduran Kurdistan STS: Belarus Chile Croatia	19 SignTyp: Brazil Estonia Kurdistan Portugal Russia Rwanda Turkey STS: Belarus Brazil Bulgaria Chile Cyprus Czech Germany Greece Iceland Poland Slovakia Urdu-1	25
Total	51	58	109

The signers grasp and pull out or up on clothing, skin, or hair to isolate these objects from the body. If the signer merely points at or contacts the item with a touch, it is more difficult to determine which item the signer is referring to. Grasping and pulling away is a functional feature which improves a viewer's perception of the named object.

Some signers produce either a grasp without moving away from the body, or a pseudo-grasp where nothing is actually grasped. These signers seem to believe that the grasping handshape is sufficient information. Grasping and pulling out are therefore not required but can occur if the signer wants functional assistance to make the sign more perceptible.

This functional feature seems to be ostensively meaningful: "Look at this!". If so, this is another example of a meaningful feature. Like the unification feature, the ostensive meaning of the isolation feature does not seem to persist at the morphemic level – the meaning is *fabric/skin/hair*, not *look at this fabric/skin/hair*.

3.5 Summary of Functional Features

Four kinds of functional features have been described: synchronizing the hands, stabilizing the arm, unifying two parts of a symbol to show that the object is a single entity, and isolating an object for display. The features function to support the iconicity of other features. They are not iconic, and they are not arbitrary.

Functional features are a completely new type of feature. Given the accidental nature of the discovery, it is difficult to determine how common they are. There are probably additional types not yet observed. Nor is there any reason to assume that only grasping features can be functional.

I have only found functional features co-occurring with iconic and exemplar features, perhaps because these two types are most likely to have physical or perceptual requirements that may benefit from some functional help. If a feature or a sign is arbitrary and needed some kind of functional assistance, parameters would probably be altered to create a simpler form that does not require assistance. It would be interesting to see if functional features can be found in older forms of a sign and dropped if and when the sign becomes arbitrary. This might explain the pseudo-grasps seem in some signers for HAIR, SKIN and CLOTHES: if signers conventionalize the sign and think of it as an arbitrary form, they discard the functional feature that isolates the object for display, because it is no longer needed.

The perceptual functions of unification and isolation have an unusual and important characteristic: they have meaning at the featural level, but this meaning does not seem to be included at the morphemic level.

4 Phonological Features or Phonetic Characteristics?

Are these proposed features truly phonological features? This section provides several diagnostics: minimal pairs for grasp, grasp as a marked category, and a lack of constraints that could predict grasp.

For simplicity, the discussion focusses on the grasps seen in BUTTERFLY, WINDMILL and SPIDER. Given that most of the proposed features are grasping, what holds for one functional grasp should hold for all. And if functional grasp is phonological, then the same arguments should hold for other non-grasp functional features.

4.1 Diagnostic 1: Are There Minimal Pairs for the Candidate?

To determine minimal pairs, the first question is whether grasp should be considered a type of contact or an aperture change.

Aperture change (van der Hulst 1996) is the degree to which fingers open or close to the palm and/or thumb. Brentari (1998) considers it a dynamic (also called prosodic) feature. Grasp can seem to involve aperture change. In CHAIN the thumb and finger open and close as the two hands join and then disconnect in order to join again to show the next link. But this aperture change is a transitional necessity and not part of the actual grasp. Furthermore, not all grasp has this type of change. The thumb grasp in BUTTERFLY and the pinky grasp in SPIDER are static features. Aperture change also seems problematic for a feature which almost always involves a grasped object – the other hand, other body parts, or clothing.

Another reason to believe that grasp is a kind of contact is that signers sometimes substitute a pseudo-grasp for an actual grasp. In that case, they usually produce a grasping handshape such as F and a touch or near touch contact as in HAIR (Portugal). Similarly, in AMBULANCE, some signers grasp the arm, but others merely contact it. These cannot be considered minimal pairs for grasp and touch because this is crosslinguistic data and there is no meaning change. But the clear relationship between an actual grasp and a pseudograsp with the same handshape for the same meaning suggests that grasp, like pseudograsp is a form of contact.

Overall, therefore grasp appears to be a contact feature.

In the transcription system SignTyp uses (a modified version of Sutton Signwriting, based on Sutton (2014), the characteristic *contact* has 4 primary subtypes of touch, rub, grasp, and brush. In a monovalent feature approach to phonology as argued for in van der Hulst (2016), signs do not have features such as [+grasp] and [-grasp], but rather the feature [grasp] is either present or absent. However, I know of no signs for the same language that differ only by having or not having a grasp. I have found a few signs that differ in the type of contact, such as grasp or brush, but even these are mostly near minimal pairs.

From my own knowledge of ASL in combination with SignTyp and STS and other websites, there are some minimal or near minimal pairs for grasp contrasting with other types of contact. The following examples are all from ASL:

1) Grasp or brush. Some versions of CHIN (though not the version in SignTyp or STS) use an all finger grasp of the chin. This may contrast with the STS version of CUTE with the same location and all finger selection but with a downward brushing contact.
2) Grasp or brush. STS CUTE and some versions of JEWISH appear to be a near minimal pair. STS CUTE is a slightly bent unspread hand with downward brushing at the chin. STS JEWISH has a grasping hand at the chin. The hand is also spread which makes it only a near minimal pair, but I have seen versions with an unspread hand.
3) Grasp or rub. The version of JEWISH with an unspread hand and grasping can contrast with versions of NAPKIN that I have seen with a similar unspread handshape and location but with a circular rubbing action.
4) Grasp or touch. SignTyp CHIN uses a thumb and index grasp on the chin. A near minimal pair for simple contact is DISAPPOINT (as seen in STS) with an extended index contacting the chin with the fingertip. It is only a near

minimal pair because CHIN has a bent index and thumb, while DISAPPOINT uses an extended index.

5) Grasp or touch. The versions of INTERPRETER and CHAIN in SignTyp are near minimal pairs. The signer touches the two thumbs and indexes together for INTERPRETER while each hand grasps the thumb and index of the other for CHAIN. However, they are only near minimal pairs, because the signer rotates only the right hand in INTERPRETER and rotates both hands in CHAIN. Furthermore, in CHAIN both hands slightly move from left to right, while INTERPRETER has no path action. Some versions of CHAIN do not have the path action as in the two versions at https://www.signasl.org/sign/chain. And some versions of INTERPRET(ER) rotate both hands as in https://www.signasl.org/sign/interpreter and https://www.signasl.org/sign/interpret. So for some signers, INTERPRET and CHAIN may be a minimal pair.

Minimal pairs are the gold standard to determine contrast or featural status. However, there are some suggestions that minimal pairs in sign languages are less common than would be expected (Liddell and Johnson 1989; Sandler 1989; Caselli and Pyers 2017). "... [D]istinctive contrasts exist, but there seem to be far fewer minimal pairs in signed languages than in spoken languages." (Eccarius and Brentari 2010).

This is my impression as well. Probable causes are the effects of iconicity, an exceptionally large set of iconic and exemplar features, signer avoidance of minimal pairs because they are too easy to confuse, and possibly a difference in the principles of economy and symmetry in sign as compared to speech (Dunbar and Dupoux 2016).[11]

To summarize, grasp is a type of contact. I have found a few near minimal pairs for grasp in ASL, but minimal pairs do not seem common. But on the basis of these near minimal pairs, grasp seems to be a feature.

---

[11] Dunbar and Dupoux (2016) explain economy as a tendency for a language to prefer a smaller set of feature combinations to a more random set of features where a smaller percentage of all possible features are used. Local symmetry is a tendency for feature systems to prefer groups of combinations that differ by only one feature. Global symmetry is a tendency to reuse certain feature combinations in balanced ways such as having approximately the same number of voiced and voiceless sounds. These properties have not been investigated for sign languages, but I suspect they may be less significant in sign than in speech.

4.2 Diagnostic 2: Is the Candidate Marked?

Another way to determine featural status is to ask if this entity is marked.

If simple touch contact is featural, then grasp is a more marked form of contact and must be featural. If, on the contrary, touch contact is merely a phonetic effect of physical constraints or derived from other features, then it still remains true that more marked versions of contact must be featural. (That simple touch is phonetic seems possible because the presence of a location feature in a sign implies that the hand contacts the location.)

In the 1,676 SignTyp signs (for 114 different prompts and 15 different languages) that have been fully transcribed and edited, some kind of contact occurs in 1,121 signs. As Table 6 shows, touch is the unmarked contact type with 58% of all signs having at least one touch contact. Grasp, rub, and brush are all less common forms of contact. Grasp, the type of interest here, occurs in only 162 signs or less than 15% of all signs.

Table 6: Sign frequencies for different contact types (more than one contact type may occur in the same sign but each contact type is counted only once for each sign).

Contact type	N	%
Grasp	162	14.5%
Brush	161	14.4%
Rubbing	267	23.8%
Touch	651	58.1%
Total contact occurrences	1121	

Thus even if touch contact is phonetic, grasp (as well as brush and rub) is marked, and therefore phonological.

4.3 Diagnostic 3: Is the Candidate Predicted by a Constraint?

If some simple physical or perceptual constraints or some feature can predict the grasp function, then grasp would be a predictable phonetic characteristic, not a feature.

Suppose that thumb grasp is somehow constrained to occur in certain hand arrangements. In the case of BUTTERFLY, might it be that once the hands are crossed, then the thumbs must be grasped? If this were the case, then the hand-crossing would be featural, not the thumb grasp.

But signers can cross their hands for various signs without thumb grasp, as in ASL BEAR and some of the STS signers' versions of SPIDER. And even though 35 of the 37 signers of BUTTERFLY who cross their hands also grasp their thumbs, there are 2 exceptions to the handcrossing – thumb grasp connection. The STS China sign is similar to the 35 thumb grasp signs, but the thumbs are straight up without grasp or any contact. The STS Belarus signer's hand crossing is more at the wrist than the thumb side of the hands, so that the hands (and therefore thumbs) are far apart. These two signers show that while thumb grasp is preferred for the crossed hand variant of BUTTERFLY, it is not obligatory, and therefore thumb grasp is not a required physical/phonetic event, but a feature.

One might still wonder why thumb grasp and handcrossing occur together for almost all BUTTERFLY signs. It may actually be hand-crossing that is nearly determined by thumb-grasp, rather than the reverse. There is little reason to cross the hands in this sign unless the signer wishes to grasp the thumbs, because thumb grasp provides the additional synchronization support for the complex movements that are often desired to display the butterfly's complex actions. In order to grasp the thumbs, and maintain close contact between the hands, the hands must be crossed.[12]

In sum, there are at least a few near minimal pairs for grasp. Grasp is a marked contact type. There is no obvious physical or perceptual constraint that would predict a grasp. On this basis, I conclude that grasp is a feature, and that therefore functional features exist.

5 Conclusion

A new type of feature, distinct from arbitrary and iconic features, has been discovered.

These new features have functions, and some also have featural meaning. Yet a change or deletion of the feature does not seem to change the meaning of the morpheme. Minimal pairs are hard to find, although a few exist. Their marked nature suggests they are features. They are unlikely to be predictable on the basis of any physical or perceptual constraint.

Functional features improve communication. Production functional features assist the signer physically by synchronizing the hands or by supporting the more active hand. Perceptual functional features assist the viewer by isolating an

---

[12] Furthermore, thumb grasping without crossing the hands does not provide the same functional support for synchronization.

object for perception or by unifying two production methods to clarify that there is a single entity being displayed and named.

This discovery is significant not just because functional features are new, but because they add to the debate on the required and the possible characteristics of features. As originally understood in spoken languages, features themselves are arbitrary and meaningless. As Hockett (1959)[13] pointed out, the lack of meaning creates *duality of patterning*. Sets of meaningless elements create meaningful morphemes, as in *tan/dan*.

But since then, there have been claims that some features can have some kind of meaning. Some spoken language features appear to have meaning or sound symbolism: Kawahara (2020) is a recent review. Many or even most sign language features are iconic and therefore meaningful at the featural level as has been hinted at or proposed (Taub 2001; van der Kooij 2002; Perniss and Vigliocco 2014; Perniss, Özyürek, and Morgan 2015; Perniss et al. 2018; Dingemanse, Perlman, and Perniss 2020; Lint 2020).

Functional features are something new: neither arbitrary nor iconic. Their existence shows that features can be more various than originally proposed and supports two different claims: 1) not all features are arbitrary, and 2) features can be meaningful.

Functional features exist in sign languages, but it is an open question whether they also exist in spoken languages. Perhaps the large and heavy muscles used in sign languages encourage codifying physical support mechanisms as features. Perhaps the problem of background noise is more significant in vision than hearing, and this encourages methods of distinguishing signs from the background.

So what is a linguistic feature? If functional (and iconic) features are accepted, a feature has a simplified definition: it is the smallest linguistic unit, limited in number, and potentially variable for each language, which combine and permute to create the morphemes of the language. The almost magical quality of duality of patterning is not a characteristic of features, but only of arbitrary features. Sets of meaningless features can create meaningful morphemes but sets of meaningful and functional features can also join to create morphemes (it is very unlikely that a morpheme could consist of only functional features).

The possible types of features are therefore expanded in two ways: there are functional, iconic, and arbitrary features, and features can be either meaningful or meaningless.

---

13 Hockett described duality of patterning in terms of phonemes, not features, but the principle (meaningless units combine into larger meaningful units) remains the same.

Appendix

Table 7 lists YouTube links for each sign discussed that occurs in SignTyp. The signs are also available on the SignTyp website https://signtyp.uconn.edu/ but readers may find these direct links easier.

Table 7: Links for all mentioned SignTyp signs.

Gloss	Signer Country	Link
ambulance	China	https://youtu.be/qEGmKcfP9lc
ambulance	Egypt	https://youtu.be/bZ4CXS58y7A
ambulance	Honduras	https://youtu.be/ToSagXGU0pM
ambulance	Nepal	https://youtu.be/-9ZidEMCBCs
ambulance	USA	https://youtu.be/oYlNwkyb4QM
bear	USA	https://youtu.be/QZpNcfl1Zeo
bracelet	USA	https://youtu.be/rWii1clsJlo
butterfly	Brazil	https://youtu.be/bJQvisi9MQs
butterfly	China	https://youtu.be/TMIF3fT1gGo
butterfly	Denmark	https://youtu.be/KFyhij0d3o4
butterfly	Egypt	https://youtu.be/ApevU4eTHMI
butterfly	Estonia	https://youtu.be/ehu8Ee5cH-g
butterfly	Ethiopia	https://youtu.be/8GEn3FCmc7g
butterfly	Germany	https://youtu.be/iZwNG0EEq_I
butterfly	Haiti	https://youtu.be/3vNsEnmlm7M
butterfly	Honduras	https://youtu.be/18msT30Ax6k
butterfly	Kurdistan	https://youtu.be/UCQ5RDhGmXU
butterfly	Lithuania	https://youtu.be/F6namO2uKKs
butterfly	Nepal	https://youtu.be/AHO5Sjg1TOU
butterfly	Nicaragua	https://youtu.be/gj4Lr8Gqzsc
butterfly	Philippines	https://youtu.be/td-ovKfmaqA
butterfly	Portugal	https://youtu.be/fJtx7bsFMj0
butterfly	Russia	https://youtu.be/lvHr6HHc5XU
butterfly	Rwanda	https://youtu.be/dNlom7dJrcs
butterfly	Turkey	https://youtu.be/XRyrmhfRJTE
butterfly	USA	https://youtu.be/2-PFvvK9Wiw
butterfly windmill fox spider	Multiple signers	https://youtu.be/Wo8AeHugAcs
button	Rwanda	https://youtu.be/k9ltVc_eq4Y

Table 7 (contiuned)

Gloss	Signer Country	Link
chain	USA	https://youtu.be/XSzLrpElDZ8
chin	USA	https://youtu.be/P9f2CFE4kAg
clothes	Brazil	https://youtu.be/gA5LA__PRlc
clothes	China	https://youtu.be/oOfolC_Uo-o
clothes	Denmark	https://youtu.be/6b_1yrQFAKg
clothes	Haiti	https://youtu.be/cGlXkOcwSX8
clothes	Kurdistan	https://youtu.be/9l3YymM7wxs
clothes	Nepal	https://youtu.be/59aM14lvZHI
clothes	Portugal	https://youtu.be/gDqdSDqqKOg
clothes	Uganda	https://youtu.be/CjDEYUBqQjw
clothes	Venezuela	https://youtu.be/4brLDdzk-Bs
clothes dryer	Egypt	https://youtu.be/dS-Um_hk9d0
clothes dryer	Ethiopia	https://youtu.be/YMq8Bc01AOk
clothes dryer	Haiti	https://youtu.be/mT1Bfv8DP7E
clothes dryer	Nepal	https://youtu.be/sOeq8XrgouU
clothes dryer	Portugal	https://youtu.be/MBkzmcJ4T8k
clothes dryer	Rwanda	https://youtu.be/Q7TufLXrf_U
Clothes washer	Brazil	https://youtu.be/WIFFHm6b99g
Clothes washer	Ethiopia	https://youtu.be/8pilnclxEZk
Clothes washer	Nepal	https://youtu.be/DQ3CsR0-QxE
Clothes washer	Rwanda	https://youtu.be/S3EA4oMbCJ4
cotton	China	https://youtu.be/k_LcvabTmmU
cotton	Ethiopia	https://youtu.be/5G7PxNZKH_E
cotton	Portugal	https://youtu.be/m3QTqlAPVoY
curtain	Portugal	https://youtu.be/Xg9QCv5aVZY
doll	China	https://youtu.be/RcxT6Osn1H0
eyebrow	Multiple signers	https://youtu.be/dSy-UjXVEUY
eyebrow	Portugal	https://youtu.be/P--hq7V-u5A
fabric	Estonia	https://youtu.be/6-iHga9Pkrl
fabric	Ethiopia	https://youtu.be/opyj4SFCMeU
fabric	Nepal	https://youtu.be/HPpwv1Fh4xM
fabric	Portugal	https://youtu.be/O7oJ8vpNKew
fabric	Uganda	https://youtu.be/4uZJ9e9zjKw
fabric	USA	https://youtu.be/rlIS60Akfm0
fingernail	Estonia	https://youtu.be/H7Uwpbh9kSQ

Table 7 (contiuned)

Gloss	Signer Country	Link
fingernail	Lithuania	https://youtu.be/LdvXxFEvcTY
fingernail	Russia	https://youtu.be/ueFSC2ys4TM
fingernail	Turkey	https://youtu.be/RUtCB_Kp7OE
fox	Brazil	https://youtu.be/NEe8Mxz2JIM
fox	China	https://youtu.be/EsuStsDZvdA
fox	Estonia	https://youtu.be/ahZ1sRuTfgQ
fox	Honduras	https://youtu.be/G03l6yfwiq0
fox	Kurdistan	https://youtu.be/0tX7P2gBE4M
fox	Nicaragua	https://youtu.be/sliD3WAnPJc
fox	Portugal	https://youtu.be/w_8GUTPV5b0
fox	Turkey	https://youtu.be/-vzTc2FuNsk
fox	Uganda	https://youtu.be/YZ317naVV6c
friend	USA	https://youtu.be/WHQUa5toFXA
hair	Brazil	https://youtu.be/FdAitZ_eqfE
hair	China	https://youtu.be/coRZjRm5qTs
hair	Denmark	https://youtu.be/-S7S53MFVEw
hair	Egypt	https://youtu.be/_kOv8qilJbI
hair	Estonia	https://youtu.be/7JGBGMeiNFQ
hair	Ethiopia	https://youtu.be/znlhHVfH3W8
hair	Germany	https://youtu.be/KaH6dlc--tA
hair	Haiti	https://youtu.be/D8z0_y6gmDI
hair	Honduras	https://youtu.be/96wKo6TkOxg
hair	Kurdistan	https://youtu.be/G6UHSDJu2Hk
hair	Lithuania	https://youtu.be/rjSoy1-jhN4
hair	Nepal	https://youtu.be/_FXd55NPApo
hair	Philippines	https://youtu.be/2WY3-f0_cVo
hair	Portugal	https://youtu.be/-rCJ-4Fmxig
hair	Russia	https://youtu.be/NHkQnoP9acY
hair	Rwanda	https://youtu.be/-jWCxja8xus
hair	Turkey	https://youtu.be/J-Zu3IB99Bc
hair	Uganda	https://youtu.be/VHh012HlDps
hair	USA	https://youtu.be/ZNyMGv3mDMs
hanger	Ethiopia	https://youtu.be/bkow7UAmemw
hanger	Honduras	https://youtu.be/YySoQ2AFcv4
hanger	Nepal	https://youtu.be/uqpoxhkSPrE

Table 7 (contiuned)

Gloss	Signer Country	Link
hanger	Rwanda	https://youtu.be/ifKirYRRFyA
hook	Ethiopia	https://youtu.be/bH20RsPebW8
hook	Nepal	https://youtu.be/3yBjDYYXYHo
hook	Rwanda	https://youtu.be/GuIbiDAkOW8
interpreter	USA	https://youtu.be/OF4pWG3Y3Xo
jeans	China	https://youtu.be/sKlUgQkgPvk
laundry	Denmark	https://youtu.be/rrXjzgO4BA8
laundry	Ethiopia	https://youtu.be/BKNRlnw316k
laundry	Haiti	https://youtu.be/luq_5W5hJnw
laundry	Honduras	https://youtu.be/kyt9EMdYNYg
laundry	Nepal	https://youtu.be/S8khRtp6FGU
laundry	Philippines	https://youtu.be/d2IpNur8j50
laundry	Portugal	https://youtu.be/4uTcMszkTAE
man	Nepal	https://youtu.be/IyqqRGoXLZE
mint	Kurdistan	https://youtu.be/7o-GlB1Tsio
patient (medical client)	Kurdistan	https://youtu.be/9bSVRxwvVvs
pen	China	https://youtu.be/lJmIG5iCSNE
plaid	Nepal	https://youtu.be/_Lc9VZyarUY
pregnant	Rwanda	https://youtu.be/6MSodAWBwHk
Sewing machine	Nepal	https://youtu.be/vTILLisIZco
shirt	China	https://youtu.be/b65ZFXYGAjw
shirt	Haiti	https://youtu.be/EWD17XP2FbE
shirt	Nepal	https://youtu.be/sebJNW57Xk8
skin	Egypt	https://youtu.be/1b0YmPDd3_o
skin	Ethiopia	https://youtu.be/rYejcnFpPmw
skin	Germany	https://youtu.be/rQYa2aBQ94A
skin	Haiti	https://youtu.be/T5fqXzhqGkM
skin	Honduras	https://youtu.be/l3smDB-DbG4
skin	Nepal	https://youtu.be/PW9yqlCqX-Q
skin	USA	https://youtu.be/pg758BKxk1U
spider	Ethiopia	https://youtu.be/lRyyNDHacgo
spider	Russia	https://youtu.be/uFybgkknkJk
spider	USA	https://youtu.be/wJq-G_q0dcw
stuffed animal	China	https://youtu.be/rAO9QzAgS7c

Table 7 (contiuned)

Gloss	Signer Country	Link
sweater	China	https://youtu.be/Yrz3QRqXYXA
sweater	Portugal	https://youtu.be/hkpYEi17tlA
towel	Portugal	https://youtu.be/01Y3qCloA-M
windmill	Denmark	https://youtu.be/JYswdl6aVOw
windmill	Estonia	https://youtu.be/rR8hwkNCcTw
windmill	Lithuania	https://youtu.be/M4v4Vcrh4TQ
wolf	Brazil	https://youtu.be/IpspRWJSooU
wolf	China	https://youtu.be/CCosdDUA418
wolf	Estonia	https://youtu.be/TdAaTMTooXo
wolf	Ethiopia	https://youtu.be/71eemz85tYw
wolf	Honduras	https://youtu.be/AYn4rVltRJM
wolf	Nicaragua	https://youtu.be/NGqT9W-EhN8
wolf	Turkey	https://youtu.be/HfyR6_eUq_E
wolf	USA	https://youtu.be/HGUpnNDfxqQ
wool	Ethiopia	https://youtu.be/L8v3-15JaZo
wool	Portugal	https://youtu.be/GwzROSyRqUo
zipper	Rwanda	https://youtu.be/4rX2kbOHugo

References

Brentari, Diane. 1998. *A Prosodic Model of Sign Language Phonology*. Cambridge, MA: MIT Press.

Caselli, Naomi K & Jennie E Pyers. 2017. The road to language learning is not entirely iconic: Iconicity, neighborhood density, and frequency facilitate acquisition of sign language. *Psychological Science* 28(7). 979–987. DOI: 10.1177/0956797617700498.

Cogill-Koez, Dorothea. 2000. Signed language classifier predicates linguistic structures or schematic visual representation. *Sign Language & Linguistics* 3(2). 153–207. DOI: 10.1075/sll.3.2.03cog.

Dingemanse, Mark, Marcus Perlman & Pamela Perniss. 2020. Construals of iconicity: Experimental approaches to form–meaning resemblances in language. *Language and Cognition* 12(1). 1–14. DOI: 10.1017/langcog.2019.48.

Dunbar, Ewan & Emmanuel Dupoux. 2016. Geometric constraints on human speech sound inventories. *Frontiers in Psychology* 7. 1061. DOI: 10.3389/fpsyg.2016.01061.

Eccarius, Petra & Diane Brentari. 2010. A formal analysis of phonological contrast and iconicity in sign language handshapes. *Sign Language & Linguistics* 13(2). 156–181. DOI: 10.1075/sll.13.2.02ecc.

Hockett, Charles F. 1959. Animal 'languages' and human language. *Human Biology* 31(1). 32–39.
Hulst, Harry van der. 1996. On the other hand. *Lingua* 98(1–3). 121–143. DOI: 10.1016/0024-3841(95)00035-6.
Hulst, Harry van der. 2016. Monovalent 'features' in phonology. *Language and Linguistics Compass* 10(2). 83–102. DOI: 10.1111/lnc3.12158.
Kawahara, Shigeto. 2020. Sound symbolism and theoretical phonology. *Language and Linguistics Compass* 14(8). DOI: 10.1111/lnc3.12372.
Kooij, Els van der. 2002. *Phonological Categories in Sign Language of the Netherlands: The Role of Phonetic Implementation and Iconicity*. Utrecht: LOT.
Liddell, Scott & Robert Johnson. 1989. American Sign Language: The phonological base. *Sign Language Studies* 1064(1). 195–277. DOI: 10.1353/sls.1989.0027.
Lint, Vanja de. 2020. From meaning to form and back in American Sign Language verbal classifier morphemes. *Word Structure* 13(1). 69–101. DOI: 10.3366/word.2020.0160.
Mandel, Mark. 1977. Iconic devices in American Sign Language. In Lynn Friedman (ed.), *On the Other Hand: New Perspectives on American Sign Language*, 57–107. New York: Academic Press.
Napoli, Donna Jo & Casey Ferrara. 2021. Correlations between handshape and movement in sign languages. *Cognitive Science* 45(5). e12944. DOI: 10.1111/cogs.12944.
Nyst, Victoria. 2018. Cross-linguistic variation in space-based distance for size depiction in the lexicons of six sign languages. *Sign Language & Linguistics* 21(2). 350–379. DOI: 10.1075/sll.00024.nys.
Padden, Carol, So-One Hwang, Ryan Lepic & Sharon Seegers. 2015. Tools for language: Patterned iconicity in sign language nouns and verbs. *Topics in Cognitive Science* 7(1). 81–94. DOI: 10.1111/tops.12121.
Padden, Carol A., Irit Meir, So-One Hwang, Ryan Lepic, Sharon Seegers & Tory Sampson. 2013. Patterned iconicity in sign language lexicons. *Gesture* 13(3). 287–308. DOI: 10.1075/gest.13.3.03pad.
Perniss, Pamela, Jenny C. Lu, Gary Morgan & Gabriella Vigliocco. 2018. Mapping language to the world: The role of iconicity in the sign language input. *Developmental Science* 21(2). e12551. DOI: 10.1111/desc.12551.
Perniss, Pamela, Asli Özyürek & Gary Morgan. 2015. The influence of the visual modality on language structure and conventionalization: Insights from sign language and gesture. *Topics in Cognitive Science* 7(1). 2–11. DOI: 10.1111/tops.12127.
Perniss, Pamela & Gabriella Vigliocco. 2014. The bridge of iconicity: From a world of experience to the experience of language. *Philosophical Transactions of the Royal Society B: Biological Sciences* 369(1651). 20130300. DOI: 10.1098/rstb.2013.0300.
Sandler, Wendy. 1989. *Phonological Representation of the Sign: Linearity and Nonlinearity. American Sign Language*. Dordrecht: Foris.
Schembri, Adam. 1996. *The Structure and Formation of Signs in AUSLAN (Australian Sign Language)*. North Rock, Sydney: North Rocks Press.
Simper-Allen, Pia. 2019. 'Cut and break'-descriptions in Swedish Sign Language: Children's and adults' depicting verb constructions. Ms.
Streeck, Jürgen. 2008. Depicting by gesture. *Gesture* 8(3). 285–301. DOI: 10.1075/gest.8.3.02str.
Sutton, Valerie. 2014. *Lessons in Sign Writing: Textbook*. La Jolla, CA: The SignWriting Press.

Taub, Sarah F. 2001. *Language from the Body: Iconicity and Metaphor in American Sign Language*. Cambridge: Cambridge University Press.
Vinson, David, Robin L. Thompson, Robert Skinner & Gabriella Vigliocco. 2015. A faster path between meaning and form? Iconicity facilitates sign recognition and production in British Sign Language. *Journal of Memory and Language* 82. 56–85. DOI: 10.1016/j.jml.2015.03.002.

Onno Crasborn and Els van der Kooij
The Emergence of the Second Hand in Sign Language Phonology: From Underlying to Surface Representations

Abstract: On the basis of corpus data of Sign Language of the Netherlands (NGT), we examine a number of issues related to the use of the non-dominant hand in signed language discourse. The prolongation of the final state of one hand of a two-handed sign while the other hand continues to produce other linguistic material (a 'hold') has been analysed in the literature as a prime piece of evidence for the presence of prosodic domains such as the phonological phrase in the organisation of sign languages. It thus provided evidence for a prosodic level of organisation more generally. It was not clear in those studies, however, how these prosodic phenomena can be represented and how they relate to the underlying lexical form of signs.

We propose a representation with three levels: lexical, surface level spell-out and post-lexical. An underlying lexical representation itself (such as provided by the Dependency Model of signs that we use here) cannot handle phenomena such as spreading across multiple lexical items. For these phenomena, an intermediate surface level is needed, to connect the underlying representation to the linear surface form (syllables) holding the spell-out of underlying features. The surface level spell-out in turn is integrated into the prosodic structure of the sequences of signs, where postlexical phenomena such as (meaningful or purely prosodic) spreading across signs and phrases occur. With regards to the second hand, the underlying lexical representation does not distinguish two independent articulators. A spell out process is needed to determine the dominant hand, as well as the position of the selected fingers, the orientation, and other features of the weak hand.

Our overall conclusion is that: a) the prolonged presence of the non-dominant hand can indeed be seen as a phonological process; b) this process can be analysed in terms of spreading of features and feature clusters of manual signs; and c) other surface phenomena (such as cross-articulator assimilation or 'echoing') can also be analysed as feature spreading, and in that sense are not fundamentally different from full holds. Thus, by creating an explicit multi-layered formal representation, heterogeneous post-lexical phenomena such as

---

Onno Crasborn & Els van der Kooij, Centre for Language Studies, Radboud University

https://doi.org/10.1515/9783110730081-016

buoys, prosodic spreading, weak prop and manual 'echoes' can be analysed in a unified manner. Our analysis strengthens the view of signed and spoken languages being similar even in the domain of post-lexical phonology, where at first sight the modality-specific phonetic differences in the surface form appear to be substantial.

Keywords: sign language, feature spreading, two-handed signs, non-dominant hand, underlying and surface representation, phonetic implementation, Sign Language of the Netherlands (NGT)

1 Introduction

With two publications in the 1990s, van der Hulst (1993, 1996) was the first (and possibly the only) spoken language phonologist to take a broad view of human language as encompassing both spoken and signed languages. The present chapter expands on a particular merit of these two early papers: the comprehensive analysis of two-handed signs. In order to account for various post-lexical phenomena that can be frequently observed in corpus data, we combine an analysis of these with earlier analyses of the prosodic phenomenon of 'full holds' (Nespor and Sandler (1999) on Israeli Sign Language, ISL). We thereby expand the underlying representation with a surface layer of representation in Section 2 and a post-lexical layer in Section 3. In this introduction, we first discuss the lexical phonology of two-handed signs (Section 1.1) and talk about some surface processes involving the two hands (Section 1.2). In Section 1.3, we discuss earlier proposals for multi-layered phonological representations for sign languages.

1.1 The Representation of Two-handed Signs in the Lexicon

Signs are specified in the lexicon as being either one-handed or two-handed. The specification for two-handed signs comes in two types: signs in which the two hands more or less look and act the same ('balanced signs') and signs in which a passive hand is the location for the active hand ('unbalanced signs').[1] The first

---

[1] These terms were introduced by van der Hulst (1993). We use the terms 'strong hand' and 'weak hand' for the two articulators in the lexicon, to express the difference in hand dominance in these signs. The terms 'dominant hand' and 'non-dominant hand' are used more generally for the two hands at the surface level, and 'left hand' and 'right hand' are used for describing the phonetic surface forms.

type is phonologically specified for the feature [symmetrical], where the two articulators are identical in shape, orientation and movement (or symmetrical with respect to the midsaggital plane). In the second type, one hand is specified as the place of articulation of the other hand (Stokoe 1960; Battison 1978; van der Hulst 1996). An example of each type is provided in Figure 1. Here and elsewhere in this article, we use the Dependency Model to represent signs (van der Hulst 1996; van der Kooij 2002). The feature [symmetrical] represents balanced signs. In unbalanced signs, the weak hand is represented as a location feature.

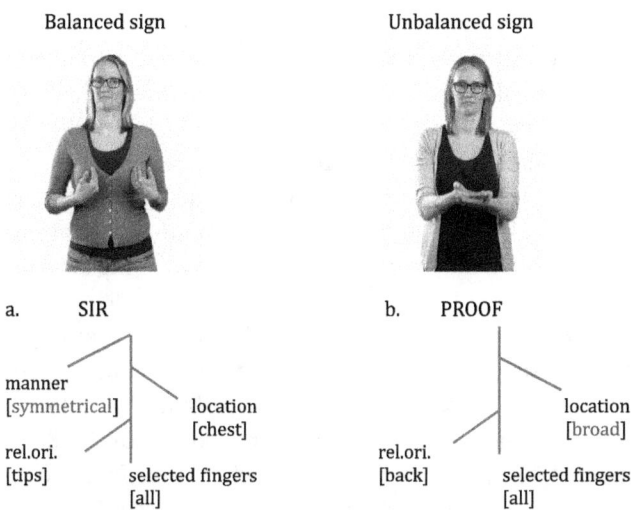

Figure 1: Two phonological types of lexical two-handed signs: the weak hand can either act as an active articulator (SIR) or as a place or articulation (as in PROOF); the relevant features in the feature geometry are highlighted in red. Both signs contain a downward movement, either of both hands or of the strong hand towards the weak hand.

Even though handedness (one vs. two-handed signs) is potentially distinctive in NGT and most likely in all sign languages, there are few minimal pairs based on this distinction. In the 1980s and 1990s, studies on two-handed signs concentrated on the number of hands required to lexically represent them (see Padden and Perlmutter (1987) and Perlmutter (1991) for discussion). More specifically: are two structural positions required in the phonological representation of the two manual articulators, or is one structural position sufficient? Several representations were proposed with two structural positions for the two-handed signs (e.g. Brentari 1990; Sandler 1989; van der Hulst 1996). Perlmutter (1991) noted several problems regarding these proposals (see also Padden and Perlmutter 1987). First of all, they over-generate the types of occurring two-handed signs. For instance, the palm of a C-hand touching the tips of a weak V-hand is not only unattested, but also an impossible lexical sign according to native intuitions. To capture these facts, constraints such as Battison's Dominance Condition (Battison (1978) on ASL) were formulated, expressing that the weak hand has no distinct movement or location and has limited shapes when it serves as a location for the strong hand. A hierarchical (dependency) relation between the structural position of the strong and the weak hand in the phonological representation reduces the overgeneration problem to some extent (van der Hulst 1996).

An alternative for a structural position for the weak hand is a featural account. The basic distinction in Battison's typology of two-handed signs is between symmetrical (balanced) and asymmetrical (unbalanced) signs. At the underlying level, symmetrical signs can easily be represented by one structural articulator position along with a feature 'symmetrical' or 'two-handed'. The implication is thus that all characteristics of the dominant hand also apply to the non-dominant hand in the surface spell-out. The representation of the non-dominant hand as the place of articulation (cf. Sandler 1989) captures the observation that, in asymmetrical signs, the non-dominant hand does not move and serves as the location for the active or dominant hand.

The size of the set of place of articulation features in this proposal might be of some concern if all possible hand configurations of the weak hand were potential place of articulation features. To this end, the distribution of different hand configurations in two-handed NGT signs was examined in van der Kooij (2002). In a review of a set of 3,084 signs, almost half of which were found to be two-handed signs; 79% of these were symmetrical. Of the 303 asymmetrical signs (21%), the hand configuration of the strong and the weak hand was the same in 59% of cases, while in another 32% of cases, the weak hand was a flat hand (all fingers selected, no finger configuration specified). The latter signs were represented with the place of articulation feature [broad] (cf. Figure 1b). In only six signs was the weak hand different from the strong hand while not being a flat hand. These signs were all analysed as being morphologically complex, in that the weak hand was a so-called classifier hand configuration: a meaningful hand configuration that can serve as an argument in post-lexical constructions (see Zwitserlood and Crasborn (under review) for further discussion). These distributional facts led to the proposal that a structural position for the weak hand as the place of articulation is only licenced by a morphemic hand configuration. In such a case, a dependent hand configuration node is generated at the lexical level, allowing for a full specification of hand configuration and orientation features for the weak hand. The full-fledged hand configuration specification for the weak hand is still placed in the location node to capture the fact that, like all other locations, the weak hand does not and cannot move by itself. On the surface, these complex two-handed signs are indistinguishable from classifier constructions. For example, the manual part of the sign TEA is indistinguishable from the classifier construction 'dip in container', as illustrated in Figure 2.

Figure 2: TEA or 'dip something small in a cylindrical container'.

However, the lexical sign and the classifier construction differ underlyingly in that the source of the two articulators in these 'homophonous' surface forms is either from one lexeme (in TEA) consisting of two morphemic hand configurations, or from two post-lexically combined one-handed morphemes (in the classifier construction 'dip in container'). We discussed the morphology of these constructions in Zwitserlood, van der Kooij, and Crasborn (2021). By providing a different underlying representation for these forms that are homophonous on the surface, we proposed a formal analysis that distinguishes the underlying representation from the surface form. Such a representational account of the source of the morphological complexity does justice to both the phonology and morphology of such two-handed signs. By contrast, for the spreading processes that we discuss in this chapter, the source of the features of the non-dominant hand is not relevant.

1.2 Some Post-lexical Phenomena that Involve the Non-dominant Hand

The articulatory potential of having two symmetrical manual articulators is not used during the realisation of one-handed signs. The non-dominant hand is inactive in these signs. Moreover, post-lexically, two-handed lexical items may sometimes be realised with just one hand ('weak drop'; see Padden and Perlmutter 1987; van der Kooij 2001; Nishio 2008). Thus, although the second articulator is phonetically available, it is inactive during some parts of utterances. This is similar to for instance the inactivity of the velar articulator during the production of non-nasal sounds. Depending on the number of one-handed articulations in sequence, this may lead to quite some potential for the non-dominant hand to perform other activities. This potential has been shown to be exploited in at least two different ways in various sign languages.

First of all, Nespor and Sandler (1999) and Sandler (2006) have argued that the non-dominant hand of a two-handed sign in ASL and ISL can maintain its final position (a 'full hold') for some time while the other hand articulates one or more new signs. Rather than contributing additional meaning, such full holds may contribute to the rhythm of the sentence, ending at specific prosodic boundaries. The perceiver thus gets an explicit phonetic cue that a certain prosodic domain has ended. This is exemplified in Figure 3 below.

Secondly, Liddell (2003) showed that, in some cases, these holds can in fact last for multiple sentences, functioning as a landmark for the ongoing discourse produced by the other hand. Liddell referred to this maintained hand as a 'buoy', which is a descriptive term that seems to be in the middle between form and function (see also Kimmelman, Sáfár, and Crasborn (2016) for arguments against this notion). An NGT example is provided in Figure 4 below. The list of 'buoys' includes pointing signs, one-handed number signs, and in principle either hand of any one-handed or two-handed sign. Although Liddell describes different types of buoys based on the source sign, these do not seem to be of a specific morphological or syntactic type; nor do there appear to be specific phonological restrictions on holds.

[PALM-UP   DEAF   CULTURE   YES]   [CORRECT . . .
'It has to do with deaf culture, yes. You're right (. . .)'

Figure 3: Short hold to mark a prosodic domain. The left hand of the two-handed sign PALM-UP is maintained during the two following signs, after which the hand relaxes during the sign YES and then continues to realise the two-handed sign CORRECT. Square brackets indicate sentence boundaries. [CNGT0538, 01:50.800–01:52.000].[2]

---

2 All examples presented in this chapter are taken from the Corpus NGT (Crasborn, Zwitserlood, and Ros 2008). References to the corpus are given in square brackets, using the four-digit session

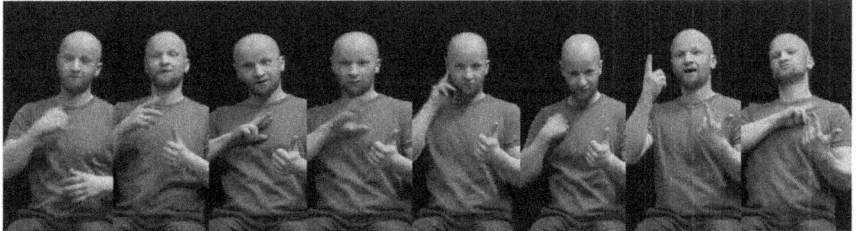

Figure 4: Long hold of a 'list buoy', where the extended thumb of the non-dominant hand ('number one on the list') is maintained during the narration of the first item on that list. [CNGT0205, 01:00.300–01:01.700].

Phonetically, these two types of full holds are identical: the final state of the articulator is frozen for some time, as it were. In both cases, the hold is categorical rather than gradient in that it maintains all properties of the sign at the end of its articulation. In terms of the phonological parameters of the sign first classified by Stokoe (1960), the handshape, orientation and location are all maintained. Sandler and Liddell look at these constructions from very different perspectives, however. Sandler considers the spreading a prosodic phenomenon, contributing to the rhythm of a sentence, whereas Liddell emphasises the discourse function of spreading. Referring to the difference in terms of larger or smaller prosodic domains is not feasible, as small domains may be motivated by discourse purposes as well. Also, larger spreading domains (larger than the phonological phrase) can be merely prosodic in nature (reflecting syntactic rather than discourse relations).

It is acknowledged that hold of the non-dominant hand across phrase boundaries occurs in classifier constructions (Nespor and Sandler 1999). These are not analysed by Sandler in the same prosodic paradigm, possibly because they have a different source, stemming from the morphosyntax rather than merely a phonological specification in the lexicon.

Nilsson (2007) discusses a broader diversity of phenomena related to the two hands. Looking at all the potential activities of the non-dominant hand in Swedish Sign Language (SSL), she proposed a continuum of phenomena that reflects the importance of the non-dominant hand in signed discourse (see Figure 5).

Nilsson emphasises the distinction between phonetic processes (everything up to and including *mirroring*) and processes that contribute to the content of the discourse, specifically in facilitating reference tracking. From *doubling* (the two-

---

code followed by the time range in mm:ss.msec. Most of the corpus sessions are publicly accessible through The Language Archive, at https://hdl.handle.net/1839/00-0000-0000-0004-DF8E-6.

                                    dominance reversals (1%)
                                buoys (17%)
                          sign fragments (6%)
                        doubling (2%)
                     mirroring (4%)
                  mirror at chest (6%)
         at chest (22%)
in lap (19%)

Figure 5: Continuum of the activities of the non-dominant hand in Nilsson (2007: 181). The percentages refer to the frequency in her Swedish Sign Language data set.

handed articulation of one-handed signs, dubbed 'weak prop' by Padden and Perlmutter (1987)) up to *dominance reversals,* the non-dominant hand articulations perform a variety of functions. They contribute to what is said in various ways: by reinforcing it; by indicating what the discourse topic is (as in *sign fragments,* or, in Sandler's terms, non-dominant hand spreading); by contributing independent information (as in *list and theme buoys* as in Figure 4); or by articulating new lexical content without activity on the other hand (*dominance reversals*).

Nilsson's terminology shows that the continuum contains two perspectives at the same time: on the one hand that of the form (phonology and phonetics), and on the other hand that of the meaning or function (contribution to discourse). Some are considered to be purely phonetic-phonological processes, while others are relevant to the discourse.

Sandler, Liddell and Nilsson differ in their relative emphasis on the form versus the function of post-lexical two-handed activities. However, none of these authors are concerned with the relation between lexical form and their realisations in discourse. That is, how can the lexical (underlying and/or surface) form be spelled out into a post-lexical representation? That is what we aim to address in this chapter. We propose an integrated representation for phonological surface phenomena such as holds, irrespective of their linguistic source. By providing a detailed surface feature representation that is linked to the underlying lexical representation, we hope to contribute to a more coherent formal basis for the surface realisation of syntactic and discourse phenomena.

1.3 Multi-layered Representations of Sign Language Phonology

The representation of the surface form of signs has not received a great deal of attention. How are all the underlying lexical features spelled out in terms of the phonetic features representing the exact configuration, position and movement of the articulators? This question has been discussed to some extent in the analysis of morphological processes. For instance, Collins-Ahlgren (1990) uses the model of Liddell and Johnson (1986, 1989) to analyse the deletion of so-called hold segments in compounds in New Zealand Sign Language, explicitly proposing a surface representation. Sandler (1993: 125) classifies various phonological processes in ASL, making a distinction between two (ordered) lexical phonological levels where various morphological processes such as verb inflection and negative incorporation take place, a post-lexical level where handshape assimilation may occur, and a phonetic level. At the latter level, movement epenthesis between signs and final lengthening take place. The levels are illustrated in Figure 6.

	Ex. of Morphological Processes	Ex. of Phonological Processes
Level X	Verb agreement	Association to skeleton
Level Y	Negative incorporation	Spread
Post-lexical		Handshape-only assimilation
Phonetic		Phrase-final lengthening

Figure 6: Levels of representation distinguished by Sandler (1993, adapted from example (32) on page 125).

These four levels primarily serve to characterise sequential processes, which affect strings of segments, without explicitly addressing two-handed signs. Interestingly, these distinctions between levels were not used in Sandler's later work on the prosody of Israeli Sign Language. The question arises how post-lexical temporal processes affecting the two hands can be represented, if there is no explicit surface representation of the two hands independently of each other.

Padden and Perlmutter (1987) discuss a variety of post-lexical processes related to the two hands and argue that the use of the left versus the right hand is fully predictable "except under discourse conditions not relevant here" (p. 338). They do not propose an explicit representation of surface forms.

Possibly the only author who has attempted to propose a phonological description of two-handed surface forms of signs is Miller (2000). Looking specifically at the rhythm of signs in terms of movement units, Miller proposed a moraic representation that accounted for various phenomena in the surface form of Langue des Signes Québécoise (LSQ). In this representation, Miller proposed two different autosegmental tiers, to specify the surface form of the left and the right hand. In the lexical surface representation that we propose below, we do explicitly mention the right and left hand, at a third stage of derivation: the post-lexical representation.

Our aim in this chapter is therefore to explicitly account for the variety of surface forms we observe with respect to the activities of the left and the right hand. We do this by differentiating between three different levels of representation. This is not unlike the proposals of Sandler (1993) and Miller (2000) in their overall approach, but we focus specifically on the realisation of two-handed signs. We see a need for a surface representation that contains a spell-out in terms of the dominant versus the non-dominant hand on the basis of the lexical specification. These dominant and non-dominant hands are realised post-lexically in terms of the left hand and the right hand: only in that way can we provide a unified account of all the surface phenomena mentioned above. These representations help us make more explicit what the second hand is doing at any given time, and may form an encouragement to look further at potential functions of low-level phonetic behaviour when lexical signs are used in context, which have so far gone unnoticed.

2 A Proposal for a Layered Representation of the Two Articulators

2.1 Lexical Underlying Representation of Two-handed Signs

Underlying representations are abstractions of surface forms that are needed to capture phonotactic patterns in the lexicon, as well as patterns in phonological processes such as feature spreading. Several aspects of the underlying representation of the Dependency Model (van der Hulst 1993, 1996; Crasborn and van der Kooij 1997; van der Kooij 2002) that are relevant for the underlying representation are the following:
- different classes of two-handed signs are captured in terms of features (see above);
- features are hierarchically organised (and are thus predicted to be amenable to spreading individually and in combination);
- the underlying representation only contains segmental features, and no temporal or syllabic structure; only in the cases of meaningful syllabicity, when features have a meaningful linear ordering, is there a 'syllabic prespecification' in the lexicon (see van der Kooij and Crasborn (2008) for discussion).

In other words, there is no notion of the two hands at all in the underlying representation: 'one hand is enough' (van der Kooij 2000, 2002). There is only one set of hand configuration features, and not two, in any sign. The focus on head-dependent relations in dependency phonology (e.g. Dresher and van der Hulst 1998) is especially well suited for capturing such distributional patterns in the lexicon.

Branching nodes represent movement, but the order of the features is not distinctive, and thus not present in the underlying representation (van der Kooij 2002). Only in cases where the movement direction and thus the order of features is meaningful (whether by morphology or by phonetic specification in the lexicon) is this lexically represented. Examples include NGT signs TO-GROW and BETTER, which both have upward movement. All segmental features of the underlying representation are associated with bipositional slots on a skeletal tier, but we suggest that this only happens at the lexical surface representation. This is discussed further in the next section. The hierarchical structuring of features is less relevant in this chapter, but is mentioned in the representation of some post-lexical phenomena in Section 3 below.

2.2 Lexical Surface Representation

The representation of two-handed signs in terms of location or symmetry features implies that there are not two actual active articulators in the underlying representation. In order to articulate these signs, they have to be mapped to the two manual articulators, the strong hand and the weak hand, and ultimately to the left and the right hand of a signer. We propose that this takes place in two steps, as the formulation in the previous sentence suggests. The *lexical surface representation* is the intermediary between the *underlying representation* and the *post-lexical representation*. In this lexical surface representation, redundant features are spelled out into a temporal structure and into a representation of the two hands that includes a notion of hand dominance (the strong hand and the weak hand).

Thus, where the underlying level allows us to express distributional generalisations, this intermediate level allows us to express Battison's Dominance and Symmetry Constraints. In contrast to the underlying representation where the two hands are not explicitly represented, the lexical surface representation includes a spell-out of the handshape for each hand. The level thus is 'intermediate' in its degree of detail and in adding the linear (syllabic) structure to the underlying representation that is needed for the integration with the post-lexical prosodic level. Further research will need to demonstrate to which extent phonological processes specifically make use of nodes in this lexical surface representation.

The lexical features of the two-handed signs illustrated in Figure 1 above are mapped to the strong hand and the weak hand. At the same time, features representing movement are mapped to a bipositional skeleton, forming a syllable. In Figures 7 and 8, this is illustrated for the two types of signs represented in Figure 1.

For unbalanced signs such as PROOF in Figure 7, the place of articulation of the sign is the weak hand. Underlyingly, this is specified with a distinctive feature

Underlying representation

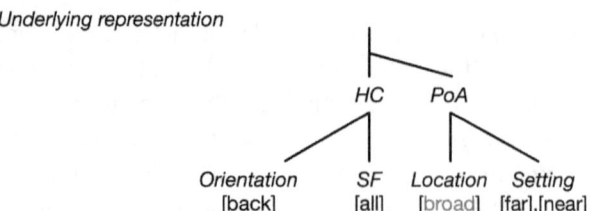

Surface representation

Strong hand
SF: [all]
Orient.: [back]
Setting: [far],[near]

[x x]σ

Weak hand
Orient.: [palm]
SF: [all]

Figure 7: Underlying and surface representation of the unbalanced lexical sign PROOF. The location feature [broad] is spelled out on the weak hand tier, as orientation feature [palm] and selected finger (SF) feature [all]. HC stands for Hand Configuration, PoA for Place of Articulation.

Underlying representation

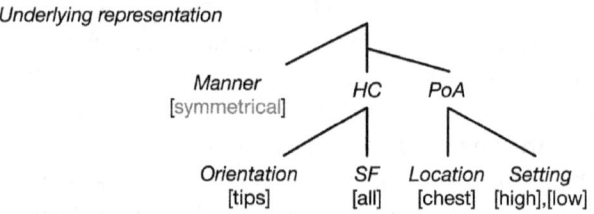

Surface representation

Strong hand
SF: [all]
Orient.: [tips]
Location: [chest (ipsilateral)]
Setting: [high],[low]

[x x]σ

Weak hand
Setting: [high],[low]
Location: [chest (ipsilateral)]
Orient.: [tips]
SF: [all]

Figure 8: Underlying and surface representation of the symmetrical lexical sign SIR. The feature [symmetrical] is spelled out as a set of tiers that is identical for the strong hand and the weak hand, and that is similarly aligned to the bipositional skeleton.

for location [broad], referring to the inside of a flat hand, which on the phonetic surface has a specific shape (or set of active fingers) and orientation with respect to the other hand. The notion 'handshape' is thus not a phonological one, but rather a descriptive shorthand for the surface form of a set of phonological features (see also Crasborn (2001) for discussion). Similarly, the location of the weak hand is spelled out on the surface as [neutral space], being the default location for either hand (see van der Kooij (2002) for discussion).

The feature [symmetrical] in the balanced sign SIR in Figure 8 spells out as a complete duplication of all features of the strong hand onto the weak hand. Since the location is now shared between the two hands, we might add 'ipsilateral' to the location feature [chest] to indicate that both hands stay on their own side of the chest.

These surface representations use the concepts of 'strong hand' and 'weak hand', expressing the generalisation that 'right' and 'left' are not lexically contrastive. The strong and weak hands can be articulated by either the left or the right hand. Only when used in context do the actual left and right hands come into play. At that level, there may also be an interaction with, for instance, locations in signing space that come from the morphosyntax.

The distinction between the underlying representation and the surface representation also makes clear that all specific weak hand handshapes (such as the 'C' hand in TEA) are surface phenomena. In most cases, they are morphologically complex forms, the weak hand being composed of a morpheme or set of morphemes (cf. Zwitserlood, van der Kooij, and Crasborn 2021).

3 A Post-lexical Representation

In this section, we look at a variety of post-lexical phenomena affecting the two hands. We propose a further spell-out of the lexical surface representation that can account for assimilation phenomena in terms of spreading of features or higher nodes. Along the way, we demonstrate how some hand-internal assimilation phenomena such as spreading of finger selection can likewise be represented in terms of feature.

For each of the examples we present in the sections below, we show how the lexical surface representation of the strong hand and weak hand in Figures 7 and 8 above is spelled out as features of the actual two articulators: the thumb (T) and four fingers (IMRP for index, middle, ring and pinky fingers) of each hand. In order to keep the representations readable, we have omitted tiers for other features such as finger configuration, aperture and manner of movement. We refer to van der Hulst (1996) and van der Kooij (2001) for the full model.

We need this lower level of representation to capture surface patterns of signs in contact. This includes spreading as discussed in this chapter, but also dominance reversal (Frishberg (1985) on ASL; Crasborn and Sáfár (2016) on NGT), which has yet to be analysed in terms of its phonological representation. This surface level is also the level where the lexical syllables get spelled out as a post-lexical syllabic organisation (see van der Kooij and Crasborn 2008).

The movements of lexical signs are either single or repeated. The actual number of repetitions (or the lack of repetition) depends on their segmental content and the prosodic position in which they are realised (see e.g. Nespor and Sandler 1999). For example, focused positions in NGT sentences may lead to repeated surface syllables, even if the lexical representation does not contain the feature [repeated] (Crasborn and van der Kooij (2013) for NGT; Nespor and Sandler (1999) for ISL). Specific morphosyntactic constructions may also lead to multisyllabic surface forms (e.g. when a repetitive action is expressed).

The spelling out of these two types of two-handed signs in terms of a more explicit surface level is needed to account for various post-lexical assimilation phenomena, as we show in the following sections. We start with an example of a weak hand hold. After spelling out the phonetic feature details of this example, we show that less straightforward examples of assimilation can also be captured in terms of feature spreading. To this end, we provide an integrated surface representation with a single process (feature spreading) that can account for all sorts of contextual phenomena.

3.1 Post-lexical Phenomena: Sequential Spreading from Different Sources

Post-lexically, lexical syllables are integrated in the prosodic structure of larger syntactic and discourse units. The segmental features that stem from the lexical syllable may be associated with the surface syllables, and the presence of some segmental features may be prolonged ('held'). The following example (Figure 9) illustrates how the weak hand of a two-handed sign may be present during the realisation of several subsequent one-handed articulations. In this case, all the features specifying the lexical surface representation of the weak hand spread over the four subsequent signs. Furthermore, the downward movement of the right hand in the sign AFTER-ALL also affects the position of the left hand. Subsequently, the left hand remains in its lower position up to the unbalanced sign RULES.

In this and further examples, we visualise and gloss the part of the sentence that is relevant to understanding the phonological processes. The references to the source of the example in the Corpus NGT is provided in the caption, so that the examples can be inspected in their full sentence context in the archived version of the corpus (see footnote 2 above).

RH:	WRITE	AFTER-ALL	FUNNY	ALL	RULES	1.ORD
LH:	WRITE—					

'(We didn't need to) write (it in a clear manner), but it was funny that we could write it for each other. The first (...)'

Figure 9: Full hold of the weak hand of the unbalanced sign WRITE during the four subsequent signs. RULES in this example could also be considered a new two-handed sign. [CNGT0004, 04:34.800–04:39.500].

In the surface representation in Figure 10 and subsequent figures below, we repeat the gloss transcription in the picture examples and, below that, represent each autosegmental feature on a different tier. Although the vertical layering of these tiers suggests that they are independent, they in fact maintain a hierarchical relation to each other, such that selected finger features and orientation jointly form part of the hand configuration node of the lexical surface representation in Figures 7 and 8 (there indicated by bracketing).

Red boxes and arrows highlight what the source (regular box) and the target (dotted line box) of the spreading process is. The left hand in RULES (used here to mean '(write) in a list') is ambiguous: it is both the continuation of the held weak hand of WRITE and the lexically specified location for RULES. For this reason, this last spreading step is visualised in a different colour. Because of the higher location of the left hand at the start of RULES, we tend towards a non-spreading analysis of that left hand; on the other hand, the orientation of the non-dominant hand would typically be fingertips up in that case.

In addition to the full hold of the left hand, two other spreading processes can be seen in the example and in the representation, to which we will come back below in Section 3.2. These latter spreading processes are visualised in grey in the figure.

Full holds (including some types of buoys) are characterised by the spreading of all hand configuration features. At the lexical level, spreading of single features (or for example of the hand configuration node in compounds) happens in assimilation processes, as discussed, for example, by Sandler (1993) for ASL. Outside

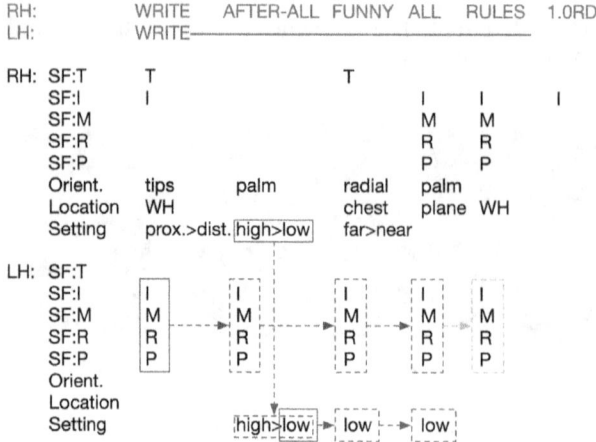

Figure 10: Surface representation of the sequence in Figure 9. All left-handed finger features of WRITE spread to the subsequent signs. In addition, the movement of AFTER-ALL is spread from the right hand to the left hand, after which the final setting (low) of the left hand spreads to the subsequent two signs (see Section 3.2 for discussion). Abbreviations used: SF = Selected Finger; Orient. = Orientation; WH = weak hand location; prox. = proximal or closer to the forearm; dist. = distal or further away from the forearm.

of morphology, post-lexically that is, we see feature spreading as coarticulation between signs that do not form a single word. This is illustrated in a sequence of one-handed signs in Figure 11, where the little finger of the right hand signing YEAR stays in place when the dominance of the hands is reversed.

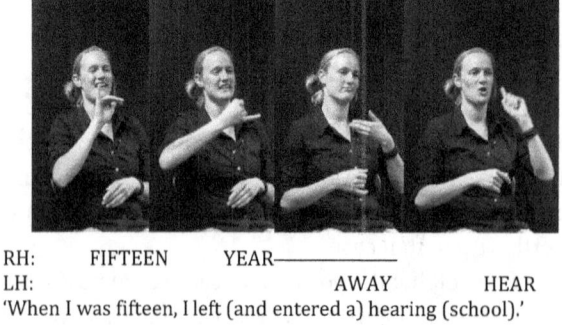

RH: FIFTEEN   YEAR———————
LH: AWAY   HEAR
'When I was fifteen, I left (and entered a) hearing (school).'

Figure 11: Spreading of the selected finger feature of YEAR to the following sign. [CNGT0411, 00:53.200–00:55.000].

In the surface representation of this example in Figure 12, the single finger feature 'Pinky' (P) spreads in a similar way as the full hold in Figure 10, from the sign

YEAR to the right hand of AWAY, which is otherwise a one-handed sign realised here by the left hand.

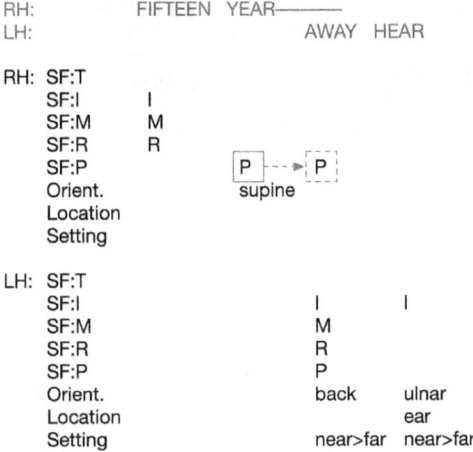

Figure 12: Surface representation of the sequence in Figure 11.

By spelling out the underlying representation into a surface representation, we formally capture various sequential phenomena such as assimilation in a unified way in terms of feature spreading (single or complex). Moreover, this analysis also paves the way for representing other assimilation phenomena in a similar manner, as we will show in Sections 3.2 and 3.3.

3.2 Assimilation across Hands: Echoing Movements

There are cases where the hand configuration of the dominant hand spreads to that of the non-dominant hand. These are what Nilsson (2007) characterised as 'mirroring'; we call them 'echoes', following Sandler's (1993) use of that term for the weak hand in symmetrical signs. In our analysis, we treat these echoes as features or feature clusters that 'vertically' spread from one articulator to the other in the post-lexical representation.

Another example of this is provided in Figure 13, represented in Figure 14. The hand configuration features (selected fingers and orientation) spread from the right hand to the left hand. The underlyingly one-handed sign CHILD thus receives a representation in which there are features on the selected fingers and orientation tiers for both hands. In addition, there are various other spreading processes, which are visualised in grey for the sake of completeness.

```
RH: PLUS      PT:1            CHILD ─────────────────────
LH: PLUS ─────────             echo:HC       PT:child        PT:1
```
'Plus, then I [don't feel that] she's the child but me [but the other way around].

Figure 13: Echoing movement of the left hand copying the selected fingers and orientation of the dominant hand (CHILD), but not the location or movement. This is glossed as 'echo:HC', referring to the hand configuration node in the representation that spreads. In addition, there's a full hold of the sign CHILD during which the left hand articulates two pointing signs. At the start of the sentence, there is also a hold of the selected fingers of the non-dominant hand in PLUS. [CNGT0134, 01:32.600–01:34.800].

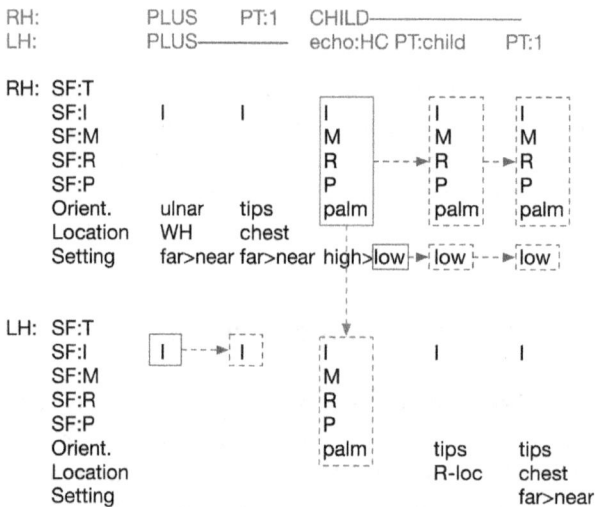

Figure 14: Surface representation of the sequence in Figure 13. The abbreviation 'R-loc' stands for a referential location in the signing space, in this case a location to the right of the signer, low in space; as these are not relevant to our present argument, we have not proposed a spell-out of this abstract feature to a phonetic one, although that will be necessary at this surface form level.

Similar to the spreading of single features in sequential spreading, we also find single feature assimilation across hands. In the following example (Figure 15), the orientation features representing the orientation change 'supination' in the sign CULTURE on the right hand spread onto the left hand. Interestingly, no echoing rotation is observed during the sign MY-OWN, which has a similar rotation movement. The rotation movement of MY-OWN, however, is not the result of a lexical orientation change specification (prone>supine), but a phonetic effect of two contacting movements on the body. At the lexical level, these double-contact signs form two syllables (cf. van der Kooij 1997; van der Kooij and Crasborn 2008), visualised in Figure 16 by the two vertical grey boxes.

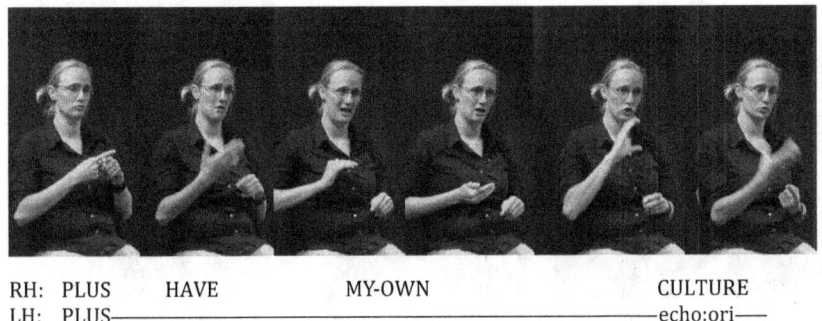

RH: PLUS   HAVE   MY-OWN   CULTURE
LH: PLUS————————————————————————————echo:ori——
'(Deaf people are very independent) and they have their own culture.'

Figure 15: Echoing movement of the orientation change in CULTURE but not in the phonetically similar movement in the double-contact sign MY-OWN. The non-dominant hand that echoes the movement itself is the result of temporal spreading. [CNGT0427, 00:58.800–01:00.600].

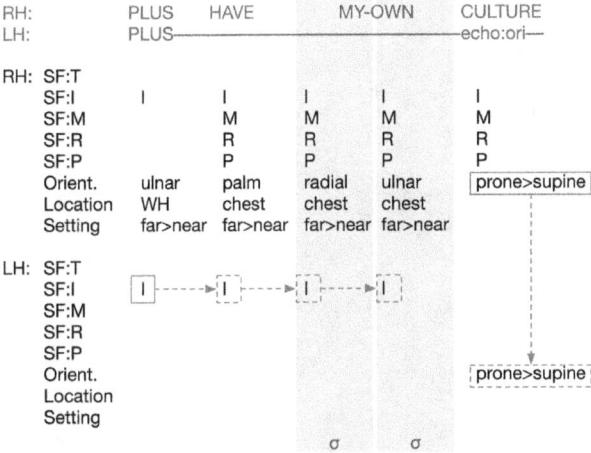

Figure 16: Surface representation of the sequence in Figure 15.

A type of echoing movement that can be frequently observed in corpus data of NGT is a non-dominant hand echo in the form of extension of the index finger. In rest position of the non-dominant hand, it seems to be common that the index finger is extended a little more than the other fingers. This is illustrated in Figure 17 for the left hand in the last four images. In cases like this example, where the left context contains a specification for an extended index (SF:I), such a rest position is indistinguishable from a feature spreading for selected fingers. The representation can be found in Figure 18. However, echoing hand configurations also often appear to happen in cases where there is no index extension.

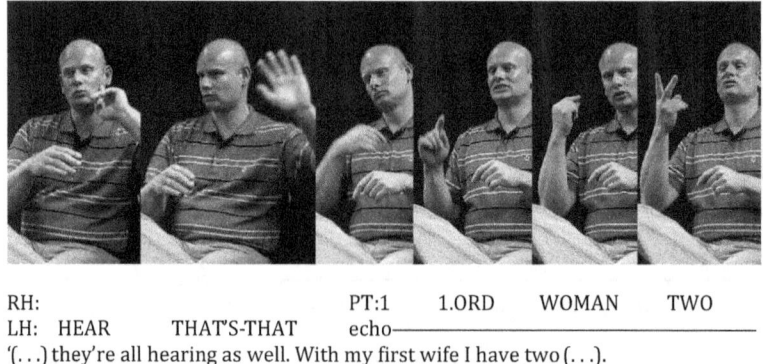

RH: PT:1   1.ORD   WOMAN   TWO
LH: HEAR   THAT'S-THAT   echo————————————————————————
'(...) they're all hearing as well. With my first wife I have two (...).'

Figure 17: Extension of index finger of resting hand, echoing the finger selection of the dominant hand. [CNGT0313, 01:46.300–01:49.900].

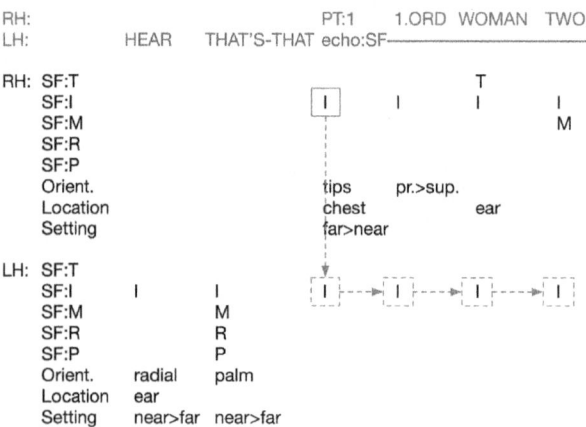

Figure 18: Surface representation of the sequence in Figure 17.

3.3 Full Copy of One-Handed Features: Weak Prop

A case of full simultaneous copy of a one-handed sign ('weak prop', as opposed to 'weak drop') was presented in Crasborn and van der Kooij (2013), where a focused position led to a two-handed pointing sign, both hands pointing to the same location in signing space. An example from the Corpus NGT is presented in Figure 19, where the first-person pronoun PT:1 is copied from the right hand to the left hand. Immediately following, the one-handed sign GOOD is also realised as a two-handed form. Further, in this example there are full holds of the signs GOOD and PALM-UP, and in the final sign PT:2, the selected finger 'pinky' is copied over (a 'finger hold') from the preceding sign YES.

| RH: | PALM-UP | PT:1 | GOOD——————— | YES——————— | PT:2 |
| LH: | PALM-UP | prop | prop | PALM-UP——————— | |

Figure 19: Two cases of 'weak prop', where one-handed signs PT:1 and GOOD are realised as symmetrical two-handed signs. [CNGT0411, 01:04.000–01.08.000].

All of these phenomena can be elegantly represented as feature spreading at the post-lexical level, as illustrated in Figure 20 below.

Note that it is not always easy, let alone self-evident, to determine what the underlying form of a sign is: a one-handed sign or a two-handed symmetrical sign (Paligot 2017). Native signer intuitions and patterns in corpora are both needed to inform this classification.

4 Summary: Overview of Spreading Processes

In Section 3, we illustrated a variety of post-lexical assimilation processes, which we argued can all be represented as feature spreading, both horizontally (between subsequent signs) and vertically (from one hand to the other). Table 1 presents an overview of these processes and the spelling out of underlying two-handed fea-

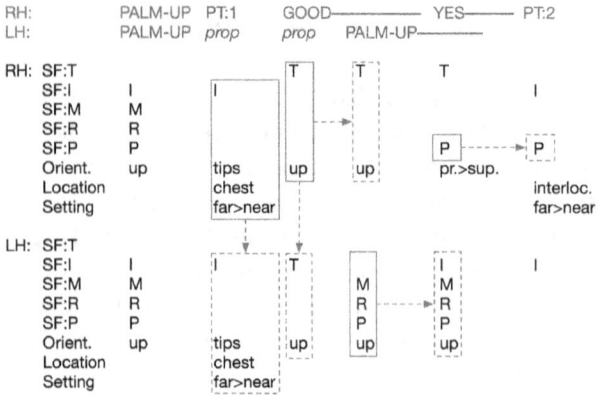

Figure 20: Surface representation of the sequence in Figure 19.

Table 1: Overview of phenomena that can be represented as feature spreading.

Layer	Sequential Spreading	Simultaneous Spreading
Lexical	Sequential compound	Spelling out of [symmetry] and location [weak hand]
Post-lexical: Root Node	Full hold: Prosodic marking Full hold: Morphosyntax / discourse ('buoys')	Full echo ('weak prop')
Post-lexical: Feature(s)	Feature spreading	Echo of feature or features

tures in terms of the spreading unit (a full segment or a subset of features), and in terms of their source, whether lexical or morphosyntactic.

As described in Section 2 above, two-handed lexical signs do not have independent representations for hand configuration or orientation for the two hands in the lexicon. Many, if not all, phonological models of signs incorporate this claim. Generalisations on distribution patterns of two-handed signs can best be captured by features such as symmetrical and weak hand as location. In the present chapter, we have argued that a spell-out to a level where the strong hand and weak hand have independent representations is necessary to be able to express further generalisations on two-handed signs in the lexicon, such as the assimilation of features in compounds. This level of representation is further needed to form an intermediate level for the representation of post-lexical processes. This latter level constitutes a third level of representation, we have argued.

At the post-lexical level, we find that the root node of signs can spread ('full holds'), as can feature clusters (for hand configuration) or individual features (for selected fingers for instance). Features can spread sequentially to neighbouring signs, and simultaneously to the non-dominant hand during one-handed signs (partial and full 'echoes'). While weak drop could in principle also be a process by which the underlying form features [symmetrical] and location [weak hand] are not spelled out onto the post-lexical level, the representation of 'weak prop' as a spreading process requires a post-lexical representation where two hands are independently represented.

5 Discussion and Conclusion

In this chapter, we have shown how an underlying representation that captures patterns across monomorphemic signs in the lexicon and that does not contain independent feature representations for the two manual articulators can be spelled out to a lexical surface representation. This surface form allows for the representation of both two-handed signs coming from the lexicon and of morphologically complex forms involving the non-dominant hand. The surface form then spells out to a post-lexical representation of the left and the right hand, necessary to capture a variety of post-lexical processes. Most of these processes have been documented for a variety of sign languages, including the prolonged presence of one of the articulators or aspects thereof. The three levels of representation together serve to make explicit and insightful how the phonotactic patterns of the language relate to what happens in context.

In addition, we have demonstrated that the spreading unit is not necessarily a full hand configuration (or h2 node in Sandler (1989)), but can also be individual distinctive features composing handshape and orientation. Neither is it the case that features or feature clusters only spread over time to neighbouring lexical items, as they can also spread from one hand to the other. Our three-level representation thus links the underlying representation of signs to surface forms, and captures all attested spreading processes in NGT.

The layered representation we propose emphasises the larger presence of feature spreading in sign language phonology than discussed in the literature. Sandler (1989) and Brentari (1990) argue for the role of autosegmental representations of signs and feature spreading within the lexical word (Brentari 1990) or prosodic word (Sandler, 1999). The proposed layered representation allows for feature spreading to also capture a broader range of post-lexical processes. Interestingly, where in spoken language phonology spreading of autosegments in prosody (Pierrehumbert 1980) formed the impetus for the development of autosegmental phonology (Clements and Keyser 1983; Clements 1985), sign language phonology has long focused solely on the representation of lexical processes. The representation of prosodic domains (the work initiated by Sandler (1999)) was not followed up by an account of phonological processes in terms of feature spreading within these domains. The explicit surface level representation interacting with the prosodic structure in sign sequences we proposed in this chapter fills that gap.

The examples in Section 3 implicitly showed prosodic domains of different sizes. We did not further discuss these domains, and leave it for future research to determine how examples like the above can form evidence for domains of different levels, such as the phonological phrase (the domain of the non-dominant hand hold in ISL, found by Nespor and Sandler (1999)), the intonational phrase or the utterance. One specific point for future research concerns the issue of supra-sentential spreading (which is probably at stake in the examples in Figures 9 and 19). Where the studies of Sandler on the prosodic hierarchy in ASL and ISL observed the utterance to be the largest unit, following Nespor and Vogel (1986), the discourse-level spreading of some examples might provide evidence for an even higher prosodic level, at least for sign languages. Nespor and Sandler point to these in passing, saying that "[w]hen [the ISL sign STREET is] reinterpreted as a classifier [. . .], h2 may spread beyond any boundary up to the level of a discourse unit" (1999: 163).

Another question that future studies will need to address is what triggers the various spreading processes. In the continuum of Nilsson (2007), discourse coherence is argued to be a major factor in this regard. Although there have been studies on post-lexical and prosodic processes for some languages (see Padden and Perlmutter (1987) for ASL and Nespor and Sandler (1999) for ASL and ISL), this is not the case for our NGT examples. One hypothesis to be tested in future research is that the amount of phonological material that is realised on the surface is dependent on the source and level of meaning that is expressed with certain features or clusters of features.

Comparison with the layered representation of Sandler (1993), presented in Figure 6 above, shows that we have evidence to distinguish two further levels of representation in addition to the underlying representation. First, the lexical surface level is the necessary spell-out of the symmetry and location features in the underlying representation. Second, the post-lexical representation allows the capture of phenomena that go beyond a single lexical item and are close to the phonetic articulation of signs by the left and right hand of an actual signer (or avatar, for that matter). The layered model on the basis of the Dependency Model of signs thus stays close to universal notions of dependency in phonology and the linguistic distinction between lexical and post-lexical representations, while at the same time allowing for the modality-specific properties of the signed modality.

References

Battison, R. 1978. *Lexical Borrowing in American Sign Language*. Silver Spring, MD: Linstok Press.
Brentari, D. 1990. *Theoretical foundations of American Sign Language phonology*. Chicago: University of Chicago PhD thesis.
Clements, G. N. 1985. The geometry of phonological features. *Phonology Yearbook* 2. 225–252.
Clements, G. N. & S. J. Keyser. 1983. *CV Phonology: A Generative Theory of the Syllable*. Cambridge, MA: MIT Press.
Collins-Ahlgren, M. 1990. Word formation processes in New Zealand sign language. In S. Fischer & P. Siple (eds.), *Theoretical Issues in Sign Language Research*, 279–312. Chicago: University of Chicago Press.
Crasborn, O. 2001. *Phonetic implementation of phonological categories in Sign Language of the Netherlands*. Leiden: Leiden University PhD thesis. Utrecht: LOT.
Crasborn, O. & E. van der Kooij. 1997. Relative orientation in sign language phonology. In Jane Coerts & Helen de Hoop (eds.), *Linguistics in the Netherlands 1997*, 37–48. Amsterdam: John Benjamins.
Crasborn, O. & E. van der Kooij. 2013. The phonology of focus in Sign Language of the Netherlands. *Journal of Linguistics* 49(3). 515–565. DOI: https://doi.org/doi:10.1017/S0022226713000054.
Crasborn, O. & A. Sáfár. 2016. An annotation scheme to investigate the form and function of hand dominance in the Corpus NGT. In M. Steinbach, R. Pfau & A. Herrmann (eds.), *A Matter of Complexity: Subordination in Sign Languages*, 231–251. Berling: Mouton de Gruyter.
Crasborn, O., I. Zwitserlood & J. Ros. 2008. *The Corpus NGT. An open access digital corpus of movies with annotations of Sign Language of the Netherlands*. http://www.ru.nl/corpusngtuk.
Dresher, E. B. & H. van der Hulst. 1998. Head-dependent asymmetries in phonology: Complexity and visibility. *Phonology* 15. 317–352.
Frishberg, N. 1985. Dominance relations and discourse structures. In W. Stokoe & V. Volterra (eds.), *SLR '83. Proceedings of the 3rd International Symposium on Sign Language Research*, 79–90. CNR.
Hulst, H. van der. 1993. Units in the analysis of signs. *Phonology* 10. 209–241. DOI: https://doi.org/10.1017/S095267570000004X.
Hulst, H. van der. 1996. On the other hand. *Lingua* 98. 121–143.
Kimmelman, V., A. Sáfár & O. Crasborn. 2016. Towards a classification of weak hand holds. *Open Linguistics* 2(1). 211–234. DOI: https://doi.org/10.1515/opli-2016-0010.
Kooij, E. van der. 1997. Contact: A phonological or a phonetic feature of signs? In J. Coerts & H. de Hoop (eds.), *Linguistics in the Netherlands 1997*, 109–122. Amsterdam: John Benjamins.
Kooij, E. van der. 2000. One hand is enough: Evidence from SLN lexical distribution. Poster presentation, 7th Conference on Theoretical Issues in Sign Language Research, Amsterdam.
Kooij, E. van der. 2001. Weak drop in Sign Language of the Netherlands. In V. L. Dively, M. Metzger, S. Taub & A. M. Baer (eds.), *Signed Languages: Discoveries from International Research*, 27–42. Washington, DC: Gallaudet University Press.

Kooij, E. van der. 2002. *Phonological categories in Sign Language of the Netherlands: The role of phonetic implementation and iconicity.* PhD Thesis. Utrecht: LOT.

Kooij, E. van der & O. Crasborn. 2008. Syllables and the word-prosodic system in Sign Language of the Netherlands. *Lingua* 118(9). 1307–1327. DOI: https://doi.org/:10.1016/J.Lingua.2007.09.013.

Liddell, S. 2003. *Grammar, Gesture and Meaning in American Sign Language.* Cambridge: Cambridge University Press.

Liddell, S. K. & R. E. Johnson. 1986. American Sign Language compound formation processes, lexicalization and phonological remnants. *Natural Language and Linguistic Theory* 4. 445–513.

Liddell, S. K. & R. E. Johnson. 1989. American Sign Language: The phonological base. *Sign Language Studies* 64. 195–278.

Miller, C. 2000. *La phonologie dynamique du mouvement en langue des signes Québécoise.* Saint-Laurent, Québec: Fides.

Nespor, M. & W. Sandler. 1999. Prosody in Israeli Sign Language. *Language and Speech* 42(2–3). 143–176.

Nespor, M. & I. Vogel. 1986. *Prosodic Phonology.* Dordrecht: Foris.

Nilsson, A.-L. 2007. The non-dominant hand in a Swedish Sign Language discourse. In M. Vermeerbergen, L. Leeson & O. Crasborn (eds.), *Simultaneity in Signed Languages*, 163–186. Amsterdam: John Benjamins.

Nishio, R. 2008. *Korpusbasierte Analyse phonologischer Aspekte der Deutschen Gebärdensprache: Zu Handformendistribution und Optionalität der nichtdominanten Hand.* Hamburg: Hamburg University MA thesis.

Padden, C. A. & D. M. Perlmutter. 1987. American Sign Language and the architecture of phonological theory. *Natural Language & Linguistic Theory* 5. 335–375.

Paligot, A. 2017. *Vers une description des registres de la langue des signes de Belgique francophone (LSFB).* Namur: Université de Namur PhD thesis.

Perlmutter, D. M. 1991. Feature geometry in a language with two active articulators. Handout of talk, Conference on Phonological Feature Organisation, UC Santa Cruz.

Pierrehumbert, J. 1980. *The phonetics and phonology of English intonation.* Cambridge, MA: MIT PhD thesis.

Sandler, W. 1989. *Phonological Representation of the Sign: Linearity and Nonlinearity in American Sign Language.* Dordrecht: Foris.

Sandler, W. 1993. Linearization of phonological tiers in ASL. In G. Coulter (ed.), *Phonetics and Phonology: Current Issues in ASL phonology*, 103–129. San Diego, CA: Academic Press.

Sandler, W. 1999. Prosody in two natural language modalities. *Language and Speech* 42(2–3). 127–142.

Sandler, W. 2006. From phonetics to discourse: The nondominant hand and the grammar of sign language. In L. Goldstein, D. H. Whalen & C. Best (eds.), *Laboratory Phonology 8*, 185–212. Berlin: Mouton de Gruyter.

Stokoe, W. C. 1960. *Sign language structure: An outline of the visual communication systems of the American Deaf* (1993 Reprint). Dept. of Anthropology and Linguistics, University of Buffalo.

Zwitserlood, I. & O. Crasborn. Under review. Simultaneous syntax: Classifier predicates in Sign Language of the Netherlands. Open Linguistics.

Zwitserlood, I., E. van der Kooij & O. Crasborn. 2021. Morphological complexity in sign languages and the classifier – core sign dilemma. Ms. Radboud University.

Shengyun Gu
Phonological Processes in Shanghai Sign Language: Contexts, Constraints, and Structure

Abstract: This study investigates phonological processes in sign language, focusing on contexts, and the implications for phonotactic constraints and sign structure. Through the lens of Shanghai Sign Language, I will show that phonological processes in sign language operate at two levels: the lexical level and the post-lexical level, with the former being frozen in complex word formation and the latter behaving like coarticulatory effects. Such a division in the property of phonological processes is ubiquitous across most established sign languages studied to date. Moreover, the sub-lexical units that undergo alternations lend support to the hierarchical structure of a sign which abstracts away from the physical instantiations of a language.

Keywords: phonological processes, coalescence, morphologically complex word, coarticulation

1 Introduction

A sign is not a holistic gesture. It is decomposable into building blocks of handshape, movement, location, orientation, and non-manual signals (Stokoe 1960; Battison 1978; Liddell 1980; Crasborn, van der Hulst, and van de Kooij 2001; Sandler and Lillo-Martin 2006). Evidence for this phonological constituency is minimal pairs in which two signs are distinguished by merely one component. Besides chunking a sign into sub-lexical units, these sub-lexical components are subject to alternations during a phonological process that manipulates the phonological shape of underlying forms in order to obtain surface forms. Such processes have several implications for sign phonology studies. First, they help corroborate the psychological reality of phonological components in a sign. Second, phonological processes occur in a certain context. Alternations are usually triggered to either follow phonotactic constraints or to satisfy ease of articulation/perception. Third, the target of modulations, namely, the sub-lexical units and their groupings during a phonological process, adds evidence to the hierarchical organization of a sign.

Shengyun Gu, University of Connecticut

https://doi.org/10.1515/9783110730081-017

This study investigates phonological processes through the lens of Shanghai Sign Language, a southern variety of Chinese Sign Language (Fischer and Gong 2010). Lexical signs and spontaneous production of narrative, lecture, and conversation by Shanghainese deaf signers were analyzed. Phonological processes are found to operate at two levels in Shanghai Sign Language: lexical and post-lexical. The former context attests to frozen processes that are obligatory in complex word formation and the latter one concerns coarticulations that are optional. I will show that a monosyllabic sign is favored in Shanghai Sign Language and demonstrate this preference with coalescence examples in both contexts. Although the sub-lexical units seem different with respect to their substance in spoken and sign languages, processes such as assimilation and coalescence in languages in different modalities parallel each other. Phonological processes provide empirical evidence for the theory of a sign's internal structure. The rest of the paper is organized as follows: Section 2 analyzes phonological processes in the formation of morphologically complex words, focusing on compounding and affixation. Section 3 is about adaptations of signs in the context of connected signing. Section 4 compares the properties of phonological processes in the two contexts and makes implications for sign structure.

2 Phonological Processes in Complex Word Formation

2.1 Coalescence in Compounding

Like spoken languages, a compound in sign languages contains at least two bases which are root morphemes. Compounding is a productive device in word formation across sign languages, including established sign languages (Bellugi and Newkirk 1981; Wallin 1983; Sandler and Lillo-Martin 2006; Lepic 2016; Quer, Cecchetto, and Donati 2017; Santoro 2018) and emerging sign languages (Tkachman and Meir 2018). To identify a compound, particularly a lexicalized compound, I use the two criteria of semantic opacity and phonological simplification (Liddell and Johnson 1986; Sandler 1989). The overall meaning of a compound is not fully predictable from the simple addition of concatenating signs. In terms of phonology, a temporal shortening is achieved so that the length of time it takes to sign a compound is about the same as the average of a single sign (Klima and Bellugi 1979). Crucially, the constituting signs of a compound are compressed (Liddell and Johnson 1986; Sandler 1987; Brentari 1990). Shanghai Sign Language is rich in compounds, which encompass both loan compounds from Mandarin and endogenous compounds. The phonological processes in compounding are characterized by the following patterns: Simplification of a compound with a strong preference for a monosyllabic form, regressive handshape assimilation, and progressive location assimilation.

The Shanghai Sign Language compound SUPERFICIAL, shown in Figure 1c, is formed by the concatenation of two free signs HEAD (Figure 1a) and FEW (Figure 1b). HEAD is produced by pointing to the center of the forehead with a '1' handshape, i.e., extended index finger. FEW is articulated in neutral space with the thumb and the index finger forming a curved closed aperture. When the two signs are put together to form SUPERFICIAL, handshape and location assimilation occurs. HEAD anticipates the handshape of FEW, a result of regressive total assimilation of handshape. In contrast, location assimilates in the opposite direction. Under the influence of the first sign HEAD, FEW is raised to a high position in neutral space parallel to the forehead. In addition to assimilation, coalescence occurs in the formation of SUPERFICIAL since the two signs are fused into a single unit by having the transitional movement between the contact location of forehead in HEAD and ending location of FEW aligned as the initial and final settings of the sole movement of the resulting compound.

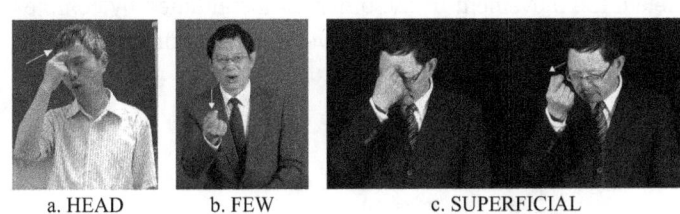

a. HEAD   b. FEW   c. SUPERFICIAL

Figure 1: SUPERFICIAL as compounded by HEAD and FEW.

Assimilation of the entire manual articulator, namely the hand, is attested as well. The formation of CLASSMATE, a concatenation of STUDY and GROW-UP, illustrates this process. As illustrated in Figure 2a and 2b respectively, STUDY is two-handed while GROW-UP is one-handed. In sign languages, the hand that is used in one-handed signs is referred to as the strong hand, while the other hand is referred to as the weak hand (Padden and Perlmutter 1987). When the two signs come together, an insertion of the weak hand is observed in GROW-UP (Figure 2c), which copies the articulation of its strong hand counterpart. Although the weak hand insertion on GROW-UP is a result of assimilation from the neighboring two-handed STUDY, what undergoes assimilation across the compound CLASSMATE is not the specific phonological features of the weak hand in the triggering sign STUDY, but the sheer fact of being two-handed. This lends support to the phonological representation of the weak hand in a hierarchically high position of a sign structure (van der Hulst 1996; Brentari 1998). The two signs are also compressed into one unit in the compound CLASSMATE. In Figure 2c, the sole location of STUDY and the ending location of GROW-UP are recombined into a single movement.

a. STUDY   b. GROW-UP   c. CLASSMATE

Figure 2: CLASSMATE as compounded by STUDY and GROW-UP.

The lexical compounds SUPERFICIAL and CLASSMATE undergo coalescence in which the two signs are blended into a single unit. The (ending) locations of each sign are recombined to form the movement in the compounds. To compress the two signs into one, it is also possible to preserve the underlying movement of one sign and simply delete the movement of the other, as instantiated by complex words that contain GOOD or BAD. These two adjectives can appear independently, as illustrated in Figures 3 and 4 respectively.

Figure 3: GOOD.   **Figure 4:** BAD.

GOOD uses an 'A' handshape, i.e., extended thumb, and is placed in front of the chest. BAD is produced with an 'I' handshape, i.e., extended pinky finger, that undergoes orientation change and downward path movement in neutral space. The two signs are different in their phonological structure, with BAD containing lexical movements and GOOD having no lexical movement other than an epenthetic movement in the surface representation. Both GOOD and BAD are productive in lexical compounding. When the two antonyms paradigmatically occur with a sign, they appeal to the same pattern of phonological adjustment despite the distinctions in their movement properties. See two such example pairs in Figures 5 and 6.

a. WIPE   b. CLEAN (WIPE^GOOD)   c. UNCLEAN (WIPE^BAD)

Figure 5: The pair of CLEAN and UNCLEAN.

a. SAILBOAT   b. SMOOTH (SAILBOAT^GOOD)   c. UNSMOOTH (SAILBOAT^BAD)

Figure 6: The pair of SMOOTH and UNSMOOTH.

WIPE (Figure 5a) involves the strong hand brushing the palm of the weak hand. SAILBOAT (Figure 6a) involves a forward path movement in neutral space. Both signs contain a lexical path movement. In Figures 5c and 6c, UNCLEAN and UNSMOOTH undergo coalescence, which deletes the movement of BAD. Meanwhile, the handshape of the first sign and that of BAD are recombined, resulting in a handshape transition superimposed onto the path movement. The same applies to CLEAN (Figure 5b) and SMOOTH (Figure 6b).

Summarizing the formational processes in a lexical compound in Shanghai Sign Language, I make the following generalizations: (1) Handshape assimilation regressively affects the first sign whereas location assimilation progressively influences the second sign; (2) The composing signs are compressed into a single unit.

2.2 Coalescence in Affixation

In addition to compounding, affixation is another device in creating new words in sign languages. An affix, which is usually a bound morpheme, attaches to a base to create a complex word. Compared with compounding, affixation is rare in concatenative morphology in sign languages (Meir 2012). Simultaneity arguably accounts for the paucity of linear affixation in sign languages (Emmorey 2002; Meier 2002). The young age of most sign languages is another factor since an affix usually historically develops as a result of the grammaticalization of a free word (Aronoff, Meir, and Sandler 2005). Provided that grammaticalization involves diachronic changes in phonological erosion and semantic bleaching, sign languages, being relatively young languages, do not display an abundance in affixes.

Despite the sparse number of affixes in sign languages due to both modality and age effects, some sequential affixations are nonetheless identified. Agentive and negative suffixes have been reported in American Sign Language (Sandler 1996; Sandler and Lillo-Martin 2006). Sense prefixes and negative suffixes are arguably genuine affixes that have been grammaticalized from free words in Israeli Sign Language (Aronoff, Meir, and Sandler 2005). My Shanghai Sign Language data confirm one type of affix that bears on negation. Following Woodward (1973, 1974), I call this affixation process negative incorporation, which occurs when "a verb is negated by a bound outward movement of the moving hand(s) from the place where the sign is made" (Woodward 1974: 22). In Shanghai Sign Language, one type of negative cannot appear on its own and it is articulated with an open palm in an outward movement. It is a bound morpheme and needs to be combined with a base sign. This negative morpheme is a suffix by consistently occurring after the base sign. Among the 2070 Shanghai Sign Language lexical items, at least nine signs are found to involve negative incorporation. I provide two examples NOT-KNOW and DISBELIEVE in Figures 8 and 10.

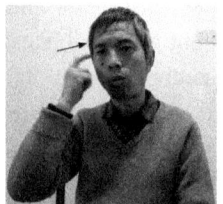

Figure 7: KNOW.

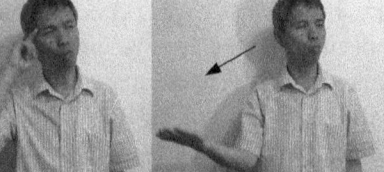

Figure 8: NOT-KNOW.

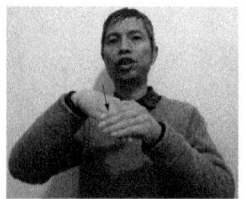

Figure 9: BELIEVE.

Figure 10: DISBELIEVE.

In Figures 8 and 10, the movement of the negative suffix is retained as the sole movement after affixation. In NOT-KNOW, the negative outward movement starts at the ending location of KNOW (Figure 7) and the same movement starts at the ending location of BELIEVE (Figure 9) in DISBELIEVE.[1]

Negative incorporation is reminiscent of lexical compounding in terms of the coalescence process. Like compounding, the base sign and the negative affix are compressed into a single unit. Such compression of units, or reduction of sequential movement, is ascribable to monosyllabicity of a sign (Coulter 1982). The notion of syllable is expressed by the movement in sign language (Perlmutter 1992; Sandler 1993; Brentari 1998). A sign is biased towards a monosyllabic form (Coulter 1982; Johnson and Liddell 1986; Wilbur 1993; van der Kooij and Crasborn 2008). That is, regardless of morphological complexity, linearly one movement (or one syllable) is the optimal form for a sign. The retention of only one movement, be it complex movement simultaneously involving multiple types or a simple movement, is arguably triggered by the phonotactic constraint of monosyllabicity.

3 Phonological Processes in Connected Signing

Apart from alternations in a complex word, phonological processes are seen in fast speech when language users utter the running stream in a simplified way. For example, in informal conversations in a spoken language like English, a phrase such as *I'm going to* is often reduced to *I'm gonna*. Studies on assimilation in fast speech in sign languages such as American Sign Language and Sign Language of the Netherlands are approached from spontaneous production in corpus (Cheek 2001; Russell, Wilkinson, and Janzen 2011; Ormel et al. 2017) or elicited production in experiment settings (Mauk 2003; Grosvald and Corina 2012; Mauk and Tyrone 2012; Tyrone and Mauk 2012, 2016). Despite a difference in methodologies, these studies report that phonological assimilations in connected signing are impacted by rate of speech and the form of neighboring units, suggesting that they are more like phonetic coarticulatory effects. I use a self-collected mini corpus of spontaneous production of Shanghai Sign Language (duration: 2 hours 56 minutes)

---

[1] One reviewer pointed out that the negative suffix can alternatively be used as a grammatical marker for negation on the sentential level. I adhere to putting this negative unit as an affix given that it invariably occurs after the negated word and cannot move. The lexicalized non-manual signal such as a head shake can occur alone or scope over a certain domain through spreading onto other manual signs. We suggest readers refer to Pfau (2008) for such an example in German Sign Language (DGS) although Pfau also analyzed this marker as a featural affix.

to examine phonological processes in connected signing. 17 Shanghainese deaf signers contributed to this naturalistic corpus from 2014 to 2017. The data involve lectures, conversations, and narratives. For all the tokens in the corpus that involve a phonological modification from their citation forms, I define those that satisfy at least one of the following two criteria as targets for investigation: First, the process must be observed in more than one signer; Second, the process must be attested for the same signer for more than one time. Despite the limited size of dataset, various types of phonological processes, including assimilation, deletion, epenthesis, coalescence, and metathesis, were identified as analogous to those in spoken languages. I report two types of phonological processes in this paper: assimilation and coalescence.

3.1 Assimilation in Connected Signing

I have shown in Section 2 that units such as handshape, location, and weak hand can undergo assimilation in complex word formation in Shanghai Sign Language. When signs occur in context, influence from one sign on another is frequently seen. Here I give examples of handshape assimilation and location assimilation.

3.1.1 Handshape Assimilation

The handshape is composed of selected fingers and joint position[2] in its internal organization. Handshape assimilation is attested in the substitution of selected fingers and joint position under the influence of neighboring signs. I provide two examples in connected signing to illustrate assimilation that targets selected fingers and joint position respectively. The sign CONFLICT (Figure 11) is produced with the index finger in citation form. CONFLICT can be modulated when it follows TINY in connected signing. TINY, as shown in Figure 12, involves the pinky finger as the selected finger in its citation form. In the running stream {IX_{3i} IX_{3j} TINY CONFLICT EXPLODE}[3] ('Tiny conflicts exploded between him_i and him_j') in Figure 13, the handshape of CONFLICT is impacted by its preceding sign TINY and thus changes its selected finger from index to pinky finger.

---

[2] By joint position, I refer to both the flexion of fingers and the aperture formed by fingers and the thumb.

[3] IX is an indexical sign which refers to a pronominal in sign languages. Canonically the index finger is used to point to the direction of the referents. The subscript 3 stands for the 3rd person. The subscripts i and j stand for two distinct referents in the discourse context.

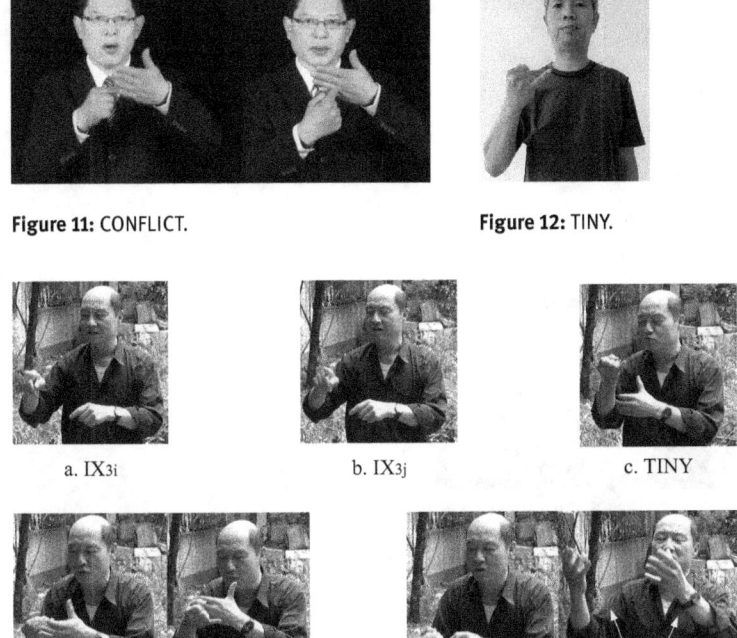

Figure 11: CONFLICT.   **Figure 12:** TINY.

a. IX3i   b. IX3j   c. TINY

d. CONFLICT   e. EXPLODE

Figure 13: Handshape assimilation of CONFLICT in context of {IX$_{3i}$ IX$_{3j}$ TINY CONFLICT EXPLODE} ('Tiny conflicts exploded between him$_i$ and him$_j$').

In addition to selected fingers assimilation, cases of joint position assimilation are observed. A crucial difference between the two subtypes of handshape assimilation resides in the fact that in assimilation of selected fingers, either total assimilation or partial assimilation is possible whereas in joint position assimilation, all selected finger joints undergo the same modulations by virtue of the Joint Position Constraint (Mandel 1981: 81), which mandates that the same set of selected fingers must take on the same joint position in sign languages like ASL. To illustrate, I provide one joint position assimilation example of OLD, which undergoes degree modification in joint flexion as a result of assimilation. OLD is articulated with a fist so that the joint position is fully closed in citation form in Figure 14. When OLD precedes GRANDMA in the running stream, its joint position converts from fully closed to curved (Figure 15), a result of copying the joint position of the following sign GRANDMA.

Figure 14: OLD in citation form.

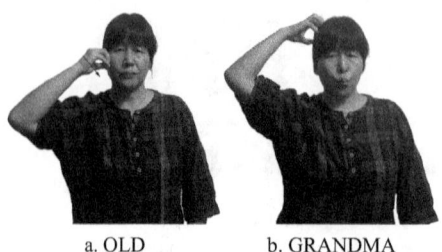

a. OLD   b. GRANDMA

Figure 15: Joint position modulation of OLD in connected signing.

3.1.2 Location Assimilation

The assimilation of location occurs when the articulation of location of one sign changes under the influence of an adjacent sign, a consequence of which the signs become more similar. In Shanghai Sign Language, signs that are articulated in neutral space are unstable by being subject to assimilation. In contrast, signs with body contact are stable and resistant to assimilation. Neutral space is construed as analogous to schwa in spoken languages whereas body location exhibits properties of full vowels in spoken languages (Grosvald 2009). Moreover, signs with body contact executes influence on the neighboring signs with respect to the height in neutral space, resulting in location raising or lowering. I explicate location raising and location lowering with examples.

Location raising frequently occurs when the sign that is produced in neutral space is in vicinity with a sign that contacts head and face, a high position on the body. The sign CHANGE (Figure 16) is produced in neutral space at the chest level. When it is followed by TANNED, a sign that involves contact with the temple, the location of CHANGE is raised to a position parallel to the temple in neutral space, a consequence of assimilation, as shown in Figure 17.

Figure 16: CHANGE.

a. SWIM   b. CHANGE   c. TANNED

Figure 17: Location raising of CHANGE in context of {SWIM CHANGE TANNED} ('(I) swam and turned tanned.').

Like location raising, location lowering is also attested in Shanghai Sign Language via assimilation from neighboring signs. The sign RAIN in Figure 18 involves a location above or equivalent to the head level in neutral space. The place of articulation also reflects the fact in the physical world that rain falls from the sky above the head, a manifestation of iconicity in location.

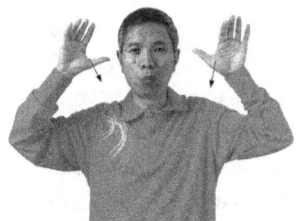

Figure 18: RAIN.

The lowering of RAIN is observed when it occurs in the string {VIOLENT RAIN KNOW} ('(He) knew about the violent rain') in Figure 19. VIOLENT is articulated in contact with the chest. Although KNOW is articulated in contact with the temple, its assimilatory strength on RAIN is weaker than VIOLENT on the account that VIOLENT and RAIN immediately constitute an extended noun phrase while KNOW is separated by a phrase boundary from RAIN regardless of their linear adjacency. RAIN there-

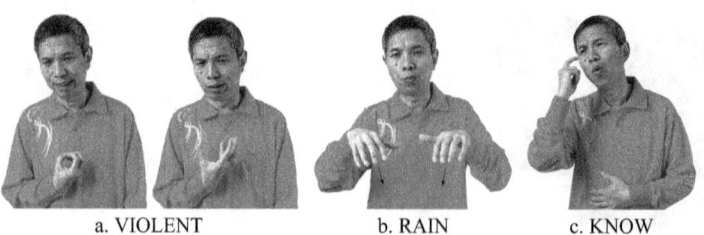

Figure 19: Location lowering of RAIN in context of {VIOLENT RAIN KNOW} ('(He) knew about the violent rain').

fore assimilates to the place of its preceding sign VIOLENT and is produced with a lowered location at the chest level. Location lowering also conforms to the principle of ease of articulation, which saves energy in manual articulation of signs.

Echoing the generalizations in McBurney (2002) on ASL, the height in neutral space in Shanghai Sign Language is not contrastive, namely, it does not differentiate lexical meanings. But the height in neutral space can carry iconic information, as in signs such as RAIN. The inclination for neutral space to undergo assimilation adds evidence to its status of being phonologically unspecified (Crasborn 2001) and meanwhile suggests that phonological processes in context can diminish the iconic motivations in lexical signs.

3.2 Coalescence

Coalescence refers to the fusion of two phonological units into a single unit. In the previous section on processes in complex word formation, I show that patterned processes regarding movement deletion, location assimilation, and handshape assimilation are involved in coalescence. When the context is extended beyond the lexical level, similar processes are attested as well in the connected signing. I report two examples of coalescence in connected signing, both of which bear on the incorporation of a negative. One negative sign in this language is a free word. The citation form of two variants of this negative sign, as illustrated in Figure 20, involves a repetitive pivotal movement of the wrist. The handshape can either be the thumb and index finger forming a curved closed aperture (Figure 20a) or the thumb and all fingers forming a curved closed aperture (Figure 20b). This negative sign is observed to undergo loss of movement and incorporation of its handshape into the preceding sign that it modifies. The sign FLEXIBLE, as illustrated in Figure 21, is an alternating sign with both hands executing circular movement in fist. The sign is articulated in neutral space at the chest level. In fast signing, coalescence of FLEXIBLE and NOT occurs in the string {HEAD FLEXIBLE NOT} ('The head is not flexible') in Figure 22.

Figure 20a: NOT (variant 1).   **Figure 20b:** NOT (variant 2).   **Figure 21:** FLEXIBLE.

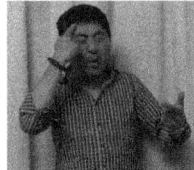 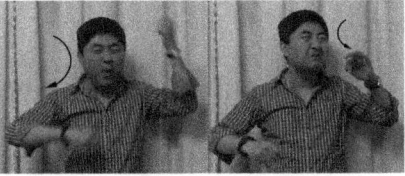

a. HEAD   b. FLEXIBLE-NOT

Figure 22: Coalescence of FLEXIBLE and NOT in context of {HEAD FLEXIBLE NOT} ('The head is not flexible').

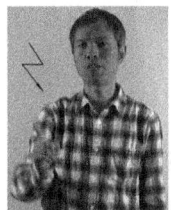

Figure 23: ELECTRICITY.

Figure 22b shows how the coalescence of the two signs FLEXIBLE and NOT is realized. At the beginning of the fused form FLEXIBLE-NOT, the sign FLEXIBLE is preserved by retaining two hands in the same configuration except that the movement manner is reduced from circular to arc movement, a lenition process in connected signing. During the weak hand movement in FLEXIBLE, a smooth transition from the handshape of FLEXIBLE to that of the following sign NOT is observed. In the arc movement of the weak hand, the handshapes of FLEXIBLE and NOT are readjusted to align with the initial and final locations of the movement, forming a handshape contrast in the coalesced form. The lexical movement of the negative NOT is deleted, and its handshape is incorporated into the preceding sign FLEXIBLE, thus realizing the fused form of FLEXIBLE-NOT. The fused form violates the symmetry condition (Battison 1978) on the two-handed lexical signs, which requires identical handshapes on the two hands. It nonetheless satisfies the Shanghai Sign Language grammar at the syllabic level, and thereby surfaces as a well-formed unit in the running stream. Apart from coalescence, location raising occurs by virtue of assimilation from the preceding sign HEAD, which is produced in contact with the forehead.

In a similar vein, when NOT is placed in vicinity with ELECTRICITY, the two signs can fuse into a compact unit. ELECTRICITY is produced with the index finger undergoing a zigzag movement in neutral space, as illustrated in Figure 23. In the running stream it can optionally be produced with two hands, with the weak hand mirroring its strong hand counterpart. When ELECTRICITY and NOT occur in a running stream (Figure 24), NOT is incorporated into ELECTRICITY by losing its underlying movement. Moreover, a smooth transition is formed between the handshape of ELECTRICITY, i.e., extended index finger, and the handshape of NOT (Figure 20b), i.e., fingers and thumb in a curved closed aperture. Such transition between two the handshapes creates a hand-internal movement (handshape contrast) that is superimposed onto the underlying zigzag movement of ELECTRICITY. The resulting coalesced form thus spans a monosyllabic unit by simultaneously having two kinds of movement, closing of the index finger and zigzag movement. Also, the weak hand of ELECTRICITY freezes in movement and is preserved as a static hand.

a. A-MOMENT-AGO   b. PHONE   c. ELECTRICITY-NOT

Figure 24: Coalescence of ELECTRICITY and NOT in context of {A-MOMENT-AGO PHONE ELECTRICITY-NOT} ('A moment ago the phone had no power').

While phonological processes such as coalescence and assimilation in connected signing are attested, these processes are all optional. Take the negative NOT for instance. Apart from examples such as FLEXIBLE-NOT and ELECTRICITY-NOT where the independent negative word NOT is incorporated into the sign it negates, many more cases that involve no phonological coalescence are observed. In Figure 25, NOT is preserved and does not undergo any phonological modulations. It is noteworthy that if coalescence does occur between LOSE and NOT, it yields a grammatical form, which involves a handshape change spanning over the arc movement of LOSE. Such processes are therefore more phonetically triggered rather than phonologically driven, and factors like formality and rate of speech impact their frequencies. My corpus data suggest that phonological processes in connected signing are more like coarticulations.

a. ZHANG   b. LOSE   c. NOT

Figure 25: No coalescence of LOSE and NOT in context of {ZHANG LOSE NOT} ('Zhang did not lose (something)').

4 Theoretical Implications

I have shown that phonological processes in Shanghai Sign Language operate in two contexts: alternations in morphologically complex word formation and processes in connected signing, which correspond to the lexical and post-lexical level respectively. While phonological processes such as coalescence and assimilation in connected signing mirror those that are attested in complex word formation, these processes are nonetheless optional and are more appropriately treated as coarticulatory effects, i.e., processes that are implemented in phonetics. The dichotomy between lexicalized processes in word formation and optional processes in connected signing is also called grammatical phonology and utterance phonology (van der Hulst and van der Kooij 2021), which seems to cut through most sign languages that have been studied. On one hand, such a ubiquitous property regarding phonological processes in sign languages contributes novel data to language studies. On the other hand, it implies that from the cross-modal typological perspective, sign languages cluster in the phonological properties where the ingredients such as lexicalized processes and coarticulatory processes are not uncommon, but the combination of these ingredients as the two levels of phonological processes are specific to sign language phonology. Such a unique property regarding "unusual recipes of common ingredients" is also identified in sign language morphology with respect to the verb agreement phenomenon (Pfau, Salzmann, and Steinbach 2018).

Phonological processes can target sub-lexical units such as handshape, location, movement, and the weak hand, thus lending support to their status as natural classes. Moreover, the modulations of sub-lexical units provide empirical evidence to a hierarchical structure in the sign representation (Sandler 1989; van der Hulst 1996; Brentari 1998; van der Kooij 2002, a.o.). The Shanghai Sign Language examples raised in this paper support the following points: Handshape assimilation can occur in its entirety or be classified into processes targeting the joint position and selected fingers, which reflects complexity in its internal organization. The sheer assimilation of the weak hand rather than its feature specifications implies a high position of the weak hand in comparison to other sub-lexical units. Unlike body locations, neutral space is subject to location assimilation. Lastly, phonological processes exhibit a strong preference for a compact unit that spans one syllable, which echoes findings in other sign languages. The variety of phonological processes indicates that sign languages, which have been reckoned as natural languages only in very recent decades, fit into and contribute to the scrutiny of the language grammar in general.

References

Aronoff, Mark, Irit Meir & Wendy Sandler. 2005. The paradox of sign language morphology. *Language* 81(2). 301–344.
Battison, Robbin. 1978. *Lexical Borrowing in American Sign Language*. Silver Spring, MD: Linstok Press.
Bellugi, Ursula & Don Newkirk. 1981. Formal devices for creating new signs in American Sign Language. *Sign Language Studies* 30(1). 1–35.
Brentari, Diane. 1990. *Theoretical foundations of American Sign Language*. Chicago: University of Chicago dissertation.
Brentari, Diane. 1998. *A Prosodic Model of Sign Language Phonology*. Cambridge, MA: MIT Press.
Cheek, Davina Adrianne. 2001. *The phonetics and phonology of handshape in American Sign Language*. Austin: University of Texas dissertation.
Coulter, Geoffrey. 1982. On the nature of ASL as a monosyllabic language. In *Annual Meeting of the Linguistic Society of America*, San Diego, CA.
Crasborn, Onno. 2001. *Phonetic implementation of phonological categories in Sign Language of the Netherlands*. Leiden: Leiden University dissertation.
Crasborn, Onno, Harry van der Hulst & Els van der Kooij. 2000. Phonetic and phonological distinctions in sign languages. *Intersign: Sign Linguistics and Data Exchange*.
Emmorey, Karen. 2002. *Language, Cognition, and the Brain: Insights from Sign Language Research*. Mahwah, NJ: Lawrence Erlbaum.
Fischer, Susan & Qunhu Gong. 2010. Variation in East Asian sign language structures. In D. Brentari (ed.), *Sign Languages*, 499–518. Cambridge: Cambridge University Press.
Grosvald, Michael Andrew. 2009. *Long-distance coarticulation: A production and perception study of English and American Sign Language*. Davis: University of California dissertation.
Grosvald, Michael Andrew & David Corina. 2012. Perception of long-distance coarticulation: An event-related potential and behavioral study. *Applied Psycholinguistics* 33(1). 55–82.
Hulst, Harry van der. 1996. On the other hand. *Lingua* 98(1–3). 121–143.

Hulst, Harry van der & Els van der Kooij. 2021. Sign language phonology: Theoretical perspectives. In Josep Quer, Roland Pfau & Annika Herrmann (eds.), *The Routledge Handbook of Theoretical and Experimental Sign Language Research*, 1–32. New York: Taylor & Francis.

Klima, Edward & Ursula Bellugi. 1979. *The Signs of Language*. Cambridge, MA: Harvard University Press.

Kooij, Els van der. 2002. *Phonological categories in Sign Language of the Netherlands: The role of phonetic implementation and iconicity*. Leiden: Leiden University dissertation.

Kooij, Els van der & Onno Crasborn. 2008. Syllables and the word-prosodic system in Sign Language of the Netherlands. *Lingua* 118(9). 1307–1327.

Lepic, Ryan 2016. The great ASL compound hoax. In A. Healey, R. Napoleão de Souza, P. Pešková & M. Allen (eds.), *Proceedings of the High Desert Linguistics Society Conference* 11, 227–250.

Liddell, Scott K. 1980. *American Sign Language Syntax*. The Hague: Mouton De Gruyter.

Liddell, Scott K. & Robert E. Johnson. 1986. American Sign Language compound formation processes, lexicalization, and phonological remnants. *Natural Language & Linguistic Theory* 4(4). 445–513.

Mandel, Mark. 1981. *Phonotactics and morphophonology in American Sign language*. Berkeley: University of California dissertation.

Mauk, Claude Edward. 2003. *Undershoot in two modalities: Evidence from fast speech and fast signing*. Austin: University of Texas dissertation.

Mauk, Claude Edward & Martha E. Tyrone. 2012. Location in ASL: Insights from phonetic variation. *Sign Language & Linguistics* 15(1), 128–146.

McBurney, Susan. 2002. Pronominal reference in signed and spoken language: Are grammatical categories modality-dependent? In R. Meier, Kearsy Cormier & David Quinto-Pozos (eds.), *Modality and Structure in Signed and Spoken Language*, 329–369. Cambridge: Cambridge University Press.

Meier, Richard. 2002. Why different, why the same? Explaining effects and non-effects of modality upon linguistic structure in sign and speech. In R. Meier, Kearsy Cormier & David Quinto-Pozos (eds.), *Modality and Structure in Signed and Spoken Languages*, 1–25. Cambridge: Cambridge University Press.

Meir, Irit. 2012. Word classes and word formation. In Roland Pfau, Markus Steinbach & Bencie Woll (eds.), *Sign Language: An International Handbook*, 77–112. Berlin: De Gruyter Mouton.

Ormel, Ellen, Onno Crasborn, Gerrit Kootstra & Anne de Meijer. 2017. Coarticulation of handshape in Sign Language of the Netherlands: A corpus study. *Laboratory Phonology: Journal of the Association for Laboratory Phonology* 8(1). 1–21.

Padden, Carol A. & David M. Perlmutter. 1987. American Sign Language and the architecture of phonological theory. *Natural Language & Linguistic Theory* 5(3). 335–375.

Perlmutter, David. 1992. Sonority and syllable structure in American Sign Language. In Geaoffrey R. Coulter (ed.), *Current Issues in ASL Phonology*, 227–261. San Diego: Academic Press.

Pfau, Roland. 2008. The grammar of headshake: A typological perspective on German Sign Language negation. *Linguistics in Amsterdam* 1(1). 37–74.

Pfau, Roland, Martin Salzmann & Markus Steinbach. 2018. The syntax of sign language agreement: Common ingredients, but unusual recipe. *Glossa: A Journal of General Linguistics* 3(1).

Quer, Josep, Carlo Cecchetto & Caterina Donati. 2017. *SignGram Blueprint: A Guide to Sign Language Grammar Writing*. Berlin/Boston: De Gruyter Mouton.

Russell, Kevin, Erin Wilkinson & Terry Janzen. 2011. ASL sign lowering as undershoot: A corpus study. *Laboratory Phonology* 2(2). 403–422.

Sandler, Wendy. 1987. Assimilation and feature hierarchy in American Sign Language. In *Papers from the Chicago Linguistic Society, Parasession on Autosegmental and Metrical Phonology* 2, 266–278. Chicago: Chicago Linguistic Society.

Sandler, Wendy. 1989. *Phonological Representation of the Sign: Linearity and Nonlinearity in American Sign Language*. Providence, RI: Foris Publications.

Sandler, Wendy. 1993. A sonority cycle in American Sign Language. *Phonology* 10(2). 243–279.

Sandler, Wendy. 1996. Representing handshapes. In William Edmondson & Ronnie Wilbur (eds.), *International Review of Sign Linguistics*, 115–158. Mahwah, NJ: Lawrence Erlbaum.

Sandler, Wendy & Diane Lillo-Martin. 2006. *Sign Language and Linguistic Universals*. Cambridge: Cambridge University Press.

Santoro, Mirko. 2018. *Compounds in sign languages: The case of Italian and French Sign Language*. Paris: l'École des Hautes Études en Sciences Sociales dissertation.

Stokoe, William C. 1960. Sign language structure. *Studies in Linguistics Occasional Paper* 8.

Tkachman, Oksana & Irit Meir. 2018. Novel compounding and the emergence of structure in two young sign languages. *Glossa: A Journal of General Linguistics* 3(1). 1–40.

Tyrone, Martha E. & Claude E. Mauk. 2012. Phonetic reduction and variation in American Sign Language: A quantitative study of sign lowering. *Laboratory phonology* 3(2). 425–453.

Tyrone, Martha E. & Claude E. Mauk. 2016. The phonetics of head and body movement in the realization of American Sign Language signs. *Phonetica* 73(2). 120–140.

Wallin, Lars. 1983. Compounds in Swedish Sign Language in historical perspective. In Jim Kyle & Bencie Woll (eds.), *Language in Sign: An International Perspective on Sign Language*, 56–69. London: Croom Helm.

Wilbur, Ronnie B. 1993. Syllables and segments: Hold the movement and move the holds. In Geoffrey Coulter (ed.), *Current Issues in ASL Phonology*, vol. 3: *Phonetics and Phonology*, 135–168. New York: Academic Press.

Woodward, James C. 1973. Inter-rule implication in American Sign Language. *Sign Language Studies* 3(1). 47–56.

Woodward, James C. 1974. Implicational variation in American Sign Language: Negative incorporation. *Sign Language Studies* 5(1). 20–30.

Language Index

African languages 152, 154–157, 160, 164–165
Afro-Asiatic 182
Akan 239
Al-Sayyid Bedouin Sign Language
  (ABSL) 276–277
Alabama 82
Aleut (Eastern) 162
Algonquian 76, 80
– Plains Algonquian 89
– Proto-Algonquian 89
Amazonian languages 244
American Sign Language (ASL) 274–276,
  279–280, 292, 294, 307–308, 310, 322,
  324, 327, 332–333, 342, 353, 350–351,
  356
Angolar 155 162
Anindilyakwa 137
Apache 182, 184–185
Apalai 82
Apurinã 75, 92–93
Arabic 116
– Cairene Arabic 162
Arawak 92
Arawakan 89
Armenian 13
Arnhem Land 133
Athabaskan 77, 80
Australian languages 133, 136, 138, 147–148
Austronesian languages 84, 91
Avar 6

Bantoid 153
Bantu 21, 153–155, 159–160, 178
Baramba 244
Basaá 153
Basque 174
Bassa 244
Belarusian 213–214
Berinmo 245–246
Biangai 77
Blackfoot 89
Bobo 175, 186
British Sign Language 280
Buriat 82–83, 92

Cahuilla 82
Cambodian 82
Cantonese 241
Capanahua 213
Cayapa 82
Chamorro 84, 90–91, 94
Cheremis (Eastern) 257, *see also* Mari
Chickasaw 87
Chinese 6
– Mandarin 99–100, 103–112, 235, 241, 347
Chinese Sign Language 346
Chukchi 255
Cree (Plains) 80
Czech 89, 296, 305

Dakota 75
Danish 244
Delaware 99
Dene 178, 182
Djambarrpuyngu 137
Dutch 58–59, 64, 152, 191, 234–235,
  238–241, 243–244, 281
Dyirbal 141

Edo 155
Edoid languages 155, 160
Efik 182–186
Ekoti 154
English 20, 26, 55–67, 76, 84–85, 93,
  102–103, 111, 152–153, 156, 163, 166,
  186, 191–194, 199, 202–203, 205, 234,
  237, 239–241, 244–246, 351
– British English 59, 67
– Present Day English 202
– General American 58
– Old English (OE) 26, 61, 63–64, 191–195,
  197–198, 203, 206
Estonian 82
European languages 152, 165

Fa d'Ambô 155, 157, 166
Fijian 84–85
Finnish 6, 82, 95, 162, 166, 233, 239
Fore 175

364 —— Language Index

Forro, *see* Santome
Franconian 240
French 57, 101, 233, 238–240, 244
– Central African French (CAF) 151–152, 154, 160–166
– Standard European French 161
Frisian 58, 244
Fula 43, 255

Gaelic 213
– Irish Gaelic 82
Georgian, 1ff.
German 22, 64, 234, 240, 244
– Old High German 192–193
German Sign Language 351
Germanic
– West Germanic 26, 52, 64, 191–193, 196, 198–199
Germanic languages 63–65, 191–192, 240, 244
Gidabal 82
Golin 173, 175–177
Gothic 26, 192, 200
Greek 6, 44, 211, 215–216
– Ancient Greek 26, 52, 219
– Classical Greek 110
– Modern Greek 110
Guaraní 213
Guineense, *see* Kriyol
Gunya 82

Hausa 162, 182–185
Hebrew 243
– Tiberian Hebrew 195
Hungarian 101, 239

Ibibio 182–185
Indic
– Middle Indic, 19ff.
  – Apabhraṁśa 33
  – Ardha-Magadhi 19, 33
– Modern Indic 45
Indo-European (languages) 44, 52, 115, 235
– Proto-Indo-European (PIE) 13
Iquito 154
Iranian (Eastern) 115
Irish 82

Israeli Sign Language (ISL) 271–274, 276–277, 320, 324, 327, 332, 342, 350
Italian 6, 25, 52, 101, 103

Japanese 6, 102, 234, 273, 282
– Tokyo Japanese 154, 211–212, 215–216, 218–219, 226–227

Kabuverdianu 166
Kartvelian 3, 12–14
Kikongo 141, 155, 159
Kimbundu 155, 159
Kinga 210–211
Kinyarwanda 21–22
Klamath 255
Kongo, *see* Kikongo
Koya 82
Kriyol 166
Kuikuro 154, 166

Lak 6
Lamba 173
Langue des Signes Québécoise 327
Latin 44, 265, 268
Laz 3, 14
Leti 14
Limilngan 138
Lithuanian 174–175, 209, 211–213, 215–221, 224–225, 227
Lung'Ie 151–152, 154–160, 164–166

Magadhi 19, 33
Maithili 77
Marathi 46
Margany 82
Margi 20
Mari
– Eastern Mari (Meadow Mari) 253, 257
– Western Mari (Hill Mari) 257
Mee 151–152, 154
Megrelian 3, 12–14
Mixtec 175, 177–178, 186
– Ayutla Mixtec 175, 177–178, 186
Mongolian
– East Mongolian 82, 92, 95
– Khalkha 71, 82
Moro 255

Munsee 71
Muskogean 87

Na-Dene 178, 182
Nakara 137
New Zealand Sign Language 327
Nez Perce 83–84
Ngankikurrungkurr 137
Ngbandi 154
NGT, see Sign Language of the Netherlands
Niger Delta 155, 164
Niger-Congo 182
Nigerian Pidgin English 156, 166
Nivkh 75
– Amur Nivkh 75
Noni 153
Norwegian 240
Nunggubuyu 138

Odawa 78
Ojibwe
– Border Lakes Ojibwe 76, 78–80
– Eastern Ojibwe 78
Ova-Himba 244

Palenquero 166
Pama-Nyungan 92, 136
Papiamentu 166, 173–174, 177
Papuan languages 151
Passamaquoddy 76–78, 88, 90
Persian 116, 239
Pichi 156, 166
Pirahã 172, 177, 244
Piro 88, 90
Polish 6, 89, 239
Portuguese 152, 154–160, 162, 164
– Brazilian Portuguese 158
– Santomean Portuguese 158, 162
Principense, see Lung'Ie
Proto-Creole of the Gulf of Guinea (PGG) 155, 157, 160

Quechua (South Conchucos) 77, 89–90, 93
Quechuan 89

Rembarrnga 137
Romance 25
– Proto-Romance 25
Russian 205, 211, 213, 215–216, 224, 256–257

Salish 219
Sama (Sibutu) 91–92
Sango 154, 160
Sanskrit 19–20, 27–28, 30–36, 38–44, 46–49, 51, 211, 215–216
– Vedic 31, 33
Santome 155, 162
Saramaccan 57, 156, 166
Saxon 63, 206
– Old Saxon 26
Selkup 202–203
SePedi (Northern Soto) 20–21
Shanghai Sign Language 299, 345ff.
Shona (Zezuru) 22
Shoshoni (Western) 82
Sign Language of the Netherlands (NGT) 274, 284, 319–322, 324, 329, 332, 338–339, 341–342, 351
Sign languages: see Al-Sayyid Bedouin Sign Language (ABSL), American Sign Language (ASL), British Sign Language, Chinese Sign Language, German Sign Language, Israeli Sign Language (ISL), Langue des Signes Québécoise, New Zealand Sign Language, Shanghai Sign Language, Sign Language of the Netherlands (NGT), Swedish Sign Language
Sinhala 43
Sino-Tibetan 182
Slavic languages 89
Spanish 213, 238
– Equatorial Guinean Spanish 161–162
– Standard Spanish 161
Sranan 166
Svan 3, 13–14
Swedish 154, 173, 177, 240
Swedish Sign Language 276, 325–326

Tagalog 213
Tahltan 77, 80–81, 95
Taiwanese 180, 186
Tanana (Minto) 175, 178
Thai 177, 241
Tibetan 175–176, 182
Trumai 75
Tübatulabal 82
Turkish 239

Ubangian languages 154
Umbugarla 137
Unami 71
Unangan 162
Uralic 253, 257

Urdu 296, 304–305
Urubú-Kaapor 138
Uspanteko 154
Uzbek 255, 268

Veps 82
Vietnamese 99–100, 102–112
Votic 82

Waalubal 81–82, 92, 95
Waanyi 137
Wakhi 115ff, 211, 215

Yanyuwa 137
Yoruba 182–186, 239

Subject Index

ablaut 120
accent 34, 58, 61–62, 69–95, 128, 133–134, 151, 153–155, 157–159, 162, 164–166, 172, 191ff., 209ff., 241–242, 253ff.
– pitch accent 110, 161, 174, 180
acquisition 14–16, 191, 201, 206, 233–234, 238, 241
allomorph(s) 9, 11–12
aperture 306–307, 331, 347, 352, 356, 358
assimilation 33, 42, 52, 65, 234, 279, 319, 327, 331–333, 335–336, 339–340, 346–347, 349, 351–356, 358–360; see also spreading

breaking 2

categorization 234, 236, 244, 247
child language 3, 14–16
clitics 111, 115, 120, 163
coalescence 219, 221–222, 225, 227, 345–349, 351–352, 356–359
compounds, compounding 15, 59–60, 63, 100, 102–103, 105–110, 153, 158, 219, 275, 278–279, 327, 333, 340, 346–349, 351
constraints 1, 7, 19–20, 23–24, 31–32, 39–41, 49, 52, 66, 83, 94, 101, 154, 160, 174, 176–177, 180, 199–200, 210, 220–226, 257, 275–278, 282, 284, 286, 291–292, 306, 309–310, 322, 329, 345ff.
contrast 21, 27–28, 42–43, 57, 60, 151–152, 154, 160–163, 165, 172–174, 178, 184–186, 205–206, 210, 233, 237, 241–243, 245, 273–274, 307–308, 357–358
corpus 182, 319–320, 324–325, 332–333, 338–339, 351–352, 359
creoles 152, 154–156, 160, 163, 165–166

Dependency Phonology (DP) 328
derivation 1, 6–7, 9, 11, 13–14, 16, 42, 48, 70–71, 84, 94, 110, 115–118, 121–122, 124, 127–129, 194, 196, 198, 206, 217, 219, 223–225, 235, 244, 265, 268, 292, 309, 327

dialects 1–3, 6, 12–13, 19, 22, 32–33, 61, 78, 119, 235, 240, 257
diphthongs 29, 55ff., 121, 172

facial expressions (in sign language) 280–281, 285
feature [back] 23, 124
feature [high] 23
feet (metrical) 60, 63, 65, 71, 99ff., 134–136, 145, 151, 176–177, 191–204, 206, 210, 212–213, 216

gemination 4, 7, 19ff., 91, 121, 191, 193, 196–200
grammar 52, 67, 104, 127, 149, 201, 209, 212, 214, 219–222, 224–227, 254, 257, 271, 282, 286, 358, 360

iconicity 14, 271ff., 292, 294–295, 297–299, 301–302, 305–306, 308, 310–311, 355–356
inflection 7, 9–10, 63, 115, 118–120, 122, 129, 196, 216–218, 222, 225–226, 235, 260, 327
intrusive stops 45
isolating languages 99ff.

laryngeals 5, 41, 45
lexicon 4, 78, 83, 120, 127, 129, 156, 233, 235, 239, 244, 247, 255, 274, 281, 284, 286, 320, 325, 328–329, 340–341

morphology 1, 6–9, 16, 62–63, 71, 76, 84, 90, 102–103, 115–116, 118–120, 122, 127, 129, 178, 205, 210–211, 215, 223, 227, 235, 253–254, 272–273, 275, 280, 323–324, 327, 329, 334, 349, 351, 359
morphophonology 206

neutral space 284, 331, 347–349, 354–356, 358, 360

Optimality Theory (OT) 15, 20, 83, 85, 94–95, 206, 221

paradigms 63, 163, 177, 242, 245, 325
perception 106, 111, 171–172, 179–181, 185–187, 233ff., 291–292, 300, 302, 305–306, 309–311, 345
phonetics 1, 4, 20, 22, 42, 52, 56, 59, 65, 69, 73, 103, 116, 120, 122, 124, 126, 152–153, 157–159, 162–165, 171ff., 203, 209–216, 218, 227, 233, 258, 277, 292, 306, 309–310, 320, 323–329, 331–332, 336–337, 342, 351, 358–359
pidgins 165
production 179–180, 234, 282, 285, 291–292, 295–296, 299, 310–311, 323, 346, 351
prominence 69–71, 73–76, 78, 81, 86, 92–94, 100–101, 103–107, 109–111, 153, 159, 166, 174–177, 179–181, 186–187, 211, 213, 264
prosody 15, 31, 34, 57, 69, 71, 74–75, 78, 86–89, 93–94, 99–101, 103–112, 151–157, 159–161, 163–166, 171, 182, 191, 203, 209–210, 212, 214, 227, 234, 240–241, 253, 278–280, 287, 306, 319–320, 324–325, 327, 329, 332, 340–342

reduplication 1, 3, 14ff, 106–107, 109, 111, 283
rhythm 69–71, 74–75, 77, 79–81, 84, 86–94, 100–101, 134–136, 138–141, 144–145, 180, 211, 254, 264, 324–325, 327

sign language 191, 271ff., 291ff., 319ff., 345ff.
sonority 2, 23–24, 27–28, 30–32, 34–37, 39, 42, 45–46, 49–51, 58, 66, 94, 125, 180
spreading 20, 23–26, 30–33, 38ff., 52, 126, 162, 211, 213–214, 319–320, 323ff., 351, see also assimilation

stress 1, 34, 52, 55–57, 59–63, 65–67, 69–75, 77–85, 87, 89–95, 100–101, 110, 115ff., 133ff., 151–155, 157–160, 162, 164–166, 171ff., 191–195, 200–206, 209ff., 233ff., 254, 300
– primary stress 69–72, 74–75, 78–85, 89–94, 101, 134–138, 153, 193, 254
– secondary stress 67, 69ff., 101, 112, 134–135, 137–138, 171, 203, 206
suprasegmental 166, 178, 237
syllables 1–2, 6, 16, 19–27, 29–32, 34, 37, 39–41, 45, 47, 50–52, 55–61, 63–67, 69–70, 72–92, 94–95, 99ff, 115–118, 120–126, 129, 134–138, 151, 153–165, 171–173, 175–180, 187, 191–197, 199–206, 210–211, 213–214, 216, 219, 238–240, 243–244, 253–255, 257–268, 278–279, 281, 319, 328–329, 332, 337, 351, 358
syntax 99, 109, 119–120, 163, 275, 280, 324–326, 332

tone 57, 104, 106, 108, 110–112, 151–166, 171–187, 209–215, 220, 227, 233, 237, 239–242, 244, 247, 281, 285

umlaut 91
universal 94, 99–101, 104–106, 111, 176, 186, 201, 287, 342

voicing 4–5, 115, 172, 187, 235, 237, 308

weight 50, 57, 65, 71, 73–74, 76, 78–79, 81–87, 92, 94, 110, 112, 116, 129, 134–136, 138–147, 149, 155–157, 159–160, 164, 171–172, 175–177, 179, 187, 203, 205, 210, 221–222, 224–226, 241, 244, 253ff.
word boundaries 73, 203

Contents of Part I

Preface —— IX

Cor van Bree
Umlaut: From Common Germanic to Dutch —— 1

Bert Botma and Maarten Mous
Vowel Copy in Iraqw Verbal Derivation —— 17

Nancy A. Ritter
Hungarian Possessive Allomorphy in the Lexicon —— 33

Markus A. Pöchtrager
The Unbearable Lightness of Being High: Openness as Structure and the Consequences for Prosody —— 71

Keith L. Snider
[+ATR] Dominance in Chumburung —— 91

Ruben van de Vijver and Agnes Benkő
Paradigmatically Conditioned Phonetic Detail in Hungarian Neutral Vowels —— 107

Bert Botma and Colin J. Ewen
Old English Breaking as Vowel Excrescence —— 133

Clemens Poppe and Jeroen van de Weijer
Diachronic Vowel Harmony: From Middle to Modern Korean —— 151

Eugeniusz Cyran
How Much Phonology in 'Laryngeal Phonology'? —— 165

Krisztina Polgárdi
The Representation of Nasal + Stop + Obstruent Clusters in English: Stop Insertion or Stop Deletion? —— 187

Norval Smith
A Perfect Mess in Ancient Greek: The Story of -*ka* —— 201

Claartje Levelt, Eline van den Brink, and Josefine Karlsson
Prompted Self-Repairs in Two-Year-Old Children —— 227

Glyne Piggott
Deriving Variable Phonological Visibility from Word Structure —— 249

Tobias Scheer
Recursion in Phonology: Anatomy of a Misunderstanding —— 265

Aida Talić
Phases and Accent Assignment Domains —— 289

Marcel den Dikken
A Phonosyntactic Representation of Hungarian 'Lowering' —— 307

John A. Goldsmith
Zellig Harris, Phonological Boundaries, and Features —— 327

Ray Jackendoff and Jenny Audring
Blends and Overlaps in Relational Morphology —— 347

Language Index —— 359

Subject Index —— 361

www.ingramcontent.com/pod-product-compliance
Lightning Source LLC
Chambersburg PA
CBHW061929220426
43662CB00012B/1846